Deschooling

A READER

IAN LISTER

Department of Education
University of York, England

Cambridge University Press

Acknowledgements

Thanks are due to the following for permission to include readings:

Aldine, Atherton Inc. for 'The school myth' by Howard S. Becker, from Learning to Work edited by Blanche Geer;
Peter Buckman for 'Deschooling', first published on 3 July 1971, © 1971 Peter Buckman;
UNESCO for 'Education: domestication or liberation?' by Paulo Freire, reprinted from Prospects, Vol. II, No. 2 (Summer 1972);
The Council of Europe for 'Permanent education - dream or nightmare?' by Hermann H. Frese, from Education and Culture, No. 19 (Summer 1972);
The Harvard Educational Review for 'Towards a political economy of education: a radical critique of Ivan Illich's Deschooling Society' by Herbert Gintis, from the Harvard Educational Review, Vol. 42, No. 1 (February 1972), © 1972 The President and Fellows of Harvard College;
Random House Inc. for 'Mini-schools: a prescription for the reading problem' by Paul Goodman, from New Reformation: Notes of a Neolithic Conservative by Paul Goodman;
Ernst Klett Verlag and Hartmut von Hentig for 'Deschooling the school' by Hartmut von Hentig, translated from 'Cuernavaca oder: Alternativen zur Schule?' by the same author, English translation © I. and K. M. Lister;
Pitman Publishing Corporation for 'Schools are bad places for kids' by John Holt, from The Under-achieving School by John Holt;
The Center for the Study of Democratic Institutions for 'Toward a learning society' by Robert M. Hutchins, from the Center Magazine, Vol. IV, No. 4 (July/August 1971);
Ivan Illich for 'The redistribution of educational tasks between schools and other organs of society' and 'Schooling: the ritual of progress';
Ivan Illich and the Australian National Union of Students for 'Ivan Illich in Australia: questions and answers';
The Association for Supervision and Curriculum Development for 'Is the school an obsolete institution' by W. Senteza Kajubi, from Educating the Young People of the World edited by Alice Miel and Louise Berman. Reprinted with the permission of the Association for Supervision and Curriculum Development and W. Senteza Kajubi, © 1970 by the Association for Supervision and Curriculum Development;
The Times Educational Supplement for 'Stick with the system' by Eric Midwinter;
Julius K. Nyerere for 'Education for self-reliance', from Ujamaa: Essays on Socialism by Julius K. Nyerere, published by Oxford University Press;
The Adult Education Association of America and John Ohliger for 'Adult education: 1984' by John Ohliger, from Adult Leadership (January 1971);
David A. Reibel and the Editors and Publishers of the Educational Journal of Applied Linguistics for 'Language learning analysis', from International Review of Applied Linguistics in Language Teaching, Vol. VII, No. 4 (1969);
Penguin Books Ltd. and Doubleday and Company Inc. for 'Networks of people', from School is Dead: Alternatives in Education, © 1971 Everett Reimer, reprinted by permission of Doubleday and Company Inc. and Penguin Books Ltd. (Penguin Education Specials);
Wildwood House Ltd. and Random House Inc. for 'The failures of educational reform in the United States' by Charles E. Silberman, from Crisis in the Classroom: The Remaking of American Education by the same author;
Fondation Européenne de la Culture for 'The "Scuola and Quartiere" movement: a case-study' by Gastone Tassinari. A translated and slightly abridged version of a paper prepared for the Florence Conference held in October 1971 and organised by the Education Project of Plan Europe 2000 for a study on 'General Secondary Education';
New Society for 'Anti-anti school' by John Vaizey. This article first appeared in New Society, The Weekly Review of the Social Sciences, 128 Long Acre, London S. C. 2, England;
Rank and File and Ludo Watson for 'Deschool off' by Ludo Watson;
The Secretariat for Social Development, Government of Ontario, Canada for 'Some doubts and some questions about post-secondary education in Ontario';
Rowohlt Verlag GmbH for 'A curriculum for working-class children' by Jürgen Zimmer, translated from Wie und was Zu lernen ist: das Curriculum by the same author, English translation, I. and K. M. Lister.

Contents

To E. N. W. and J. H. P. – my teachers

The challenge of deschooling

Since 1971, in a remarkably short space of time, deschooling has entered the educational debate. The word itself has gone into several languages and its related concepts, such as 'networks' and 'peer-matching', are to be found in the committee prose of international organisations as well as in the leaflets of radical and underground groups. From Mexico and the USA, to West Germany, Italy and Australia, 'deschooling' has itself become part of the rhetoric of educational reform.

The responses to the challenges of deschooling have varied in different countries, and among different groups. Some people in 'advanced' countries have argued that it is all right for Third World countries, but not for them. Others have argued that deschooling is itself a feature of the contradictions of capitalist society and that it might be all right for the USA, but not for Europe. Reactions were often emotional - both deschooling theory and its attackers were characterised by a lack of appeal to empirical evidence. Deschooling touched many raw nerves in the educational world for two main reasons: because of the way that education was organised and perceived in many countries, and because of the 'unfolding world crisis in education' that Philip H. Coombs wrote about in 1968. [1]

In most countries educationists had long since given up asking the kind of first-order questions about purposes raised by people like Illich, Nyerere, and Paulo Freire. Instead they had confined themselves to second-order questions about the activities of others. Theory was set apart from practice - each encapsulated in its own institution, guaranteeing actionless thought in the one and thoughtless action in the other. The sub-disciplines through which educational studies struggled for academic respectability were sometimes populated by those who were regarded as second-rate by practitioners of the main discipline, and in most programmes they were kept well apart. The history of education, something that might have helped teachers in training to relate the parts to a whole, was a version of Whig history, held together by the idea of progress (organised from above by acts of parliament) and its main end was to celebrate the present. The message, as received from the new holy trinity of educational sub-disciplines was: the sociology of education shows us that large sections of the population cannot speak and are virtually ineducable; educational psychology tells us how to motivate them; and the philosophy of education justifies what we do. In many countries the area of the political economy of education, where deschooling theory raises some of its most vital questions, is merely a gap in the intellectual training of educationists and teachers. This, plus the prevailing specialisation in schools and universities which encourages one-dimensional men, left many ill-equipped for a debate with multi-dimensional, eclectic theorists like Paul Goodman and Ivan Illich, people who, in deschooling fashion, make their starting point a problem, and not a theory of knowledge. If the educationists were vulnerable to general theories produced by mavericks of the disciplines, teachers were often in an even weaker position. Their training had seldom encouraged them to see their work in a general historical and social context and the nature of their work tied them up with immediate problems.

Many felt that educational theorists failed to understand their everyday life-situations; and some felt daily and bitterly the gap between the rhetoric of educational reformers and the reality they saw happening in their own schools. The reaction of many teachers to deschooling theory was either to be confused and demoralised, or else to say: 'Thank God. Someone's said it at last!' Leaders of teachers' trade unions responded with religious fervour to deschooling theory, and they, and several educational journalists, denounced 'deschoolers' as 'enemies of education, intellectual quislings':[2] 'anti-educationists with a programme for educational anarchy';[3] and declared that children should be protected from them.

The general crisis in education was first argued by economists who pointed out the growing costs of education in formal institutions. At first the simple growth philosophy was questioned in the context of Third World countries by people like Coombs, Nyerere,[4] Callaway[5] and Kajubi.[6] Then similar questions were asked about educational provision in the USA and Canada. In Western Europe, too, there is evidence of crisis. In France since 1968 the crisis is an assumed starting point of any educational discussion, and Alain Drouard has predicted that 'the fundamental crisis in all educational systems will last for many years to come'.[7] In Italy the traditional system has been radically criticised by the children of the School of Barbiana:[8] by Gastone Tassinari;[9] and by the work of Mario Borrelli at the House of Urchins in Naples. In West Germany the 'Schulmisere' is a term of everyday speech and Hartmut von Hentig, the leading school-reformer, has advocated deschooling the school.[10] In Sweden, Torsten Husén, who used to be a high-priest of the schoolmen and who in 1970 was confidently predicting a dominant role for the school in tomorrow's educational system, has now turned his attention to the crisis in his latest book Skolans Kris.[11] In England, with its belief in conservative change, there is growing evidence that things are far from well. 'School refusal', 'lesson refusal', truancy from urban schools, and damage to school buildings are growing features of the system. More and more people are beginning to notice that majorities fail to learn what schools pretend to teach. Commentators as diverse as Geoffrey Bantock, a conservative professor, Tom Lovett of the Workers' Educational Association, and radical London teachers all speak of the failures of popular education and of a crisis in the system.

In this general context it is difficult to know how much reforms - and the movements for reschooling, freeschooling, and deschooling - are themselves part of the crisis, and how much they are a way beyond the crisis. It is possible that deschooling, like 'comprehensive education' or 'community control' - those slogans of yesteryear - might itself be a passing phase, but the problems it attempts to deal with are likely to be with us until the end of the century. Some deschooling analysis and some deschooling practice might help us to get beyond the present crisis. For those reasons it is important not to dismiss deschooling with epithets, and to raise the discussion above the superficial level seen hitherto.

Although the word deschooling is frequently used in educational argument, and although 'the deschoolers' have a shadow existence as devils in the school theology of some educational preachers, there are no easy answers to questions like: Who are the deschoolers? What is the deschooling movement? And what is deschooling?

There have been school-critics as long as there have been schools. Some of them have been disappointed schoolmen. Some have been anti-schoolmen, like the Irish playwright Bernard Shaw. None - with the disputable exception of Rousseau - have been deschoolers. The first deschooler seems to have been Paul Goodman, the US social critic. As early as 1947, in Communitas, Goodman was raising questions about the relationship of man to the modern urban, industrial environment; in 1960, in Growing Up Absurd, [12] he argued that the young in the USA failed to grow up because they lived in a society unfit to grow up in; in 1962, in Compulsory Miseducation, [13] he asked: 'Since schooling undertakes to be compulsory, must it not continually review its claim to be useful?' Other of his major themes - such as the natural ability of children to learn, mini-schools, learning from apprenticeships, by doing, from the city, and from life itself - were to recur throughout later deschooling writings, and some of his main concerns - transformed into new phrases like 'the youth culture' and 'environmental education', have entered into common currency. It was Goodman, too, who first began the serious search for alternatives which is one of the central elements of deschooling. Some of the later deschooling dilemmas are also evident in Goodman: it is never clear whether he is trying to deschool society or to turn all the world into a school; whether his real understanding is of 'the community of scholars' rather than of ordinary people: or whether he is looking backward, to a world of cottage industry, as a means of escape from the world of late industrialism. His faith in people, and his lack of faith in institutions, is something shared by later deschooling writers. It is also the cause of several paradoxes and ambiguities in deschooling theory.

A self-declared deschooler is John Holt who wrote in April 1971: 'For the last year I have been completely convinced of the necessity for deschooling society.'[14] Holt, however, started life and is better known as a schoolman-reformer. How Children Fail, 1964, [15] made his reputation. It is a book of powerful insights, trying to see learning from the learner's point of view; revealing the strategies of teachers' questions and pupils' answers; studying failure; asking questions about interactions between teacher and pupil, and asserting that 'What goes on in class is not what teachers think'. The implication throughout is that children fail because of bad teachers and bad schools, not because of the process of schooling and society as such, and that, therefore, the way ahead is to improve teachers and make better schools, not to deschool. This is confirmed in Holt's next book How Children Learn, 1967, [16] where he writes: 'When we better understand the ways, conditions, and spirit in which children do their best learning, and are able to make school into a place where they can use and improve the style of thinking and learning natural to them, we may be able to prevent much of the failure that takes place in school. ' In the more polemical The Underachieving School, 1970, [17] even when he states that 'school is a long lesson in How To Turn Yourself Off' the implication is that schools should find ways to turn people on. It is true that he goes on to advocate the end of compulsory attendance but this is so that we would then make schools into 'places where children would want to be'. In his most recent book, What Do I Do Monday?, 1970, [18] Holt was still advocating 'a New Schooling', the essence of which he seems to have found in that shrine in England visited by so many US school pilgrims - 'Leicestershire County'. In short, he was still in the same camp as such leading schoolmen-reformers as Vincent Rogers, Professor of Education at the University of Connecticut, who is currently trying to import English progressive primary schools into the USA. Holt's writings are about children, whereas deschooling theory concerns itself with educational provision in the whole of society, and even challenges the idea of 'childhood' itself. Holt writes for teachers - this is his great strength: he knows the teacher's everyday work situation, and the teacher's worries, and offers some positive and practical suggestions. But from a deschooling point of view Holt's writings do not see beyond the chalk-dust, and fail to tackle general, structural questions: they are 'all schooled-up'. Although he has seen some of the dangers of free schools Holt's deschooling writings are still to come.

Fortunately for anyone in search of 'the deschoolers', and an idea of what deschooling might mean, there are two men who both regard themselves as deschoolers, and who have written plenty on the subject. Ivan Illich and Everett Reimer have been engaged on a dialogue on deschooling for over fifteen years. Illich is the person who first publicised the term 'deschooling' - first in articles in the New York Review of Books and then in his book Deschooling Society, 1971. [19] For Illich deschooling 'must be the secularization of teaching and learning'; it should be 'creative, exploratory learning'; its concern is 'personal growth' - 'The learning I prize is immeasurable re-creation. ' It involves the disestablishment of schools; the building of an educational world: and 'a new approach to incidental or informal education'. In spirit it will be 'convivial' and not 'manipulative'. In the deschooled society 'recreation will regain its real meaning i. e. to re-create oneself'. Most of Deschooling Society is a critique of present systems. Illich bases his analysis on the 'phenomenology of the school' - the general characteristics that schools have, be they in the United States or the Soviet Union: 'I shall define school as the age-specific, teacher-related process requiring full-time attendance at an obligatory curriculum. '

Like Illich, Reimer[20] starts from a functional analysis of what schools do: their main functions, according to both Illich and Reimer, are custodial care; social-role selection; indoctrination; and education/learning. In performing the first three functions mass-education systems negate any hope for learning and education. Reimer's definition of 'school' is similar to that of Illich: 'We define schools as institutions which require full-time attendance of specific age groups in teacher-supervised classrooms for the study of graded curricula. ' Looking towards the future, Reimer continues: 'Alternatives in education can be most generally defined as moving away from this stereotype. ' At the moment, writes Reimer, 'perhaps the most important thing that individuals can do is to take back responsibility for the education of their children. ' Illich goes further. Arguing that 'school makes alienation preparatory to life, depriving education of reality and work of creativity', and that 'the New

World Church is the knowledge industry', he goes on to assert that 'deschooling is... at the root of any movement for human liberation' and that 'each of us is personally responsible for his or her own deschooling'. Illich explains the origins of the term 'deschooling' as caused when he misheard the answer given by someone in an audience when he asked them what they felt schools did. The person said: 'Schools screw you', but he heard 'Schools school you' and afterwards they began to talk of deschooling. Elsewhere Illich has said of the word 'deschooling': 'I am so sorry that I used that word in one of my sentences somewhere in my book. My editor said on the telephone that this is the title we will give the book. I said yes, leave me alone, I'm conducting a seminar on something else. And now I am responsible for an ugly neologism!' The further descriptions of deschooling are readily available in the writings of Illich and Reimer but enough has been said here to show that deschooling is not a precise concept. It is rather a general drift of thinking. Thus, a phrase like 'the deschooling movement', which is in current polemical use, might have some meaning if firstly one could distinguish a direction and secondly if it followed the general drift. This opens up the possibility of linking with the two indubitable deschoolers others who embody certain elements of deschooling theory and whose works move 'in a deschooling direction'. These include people like Paulo Freire from Brazil; Michael Huberman, formerly of UNESCO and now Professor of Pedagogy in Geneva; Gastone Tassinari in Italy; and Jürgen Zimmer in West Germany. Freire, with his adult literacy projects, promoted learning in non-school settings. Huberman's key question: 'How much longer can countries... afford to support school systems whose curriculum is abstracted from the activities of life and divided into texts, lessons, scheduled learning periods and graded promotions?'[21] reflects aspects concentrated on by deschooling analysis. Tassinari is seeking to build alternatives to the traditional school system in non-school contexts. Zimmer is planning, and operating, deschooled curricula through projects - Illich himself talks of 'planning for non-schooled learning'. Apart from these people deschoolers are hard to find. Free schools preserve the rhetoric of schooling in a yet more extreme form. According to Illich: 'Free schools, which lead to further free schools in an unbroken chain of attendance, produce the mirage of freedom. Attendance as the result of seduction inculcates the need for specialized treatment more persuasively than reluctant attendance enforced by truant officers.'[22] They push the classroom into the street, which itself takes on mystical qualities. They can be more manipulative than traditional schools, with leaders who speak of freedom and operate on charisma, encouraging guru-figures who, Pied Piper like, lead their charges over the hills and far away. Of English progressive schools Reimer says: 'Summerhill and schools patterned after it... still... teach dependence on the school. ' If freeschooling is not deschooling, a point which many present critics miss, what is left? The Open University brings 'education' in new ways and to new audiences, but - by and large - they are audiences and the learning comes in the kind of packaged curriculum which is an anathema to Illich. Often those who talk of deschooling are really schoolmen-reformers; others pick out the bits of deschooling theory which support their current purposes and practices. Maybe there are some deschoolers, like some Catholics in Poland today - 'believing but not practising'; equally there

may be teachers in the system, like some Polish communists - 'practising but not believing'. The actual numbers of deschoolers are few, but the challenges raised by deschooling are serious. Instead of regarding deschoolers as devils, to be exorcised by conventional rituals, or incorporating deschooling in a new liturgy, we need to analyse the challenges in order to meet them, and get beyond them. For clarity's sake I will attempt to identify, isolate, and list the challenges of deschooling:

1. **The shaking of assumptions**

This is the general challenge of people like Goodman, Reimer, Illich and Freire - the shaking of the community of assumptions hitherto shared by most educational planners in most countries, particularly the assumption that more schools equals more education (and that more GNP equals more prosperity).

2. **Schools and education**

'To identify schools with education, ' says Illich, is 'to confuse salvation with the church. ' If schools and education are seen to be not necessarily the same thing it is also possible for schools to be anti-educational, to prevent learning instead of encouraging it. Illich argues: In that schools are unworldly, and make the world non-educational, and in that they discourage the poor from taking control of their own learning, 'all over the world the school has an anti-educational effect on society'.

3. **School failure**

Schools fail to teach what they pretend to teach. Most of their inmates spend years failing to learn things like Mathematics, Science, and French. In England to reach 'Ordinary Level', an examination taken by some children in the schools, is a highly extra-ordinary achievement. But, says Illich, 'if schools are the wrong place for learning a skill they are even worse places for getting an education'. Teachers have a vested interest in failure (if everyone succeeded the suspicion might arise that teachers were superfluous) but they need excuses for the continuation of failure at such a rate.

4. **Labelling**

Failure is individualised and personalised and 'failures' are given labels to explain that the origins of their failure lie within themselves: they were born in original stupidity ('low IQ'). Or, at best, the sins of their fathers were visited upon them ('bad home background', 'poor environment'). For them, educational reform often means giving them new names - 'the culturally deprived', 'the culturally disadvantaged', 'those in need of nurture', 'those below the 60th percentile', and recently in England, discovered in 1963, 'the Newsom child'. Teachers who live with failure on a large scale need such explanations in order to preserve their mental health. That is part of the human tragedy of such labelling.

5. **Definitions**

Institutional apologists who do not question their own operations define situations, and other people, according to their own assumptions. Thus children who leave school as soon as it is allowed by law are called 'early leavers' (when they themselves regard those who remain as 'late stayers'). We talk of 'the school-leaving age', not 'the school-staying age'; and of 'lesson refusal' and 'school refusal'. Some official reports even refer to the numbers who leave school 'prematurely' as 'attrition', recalling the horrors of the First World War.

6. To fail is to expand

When school systems fail to teach assessable skills they succeed in expanding their activities by raising funds for 'curriculum development'. Thus, millions of pounds go into 'New' Mathematics, Science, and Modern Language Projects. According to an educational law of eventually diminishing returns increased investment leads to increased failure and, in its turn, to arguments for yet more investment. This creates an exponential increase in the cost of failure. A developed country is one that can afford failure at the highest per capita cost.

7. School as a modern invention

'Medieval society... had no idea of education', writes the French historian Philippe Ariès. [23] School, as we know it, is only about 200 years old and arose as part of the apparatus of the modern, bureaucratic state. Its origins are Prussian and Napoleonic, and it may be viewed as a German invention. The Germanic grade system, whereby the 'Jahrgang' (the year group) moved forward as a cohort, was imported into the USA in the nineteenth century; Matthew Arnold tried, and failed, to introduce the German organic approach to educational planning in England. Thus, the question arises whether the school, far from being an eternal institution, is in fact something connected with a particular period in history and may, in a future of changed conditions, disappear.

8. The school as a political educator

Although in some countries it is usual to assert the political neutrality of schools, as Paulo Freire argues 'Education cannot be neutral.'[24] As soon as we consider the question with critical distance, by examining the structures, programmes and even the history textbooks of schools in countries other than our own, we realise that schools are used, both explicitly in the written curriculum and implicitly through the hidden curriculum, to educate their people politically. In general they teach allegiance to the government; the history books of all countries are self-justifying and, like most histories of education, celebrate the present. Schools have been used intentionally as political educators to make immigrants into Americans; the school was the melting pot by which social alchemists hoped to transform the rejected of Europe into New American Man. In nineteenth-century England the newly revived public schools were used to turn the sons of the English middle class into 'gentlemen': monastic and monosexual (and often homosexual) they produced leaders for three other monastic and monosexual enterprises of the time - the empire, the army, and, for 'the weaker brethren', the church. [25] In the twentieth century we have seen attempts to make schools produce leaders for the thousand years' Nazi Reich;[26] a meritocracy of Platonic guardians in Britain;[27] and leaders, and nations, in Third World countries. [28] But if élites were educated to lead, majorities were educated to be led. For the first group teachers served as role-models of the leaders they themselves were to become; for the second group

teachers appeared as authority figures, forerunners of the officers, bosses, and policemen who were to order them around for the rest of their lives. The pupils of the first group role-played the servant in order later to become a more effective master. The pupils of the second group were in a general state of confrontation with their teachers. For these majorities schools taught the passive virtues of 'Gehorsam' and 'Ruhe' - obedience and silence - as Tolstoy noticed when he visited the Prussian schools. [29] This political education in acquiescence was achieved less by the written curriculum than by the structures and operational methods of the institution. In England, for example, the tradition of the great headmaster is so strong that it has gone from Thomas Arnold of Rugby School, into the grammar schools, the comprehensive schools, and even the free schools, all of which share with monarchy the major features of charismatic leadership and succession crises. In Germany Bismarck regarded every teacher as his representative in the classroom: the system produced what he called, with pride, 'a race of non-commissioned officers'. [30] The inflexible grade-system almost prevented Einstein from continuing his studies: it probably encouraged others to march on, in step, towards Stalingrad and Auschwitz. The question arises: if we want to change the kind of political education offered by many schools will we have to change 'the hidden curriculum' so much that it will be no longer school?

9. The school as an educator for the economy

The great achievements of nineteenth-century schools included schooling European peasants to accept American urban society, and getting the masses used to the dull, repetitive work that they had to suffer for the rest of their born days. The school taught the supreme virtue of attendance - this alone won medals. (Today, in contrast, truancy from schools is paralleled by absenteeism from the factories.) It taught the virtue of punctuality, and of time dictated by the clock and not by the seasons. It taught people to know their place, and to sit still in it. (Today, in several countries, there are schools that label children 'hyper-active' if they want to walk around the classroom, and some even treat them with tranquillising drugs.) The economy to which many schools still relate is that of early industrialism - of labour-intensive production, and of the production-line of one man, one place, one task. (This was reflected in the Battersea system, described by Matthew Arnold, [31] of one pupil, one desk - a nineteenth-century British invention that conquered the world.) Nowadays Volvo, the Swedish motor manufacturers, have workers doing a number of tasks, moving around an area of the factory. (This may be reflected in some English progressive primary schools where pupils are allowed to move around the room as they take part in project production.) The question arises, as the economy moves rapidly towards a future which is capital-, not labour-intensive, and in which service industries will expand, isn't 'the hidden curriculum' of schools related to a passing, and perhaps bygone age? Again, if the hidden curriculum is changed, will there be schools?

10. The teacher as prostitute, bureaucrat, and political educator

Teachers, argues Illich, are professionals - at least in the sense that they are paid - and the hallmark of a professional is that he or she works for the owner of the house (in this case, the house of knowledge). Thus, according to Illich, the patron saint of teachers ('the second oldest profession') ought to be Mary Magdalene, for they are not only in the game, but also on the game. But in all countries the teacher is a political educator: in West Germany a teacher swears an oath of allegiance to the state;[32] in Liberia a teacher is a political appointee and has to give one month's salary each year to the ruling True Whig Party;[33] in England it is better hidden but essentially the same - a main function of teachers is to endorse the status quo, not to challenge it. The teacher is the first political figure a child meets - that is, a figure whose authority attaches to the office, not the person: a father dies and the child has lost his father; one teacher dies (or leaves) and another pops up to take his place. Put another way, a naked father might still have personal authority but an Emporor-teacher without his clothes loses in stature (the basic reason why the vestiarian controversy over gowns, suits, and uniforms is so bitterly fought in so many schools).

In most countries the teaching profession attracts those with conservative personalities, those who choose the one job they have really seen in action, majorities of whom journey in life from school, to college, and back to school again. They have chosen a profession which offers security and a pension, as well as a limited degree of social mobility. In fact, many have climbed up the social ladder to become teachers and they are grateful to have arrived. In rigidly stratified societies they become, in the Austrian phrase 'cyclists' - bowing to those above them, and trampling on those below, a mixture of deference and arrogance.

But although teachers have chosen to live in a school environment in which they were relatively successful themselves, most of them have experienced some form of failure in the educational system, and in some countries many have failed to gain entry to a university, or to get a degree (something that puts them on a lower level in the school hierarchy, and a lower pay scale). In most countries teachers are 'produced' by second- or third-grade institutions ('less noble institutions', an OECD report calls them) and they are subjected to the hidden curriculum of schools in a yet more extreme form: knowledge is mediated to them - 'R. S. Peters says... Bernstein says... Piaget says... O'Grady says...'; progressive methods and individual choice are recommended to them in compulsory lectures: and School is Dead is prescribed reading on the booklist. They are put through a sequential curriculum, and the various 'rites de passage' provide a pathway for some, and a means of screening out others. The dilemma of 'the progressive teacher' is that the teacher is asked to be a political educator, but in a particular sense: he is asked to disseminate consensus values but forbidden to disseminate partisan values. [34] The problem for socialist teachers who believe that the answer to present problems is to 'produce' socialist teachers is that this analysis applies to them as well as to anyone else. At a time when the language of cycling teachers (the James Report in England and Wales) and recycling people (the USA) is current in discussions about professional training, the question arises whether the 'production' of a different kind of teacher is possible without a radical alteration of the structures within which teachers are 'produced'.

11. Childhood - a recent creation

There have always been children but childhood is a recent creation. 'In medieval society the idea of childhood did not exist', writes the French historian Philippe Ariès. [35] J. H. Plumb, the British historian, writes: 'The very idea of childhood is a European invention of the last four hundred years. [36] In pre-industrial society, and in Third World countries today, children performed and perform real tasks. Industrial society first used children as cheap labour but later, as a result of protective legislation and the mechanisation of production, children became superfluous. Childhood began among the upper classes, where children were first superfluous, and has spread downwards to the middle and working classes. In the nineteenth century the 'needs' of childhood were met by a new service-industry which made toys and dolls, and whose development is chronicled in a special museum of childhood in Edinburgh. In England, the mass provision of schools from 1870 onwards was seen by some as a means of protecting children from factory exploitation: but they were also places to put children who otherwise would have been on the street. Today, when the raising of the school-leaving age is partly related to youth unemployment, in several ways children would be better protected by legislation governing factories than by legislation governing schools. When childhood was invented children were dressed up to suit adult fantasies. In common with other groups who came to be regarded as irrational and superfluous in Western Europe, they became subjected to special treatment in houses of confinement. The unemployed were put in the workhouse; the mentally ill in asylums; the criminals in prisons; and children were put in schools. Those who suffered the extreme treatments were the sons of the European bourgeoisie who were sent to institutions in the remote parts of the country to undergo a planned course of deprivation to cure them of their childhood. All these groups were victims of what the French historian Michel Foucault calls 'the great lock up'. [37]

Attitudes to childhood varied between groups, and sometimes adults held within themselves ambivalent views of childhood - romanticising it one moment, and punishing it the next.

The general development saw a separating of the generations: the able-bodied who could work were given work; all other groups received social services. In several societies now the old are put in 'homes'. In the process school became a place unfit for adults, inhabited by peculiar people, women among children, 'men among boys', a doll's house full of pretence and simulation. At the same time a world was built that was unfit for children. Today, as the environment becomes ever more hostile to them, children all over the world are offered their own refuges in the form of playgrounds. A playspace project proclaims: 'The child is liberated within the confines of the playground', [38] paradoxically combining the rhetoric of freedom with the realities of incarceration.

In Education 'the child' became the centre of the great debate of the first half of the twentieth century, and it was essentially a debate about the nature of man. Was the child born in original stupidity (sin) and therefore in need of the extrinsic motivation of stick and carrot in order to learn? The progressives denied it, A. S. Neill stating: 'A child is innately wise and realistic. '[39] This has been a basis of the progressive argument from Rousseau and Tolstoy, to Dewey and Neill, and to Goodman and Holt. The other great secular-religious debate of the eighteenth century also came to be applied to the child -

'human rights' (the notion that a man has rights because he is a man, not because they are granted by society) were adapted to create a doctrine of 'children's rights'. The implications were similar: 'human rights' shook kings, and 'children's rights' shake schoolmasters.

Both the progressives and the traditionalists assert that they want to protect children - from each other. They have become, ironically, complementary parts of the same protection racket.

Some of the progressives put their faith for a better future with the children: while the social · structures into which the children enter remain essentially unchanged their hopes and their disappointments will be eternal. Indeed the utopian hope of a society reformed by children is a common part of the romantic schoolman's creed, whatever his particular sect. Some hope that children will create the libertarian society; some that they will create the classless society. Politically, though, children are a marginal group - the younger they are the more marginal they become. This is why educational reformers are allowed to indulge their fantasies most with the very young. It is the political weakness of the young that has itself made them so vulnerable to educational researchers and to utopian experiments.

It is not only the schools that are affected by childhood. If industrial society created childhood late industrial society has preserved and extended it into adolescence and studolescence, and has made what the Ontario Report calls 'academic playpens'[40] for the young, who grow older in each generation. The universities in many countries have become 'youth cities' in which childhood is prolonged into middle age. As the prospects of old-time 'employment' decrease, the prospects of further extensions of 'childhood' increase. By the end of the century in several countries it might be possible to go straight from childhood to the old folks' home.

12. 'School Age'

'School age' is a very odd concept - little more than a legal term. It is prescriptive, not descriptive. Large sections of the school population behave as if they were not of 'school age' at all. Certainly 'school age' is extending - the school-starting age is lowered and the leaving-age is raised, and some theorists of 'permanent education' raise the spectre of lifelong schooling.

13. School as an institution

Paul Goodman and Ivan Illich have compared schools to prisons, hospitals, asylums, and the church. These all have their supervisors and mediators and, in the case of the first three now and the church when attendance was compulsory, their inmates. They all offer value-packages. They all have their own institutional logic. The American sociologists Howard S. Becker and Erving Goffman both expose the disparity between the rhetoric and the reality of institutions. Becker writes: 'The rhetoric institutional apologists produce diverts our attention from the way the very organisation of an institution produces the failures so excused.'[41] Goffman writes: 'The contradiction between what the institution does and what officials must say it does forms the basic context of the staff's daily activities.'[42] What puts the school in such a vulnerable position, according to Illich, is that is has become the repository of society's hopes. School is the world church of secular society, offering salvation to the masses. Just as the church distributed eternal-life chances, so the school distributes life-chances. The 'elect' are chosen (or are the chosen) and they recognise themselves, as Weber said the Calvinist elect recognised themselves, by their earthly prosperity. School certificates are received and taken as a sacrament - an external and visible sign of internal grace. Those born in grace - of the right sex, to the right parents, in the right place and at the right time - consume more formal schooling and go on to consume more houses, cars, and wives than the damned whose in-born ignorance the school has confirmed and certified. The church, which promised life-after-death, was in a better position than schools which offer life after school. The first could not be falsified empirically. However, in Third World countries and in post-industrial societies today unemployed school and university graduates reflect bitterly on the school's false promises. While any compulsory institution, be it the church in times past or an army founded on conscription in time of peace, is likely to have an agnostic congregation, the comprehensive school-church is likely to lose its congregation altogether if it consistently fails to match promise with performance.

The two main questions that this aspect of deschooling raises are: Can institutions change and renew their purposes? What would happen to schools if compulsion was taken away?

14. Teaching and learning

'An illusion on which the school system rests,' writes Illich, 'is that most learning is the result of teaching.' Certainly it seems that a lot of teaching, but not much learning of what is taught, goes on in school. If this is true the possibility arises that the teacher, whether performing classical theatre in front of or street theatre moving round the class, is engaged in a charade or non-interaction ritual. In mass systems, as majorities clearly do not learn what the school pretends to teach, the school creates alibis. A large number of explanations are possible. James Herndon, the US radical educational reformer, has argued the extreme thesis: 'Nobody learns anything in school, but middle-class children learn enough elsewhere to be able to pretend that school has taught them something; since lower-class children have nowhere else to learn what school is supposed to teach them they just do not learn it; the middle-class 'success' allows the schools to believe that they are effective and that the trouble lies in lower-class children rather than in the schools.'[43] In similar vein the children of the School of Barbiana attack the traditional Italian school, saying: 'It remains a school cut to measure for the rich. For people who can get their culture at home and are going to school just in order to collect diplomas.'[44] Illich writes: 'School teaches us that instruction produces learning' but 'most learning is not the result of instruction. It is rather the result of unhampered participation in a meaningful setting.' Schools give the impression of maintaining a continuity of enterprise by assumed or enforced regular attendance. Deschooling theory raises the question of whether schools provide bad learning environments. A lot of their organisation is explicable in terms of housing and moving large numbers around in a building - that is, administrative convenience - and not in terms of a concern to promote learning or what we know about processes of learning. Elaborate timetables in multi-coloured plastic, which now stand as icons in some schools, might well be part of the mystification of teaching and learning in which most schools indulge. In England, the dominant factors in the general school reorganisation now taking place have been the concern to fit children into existing buildings and to make sure that teachers do not have to change their jobs or lose job opportunities. I have on record a thought-provoking statement by a headmaster who speaks of difficulties in 'fitting children into the timetable'.

15. Non-school and deschooled learning

Deschooling theory has pointed out that many of the resources for learning, both in things and people, are to be found outside the school. It has also stressed the amount of learning that goes on outside the school - in the family, the peer-group, in pubs, clubs, and churches, in interest groups, and in learning on-the-job. Modern technology has further increased the possibilities of learning outside the school. Unlike the nineteenth century, our society is information-rich - with easy access for many to libraries, recordings, and sometimes even to skill-centres: newspapers and television spread news more quickly than ever before in history. The potential of information services via the telephone is only just beginning to be explored. Schools tend to invalidate things learned outside the school, declare them uneducational, or else regard them as a threat. Deschooled learning presupposes a positive move away from school as we have known it hitherto. Deschooling theory has raised questions about how non-school learning might be further promoted and its vitality increased, and about the possibilities of deschooled learning: the latter might involve using the school building more as an operational base and as a forum for dialogue; it would certainly involve making the world outside the school much more accessible than it is today, and not only to privileged minorities.

16. What schools teach

For majorities schools fail to teach assessable skills: teachers often therefore explain their activities in other terms whose common characteristics are that they need to be both grandiose and vague. Thus they are teaching pupils 'how to learn' (they never say what); how to get on with other people; tolerance; or citizenship. Schools, claims Illich, teach the hidden curriculum of schooling. Thus those teachers are right who say that schools teach something other than what most people think they teach. But it is also true that teachers 'know not what they do'. Most of them are social workers, and political educators, without knowing it. As Robert Silman has written about doctors, so with teachers: they 'confuse for themselves, as well as for others, the knowledge they have with the social role they enact'. [45]

17. Schooling as a service-industry

As societies modernise, workers move from the agricultural to the industrial sectors of the economy, and from the countryside to the towns. With the development of mechanisation and automation, employment decreases in primary producing industries, such as coal and steel, and service industries expand, particularly those connected with education and leisure. Technical problems of production are fairly easy to overcome but, in order to stimulate and maintain consumption, the advertising industry becomes the key industry - often persuading people to buy things they don't need with money they haven't got. The school, as a place where society conserves and reproduces itself, is a part of the advertising industry. Education is the mass-service-industry of modern society. It creates the need for its own products, and it validates its own activities. At a time when the economy is becoming more capital- and less labour-intensive, education is becoming more labour-intensive, and that from an already labour-intensive base. It is able to absorb redundant workers from other industries - as it did with Rolls Royce engineers and ICI chemists - into its work force. Non-polluting (at least physically, for the education industry deals mainly in the redistribution of things that already exist) this points to a future where we will all sell services to each other.

The two most striking features of this service industry are that up to now its activities have been assumed to be legitimate, and that each of its failures is made a pretext for further expansion. Few critics have even noticed the schoolman imperialism that is a characteristic of our times. Failures in the teaching of 'hard knowledge' - like Mathematics, Science, and Foreign Languages - have led to major and expensive projects in many countries, reflecting a general rule - the greater the failure, the greater the expansion. Indeed the prosperity built on failure has led to the rise of a new sector of the service-industry - Curriculum Development. Here, during the last decade, a thousand Blooms have flowered. Entrepreneurial knowledge capitalists, reminiscent of the projectors and patentees of seventeenth-century England, have sought their fame and fortunes. Their curriculum cargo has become part of the import and export business, although their main speciality is selling obsolete models from the USA. Just as neo-colonialism uses methods of economic control which are more sophisticated than the old forms of imperialism which involved physically occupying colonies, so advanced countries no longer export schools or whole school-systems; instead they practise a form of neo-colonialism through the export of teaching materials and curriculum advisers. In fact, it is the people who, before the new rhetoric, used to be called the poor who have usually been the main victims. Often social scientists, curriculum and community developers have been used by governments (or government agencies) to treat the illnesses (or the symptoms of the illnesses) of modern society. As systems-maintenance men they have subjected education to the language of systems-engineering - of 'inputs' and 'outputs', 'flows' and 'feedbacks': dominated by the image of the production-line they have broken the curriculum and teaching down into component parts, and treated both learning and people as commodities to be produced. They have determined other people's interests and needs and engineered environments for others to live in. Generally speaking they have reinforced rather than questioned the hidden curriculum. Assessment of projects was done by project members, who were part of the project hierarchy and dependent on the goodwill of the director for their further career prospects: like the research of retail industry generally it was aimed to improve delivery systems. Rather than question the structures and definitions in which they operate, they have consistently chosen to expand their activities until, like industry in late-capitalism generally, they have finally achieved in-built obsolescence, making their products ephemeral, but themselves eternal. Like much of consumer industry in general, the education industry fails to serve its clients; rather it consumes the consumers. Even on a personal level, the insight of the playwright

Ionesco as portrayed in his play La Leçon is correct: there is consumerism in formal education, but it is not that students consume curricula, but rather that teachers consume their pupils.

18. Certificates as passports and credit cards

Certificates are used to label the product, and to validate the activity. For 'the scholarship boy', with high-grade certificates, they have served as passports to new parts of the country, and new social strata. With the International Baccalaureate credit cards have been printed for Europe's would-be elite. But for many, even though they had sat, served and waited through ten years of school, there were no certificates. For them new certificates were created, a soft currency, an identity card rather than a passport. Curiously, those very systems of internal assessment which in Europe were recognised as being Prussian, bureaucratic, and Kafkaesque, were taken up by English reformers in the name of progress, encouraging pupils to cease to study subjects and to study their teachers instead. If the community school is the ultimate arrogance of the schoolmen, trying to print their own money is their final folly, for it may very soon prove counterfeit. Works like Ivar Berg's Education and Jobs: The Great Training Robbery[46] have exposed the negative correlation between certification and subsequent job-performance. Employers themselves are becoming ever more suspicious of school and university certificates and several firms have created their own training systems and skill-centres - described as 'shadow systems of education' in some documents. The future is likely to see job-related tests taking the place of school certificates in the selection of personnel. A 'mandarin curriculum' (which deals in arcane knowledge, and does not relate to the life-situations of the learner) has already failed in the mass school system. However, a do-your-own-thing curriculum offers no real answer to the schoolmen because socially only the rich can afford to do their own thing, and at a school level most people will probably want to do it somewhere other than school.

19. Schools and equality: élites and the poor

That the poor of the earth have at times seen the school as the path to secular salvation, there can be no doubt. Booker T. Washington, the spokesman for the emancipated slaves of the USA in the nineteenth century, wrote: 'I had no schooling whatever while I was a slave, though I remember on several occasions I went as far as the schoolhouse door with one of my young mistresses to carry her books. The picture of several dozen boys and girls in a schoolroom engaged in study made a deep impression on me, and I had the feeling that to get into a schoolhouse and study in this way would be about the same as getting into paradise.'[47] In their moving plea for better schools the Italian peasant children who ran their own school at Barbiana in Tuscany go beyond the basic defence - 'School will always be better than cow shit' - to point out that 'in Africa, in Asia, in Latin America, in southern Italy, in the hills, in the fields, even in the cities, millions of children are waiting to be made equal.'[48] In African and Indian villages many children see the school as a way out, and they are willing to learn the vain repetitions of the new religion (which has taken the place of the missionaries' catechisms) in order to gain a passport to the towns.

The reality is that only a small minority 'escape': whereas some escaped before by becoming priests, several now escape by becoming schoolmasters. Some of these reinforce the system, believing it to be good because they succeeded through it, and believing it to be a significant instrument of social mobility because of their own mobility. Sometimes they are even more conservative than schoolmasters from the middle or upper strata of society. This phenomenon is expressed in different countries and climes in different ways. Paulo Freire says: 'It is a rare peasant who, once "promoted" to overseer, does not become more of a tyrant towards his former comrades than the owner himself.'[49] The British social historian R. H. Tawney said the educational system was like a pond full of frog-spawn: those tadpoles who grew legs, and became frogs, jumped on to the bank and croaked the message that any tadpole with drive and ability could become a frog. The sentiment is put more bluntly in an English folk song:

Working class can kiss my arse,
I've got the foreman's job at last!

School systems generally have served not to promote equality, but to legitimise inequality. Like religion, schooling has provided 'the theodicy of good fortune for those who are fortunate', and has offered either expulsion or consolation to the oppressed. Just as the mandarin activities of the English public schools in the nineteenth century legitimised the power of the ruling groups, so today in some Third World countries the power of ruling élites is bolstered by a literary culture as well as by guns. In reformed school systems run according to contest rather than sponsored mobility - that is, where the competition is made to look open and where everyone seems to have an equal chance - the legitimising process is even more secure. People believe they are social failures because they are social failures, and not because society has done them down. Meanwhile, the poor become victims of some educational planners who in literacy projects deny their word and subject them to 'linguistic enrichment programmes', and who offer them 'communities' planned in Paris or the town hall. In some countries, those who succeed by school standards depart clutching their certificates to join the urban poor, or to sit with several of their fellows in white collars around a desk, producing nothing and consuming little, desperately simulating activity. Even in England, where the influence of the nineteenth-century public schools has gone into the grammar and the comprehensive schools, the strange truth is beginning to dawn: ruling élites did not become ruling élites because they went to public schools: the reverse was the case - public schools were places where ruling élites sent their sons. Sadly, the evidence is that the centuries of mass school systems have seen growing inequalities, both within countries (the USA has its own Third World, and Canada its 'grey belts') and on a world scale.

20. Rhetoric, myth, and ritual

Schools can do relatively little to promote equality as the ways to greater equality lie more outside schools, with access to jobs, housing, transportation and health services, and through political action, legislation, and changed social organisation. Schools, however, can deny to many the opportunities of changing their lot by failing to offer 'hard knowledge', particularly the knowledge of political economy, and instead offering to majorities either mandarin knowledge - which does not relate to their lives, and whose use they cannot see - or the consolations of therapy. Nevertheless, in societies characterised by inequality it is both essential and strategic to locate the central myth of the system - that of equality of opportunity - in the schools. Unequal provision, even within the educational system, is justified in terms of the myth ('equal opportunity to become unequal') and reports manage both to recognise the existence of gross inequality and keep the myth going ('equal opportunity of acquiring intelligence'[50]). The function of the myth, and its supporting rhetoric and associated rituals, is to veil the disparity between the promise and the performance of the system. In similar fashion, the school curriculum is specialist, but all the talk is about general education; some progressive teachers manipulate children and call it 'free drama'; and a system whose reality was often the social pacification of poor people was run by an 'education service' describing its work as 'educating our masters'.

21. Schooling and democratisation

That education today has its religious dimensions is proved by the current 'theological' debate concerning the nature of intelligence. Its political importance is shown in the way that rival groups try to control the school, as in former times they struggled to control the church. The central issue which combines the 'religious' and the 'political' aspects of the present system is democratisation. Michael Huberman in 1970, at a time when he was an employee of UNESCO, produced a paper called Reflections on Democratisation in Secondary and Higher Education[51] in which he pointed out that education systems could not democratise merely by expanding the old élite models. If UNESCO didn't put his paper on a modern equivalent of the index librorum prohibitorum, neither do they want it republished. Huberman later found himself, not on the heretic's pyre nor in the mental asylum, but as a professor a pedagogy (perhaps a worse fate). He had raised political and structural questions which international organisations, and most political parties, do their best to evade. Put simply, most people view social mobility (in which we are all supposed to believe) only as mobility upwards. Most people have long since stopped talking about the redistribution of wealth in society. Groups at the top of society, for their part, consolidate their power through property and capital, and do not move over simply because political theorists point out that they are there, or because others have consumed more formal schooling. Democratisation would involve positive discrimination on a scale unheard of so far (and it is doubtful in many countries if this is a political possibility) or a change in the social structures. These are difficult questions and many people still prefer to talk about democratisation rather than answer them.

22. Compulsion and therapy

A result of the mass system of compulsory schooling in many 'advanced' countries is a confrontation between teachers and pupils. For these teachers 'discipline' is a major concern and their weapons include hitting the children with sticks (defended in Britain by many 'as a last resort'[52]), sarcasm, humiliating pupils in front of their fellows, or sentencing (as judge, jury, and executioner) wrong-doers to periods of physical detention. The alienation from work that many of these children will later suffer is first learned in the classroom where teachers use the word 'work' as a threat ('Be quiet, or I'll set you some work!'). The situation tends to grow ever worse, until any humanist hopes that the teacher might have possessed are lost in a spiral of mutual resentment. There is a cold war in the classroom, in which the teacher's main aim is containment, and his policy one of crisis management. In the classroom the main problem is the teacher's problem and he tries to overcome it in new, and more sophisticated ways - joining with other teachers in a team ('Teaching from Strength', reminiscent of the Cold War 'Negotiation from Strength'); individualising learning ('Divide et Impera'); electrifying the classroom to create McLuhanesque happenings; or - more likely - turning the pupil's life into an endless succession of worksheets. To take the tension out of the situation other teachers get on Christian-name terms with their pupils, and speak of learning from each other. (But, although they try to deny much of their role it is still the teachers, and not the pupils, who draw pay at the end of the month.) Some schools instal coffee-bars and discos (pretending that the school is not a school, but 'a community centre') and teachers follow the latest trends in hair and dress styles - the rock-priest syndrome. At a time when the classical proletariat is being made redundant (by automation, and by the import of immigrant labour from poorer countries to form a sub-proletariat) it is found that the therapy education of the private 'progressive' schools, formerly only suitable for the disturbed children of neurotic upper-class parents, is now suitable for the masses. Hard knowledge is as difficult to come by as ever, but neurosis has been democratised. Thus, the masses are gentled in a new way, towards a future of enforced 'leisure' and welfare benefits. Already in adult education some of these social therapists offer pottery to the workers, and cottage industry to the urban unemployed.

At school level one sees the paradox of compulsory therapy, as part of the general policy of changing the consciousness of the oppressed, instead of changing the structures which cause the oppression.

The strength of teachers who teach the upper strata of society, those about to enter into leadership positions, is that the pupils see the purposes and ends of the operation (and that they are their purposes and ends), and therefore teachers and pupils are essentially on the same side. The fundamental weakness of teachers of large sections of the school population and one that all the teachers' stratagems fail to hide from the pupils, is that they are not on the same side. For these pupils, too, their education has an instrumental quality, but it is instrumental to serve the purposes and ends of others. In such institutions there is often a lot of deliberate damage done by the pupils to the building; some pupils still regard the lavatory as a place of refuge; and truancy rates are high. Here, some progressive schools turn what to some children looks like a prison into an open prison, either with a relaxed régime within conditions of 'maximum perimeter security' or else by redefining school as something which includes the whole area. In this latter case there may well seem to be no way out.

23. The challenge of media technology

Although the schoolmen have developed new empires devoted to 'educational technology', and although some preach salvation for teachers through its application, the fact is that the revolution in media technology has made the school obsolete as a transmitter of information. Teachers have almost lost control over their 'vertical' transmission of knowledge, as priests did once before with the invention of printing. The degree of lingering control which teachers enjoy depends on the social recognition of the certificates they issue. (In the past 'the right to exclude from the sacraments was the last priestly control left in England'.[53]) The book raised the possibilities of decentralised and deinstitutionalised learning: it threatened a know-ledge-social system ruled over by a tiny, reading élite (called 'lecturers'); and it broke the church. Just as printing was followed by Luther's religious heresy - 'Everyman his own priest', so the new media have been followed by Illich's educational heresy - 'Everyman his own teacher'. The church feared the book, not as a medium of communication as such - after all, throughout the centuries and on a regular basis the church organised multi-media happenings unequalled in the dreams of media tech-nologists - but because of its political implications. The church therefore drew up an index of prohibited works, and burned books (something which only totalitarian states do today). The schools, however, treat the new media with a combination of denial and domestication. Many teachers have asserted that they have qualities that the new media have not (which is true, for the new media are <u>potentially</u> more susceptible to learner control: you can turn off a television with a flick of the wrist, but you have to indulge in mental truancy to turn off a teacher). Some teachers see their future role as mediating the media to their pupils; others see the media liberating them from all the aspects of their work they don't like and allowing them to get on with 'the real job of teaching' (although they never say what that is). Many teachers have used the new media to strengthen their hand vis-à-vis their pupils, developing 're-sources banks', full of hardware and information sheets, where they are the bank managers. Alongside this, new teaching systems are developed, in which the teacher deals out the worksheets, like a banker in a game of cards, better set for a win than the ordinary player.

The Open University in Britain has taken up the <u>technical</u> challenges of new ways of teaching and learning. But the main questions raised by the new media technology are <u>political</u> questions, concerning the horizontal versus the vertical transmission of knowledge, centralism versus decentralisation, and problems of control. (So far, radio and television have been used for hierarchical, one-way communica-tion, although phone-ins are now used to give an impression of dialogue. In some large schools, headmasters and headmistresses communicate with staff and pupils through loudspeakers fitted in each classroom - god out of the machine.) High technology raises the power of the institutions, and reinforces the message of the hidden curriculum that only by attending the (now electronic) learning centre can a person learn. Intermediate and low-profile technology offer possibilities of decentralised learning, under learner control.

24. School and the cultural revolution

Once I wrote that we needed a cultural revolution - in which old concepts like 'education', 'work' and 'leisure' would be looked at in a new way - to take us beyond the cultural crisis of our times.[54] Now it seems that one of the causes of the school crisis itself is that a cultural revolution is actually going on in modern society. The reference points change rapidly - in England, for example, sex, Europe, and the penny are not what they were, and for some the

days of 'work' are over and the age of 'leisure'/ 'unemployment' has already begun. Technological progress is exponential, not linear, and the speed of change constantly increases. In education the reform which it has taken a decade to achieve politically is declared obsolete by current research (which is as well, as running inflation has made it too costly to afford). The school has been a culture-lag institu-tion suitable in minority and non-compulsory systems for transmitting the high-culture and dealing in arcane knowledge. In a time of rapid change, with a mass-clientèle, the school has the dilemma of whether it should promote its own peculiar purposes, or whether it should chase after change, and perhaps even offer life-adjustment education throughout life with permanent schooling. The first course tends to ignore majorities: the second is in danger of chasing a will o' the wisp.

25. A new look at the underground

Deschooling theory and alternative projects have forced us to take a new look at the underground. Alternative programmes reflect perceived weaknesses in present society. I have written elsewhere that 'today in the catacombs of educational thought the deschooling underground might be revealing to us the outlines of tomorrow's world.'[55] Daniel Berrigan has suggested: 'Instead of thinking of the underground as temporary, exotic, abnormal, perhaps we should start thinking of its implication as an entirely self-sufficient, mobile, internal-revival community; the underground as a definition of our future.'[56] Although it is dependent on the system it opposes, and is in danger of being a complementary part of the dominant reality, the underground does offer a <u>variety</u> of alternatives for consideration. Schooling tends to be a closed system, sanctified rather than evaluated by the internal assessments of the schoolmen them-selves. What is needed now is much more counter-foil research on schools, and much more research on the underground.

26. Alternative futures: the delimited school versus the escalating school; the schooled society versus the learning society; economy-centred versus man-centred educational planning

The response of many schoolmen to the present educational crisis is either to build schools which attempt to encapsulate the world, or else to try to turn all the world into a school. Both usually operate under a 'community' rhetoric. The first group invite 'the community' into the school; they reconstruct the world inside the school - with flats, workshops (usually specialising in obsolete machinery), and dis-cotheques. In more 'advanced' countries these schools will eventually also contain sex rooms, for the golden rule of the institution will be that every-thing is allowed, as long as it is performed on the premises, under teacher supervision. The second group turn 'the environment' into part of their imperium, and every human act into 'a learning experience'. Like the Austro-Hungarian Empire both these groups, when in doubt, expand. They attribute to the school yet more tasks which it cannot perform. The major alternative to this policy is for the school to reduce its tasks, and to delimit its activities. However, in England and the USA this does not seem to be the way things are going.

The main choice for the future can be character-ised as being between Illich's nightmare scenario for 'the schooled society' and Robert M. Hutchins' vision of 'the learning society'. [57] In the first, teachers and mediators would dominate, and individuals would be subjected to institutional treatments from cradle to grave, and school would expand until it was co-terminous with society, the world, and with life itself. The major preconditions for the second are a decentralisation and a debureaucratisation of educational provision. School would have a place, but it would be a delimited school whose tasks would be related to lifelong learning provision. From the school teacher's point of view this is the central question.

The key question for educational planners is whether their plans are economy-centred (based on projected manpower requirements) or man-centred (based on a vision of man). The field of permanent education is the arena where this battle is already being fought.

27. Permanent education: man or manpower?

Permanent education is the area of education of most interest to international planners, to international organisations like OECD, the European Cultural Foundation, the Council of Europe, and UNESCO, as well as to the multi-national corporations. Although to some it may provide a new alibi - using the dream of lifelong learning to divert attention away from the reality of school failure, the schoolmen need to de-school their analysis enough to recognise this major field. For us all, permanent education illustrates the dilemmas for the future, and a consideration of its developing theory is instructive.

Its origins were mainly concerned with job training and retraining, and this has been a dominant theme throughout. The Austrian Education Minister, Piffl Percevic, stated in Continued Education, [58] 1965: 'The present development of economic production calls for an increasing number of skilled workers. The training and shaping of a type of human personality [my underlining] which... will functionally and numerically supersede the relatively unskilled labourer of earlier days, constitutes a problem the solution of which is of vital importance for all States of the free world. ' E. W. Sudale, developing this theme in Continued Education, 1971[59] wrote: 'The basic thesis of lifelong education is that the pace and pervasiveness of socio-economic change have rendered obsolete any traditional educational system which assumes that man's initial schooling in his youth can endow him with a store of knowledge and skill which will be valid for the rest of his life. It should therefore be progressively replaced by a system of "recurrent" education, which provides a succession of varied opportunities for people of all ages consciously to resume their personal, vocational and general education. This, in turn, requires a radical rethinking of the purpose, content and method of initial schooling. ' Bertrand Schwartz, a major theorist of permanent education, has argued for education throughout life, not education for life, so that man can keep abreast of the rapidly changing environment, not only in terms of professional re-training but also in terms of changed values and adapt to new ways of life. [60] The re-licensing and re-certification of doctors and dentists is already common practice in the USA, and there is talk of 'topping up' degrees. Rapid technological changes in production have created growing 'career obsolescence', a personal and a social problem that some theorists have suggested might be dealt with in the following way: 'An important role for adult education... is resocializa-

tion. Resocialization is a process in which allegiances, perceptions, and habits are altered. It involves a change in personal and social identity [my underlining]. '[61] In the USA there is already talk of compulsory adult education and of recycling people[62] [my underlining]. As Dragomir Fillipovic of Yugoslavia has written: 'The concept of permanent education entails undreamt-of expansion of the educational system. '[63] It is little wonder that humanists like Ohliger[64] and Frese[65] have got frightened. Frese has asked the pertinent question: 'Is the new permanent education meant to be a superior instrument for moulding people?... Its uses will reinforce the established social order... controlling and manipulating the destiny of whole populations. ' Nor can we wonder that, at a time when education is becoming the biggest national industry and less a preparation for life than a way of life, that another humanist has asked the question: 'Is there school after death?'[66]

Permanent education focusses more clearly some of the dilemmas of the school system - conflicts between a production-centred and a person-centred approach, between economic and humanistic goals. Willis Harman warns: 'Those who wish not only to fit in with the future, but also to participate in the choosing of it, need to understand what is at stake in the choices - "the issues beneath the issues"... ' While some theories of resocialisation come close to the kind of 're-education' practised in Mauthausen concentration camp we would be unwise to dismiss the nightmare scenarios of Ivan Illich out of hand.

28. The limitations of deschooling theory

In spite of its profound insights deschooling theory has serious weaknesses. The most serious of these are that the arguments lack a firm basis of empirical evidence and practical alternatives; they evade central questions of political power; and they offer critiques, rather than operational strategies or programmes. Much of the evidence is circumstantial, or anecdotal: both Goodman and Holt tend to buttress their assertions with the statements of friends who agree with them. When 'hard' data - such as statistics of economic costs of education - are presented they have often been selected to support the thesis being argued. Too much of the deschooling argument at the moment is based on general theories, standing on other general theories - particularly general theories about institutions and professionals - that is, it is a framework of assertions. The dominant ideology of both Goodman and Reimer is that of the libertarian anarchist: this position, although reflecting from Kropotkin on some of the highest ideals and best visions of man, has yet to reconcile its central paradox - society without the state, and major, common human activities without institutions. Both seem to believe in the myths of the American history books - the self-reliant frontiersman often appears to be their model - and perhaps they, as much as the schoolman-believer Silberman, are products of the Great American Dream Machine. Are they trying to salvage an American dream in which a Jeffersonian, independent yeomanry have mod. cons. at their disposal? If so, they should remember that Jefferson in office was different from Jefferson in opposition: few did more to enhance the power of the state. In 'advanced' countries our crisis is one of mass, urban education. We should remember Jefferson's attitude: 'The mobs of great cities add so much to pure government as sores do to the strength of the human body. '

Goodman uses language in his own way, and for

his own ends - 'natural' and 'human' are good, 'unnatural' and 'inhuman' are bad. Goodman, Reimer, and Illich all use a reality principle in which the 'real' is not what is, but what ought to be. Their ultimate appeal is to 'real education', but what that might be is stated in extremely vague terms. In Reimer's book it is Paulo Freire who carries a heavy burden as a rare example of what deschooling might achieve in practice. In Goodman's works apprenticeships are offered as a better way of learning than school in spite of the fact that he recognises that at present they are exploitative. (Social historians, like Peter Laslett, [67] and West German radicals, confirm that they were and are a means of exploitation and cheap labour. Howard S. Becker suggests that they are a very inefficient form of learning. To adapt Goodman's argument about schools, I would suggest that they are often a way of keeping youth at least half off the labour market.) The point raises the question of just how much the classic deschoolers contrast a reality (or a distorted reality) of schooling with an alternative, deschooling ideal. We need also to ask how much the concept of school, on which much of Reimer's and Illich's arguments are based, is essentially true in practice, and how much of it is stereotype and caricature. What is certain is that all the deschooling theorists, in their arguments about 'natural' learning, overuse the model of learning the native language, and base on it sweeping assertions that it cannot support.

It is Ivan Illich, the most important of the deschooling theorists, who embodies most of the ambivalences, paradoxes, and contradictions of deschooling theory. His fundamental attack on schools has two dimensions: from his functional analysis he claims that schools fail to carry out their functions efficiently; from his idealistic position he claims that schools fail to fulfil the ideal of true education. On one level this may seem a subtle, two-pronged argument, that will catch the school on one hook, if not on the other. But there is, in the two dimensions, a fundamental ambiguity that runs right through his whole analysis. It concerns the political economy of education or, put more simply, the relationship of school to our present industrial society. If there are major elements about the organisation of work in that society which are alienating we should rejoice that aspects of the school are dysfunctional, and that their job-slotting work is inefficient. There are times in history when liberal education is a threat to the established order. The idealistic premisses of the second position, which proceeds from a vision of man and not a need for manpower, are curious bedfellows for the crude, reductionist arguments stemming from the sociological school of structural functionalism. One wonders whether he employs the device mainly for polemical purposes, or whether Illich really believes that major human institutions can be simplistically reduced to their alleged functions. This is not to deny that institutions have functions, but it is to assert that that is only one level of their reality as perceived by people. A functional analysis of any institution can help us to imagine alternative ways of carrying out its activities, as functionally defined. (The family's 'functions' of economic support, feeding, sex, love, and child rearing might be paralleled in the commune.) Illich naturally chooses 'better' alternatives; but worse alternatives can also be imagined: custodial care, social role selection, and indoctrination - three of Reimer's and Illich's main school 'functions' - could be carried out in a worse form in a society without schools. They might be done by families (often more

manipulative and restrictive than schools); by people giving jobs to their relatives (blood being thicker than water, and more influential than certificates) and to their friends (a continuation, and revival of 'the old pals act'); indoctrination would be done, as it is now, by the media, which mediate a pre-packaged reality more effectively than schools have ever done. If schools have taken the place of the church in being the major legitimating institution of our society we could surmise that the passing of schools would be marked by the rise of a new legitimating institution.

Illich also uses language in his own way - the word 'schooling' itself is often an assertion masquerading as a descriptive statement. The word 'deschooling' itself, for which Illich has apologised, in its best moments is multi-dimensional, but at its worst moments leads to conceptual confusions. Illich uses associative arguments; he insinuates that because something follows something else, it has been caused by it (e.g. higher educational expenditure causes increased educational failure); and that because two things exist at the same time they are necessarily connected.

The argument that schools 'school people' - a central feature of Illich's position - is based on a characteristic lack of empirical evidence. It seems to rest on the simplicities of early American political socialisation theory. Linkages between children's political learning and adult political behaviour were then assumed: they still need to be demonstrated. [68] Adult political socialisation might be much more important. [69] This suggests that we need to look at life-situations in the working world, the real life curriculum, rather than at schools. If schools have a derivative, rather than a primary function in society - that is, if the school is a dependent variable - a lot of Illich's argument falls or loses its force. Illich treats schools as a metaphysical category in his analysis: but schools are not metaphysical, they exist in a social context. To claim that schools are bad by their very nature, that in their essence they are evil, is to make them part of a demonology, a mirror version of the commodity-fetishism that he himself decries.

Illich, like many contemporary educational reformers, must be viewed as a religious figure, and their reform movements are the major religious movements of our time. In many countries the great traditional religions and the great secular religion of Marxism meet in these movements, which have provided an umbrella as well as new purposes for groups as diverse as the World Council of Churches and the survivors of the New Left. Like Marxism, many of the reform movements combine the two heresies of the two major Western religions. Judaism preached the messiah: the great heresy was to believe he had actually arrived. Christianity preached heaven: the great heresy was to believe that heaven can exist on earth.

The style of Illich's writings is reminiscent of the Talmud and the scriptures: they are discursive, didactic, dealing in parables and allegories, something which he shares with the schoolman-reformer Silberman. Also similar is the way in which the rabbi-model of the great educator seems to run through their writings.

Although he exposes the rhetoric of the schoolmen, it is Illich himself who has raised the rhetoric to unprecedented heights. It is Illich who has created a new liturgy. '[I believe] schools confuse process and substance, teaching with learning, and fluency with the ability to say something new' might be regarded as Illich's anti-creed. With Illich, the evangelical tone, and the salvationism, are stronger than ever before. Illich himself has accepted the schoolman's promises of secular salvation, and offered alternative paths to realising them. Max Weber, the great sociologist of religion, once wrote: 'The annunciation and promise of religion have naturally been addressed to the masses of those who were in need of salvation... Frequently the very next generation reinterprets these annunciations and promises in a fundamental fashion.'[70] Parallel groups to free-schoolers and deschoolers had their parallels in seventeenth-century England where groups set up their own free churches, and some tried to de-church religion. Then, too, there were mystics and messiahs offering hell-fire ('the schooled society') on the one hand and paradise ('the learning society') on the other. As in other periods of rapid social change the vision was, and now is, both apocalyptic and millenarian. In those times, with their restructuring of knowledge and radical questioning of established institutions, it was those with internal discipline who flourished, and the early Quakers (probably the de-schoolers of the day) survived by becoming even more respectable than their opponents. In the light of history we should be wary of the way in which Illich fails to face up to the central problem of political power and, instead, makes deschooling an act of faith. It is the fate of those who fail to learn from history that they have to relive it.

Although he operates mostly on a religious plane, Illich is aware that deschooling has its own dangers. In suggesting that it is no longer a question of whether deschooling will happen but how it happens he is right. Deschooling is already occurring in three significant ways - most of the transmission of knowledge now takes place outside schools; industries are setting up their own systems of education; and permanent education is being planned, and developed. Although Illich denounces the service-industry of schooling, other service-industries perhaps offering worse futures - such as the Pentagon and the multi-national corporations - might be more in the running for success than Illich's 'convivial groups'. It is the lack of such political realism in Illich's proposed alternatives that have led people to dismiss them as utopian, not that the people themselves are so 'schooled up that any alternative seems unreal'. That schools do not stand in a simple, direct, and sub-servient position to industry may offer a little hope. Meanwhile, Reimer and Illich give the impression of being men who would burn our boats before they have built a raft.

Illich himself shares the schoolman quality of over-rating the possibilities of schools. However, he is also aware that many of the problems lie outside the schools, and he has moved on, or away, from education to questions of a convivial society guaranteed by law,[71] and of 're-tooling society'.[72]

29. The problems and possibilities of alternative projects

If one of Reimer's embarrassments in 1971 was the poverty of alternative projects to point to, today the embarrassment is the large number, and the variety of alternative projects which exist. They are difficult to classify, and even more difficult to assess. Some of the projects include elements of deschooling; some move more positively in a deschooling direction; and some are actually deschooling projects. The general flourishing of alternative projects has less to do with deschooling as such than with the general crisis of education, and the general reform movements; in relation to both deschooling is a subordinate category. It is almost impossible to sort out the many strands of the reform movement but it is important to realise that many of them pre-dated Illich's Deschooling Society, particularly the concern for environmental education (and the growth of urban studies), the French ideas of permanent education, and the ideal of a learning society.

Alternative projects operate within the system, outside the system, or sometimes on the tightrope between the two: although the rhetoric of most projects usually places them in one camp or the other, in reality the distinction is usually blurred - it is the down-to-earth question of finance that gives many projects the tightrope element. The projects have worked with pre-school children; with children of school age; and with adults.

Projects with pre-school children have included the pre-school playgroup movement in Britain, and the work of Jürgen Zimmer in West Germany which explicitly stresses deschooled learning. There have also been a number of literacy projects (often in a non-school setting) in countries like Britain and the USA.

At school level there are major examples of children largely running their own schools in Italy (the School of Barbiana in Tuscany) and in Spain (Bemposta). There has been a great growth in environmental and urban studies which use the world outside the school as a resource (although schools by and large have no adequate system for using people from outside the school to aid learning). The progressive primary schools in England are a long way from Reimer's and Illich's stereotype of 'school' - they tend to be vertically-grouped and/or interest-grouped; a lot of the work is collaborative, rather than individually competitive; and they attempt to accept the experience of children, not to invalidate it. The school crisis is really in the compulsory secondary schools. Even here, there is evidence of an opening up of choices to learners, and an attempt to construct institutional structures that are based more on learning needs than on administrative convenience.

At university level there have been moves to deschool curricula, by extending the range of choice, sometimes by the introduction of course unit systems, sometimes by the setting up of schools of independent studies, and by questioning compulsory courses where the compulsion cannot be justified, either in terms of the nature of the learning or in terms of being related to job-performance. The Open University in Britain, the University Without Walls in the USA and other countries, have opened up access to knowledge and are facing up to the challenges of mass education: their best elements are already making a major contribution to the building of the learning society. In teacher training some selectors are discriminating in favour of those who have had experience outside the confines of school and university (i.e. in favour of those who have been deschooled) and more training programmes now include visiting and studying mines and factories, partly in the hope that teachers will understand the everyday life-situations of the parents of many of their pupils.

Many of the most impressive alternative projects have taken place with adults. These include the literacy projects of Paulo Freire in Brazil and Chile; the literacy programme in Cuba; and in England the Adult Literacy Scheme, run by student-volunteers in Liverpool.

Some projects operate under a community rhetoric. These include community-action projects; community centres which offer a variety of educational and social provision, examples of which are to be found in several countries, including Australia, Britain, and the USA.

A kind of non-school project which is now common is the use of street-theatre (de-theatred theatre) as a means of involving ordinary people in social and political questions. Examples of theatre projects are to be found in several countries, including Britain, Italy, and West Germany. There are also examples of children making their own television programmes - to develop 'teleliteracy' and to help them control this aspect of the modern environment - in Britain and West Germany.

Projects which specifically base themselves on deschooling theory, or which relate their activities to that theory, include various documentation service networks, such as that of the Centro Intercultural de Documentacion (CIDOC) at Cuernavaca, Mexico and the ERIC Clearinghouse in the USA, and Learning Exchanges (a kind of switchboard which attempts to match those who want to teach something, with those who want to learn it) such as those at the Australian Armadale in Victoria, Evanston in Chicago, and Hackney, London.

Alternative projects face many difficulties; they have limitations, as well as possibilities; and some of them might even contain inherent contradictions. In general, they are difficult to assess, and some of their operators - who view themselves as being involved in a kind of religious enterprise - resist assessment even more than the traditional schoolmen. Some projects do not get much further than creating an alternative rhetoric and alternative rituals.

There are detailed questions to be asked about particular projects. The pre-school playgroup movement might be viewed as the middle class giving their own children a 'two-head start' programme on the way to winning school and life honours at the expense of less privileged groups. Jürgen Zimmer's projects could be viewed as manipulative and as suffering from hidden élitism. Aspects of progressive primary education in England reflect new mystifications of teaching and learning. Open University schemes could be used by certain governments, not 'to provide education on the cheap', but for the domestication of teaching and learning. (Indeed, it was partly because the fact that traditional universities, by gathering students together, had facilitated protests, that René Maheu of UNESCO greeted the University Without Walls.)[73] At the moment, at a time when our crisis is caused by the problems of mass education in an urban society, many of the projects - particularly the free schools and the deschooling projects - concern tiny groups of people. Some advocate a policy of rural retreatism, which is just not a possibility for the majority. Many have an ambivalent attitude to 'the system', opposing and attacking it, and wanting to be supported by, and part of it.

The major weaknesses of alternative movements to date are political. They fail to attack, or force change in the central structures of the educational system, and instead operate round its periphery, becoming themselves a fringe activity. In general,

their challenges have been accommodated among politically marginal groups - pre-school children, the truant and 'the less able' at school level, and with 'the deprived' in the towns. The political danger of apparent increased choice in societies where dominant groups continue to dominate is that it could lead to the privatisation of education, which would become no more a matter for political debate than an individual's motor car or his job is today. It would become as difficult to raise the discussion to the level of 'education' as it is to maintain discussion now about 'transportation' or 'work'. Thus, the greatest political danger in Illich's work, and in that of A. S. Neill, lies in their individualist ideology. The evasion of this central question of political power by Illich does not actually circumvent it, for its reality remains. Those who have faced up to it directly, like Paulo Freire, have usually been beaten. This is not to dismiss alternative enterprises, or the people who work in them. It is only to say that we must not be politically naïve. If both evasion and confrontation are incorrect strategies, we have to find another strategy. Here we have to be wary of the rhetoric of 'the long march through the institutions', for the people who use it - like Dutschke and Gintis - need themselves to remember that its prerequisite is getting in to the institutions in the first place.

30. Two alternative futures: Sweden and Ontario

It would be politically realistic to assert that, at the moment, changes in the central structures of educational systems in advanced countries are less likely to be caused by alternative movements than by changes in the economy's systems of production and by the planning of permanent education which is already leading to a radical reassessment of the school. We should also recognise that the two most impressive alternative plans have been produced by governments - the U-68 plan for recurrent education in Sweden, and the Ontario plan for post-secondary education. The two plans have important common elements: they both reject the old, once and for all view of education provided by schools; they aim at flexibility - 'with as few cul-de-sacs as possible' - and both alternate periods of work with periods of formal education. Both are coherent plans (even England is now moving towards organic planning in education) and both pay attention to fundamental questions of financing the new systems.

The Swedish analysis, which appears to be more economy-centred than man-centred, does ask some awkward questions: will the people to benefit from recurrent education in fact be the same people who benefited through schools - i. e. Will it provide more advantages for the already advantaged? Is the term 'secondary education' meaningful if we have a system of recurrent education which takes the present compulsory school as its starting point? What will be the relationship between the recurrent education provided by the state and the increasing formal recurrent education already carried out inside large industrial enterprises?[74]

The Ontario plan is explicitly man-centred, and some of its thinking has been influenced by Ivan Illich. Essentially its approach is to ask: What kind of educational provision ought to exist in our society? What provision exists now? How do we open access to the provision which already exists, and add to that provision? The programme is a blueprint for deschooling a system from within.[75]

14

31. Beyond deschooling

There is no single, magical way out of the education crisis. It is difficult even to draw up general guidelines as situations vary according to context, and it is within particular contexts that strategies need to be worked out. Third World countries have their own peoples and it is for them, in dialogue with others if they want it, to work out their own ways to the future: several alternative models already exist, such as China, Cuba, Ontario and Tanzania. In advanced countries a major question confronting us is whether mass school systems can offer to majorities an education which the majorities themselves see as instrumental to their purposes. If we continue to fail to do this then mass secondary schooling will indeed have lost its moral base. There are still tasks for schools in our societies: there is a moral argument for schools guaranteeing citizens good levels of literacy (including political literacy) and an ability to understand and manipulate numbers, and to provide for everyone a common core of learning and experience (something important if multi-cultural societies are to hold together positively, without using the device of having common enemies to promote unity). Such morally defensible schools would be accepting, not rejecting institutions; pupils and teachers would work together, instead of against each other; there would be more assessment, not less, but it would be diagnostic assessment, aimed to help learning, and not the grading of pupils in constant competition; they would be open to the world, not cut off from it; and they would relate to the future, and the kind of world we want to create, and not simply reflect a society of the past. Schools can still potentially liberate from the restrictions of family and locality, and they can still potentially offer a kind of knowledge that is not on offer, incidentally, in society. This includes such hard-knowledge as political economy, languages, science and mathematics: it is here that these schools which mainly offer therapy are committing yet one more 'trahison des clercs'.

As far as school systems in general are concerned the question is not whether the deschooling criticisms are true or false, but how true they are in particular contexts. As far as the school crisis is concerned the way out is for teachers - who are now a mixture of policeman, priest, therapist and elder - to reduce their tasks, and for schools to delimit their activities. Not only do we need to recognise the limitations as well as the possibilities of schools (they cannot build a New Jerusalem) but we have to recognise that while some schools get carried away with community rhetoric, plans for permanent education are in fact delimiting their tasks for them.

At the same time, alternative enterprises need to be encouraged and realistically funded. We need to investigate further the possibilities of informal learning; non-school learning; and deschooled learning. In our attempt to build a better society we should evaluate, by empirical research, both programmes within the system and alternative programmes.

The general need now is for us to go beyond Ivan Illich, and get beyond the general crisis in education which now confronts us.

1

HOWARD S. BECKER

The school myth

Source: Draft text for <u>Learning to Work</u>, edited by Blanche Geer (Aldine Press, 1972). This extract is from the essay 'A school is a lousy place to learn anything in'.

* *

Howard S. Becker is one of the best known sociologists in the USA. He has the ability, rare among sociologists, of being able to write a language that ordinary people can understand and to say things that are worth saying. He asks basic and pointed questions. Whereas most of the arguments about learning are vague, and are in terms of learning as a general category, Becker asks: 'Learning what?' He applies his assertions in this passage not only to schools, but to institutions generally. He goes on to argue that, although majorities fail to learn what schools pretend to teach, on-the-job training, as at present organised, does not do a very effective job

either. See also the Quotational Bibliography - BECKER, Howard S.

* *

Institutions create myths to explain, to their participants and the public generally, what they do, how they do it, how much society needs it done, and how successfully they perform the function. Every institution fails in some measure to do the job it promises to do, and its functionaries find it necessary to explain both that they are trying to do better and that the disparity between promise and performance does not exist, is not serious, or occurs only rarely. The rhetoric institutional apologists produce diverts our attention from the way the very organization of an institution produces the failures so excused. Further, it diverts our attention from comparisons which might show how others, under a different name and rhetoric, actually perform the institution's characteristic function more effectively.

The myth schools produce tells us that in a school people learn something they would not otherwise know. Teachers, who know that something, teach it to their pupils. The myth further explains that schools pass the cultural heritage of our society on to succeeding generations, both the general heritage we acquire in elementary and high school and the more differentiated aspects taught in colleges and graduate and professional schools. Finally, while educators readily admit the shortcomings of schools, they do not conceive that anything in the essence of a school might produce those shortcomings or that any other institutional form might do the job better.

2

PETER BUCKMAN

Deschooling

Source: Article in <u>Ink</u>, 3 July 1971.

* *

Deschooling theory appealed to the underground, and to those trying to build 'an alternative society'. This extract is a good example of one particular genre of deschooling writings. It is a mixture of anarchism, libertarianism, and romantic populism. It offers a lot of polemics, but little evidence. The dominant learning model is that of learning the native tongue, and this is assumed to apply to all other kinds of learning. See also the Quotational Bibliography - BUCKMAN, Peter.

* *

Compulsory schooling has achieved none of the things it set out to do. Throughout the world - with a handful of exceptions who are either ridiculed or regarded as 'backward' - a 'sentence' of at least ten years for every child is considered the most elementary sign of progress and civilization. Yet after a century of compulsory education, we are even further from a

more equal society, one where all jobs are open to the best 'qualified' people.

A growing number of kids play truant. A huge number forget how to read within three years of leaving school. Unemployment amongst schoolleavers - and graduates, for that matter - is leaping upwards. And as for all those 'qualifications' that school exists to provide - 90 per cent of the kids who leave school at 15 (which is about half the school population) do so without any exam pass whatsoever, according to statistics released by the Department of Education.

We need to abolish compulsory schooling altogether, at the same time as we must make discrimination by education illegal. Employers should no longer be permitted to ask about an applicant's school record, any more than they are allowed to ask about religion, politics, or race. The only tests applied should strictly concern ability to perform the job available. The relevant skills would remain important, of course: if you go to a doctor you have a right to expect a skilled knowledge of medicine. But whether a doctor has attended school for two or twenty years doesn't matter in the least. The test is whether she or he can make you well.

Education should be a life-long process of discovery. Instead, it is what the American writer Ivan Illich - who has pioneered the idea of deschooling - calls a grand 'initiation rite' into a society that thrives on 'mystery'. Everything somehow has a 'secret' which can only be revealed to those who have the 'right qualifications'. These 'secrets' are only necessary to maintain things as they are. School, of course, trains kids to accept this situation, both by its rigid, hierarchical structure and by the demands of the curriculum. If compulsory schooling were abolished, and if jobs were awarded on merit rather than the possession of irrelevant certificates, education could be freed from the tyranny of a curriculum. Which would mean that those good teachers, of whom there are so many, would be free to follow their enthusiasms, and to enthuse others at a pace that suited both of them. The pupil would once more become the centre of the education process, instead of just being a nut on a conveyor belt that is either tightened by the spanner of exams or rejected altogether.

All this may sould a bit romantic. But consider the imminent breakdown in education - as well as that in employment, to which education has traditionally been linked. You don't need a confusion of statistics to know that there aren't enough teachers, that the quality of education is declining, especially in schools peopled by the poor, that resentment at the compulsion of school is showing in increasing violence - the number of delinquents of school age is increasing compared to those who have left school - and that, with increasing unemployment, we are hurtling backward towards the elitism that universal schooling was supposed to eliminate. As for the purpose that leftwing cynics have always accused schooling of serving, that of simply providing technical expertise for the managerial society, technology is simply moving too fast for rigid institutions like schools to adapt to it.

In all, how could anyone expect a revolution, of whatever sort, from institutions so cumbersome, rigidly traditional, and into which so much investment has been sunk - the schools? The true revolutionaries must now press for the abolition of these dinosaurs (was that the one that died because its brain was too small for its body?) - even if their collapse looks inevitable anyway.

Most people learn better when they can pursue their own interests at their own pace. The few progressive primary schools are an example of this, being places where there is a lot of stuff that might interest different kids, plus people who know about this stuff and who can help an interested kid towards further discovery. A. S. Neill's Summerhill is an obvious champion of this method, as are adventure playgrounds, and - for some - the privileges of scientific research, where those students who have shown ability for the tasks in hand are allowed a free run of the labs and access to those who know more than they do.

An American reading programme for ghetto kids proved that literacy progressed dramatically - and showed every sign of permanence - when the kids were simply taught to read words they asked about, that had a bearing on their everyday lives. In this context, the American writer and educator John Holt has a simple proposal to encourage literacy: those who could read and write would carry badges saying something like 'Reader's Guide', which would oblige them to pronounce, write down, and spell out any word on request. Time and again, when motivation to learn is a person's own, and not something forced

on him, his curiosity, absorption, and responsibility for progress is immeasurably greater than when he is required to learn and proceed at someone else's behest.

It is this personal motivation that must be the core of education in the future. The basis of learning is imitation: people who possess skills - and the ability and enthusiasm to teach them to others - must be available to those who want to learn.

Abolishing compulsory schooling does not mean an abdication on the part of the state: far from it. The problems it will soon face - is facing, indeed - are of a massive 'leisured' (= unemployed) class, which will include kids as well as adults. All these people must be given the opportunity to explore and expand their knowledge of what interests them. The father who is a carpenter may teach his children his trade better, he would teach anyone who came to him, and he and his children would learn together about biology, or greyhounds, or whatever they felt like. Such learning would proceed by means of the exchange of information: there would be places - school buildings, for example - where those who knew came to trade knowledge, and to answer questions from those who didn't know. And if this simple idea sounds ridiculous, consider the 'specialist' clubs for those interested in photography, stamps, bicycling, or whatever. They work on an exchange of information and a two-way flow of interest between members. That is how education could be a lifelong pursuit.

But society would have to change too. Not only would equipment have to be provided, of all sorts, so that interested parties would have access to it (the way some schools now provide courses for 'star' pupils in subjects of their choice), but also it would have a responsibility to pay and provide for books and teachers who would be available to all, in the same way - as John Holt points out - that the public libraries are open to all, at state expense. More than that, the workings of the community itself would have to be opened to inspection, so that those whose interests lie towards civic work, journalism, banking, buying and selling, would be able to see these jobs being performed. This is no more revolutionary than proposing that what the taxpayer pays for should be open to inspection by him or her, and it need be no more 'inconvenient' than a steady increase in the Open Days that are offered by the armed services, hospitals, jails, schools, police and fire stations, and so on.

The important point is that 'work' and 'education' are not two separate parts of a process in which you have to finish the one before beginning the other: they are part of the same process, and if the community is to make any progress, and if its citizens are to be allowed to contribute to its development, their education and their participation in all aspects of its work is an urgent necessity.

We learn to talk by immersion, imitation, exploration, and practice. Is there any reason why all education should not proceed on the same lines - at 'Our' pace, not 'Theirs'?

3

PAULO FREIRE

Education: domestication or liberation?

Source: Article in Prospects, Vol. II, No. 2
(Summer 1972).

* *

Paulo Freire, who now works with the Programme
Unit Education and Communication of the World
Council of Churches in Geneva, has been a university
professor in Brazil, Chile, and the United States.
He is best known for his adult literacy projects in
his native Brazil, from which he was forced into
exile in 1964, and for his work Pedagogy of the
Oppressed. In this article he presents the essence
of his thesis - 'Education cannot be neutral'. See
also the Quotational Bibliography - FREIRE, Paulo,
GRABOWSKI, Stanley M. , and LISTER, Ian: A
Conversation with Paulo Freire.

* *

I am convinced that the so-called commonplace is not
always just the cliché suggested in its verbal expression. The commonplace on the contrary is very
often found only in the formal expression of the
language, and is therefore merely apparent. When
language is 'bureaucratized' into conventional for-
mulae, it satisfies the need we sometimes experience
of concealing in the cliché the importance of some
theme which is awaiting its critical perception.

On other occasions there is not even the formal
expression of the language - the verbal expression
describing the fact becomes a commonplace from the
very obviousness of the fact. Whichever the case,
our principal task is to transcend the naïveté which
allows itself to be deceived by appearances; we
thus acquire the critical attitude which breaks through
the obscurity of the commonplace or of the apparent
commonplace and brings us face to face with the fact
until now concealed. This is the attitude of this
essay - that of seeking to apprehend the deeper meaning of facts and at the same time to strip them of
their disguises.

Thus, the first apparent commonplace, on the
critical analysis of which will depend the understanding of this essay, can be expressed thus: education
cannot be neutral.

If we claim to go beyond the naïve, formal interpretations of the human task of education, this must
be the starting point of a critical or dialectical reflection. Lacking this critical spirit, either because we
are alienated to thinking statistically and not dynami-
cally, or because we already have ideological interests, we are incapable of perceiving the true role of
education, or if we do perceive it, we disguise it.
We tend to ignore or to obscure the role of education,

which, in that it is a social 'praxis' will always be
in the service either of the 'domestication' of men or
of their liberation. Thus we almost always lose
ourselves in verbalistic considerations on the subject
of what is termed 'the educational crisis'; or on the
subject of the need for reforms in the didactic processes; in the face of the fundamental problems of
structure, with which the educational process is
concerned, we indulge ourselves in these amuse-
ments.

At other moments, alarmed by the inevitable
choice we have to make between education as a
domesticating praxis and education as a liberating
praxis, we seek a third way - which is non-existent
per se. We declare education to be neutral, as if
it were not a human obligation, as if men were not
beings in history, as if the teleological character of
the educational praxis were not the factor which
determined the non-viability of its neutrality.
Furthermore, all we do in affirming this neutrality
is to opt for domestication which we simply proceed
to disguise.

Neutral education cannot, in fact, exist. It is
fundamental for us to know that, when we work on the
content of the educational curriculum when we discuss methods and processes, when we plan, when we
draw up educational policies, we are engaged in
political acts which imply an ideological choice;
whether it is obscure or clear is not important. To
recognize that neutral education is not viable involves
a critical form of thinking and of perceiving reality,
and demands an ever-growing practice of that manner
of thinking which continually revises itself, seeking
always to overcome its opposite, which is the naïve
manner of thinking. It is this requirement, stemming
from critical thinking, which imposes on us the need
of taking our earlier affirmation that education is not
neutral, as a problem to be 'unveiled' as a problem,
and not seeing it as a set phrase or as a mere
'slogan'. It is this critical manner of thinking which
always desires to go beyond the deceptive appearances, to seek the raison d'être of facts, and the
relationships between different facts, within the
totality of which they are a part. However, for the
critical mind, the simple affirmation that 'neutral
education' is not viable should not stop at the level
of merely being aware of the fact. The mere awareness of the fact does not constitute a full knowledge
of it. What is necessary is a penetration into the
reality of which the fact is a dimension, so that mere
opinion about it can be transcended by the precise
knowledge of it through the apprehension of the
'reason for its being'.

For example, at the moment in which we see the
educational act as the object of our critical reflection,
and not as something we are merely aware of, we
perceive that this act, temporally and spatially, does
not restrict itself to the limitations of the description
which the naïve consciousness sometimes makes of
it. That is to say, it is not constituted solely by the
effort which societies make for its cultural preservation. If one considers the case of the dependent
societies, education is on the one hand the expression of their alienation, and on the other the instrument of a further alienation which is an obstacle to
its being genuine. Thus the expression 'cultural
preservation', for the critical consciousness, is
vague and obscure, and conceals something which
needs to be clarified. In fact, the vagueness of the
expression 'cultural preservation' can be explained
with exactness as the perpetuation of the values of
the dominating classes who organize education and

determine its aims. In that it constitutes a super-structure, systematic education functions as an instrument to maintain the infrastructure in which it is generated. Hence the non-viability of its neutrality. When education is oriented toward this preservation - and educators are not always aware of this - it is obvious that its task is to adapt new generations to the social system it serves, which can and must be reformed and modernized, but which will never be radically transformed.

It is impossible for the power-élites to organize, plan or reform education with the aim of laying open to question the essence of the social system in which precisely they are élites. Their real desire, on the contrary, must be, let us repeat, to 'recuperate' the educatees, which is as much as to say, to adapt them to the system. Their ideas and values, their way of being, are announced as if they were - or should be - the ideas, values and way of being of all society, even though the popular classes cannot share them, perhaps because of their ontological inferiority.

It is without question that the concretizing of these aims requires at one and the same time the 'domesticating' character of this education and the explanation of it. As the social order is 'sacralized', systematic education must necessarily become a powerful instrument of social control.

The point of departure of this domesticating education (which requires the de-dialectization of thought) must be, paradoxically enough, in the very dialectization which exists between the consciousness of the world, or in other words, in the relationship between man and the world. It is curious to observe that the act of de-dialectization, of reducing thought to a state of naïveté, must have the same radical origin as the dialectizing and critical-making force of thought which is at the base of education as the praxis of liberty. None of these antagonistic forms of education or of cultural action can escape the consciousness-world dialectization, even though their practices are diametrically opposed with regard to this dialectization. Thus, education or cultural action for domestication is bound to divide the consciousness from the world, and to consider the consciousness as an empty space within man which is to be filled with contents. This separation, which results in the consciousness and the world being taken as statically opposed separate entities, implies the negation of the power of reflection of the consciousness, which is transformed into the empty space referred to. In fact, 'world and consciousness are not statically opposed to each other, they are related to each other dialectically, within their original and radical unity. For this reason the truth of one is to be gained through the other; truth is not given, it conquers itself and makes itself. It is, at once, discovery and invention.'

This is precisely what education, or cultural action for domestication cannot claim. Instead, as an ideologizing instrument it imposes the mythification of the world instead of its truth, through the truth of the consciousness which critically 'unveils' this world. Thus, the mythification of the world - the world of the consciousness - means the mythification of the consciousness: consciousness of the world.

It would then be an unpardonable contradiction on the part of the power-élites if they consented to the kind of cultural action on a large scale which considered social reality (which mediates men) as the object of their truly critical analysis.

This is because this type of cultural action implies an epistemological practice which would be the contradiction of the one which characterizes cultural action for domestication.

The epistemological practice of cultural action or education for domestication divides teaching and learning, knowing and working, thinking and doing, informing and forming, re-knowing existing knowledge and creating new knowledge. In this kind of action, knowing is receiving information, or stocking 'deposits' made by others.

Hence the form of action has the characteristic - which it never loses - of being a mere act of transferring knowledge. In this act, the educator - he who knows - transfers existing knowledge to the educatee: he who does not know. In this practice, knowledge is a mere given fact and not a permanent process which entails the praxis of men on the world. In this strange epistemology, there is no knowable object, but complete knowledge which the educator possesses. Thus it is incumbent on him to transfer, bring, extend, give and hand over to the 'ignorant' educatee, the 'knowledge' he possesses. In this way, the active character of the consciousness, when it is 'intentionality' towards the world, becomes passive; it is this active character which on the one hand explains man's ability for 're-knowing' existing knowledge, and on the other his ability for creating new knowledge. This practice of 'anaesthetizing' of de-dialectizing thought can also be seen in the emphasis laid on the 'focalist' rather than the totalizing perception of reality. This twisted view of the facts, which is not only unable to apprehend the relationships existing between them, but not even the relationships existing between the parts which constitute the totality of each of them either, is profoundly alienating. This way of seeking knowledge, which implies a conception of an immobile reality, can only lead us to a distorted view of things, which thus 'empty themselves' of their unquestionable temporality. Thus, we never get beyond the superficiality of the phenomena which we do not manage to understand in all their complexity and dynamism.

This way of acting is both alienating and 'domesticating', no matter whether the educators are or are not conscious of this.

It is not difficult to come on the practice of 'domestication' which we are analysing in systematic education, whatever its level. In the primary and secondary schools, in the university (and also in adult-education campaigns) we are witness to the transfer of knowledge, and not the search for knowledge as a process, to knowledge as something without conditions, taken as chaste and universal, to the split between teaching and learning, to the understanding of reality as something immobile, where reality is seen as a given fact and not as a process or a state of 'becoming' in order to be able to 'be'.

We could add to all this the myth that science is neutral, that the scientist is impartial, the myth of what must necessarily come out of his lack of preoccupation with the aims laid on the results of his activity as a scientist.

Let us see, in more concrete terms, although not extensively, how, and in what areas, education figures as the practice of 'domestication'.

First of all, since the school is an instrument of social control, it cannot be a theoretical context, dialectically related to a concrete or objective context in which facts occur. Instead of permanently seeking the reason for the existence of the objective facts, in order to theorize them, the school becomes an agency specialized in the formal enunciation of them. Its false point of departure implies the epistemological distortion we have already spoken of, in which to know is reduced to a mechanical dualism expressed in the transference-reception of given facts.

Thus the relations between educator and educatee are the relations of a subject to an object, which means that the latter is the mere recipient of the contents of the knowledge of the former. The educator, he who knows, he who separates the act of teaching from the act of learning, is therefore always the educator of the educatee, while the latter is always the educatee of the educator. This explains the antidialogical character of this form of education. This situation of antidialogue is not only present in the epistemological relationship already referred to, but is also present in the disciplinary relationship. The educator is the one who thinks, who says his word, who knows; the educatee has the illusion that he is thinking, through the thinking of the educator; he has the illusion that he is saying his word, in repeating what the educator says; he has the illusion that he knows, because the educator knows. Inasmuch as the school cannot be a genuinely theoretical context; inasmuch as the educator is the transmitter of a knowledge which merely describes reality as a given fact; inasmuch as the educator declares that he knows what ought to be taught, and does not recognize that he learns as he teaches, it seems obvious to him that it is incumbent on him to choose the content of the educational curriculum. The educatee can do nothing but let himself docilely be filled with this content. 'Because of this, in general, the good educatee is neither restive, nor indocile; he does not show doubt, he does not wish to know the reason for facts, he does not go beyond set models, he does not denounce "mediocratizing" bureaucracy, he does not refuse to be an object. The good educatee, in this type of education, on the contrary, is he who repeats, who refuses to think critically, who adapts to models, who finds it nice to be a rhinoceros. ' (See Ionesco: Rhinoceros.)

Before all this force of domestication, stands one really important question: Why is it possible for man, in spite of everything, to emerge critically, denouncing the ways of domestication? The answer to this basic question sends us back again to the problem of the consciousness, of its reflective character (and not only its reflective character), of its intentionality.

If all this attempt at alienating, at de-dialectizing thought 'domesticates' the capacity of the consciousness for reflection and criticism, or of man to be a conscious being, it cannot however make this capacity disappear. Sooner or later, the power of reflection and criticism reconstitutes itself in the very process of its 'domestication'. This is why we are able to talk about the liberation of man, even when we have to say that this does not stem from the mere recognition that it is necessary, but rather from the praxis which transforms the world in which we are not free. Contrary to education for domestication, education for liberation is an eminently Utopian praxis. This does not mean that it cannot be carried out. The Utopian nature of this type of education is expressed in the permanent state of unity which exists between the acts of denouncing and announcing, which give it life. In fact, domesticating education, which satisfies the interests of the dominating élites and corresponds to their ideology, can never be Utopian in the sense discussed here.

20

What denunciation can those who dominate make, unless it is the denunciation of those who denounce them? What can they announce except their own myths? What does their future as dominators consist of but the preservation of their present as privileged beings? Only education for liberation can be Utopian, and because it is Utopian, prophetic and hopeful. I cannot be prophetic or hopeful if my future is to be the repetition of a 'well-conducted' present, or of this present simply 'reformed' in some of its secondary aspects. Only those who are dominated can truly denounce and announce - denounce the world in which they exist but are forbidden to be, and announce the world in which they are able to be, and which demands their historical commitment in order for it to be brought into being. It is only they who have a future different from the present, an aspiration to be created and re-created. In their present as dominated beings can be found the plan of their liberation, which can be identified with the future which they must build.

Contrary to education for domestication, education for liberation, Utopian, prophetic and hopeful, is an act of knowing and a means of action for transforming the reality which is to be known.

The epistemological focus of attention changes radically from one to another of the opposing forms of education or cultural action.

While in education for domestication one cannot speak of a knowable object but only of knowledge which is complete, which the educator possesses and transfers to the educatee, in education for liberation there is no complete knowledge possessed by the educator, but a knowable object which mediates educator and educatee as subjects in the knowing process. Dialogue is established as the seal of the epistemological relationship between subjects in the knowing process. There is not an 'I think' which transfers its thought, but rather a 'we think' which makes possible the existence of an 'I think'. The educator is not he who knows, but he who knows how little he knows, and because of this seeks to know more, together with the educatee, who in turn knows that starting from his little knowledge he can come to know more. Here there is no split between knowing and doing; there is no room for the separate existence of a world of those who know, and world for those who work.

While in the domesticating practice the educator is always the educator of the educatee, in the liberating practice the educator must 'die' as exclusive educator of the educatee in order to be 'born' again as educatee of the educatee. At the same time, he must propose to the educatee that he 'die' as exclusive educatee of the educator in order to be 'born' again as educator of the educator. This is a continual passage back and forth, a humble, creative movement, which both have to make.

Because educator-educatee accept in communion with each other the role of subjects in the educational act which is a permanent process, the educator no longer has the right to establish the curriculum-content of education, which does not belong exclusively to him. The organization of the curriculum, which must be regarded as a 'knowable object' by both educator-educatee and educatee-educator, requires the investigation of what we usually term the 'thematic universe' of the educatees. Taken as the point of departure of the process, the investigation of the 'thematic universe' not only reveals to us the preoccupations of the educatee, but also their state of perception of their world.

When the curriculum whose structure is based on the themes investigated, becomes for the educatees a series of problems to be 'unveiled' as such, education for liberation takes the form of the permanent unity existing between the investigation of the thematic and its presentation as a problem. If, in the moment of our investigation - which is already cultural action - we come on the themes and the levels of perception of reality, in the moment when the problematization of these themes is presented as a knowable object, the perception of reality undergoes a change, and a new set of themes emerges, through a new vision of old themes or through a perception of themes hitherto not perceived.

Thus, education (or cultural action for liberation, which it cannot fail to be) reproduces the dynamism which characterizes the historical-social process. Its mobility depends on the mobility of the facts which must genuinely be known in the practice of education. It is only through an education which does not separate action from reflection, theory from practice, consciousness from the world, that it is possible to develop a dialectic form of thinking which contributes to the insertion of men as subjects in their historical reality.

In that it is Utopian and demythologizing, education or cultural action for liberation implies a constant risk which we do not always want to run, since we are tempted by the stability we fear to lose. In the long run, in preferring stability, immobility, self-censure, conspiratorial silence, all we do is renounce liberty because we are afraid of it. We shall thus not be able critically to have 'unusual ideas about education', since thinking in this way is to be committed, and requires of us a greater risk: that of putting into practice some of the unusual ideas.

4

HERMAN H. FRESE

Permanent education - dream or nightmare?

Source: Article in Education and Culture, No. 19 (Summer 1972).

* *

Permanent education is the area in education of most current concern for the international organisations - OECD, the European Cultural Foundation, the Council of Europe and UNESCO, as well as of the multinational corporations like Shell and Phillips. Many see it as an escape from the failure of school education. As yet few have pointed out some of the dangers. Hermann Frese is one of them. See also Reading 21 - John Ohliger: Adult Education: 1984.

* *

During a course on the methods of adult education for a group of adult part-time students the discussion turned towards the concept of permanent education. The students were fascinated by the width and depth it offered to the development of life-long learning and subsequent educational provisions. At the next meeting, however, one of them, an elderly lady, confessed that the idea had kept her awake. She did not like, she said, the idea of everybody having to go to school for a lifetime. The school she remembered from her childhood was about enough for her. The others agreed with this. Yet they had to admit that while being critical of permanent education in this respect they were benefiting from it in another, their own course being the example.

The expansion of formal education

Does the development of permanent education necessarily mean the continuation of the traditional school? It is not likely. The expansion of formal education on such a scale, with its teachers, classes and special buildings, would virtually result in blowing up the system. The present number of teachers would have to be multiplied. Where to find them, how to train them? And where to find the room facilities for educational classes on such a scale? Finally, it would be impossible to get the money needed for financing this development. The problems of extending compulsory education today are sufficient evidence of this conclusion. So are those experienced with developing our universities. The institutions, once a privilege for the few, now have become means for mass education, a function for which they are ill-equipped.

For our understanding of the scale of the problems with which we are confronted the figures presented by Jankovich are of interest. They show that the institutions for higher education in the 17 member-states of the Council of Europe counted 4 million students in 1970-71. This number is predicted to increase by 1980-81 to 9 million, only half of which can be accommodated by institutions of the present type. The other half, i. e. 4.5 million, plus some 1.3 million postacademic students, must be served by other means. To them must be added 16 million students in out-of-school education.

Educational technology

It is obvious that for the mere sake of the increased scale and scope the existing model of formal education has to be changed. So the fear of having to return as an adult to the old school is unwarranted. It is to be doubted, however, whether the alternative which is under preparation now offers a more pleasant and beneficial perspective. It represents the application of the new educational technology, defined by Schmidbauer in a working paper for the Council of Europe as 'the new media and technological systems born of the communication revolution, which can be used for educational purposes. Educational technology, as a term, comprises a great variety of hard-ware and related soft-ware. It refers to the telemedia (television, radio, telewriting, telephone, teletype, etc.) as well as to the recording media (video tape, audio tape, disc, film, microform, etc.); to the digital computer and the various types of mechanical teaching machines, as well as to the different systems for the distribution of electronic signals (microwave, satellite, laser beam, etc.).'

According to Schmidbauer and others permanent education can only be developed as a comprehensive system, using a multi-media approach and organized as an education network. A contemporary example of such a system is the Open University. Earlier examples are the German Telekolleg and Teleac of the Netherlands. They have truly opened a road to education for people otherwise deprived of further study. Economising on teaching staff and buildings the expenditure per student of the Open University, for instance, is said to be half that of students at the traditional universities. Telekolleg students cost 40% of a student in primary education, 20% of one in secondary education. Moreover, these students work while they study and so contribute to the national product.

Centralisation and the power of decision-making

Whatever their advantage in accommodating large numbers of students at reduced costs, these systems present the risk of being centralised forms of technically advanced manipulation. For who sets the aims and who decides as to the content and methods of the education involved? I tried to answer this question with regard to such a worthwhile initiative as that of the Open University. The production scheme used for the preparation of its courses shows a total of 155 units divided over 34 consecutive steps that have to be cared for. The scheme is operated by a multi-disciplinary team of subject-specialists, educational experts and media-producers. The students, however, are notably absent. They are referred to in one unit in the first step only, which says: 'Collate and analyse information about learner characteristics' and in units in step 21 and 23 requiring the 'developmental testing' of the material on a student sample. Perhaps the lack of opportunity to have a vote in deciding the aims and means is compensated to a certain extent by a student representation in the Regional Assemblies and the General Assembly of the Open University. From my own experience with a similar body, the Advisory Council of Teleac, I know that such influence remains insignificant compared to the expertise power of the production staff. The present trend of democratising education internally by granting students certain rights to decide upon the ends and means of their own education, seems to be reserved for the schools that are about to disappear. In the newer systems of mass education, said to be the promise of our future, such rights are forsaken. Their place is being taken by audience and market research and developmental testing. Some would reply that the feedback from the student, on which these systems are based, represents a form of influence on their part. Essentially, however, the feedback is a technical feature of didactical significance. It will improve the system but does not offer a power input on the side of the students.

The education industry

The Open University and similar institutions still are favourable examples of such systems. As public corporations they work on a non-profit basis. The new systems of mass education are of great interest, however, to commercial enterprise. Their development opens a potential market of colossal size for the rapidly expanding education industry. This is indicated by the present boom in educational publishing, necessitating national and international mergers between the larger companies with the disappearance of the smaller houses. The production of multi-media systems, i.e. the software, is of great interest to the producers of electronic hard-ware. This leads to still larger mergers. Some time ago the Radio Corporation of America (RCA), producers of the Selecta-Vision cassette system, bought Random House. Similarly Columbia Broadcasting System, producer of Electronic Video Recording (EVR), acquired the publishing house of Holt, Rinehart. In Europe a number of large publishing companies have started a joint-venture for the same reasons. On the hard-ware side the spacecraft and communication industry, too, is interested in the deployment of such systems. In his study on satellite communication services for education in Europe, Jankovich, after specifying the need for such a system, estimates its cost of investment between 3,500 and 5,500 million dollars.

Again one may ask who is to decide the aims, content and methods of the education involved? In the commercial setting the market and price mechanism together with the profit criterion are supposed to regulate the production. In a free market situation the consumer, i.e. the students, can exert their influence on such decisions. The mergers we indicated before, however, suggest a monopolizing of the market by giant producers. This leaves the customer with little choice ultimately. It means that the consequences of the centralised nature of the systems which we noticed when discussing non-profit making institutions, are aggravated when the systems are commercially operated. And let us be sure: the preparations for such an operation are well under way.

Compulsory education and control

The situation becomes really serious when the new systems of permanent education, designed for use in free adult education, will be applied to compulsory education. The first signs of unrest can already be noticed. At the recent National Education Exhibition in the Netherlands, for instance, the producers of educational material were severely criticised by the Undersecretary of Education and by representatives of educational and consumer organisations. The industry was blamed for producing its material according to commercial considerations only, flooding the market with a confusing offer of books, films and other means of which both the price and the quality were disputed. This leads to the more general question as to who is to control the production and distribution of these means? Should it be taken over by the government, or by non-profit making organisations? Are the products to be inspected on behalf of the Ministry of Education? Or would a State guarantee be sufficient? It leaves the question as to who is to set the criteria to be used in such cases. The students will hardly have a chance to have a say in this matter. Does it then make any difference if one is bitten by the dog or by the cat?

Like others I, too, was initially fascinated by the idea of an integrated system of educational provisions for life-long learning. The fascination has remained but I have come to distrust the centralisation of power which the systems evidently display when they are left to develop on their own. Parliamentary control is too slow to be effective. Government control tends to be prohibitive of innovations. Moreover, there are many reasons why one should distrust education by the state, especially on a life-long basis. As to the commercial development, education is not to be treated as a consumer good.

An alternative view on education

The most essential criticism of the systems that were described so far, however, stems from our view of education itself. Education, in our opinion, should contribute to the formation of personality by offering optimal opportunities for the development of each individual's potential. To safeguard such education from manipulation and indoctrination it assumes the individual's rights of decision on aims, content and methods, and the consequent limitation of external influences in this respect. This assumption is a basic condition. Recognising individual differences of motivation and interest the function of educational provisions is to stimulate divergent learning. This implies a design of educational facilities which start at the basis, i. e. individuals and local groups. In a paper for the Council of Europe on 'Permanent education, a strategy of social action' I have tried to outline such a design and its underlying reasons.

Instead of schools and multi-media systems, with their emphasis on task-oriented convergent learning, forcing pupils to submit to social conformity, my design consists of a local network of centres for learning and community development, using methods for self-study and group-work. Teachers are replaced by teams of subject-specialists and specialists in learning methods or tutors. To them must be added the aid by volunteers whose work in this respect is part of their own learning by means of helping others. Free information, if not locally available, is to be obtained from centralised sources according to local needs in which students and staff have an important say. Such views are neither new nor original. Many reformers have pleaded what we now call 'deschooling', developing practical ways for its realisation. What is new in the views defended by Illich and others, however, is the analysis of education in terms of systems serving the larger social systems of which they are a part. The outcome of contemporary research by educational sociologists indicates the function of continuation and reinforcement which education has for the social system as a whole. Especially the extensive research done with regard to the school success of children from working class families bears ample evidence of the significance of social handicaps and their continuation through education.

Changing systems

Simplified, the conclusion is that the educational system prepares for specific positions in society and so serves the reproduction of a given social order. In doing so its human effect is one of alienation, both for the privileged who are prepared for their future function of domination, and for the underprivileged who learn little and leave early ready for a life of submission. Of course this analysis is very unjust to the great number of well-meaning teachers who do whatever they can to help their pupils to get the best opportunities there are. It also seems to ignore the increased social mobility which allows talented boys and girls to have a further education and so to move up. The analysis, however, does not deal with people. It is meant to uncover the nature and functioning of our social system and that of the educational system serving it.

The essence of the analysis is that a change in the educational system will affect the social system. Change always creates resistance. If only the educational system is involved and the basic values and structure of the social system are left relatively unharmed the resistance still is considerable. The introduction of the large scale educational systems resulting from the systematic application of present educational technology provides an example. Even they, however, put the social system to the test by redistributing the power of knowledge, for instance. Still they tend to improve and refine the educational functions of a given social system.

Illich's proposals are of a more drastic nature, reflected in his aim of 'deschooling society'. They attack the social system at its very centre through its reproductive mechanism, education. Consequently the resistance will be enormous. The more so since these ideas stem from humanistic values that are basic to the same social system they attack: the right of self-determination and developing one's own potential, in a general solidarity with others, requiring a just society pursuing the common good. To many people the ideas by Illich and others will represent a frustrating memory of ideals repressed by the facts of life. If the revival survives the aggression generated by this frustration, we have gained adherents for this alternative development of educational and social change. Instead of largescale solutions the only way to succeed is by initiating a large number of small-scale activities stimulating the forces of change that are already at work within the system itself. It will be a time-consuming and energy-demanding job. Let us hope we will have the time and find the people to do this work.

5

HERBERT GINTIS

Towards a political economy of education: a radical critique of Ivan Illich's <u>Deschooling Society</u>

Source: Article in the <u>Harvard Educational Review</u>,
   Vol. 42, No. 1 (February 1972).

* *

Herbert Gintis, according to <u>The Times Higher
Education Supplement</u> of 16 March 1973, 'much to his
surprise was rehired last month as an assistant
professor (at Harvard University) with a guaranteed
promotion to the untenured rank of associate professor'. This neo-Marxist critique asserts that Ivan
Illich misunderstands the relationship between schools
and society and that Illich's analysis has serious
weaknesses in the political and economic sphere.
Although I think that Illich overestimates the significance of schools, and that work in the field of the
political economy of education could help to take us
beyond Illich, I don't think that Gintis meets Illich's
argument that today the educational system is a
major service-industry, creating demands for its
own services and validating its own activities, and
that the expansion of that service-industry (through
permanent education) is itself a major element in
current economic planning. Gintis's Marxist ideology provides him with insights, but it also imposes
limitations on his own analysis. His arguments have
been taken up by West German neo-Marxists. See
also Quotational Bibliography - BOWLES, Samuel.

* *

The author gives a critique of Ivan Illich's
Deschooling Society, arguing that, despite his
forthright vision of the liberating potential of
educational technology, Illich fails to understand
fully how the existing educational system serves
the capitalist economy. Gintis evaluates and
rejects the book's major thesis that the present
character of schooling stems from the economy's
need to shape consumer demands and expectations. Instead, he offers a production orientation which maintains that the repressive and unequal aspects of schooling derive from the need
to supply a labour force compatible with the social
relations of capitalist production. Gintis concludes that meaningful strategies for educational
change must explicitly embrace a concomitant
transformation of the mechanisms of power and
privilege in the economic sphere.

Ivan Illich's 'Deschooling Society', despite its bare
115 pages, embraces the world. Its ostensible focus
on education moves him inexorably and logically
through the panoply of human concerns in advanced
industrial society - a society plainly in progressive
disintegration and decay. With Yeats we may feel
that 'things fall apart/The centre cannot hold', but
Illich's task is no less than to discover and analyse
that 'centre'. His endeavor affords the social scientist the unique and rare privilege to put in order
the historical movements which characterise our
age and define the prospects for a revolutionary
future. Such is the subject of this essay.

This little book would have been unthinkable ten
years ago. In it, Ivan Illich confronts the full spec-
trum of the modern crisis in values by rejecting the
basic tenets of progressive liberalism. He dismisses
what he calls the Myth of Consumption as a cruel and
illusory ideology foisted upon the populace by a manipulative bureaucratic system. He treats welfare and
service institutions as part of the problem, not as
part of the solution. He rejects the belief that education constitutes the 'great equaliser' and the path to
personal liberation. Schools, say Illich, simply
must be eliminated.

Illich does more than merely criticise; he con-
ceptualises constructive technological alternatives to
repressive education. Moreover, he sees the present age as 'revolutionary' because the existing social
relations of economic and political life, including the
dominant institutional structure of schooling, have
become impediments to the development of liberating,
socially productive technologies. Here Illich is relevant indeed, for the tension between technological
possibility and social reality pervades all advanced
industrial societies today. Despite our technological
power, communities and environment continue to
deteriorate, poverty and inequality persist, work
remains alienating, and men and women are not
liberated for self-fulfilling activity.

Illich's response is a forthright vision of participatory, decentralised, and liberating learning
technologies, and a radically altered vision of social
relations in education.

Yet while his <u>description</u> of modern society is
sufficiently critical, his <u>analysis</u> is simplistic and
his program, consequently, is a diversion from the
immensely complex and demanding political, organisational, intellectual, and personal demands of revolutionary reconstruction in the coming decades. It
is crucial that educators and students who have been
attracted to him - for his message does correspond
to their personal frustration and disillusionment -
move beyond him.

The first part of this essay presents Illich's
analysis of the economically advanced society - the
basis for his analysis of schools. Whereas Illich
locates the source of the social problems and value

crises of modern societies in their need to reproduce alienated patterns of consumption, I argue that these patterns are merely manifestations of the deeper workings of the economic system. The second part of the essay attempts to show that Illich's over-emphasis on consumption leads him to a very partial understanding of the functions of the educational system and the contradictions presently besetting it, and hence to ineffective educational alternatives and untenable political strategies for the implementation of desirable educational technologies.

Finally, I argue that a radical theory of educational reform becomes viable only by envisioning liberating and equal education as serving and being served by a radically altered nexus of social relations in production. Schools may lead or lag in this process of social transformation, but structural changes in the educational process can be socially relevant only when they speak of potentials for liberation and equality in our day-to-day labours. In the final analysis 'de-schooling' is irrelevant because we cannot 'de-factory', 'de-office', or 'de-family', save perhaps at the still unenvisioned end of a long process of social reconstruction.

The social context of modern schooling: institutional values and commodity fetishism

Educational reformers commonly err by treating the system of schools as if it existed in a social vacuum. Illich does not make this mistake. Rather, he views the internal irrationalities of modern education as reflections of the larger society. The key to understanding the problems of advanced industrial economies, he argues, lies in the character of its consumption activities and the ideology which supports them. The schools in turn are exemplary models of bureaucracies geared toward the indoctrination of docile and manipulable consumers.

Guiding modern social life and interpersonal behavior, says Illich, is a destructive system of 'institutionalised values' which determine how one perceives one's needs and defines instruments for their satisfaction. The process which creates institutional values insures that all individual needs - physical, psychological, social, intellectual, emotional, and spiritual - are transformed into demands for goods and services. In contrast to the 'psychological impotence' which results from institutionalised values, Illich envisages the 'psychic health' which emerges from self-realisation - both personal and social. Guided by institutionalised values, one's well-being lies not in what one does but in what one has - the status of one's job and the level of material consumption. For the active person, goods are merely means to or instruments in the performance of activities; for the passive consumer, however, goods are ends in themselves, and activity is merely the means toward sustaining or displaying a desired level of consumption. Thus institutionalised values manifest themselves psychologically in a rigorous fetishism - in this case, of commodities and public services. Illich's vision rests in the negation of commodity fetishism:[1]

> I believe that a desirable future depends on our deliberately... engendering a life style which will enable us to be spontaneous, independent, yet related to each other, rather than maintaining a life style which only allows us to make and unmake, produce and consume. ('De-Schooling Society', hereafter 'DS', p. 52)

Commodity fetishism is institutionalised in two senses. First, the 'delivery systems' in modern industrial economies (i. e. the suppliers of goods and services) are huge, bureaucratic institutions which treat individuals as mere receptors for their products. Goods are supplied by hierarchical and impersonal corporate enterprises, while services are provided by welfare bureaucracies which enjoy '... a professional, political and financial monopoly over the social imagination, setting standards of what is valuable and what is feasible... A whole society is initiated into the Myth of Unending Consumption of services' ('DS', p. 44).

Second, commodity fetishism is institutionalised in the sense that the values of passive consumerism are induced and reinforced by the same 'delivery systems' whose ministrations are substitutes for self-initiated activities.

> ... manipulative institutions... are either socially or psychologically 'addictive'. Social addiction... consists in the tendency to prescribe increased treatment if smaller quantities have not yielded the desired results. Psychological addiction... results when consumers become hooked on the need for more and more of the process or product. ('DS', p. 55)

These delivery systems moreover 'both invite compulsively repetitive use and frustrate alternative ways of achieving similar results. ' For example, General Motors and Ford

> ... produce means of transportation, but they also, and more importantly, manipulate public taste in such a way that the need for transportation is expressed as a demand for private cars rather than public buses. They sell the desire to control a machine, to race at high speeds in luxurious comfort, while also offering the fantasy at the end of the road. ('DS', p. 57)

This analysis of addictive manipulation in private production is, of course, well-developed in the literature. Illich's contribution is to extend it to the sphere of service and welfare bureaucracies:

> Finally, teachers, doctors, and social workers realize that their distinct professional ministrations have one aspect - at least - in common. They create further demands for the institutional treatments they provide, faster than they can provide service institutions. ('DS', p. 112)

The well-socialised naturally react to these failures simply by increasing the power and jurisdiction of welfare institutions. Illich's reaction, of course, is precisely the contrary.

The political response to institutionalised values

As the basis for his educational proposals, Illich's overall framework bears close attention. Since commodity fetishism is basically a psychological stance, it must first be attacked on an individual rather than political level. For Illich, each individual is responsible for his/her own demystification. The institutionalisation of values occurs not through external coercion, but through psychic manipulation, so its rejection is an apolitical act of individual will. The movement for social change thus becomes a cultural one of raising consciousness.

But even on this level, political action in the form of negating psychic manipulation is crucial. Goods and services as well as welfare bureaucracies must be prohibited from disseminating fetishistic values. Indeed, this is the basis for a political program of de-schooling. The educational system, as a coercive source of institutionalised values, must be denied its preferred status. Presumably, this 'politics of negation' would extend to advertising and all other types of psychic manipulation.

Since the concrete social manifestation of commodity fetishism is a grossly inflated level of production and consumption, the second step in Illich's political program is the substitution of leisure for work. Work is evil for Illich - unrewarding by its very nature - and not to be granted the status of 'activity':

> ... 'making and acting' are different, so different, in fact, that one never includes the other... Modern technology has increased the ability of man to relinquish the 'making of things to machines, and his potential time for 'acting' has increased... Unemployment is the sad idleness of a man who, contrary to Aristotle, believes that making things, or working, is virtuous and that idleness is bad. ('DS', p. 62)

Again, Illich's shift in the work-leisure choice is basically apolitical and will follow naturally from the abolition of value indoctrination. People work so hard and long because they are taught to believe the fruits of their activities - consumption - are intrinsically worthy. Elimination of the 'hard-sell pitch' of bureaucratic institutions will allow individuals to discover within themselves the falsity of the doctrine.

The third stage in Illich's political program envisages the necessity of concrete change in social 'delivery systems'. Manipulative institutions must be dismantled, to be replaced by organisational forms which allow for the free development of individuals. Illich calls such institutions 'convivial', and associates them with leftist political orientation.

> The regulation of convivial institutions sets limits to their use; as one moves from the convivial to the manipulative end of the spectrum, the rules progressively call for unwilling consumption or participation... Toward, but not at, the left on the institutional spectrum, we can locate enterprises which compete with others in their own field, but have not begun notably to engage in advertising. Here we find hand laundries, small bakeries, hairdressers, and - to speak of professionals - some lawyers and music teachers... They acquire clients through their personal touch and the comparative quality of their services. ('DS', pp. 55-6)

In short, Illich's Good Society is based on small scale entrepreneurial (as opposed to corporate) capitalism, with perfectly competitive markets in goods and services. The role of the state in this society is the prevention of manipulative advertising, the development of left-convivial technologies compatible with self-initiating small-group welfare institutions (education, health and medical services, crime prevention and rehabilitation, community development, etc.) and the provisioning of the social infrastructure (e.g., public transportation). Illich's proposal for 'learning webs' in education is only a particular application of this vision of left-convivial technologies.

Assessing Illich's politics: an overview

Illich's model of consumption-manipulation is crucial at every stage of his political argument. But it is substantially incorrect. In the following three sections I shall criticise three basic thrusts of his analysis.

First, Illich locates the source of social decay in the autonomous, manipulative behaviour of corporate bureaucracies. I shall argue, in contrast, that the source must be sought in the normal operation of the basic economic institutions of capitalism (markets in factors of production, private control of resources and technology, etc.)[2] which consistently sacrifice the healthy development of community, work, environment, education, and social equality to the accumulation of capital and the growth of marketable goods and services. Moreover, given that individuals must participate in economic activity, these social outcomes are quite insensitive to the preferences or values of individuals, and are certainly in no sense a reflection of the autonomous wills of manipulating bureaucrats or gullible consumers. Hence merely ending 'manipulation' while maintaining basic economic institutions will affect the rate of social decay only minimally.

Second, Illich locates the source of consumer consciousness in the manipulative socialisation of individuals by agencies controlled by corporate and welfare bureaucracies. This 'institutionalised consciousness' induces individuals to choose outcomes not in conformity with their 'real' needs. I shall argue, in contrast, that a causal analysis can never take socialisation agencies as basic explanatory variables in assessing the overall behaviour of the social system. In particular, consumer consciousness is generated through the day-to-day activities and observations of individuals in capitalist society. The sales pitches of manipulative institutions, rather than generating the values of commodity fetishism, merely capitalise upon and reinforce a set of values derived from and reconfirmed by daily personal experience in the social system. In fact, while consumer behaviour may seem irrational and fetishistic, it is a reasonable accommodation to the options for meaningful social outlets in the context of capitalist institutions. Hence the abolition of addictive propaganda cannot 'liberate' the individual to 'free choice' of personal goals. Such choice is still conditioned by the pattern of social processes which have historically rendered him or her amenable to 'institutionalised values'. In fact, the likely outcome of de-manipulation of values would be no significant alteration of values at all.

Moreover, the ideology of commodity fetishism not only reflects the day-to-day operations of the economic system, it is also functionally necessary to motivate men/women to accept and participate in the system of alienated production, to peddle their (potentially) creative activities to the highest bidder through the market in labor, to accept the destruction of their communities, and to bear allegiance to an economic system whose market institutions and patterns of control of work and community systematically subordinate all social goals to the criteria of profit and marketable product. Thus the weakening of institutionalised values would in itself lead logically either to unproductive and undirected social chaos (witness the present state of counter-culture movements in the United States) or to a rejection of the social relations of capitalist production along with commodity fetishism.

Third, Illich argues that the goal of social change is to transform institutions according to the criterion

26

of 'non-addictiveness', or 'left-conviviality'. However, since manipulation and addictiveness are not the sources of social decay, their elimination offers no cure. Certainly the implementation of left-convivial forms in welfare and service agencies - however desirable in itself - will not counter the effects of capitalist development on social life. More important, Illich's criterion explicitly accepts those basic economic institutions which structure decision-making power, lead to the growth of corporate and welfare bureaucracies, and lie at the root of social decay. Thus Illich's criterion must be replaced by one of democratic, participatory, and rationally decentralised control over social outcomes in factory, office, community, schools, and media. The remainder of this essay will elucidate the alternative analysis and political strategy as focused on the particular case of the educational system.

Economic institutions and social development

In line with Illich's suggestion, we may equate individual welfare with the pattern of day-to-day activities the individual enters into, together with the personal capacities - physical, cognitive, affective, spiritual, and aesthetic - he or she has developed toward their execution and appreciation. Most individual activity is not purely personal, but is based on social interaction and requires a social setting conducive to developing the relevant capacities for performance. That is, activities take place within socially structured domains, characterised by legitimate and socially acceptable roles available to the individual in social relations. The most important of these activity contexts are work, community, and natural environment. The character of individual participation in these contexts - the defining roles one accepts as worker and community member and the way one relates to one's environment - is a basic determinant of well-being and individual development.

These activity contexts, as I shall show, are structured in turn by the way people structure their productive relations. The study of activity contexts in capitalist society must begin with an understanding of the basic economic institutions which regulate their historical development.

The most important of these institutions are: (1) private ownership of factors of production (land, labour, and capital), according to which the owner has full control over their disposition and development; (2) a market in labour, according to which (a) the worker is divorced, by and large, from ownership of non-human factors of production (land and capital), (b) the worker relinquishes control over the disposition of his labour during the stipulated workday by exchanging it for money, and (c) the price of a particular type of labour (skilled or unskilled, white-collar or blue-collar, physical, mental, managerial, or technical) is determined essentially by supply and demand; (3) a market in land, according to which the price of each parcel of land is determined by supply and demand, and the use of such parcels is individually determined by the highest bidder; (4) income determination on the basis of the market-dictated returns to owned factors of production; (5) markets in essential commodities - food, shelter, social insurance, medical care; and (6) control of the productive process by owners of capital or their managerial representatives.

Because essential goods, services, and activity contexts are marketed, income is a prerequisite to social existence. Because factors of production are privately owned and market-determined factor returns are the legitimate source of income, and because most workers possess little more than their own labour services, they are required to provide these services to the economic system. Thus control over the developing of work roles and of the social technology of production passes into the hands of the representatives of capital.

Thus the activity context of work becomes alienated in the sense that its structure and historical development do not conform to the needs of the individuals it affects. Bosses determine the technologies and social relations of production within the enterprise on the basis of three criteria. First, production must be flexibly organised for decision-making and secure managerial control from the highest levels downward. This means generally that technologies employed must be compatible with hierarchical authority and a fragmented, task-specific division of labour. The need to maintain effective administrative power leads to bureaucratic order in production, the hallmark of modern corporate organisation. Second, among all technologies and work roles compatible with secure and flexible control from the top, bosses choose those which minimise costs and maximise profits. Finally, bosses determine product attributes - and hence the 'craft rationality' of production - according to their contribution to gross sales and growth of the enterprise. Hence the decline in pride of workmanship and quality of production associated with the Industrial Revolution.

There is no reason to believe that a great deal of desirable work is not possible. On the contrary, evidence indicates that decentralisation, worker control, the re-introduction of craft in production, job rotation, and the elimination of the most constraining aspects of hierarchy are both feasible and potentially efficient. But such work roles develop in an institutional context wherein control, profit, and growth regulate the development of the social relations of production. Unalienated production must be the result of the revolutionary transformation of the basic institutions which Illich implicitly accepts.

The development of communities as activity contexts also must be seen in terms of basic economic institutions. The market in land, by controlling the organic development of communities, not only produces the social, environmental, and aesthetic monstrosities we call 'metropolitan areas', but removes from the community the creative, synthesising power that lies at the base of true solidarity. Thus communities become agglomerates of isolated individuals with few common activities and impersonal and apathetic interpersonal relations.

A community cannot thrive when it holds no effective power over the autonomous activities of profit-maximising capitalists. Rather, a true community is itself a creative, initiating, and synthesising agent, with the power to determine the architectural unity of its living and working spaces and their coordination, the power to allocate community property to social uses such as participatory childcare and community recreation centers, and the power to insure the preservation and development of its natural ecological environment. This is not an idle utopian dream. Many living-working communities do exhibit architectural, aesthetic, social and ecological integrity: the New England town, the Dutch village, the moderate-sized cities of Mali in sub-Saharan Africa, and the desert communities of

Djerba in Tunisia. True, these communities are fairly static and untouched by modern technology; but even in a technologically advanced country the potential for decent community is great, given the proper pattern of community decision mechanisms.

The normal operation of the basic economic institutions of capitalism thus render major activity contexts inhospitable to human beings. Our analysis of work and community could easily be extended to include ecological environment and economic equality with similar conclusions.

This analysis undermines Illich's treatment of public service bureaucracies. Illich holds that service agencies (including schools) fail because they are manipulative, and expand because they are psychologically addictive. In fact, they do not fail at all. And they expand because they exist as integral links in the larger institutional allocation of unequal power and income. Illich's simplistic treatment of this area is illustrated in his explanation for the expansion of military operations:

> The boomerang effect in war is becoming more obvious: the higher the body count of dead Vietnamese, the more enemies the United States acquires around the world; likewise the more the United States must spend to create another manipulative institution - cynically dubbed 'pacification' - in a futile effort to absorb the side effects of war. ('DS', p. 54)

Illich's theory of addiction as motivation proposes that, once begun, one thing naturally leads to another. Actually, however, the purpose of the military is the maintenance of aggregate demand and high levels of employment, as well as aiding the expansion of international sources of resource supply and capital investment. Expansion is not the result of addiction but a primary characteristic of the entire system.

Likewise from a systematic point of view, penal, mental illness, and poverty agencies are meant to contain the dislocations arising from the fragmentation of work and community and the institutionally determined inequality in income and power. Yet Illich argues only:

> ... jail increases both the quality and the quantity of criminals, that, in fact, it often creates them out of mere nonconformists... mental hospitals, nursing homes, and orphan asylums do much the same thing. These institutions provide their clients with the destructive self-image of the psychotic, the overaged, or the waif, and provide a rationale for the existence of entire professions, just as jails produce income for wardens. ('DS', p. 54)

Further, the cause of expansion of service agencies lies not in their addictive nature, but in their failure even to attempt to deal with the institutional sources of social problems. The normal operation of basic economic institutions progressively aggravates these problems, hence requiring increased response on the part of welfare agencies.

The roots of consumer behaviour

To understand consumption in capitalist society requires a production orientation, in contrast to Illich's emphasis on 'institutionalised values' as basic explanatory variables. Individuals consume as they do - and hence acquire values and beliefs concerning consumption - because of the place consumption activity holds among the constellation of available alternatives for social expression. These alternatives directly involve the quality of basic activity contexts surrounding social life - contexts which, as I have argued, develop according to the criteria of capital accumulation through the normal operation of economic institutions.

What at first glance seems to be an irrational preoccupation with income and consumption in capitalist society, is seen within an activity context paradigm to be a logical response on the part of the individual to what Marx isolated as the central tendency of capitalist society: the transformation of all complex social relations into impersonal quid pro quo relations. One implication of this transformation is the progressive decay of social activity contexts described in the previous section, a process which reduces their overall contribution to individual welfare. Work, community, and environment become sources of pain and displeasure rather than inviting contexts for social relations. The reasonable individual response, then, is (a) to disregard the development of personal capacities which would be humanly satisfying in activity contexts which are not available and, hence, to fail to demand changed activity contexts and (b) to emphasise consumption and to develop those capacities which are most relevant to consumption per se.

Second, the transformation of complex social relations to exchange relations implies that the dwindling stock of healthy activity contexts is parcelled out among individuals almost strictly according to income. High-paying jobs are by and large the least alienating; the poor live in the most fragmented communities and are subjected to the most inhuman environments; contact with natural environment is limited to periods of vacation, and the length and desirability of this contact is based on the means to pay.

Thus commodity fetishism becomes a substitute for meaningful activity contexts, and a means of access to those that exist. The 'sales pitch' of Madison Avenue is accepted because, in the given context, it is true. It may not be much, but it's all we've got. The indefensibility of its more extreme forms (e. g. , susceptibility to deodorant and luxury automobile advertising) should not divert us from comprehending this essential rationality.

In conclusion, it is clear that the motivational basis of consumer behaviour derives from the everyday observation and experience of individuals, and consumer values are not 'aberrations' induced by manipulative socialisation. Certainly there is no reason to believe that individuals would consume or work much less were manipulative socialisation removed. Insofar as such socialisation is required to stabilise commodity fetishist values, its elimination might lead to the overthrow of capitalist institutions - but that of course is quite outside Illich's scheme.

The limitations of left-convivial technologies

Since Illich views the 'psychological impotence' of the individual in his/her 'addictedness' to the ministrations of corporate and state bureaucracies as the basic problem of contemporary society, he defines the desirable 'left-convivial' institutions by the criterion of 'non-addictiveness'.

Applied to commodities or welfare services, this criterion is perhaps sufficient. But applied to major contexts of social activities, it is inappropriate. It is not possible for individuals to treat their work, their communities, and their environment in a simply instrumental manner. For better or worse, these social spheres, by regulating the individual's social activity, became a major determinant of his/her psychic development, and in an important sense define who he/she is. Indeed, the solution to the classical 'problem of order' in society is solved only by the individual's becoming 'addicted' to his/her social forms by participating through them. In remaking society, individuals do more than expand their freedom of choice - they change who they are, their self-definition, in the process. The criticism of alienated social spheres is not simply that they deprive individuals of necessary instruments of activity, but that in so doing they tend to produce in all of us something less than we intend to be.

The irony of Illich's analysis is that by erecting 'addictiveness vs. instrumentality' as the central welfare criterion, he himself assumes a commodity fetishist mentality. In essence, he posits the individual outside of society and using social forms as instruments in his/her pre-existing ends. For instance, Illich does not speak of work as 'addictive', because in fact individuals treat work first as a 'disutility' and second as an instrument toward other ends (consumption). The alienation of work poses no threat to the 'sovereignty' of the worker because he is not addicted to it. By definition, then, capitalist work, communities, and environments are 'non-addictive' and left-convivial. Illich's consideration of the capitalist enterprise as 'right-manipulative' only with respect to the consumer is a perfect example of this 'reification' of the social world. In contrast, I would argue that work is necessarily addictive in the larger sense of determining who a man/woman is as a human being.

The addictive vs. instrumental (or, equivalently, manipulative vs. convivial) criterion is relevant only if we posit an essential 'human nature' prior to social experience. Manipulation can then be seen as the perversion of the natural essence of the individual, and the de-institutionalisation of values allows the individual to return to his/her essential self for direction. But the concept of the individual prior to society is nonsense. All individuals are concrete persons, uniquely developed through their particular articulation with social life.

The poverty of Illich's 'addictiveness' criterion is dramatised in his treatment of technology. While he correctly recognises that technology can be developed for purposes of either repression or liberation, his conception requires that the correct unalienated development of technological and institutional forms will follow from a simple aggregation of individual preferences over 'left-convivial' alternatives.

The same analysis which I applied to the atomistic aggregation of preferences in the determination of activity contexts applies here as well: there is no reason to believe that ceding control of technological innovation and diffusion to a few, while rendering them subject to market criteria of success and failure, will produce desirable outcomes. Indeed this is precisely the mechanism operative in the private capitalist economy, with demonstrably adverse outcomes. According to the criterion of left-conviviality, the historical development of technology in both private and public spheres will conform to criteria of profitability and entrepreneurial control. Citizens are reduced to passive consumers, picking

and choosing among the technological alternatives a technological elite presents to them.

In contrast, it seems clear to me that individuals must exercise direct control over technology in structuring their various social environments, thereby developing and coming to understand their needs through their exercise of power. The control of technical and institutional forms must be vested directly in the group of individuals involved in a social activity, else the alienation of these individuals from one another becomes a postulate of the technical and institutional development of this social activity - be it in factory, office, school, or community.

In summary, the facile criterion of left-conviviality must be replaced by the less immediate - but correct - criterion of unalienated social outcomes: the institutionally mediated allocation of power must be so ordered that social outcomes conform to the wills and needs of participating individuals, and the quality of participation must be such as to promote the full development of individual capacities for self-understanding and social effectiveness.

Schooling: the pre-alienation of docile consumers

Everywhere the hidden curriculum of schooling initiates the citizen to the myth that bureaucracies guided by scientific knowledge are efficient and benevolent... And everywhere it develops the habit of self-defeating consumption of services and alienating production, the tolerance for institutional dependence, and the recognition of institutional rankings. ('DS', p. 74)

Illich sets his analysis of the educational system squarely on its strategic position in reproducing the economic relations of the larger society. While avoiding the inanity of reformers, who see 'liberated education' as compatible with current capitalist political and economic institutions, he rejects the rigidity of old-style revolutionaries, who would see even more repressive (though different) education as a tool in forging 'socialist consciousness' in the Workers' State.

What less perceptive educators have viewed as irrational, mean, and petty in modern schooling, Illich views as merely reflecting the operation of all manipulative institutions. In the first place, he argues, the educational system takes its place alongside other service bureaucracies, selling a manipulative, pre-packaged product, rendering their services addictive, and monopolising all alternatives to self-initiated education on the part of individuals and small consenting groups.

Yet, argues Illich, schools cannot possibly achieve their goal of promoting learning. For as in every dimension of human experience, learning is the result of personal activity, not professional ministration:

Most learning is not the result of instruction. It is rather the result of unhampered participation in a meaningful setting. Most people learn best by being 'with it', yet school makes them identify their personal, cognitive growth with elaborate planning and manipulation. ('DS', p. 39)

Thus, as with all bureaucratic service institutions, schools fail by their very nature. And true to form, the more they fail, the more reliance is placed on them, and the more they expand:

Everywhere in the world school costs have risen faster than enrollments and faster than the GNP, everywhere expenditures on school fall even further behind the expectations of parents, teachers, and pupils... School gives unlimited opportunity for legitimated waste, so long as its destructiveness goes unrecognised and the cost of palliatives goes up. ('DS', p. 10)

From the fact that schools do not promote learning, however, Illich does not conclude that schools are simply irrational or discardable. Rather, he asserts their central role in creating docile and manipulable consumers for the larger society. For just as these men and women are defined by the quality of their possessions rather than of their activities, so they must learn to 'transfer responsibility from self to institutions...'.

Once a man or woman has accepted the need for school, he or she is easy prey for other institutions. Once young people have allowed their imaginations to be formed by curricular instruction, they are conditioned to institutional planning of every sort. 'Instruction' smothers the horizon of their imaginations. ('DS', p. 39)

Equally they learn that anything worthwhile is standardised, certified, and can be purchased.

Even more lamentable, repressive schooling forces commodity fetishism on individuals by thwarting their development of personal capacities for autonomous and initiating social activity:

People who have been schooled down to size let unmeasured experience slip out of their hands... They do not have to be robbed of their creativity. Under instruction, they have unlearned to 'do' their thing or 'be' themselves, and value only what has been made or could be made... ('DS', p. 40)

Recent research justifies Illich's emphasis on the 'hidden curriculum' of schooling. Mass public education has not evolved into its present bureaucratic, hierarchical, and authoritarian form because of the organisational prerequisites of imparting cognitive skills. Such skills may in fact be more efficiently developed in democratic, non-repressive atmospheres. Rather, the social relations of education produce and reinforce those values, attitudes, and effective capacities which allow individuals to move smoothly into an alienated and class-stratified society. That is, schooling reproduces the social relations of the larger society from generation to generation.

Again, however, it does not follow that schooling finds its predominant function in reproducing the social relations of consumption per se. Rather, it is the social relations of production which are relevant to the form and function of modern schooling.

A production orientation to the analysis of schooling - that the 'hidden curriculum' in mass education reproduces the social relations of production - is reinforced in several distinct bodies of current educational research. First, economists have shown that education, in its role of providing a properly trained labour force, takes its place alongside capital accumulation and technological change as a major source of economic growth. Level of educational attainment is the major non-ascriptive variable in furthering the economic position of individuals.

Second, research shows that the type of personal development produced through schooling and relevant to the individual's productivity as a worker in a capitalist enterprise is primarily non-cognitive. That is, profit-maximising firms find it remunerative to hire more highly educated workers at higher pay, essentially irrespective of differences among individuals in cognitive abilities or attainments. In other words, two individuals (white American males) with identical cognitive achievements (intelligence or intellectual attainment) but differing educational levels will not command, on the average, the same income or occupational status. Rather, the economic success of each will correspond closely to the average for his educational level. All individuals with the same level of educational attainment tend to have the same expected mean economic success (racial and sexual discrimination aside). This is not to say that cognitive skills are not necessary to job adequacy in a technological society. Rather, these skills either exist in such profusion (through schooling) or are so easily developed on the job that they are not a criterion for hiring. Nor does this mean that there is no correlation between cognitive attainments (e.g., IQ) and occupational status. Such a correlation exists (although it is quite loose), but is almost totally mediated by formal schooling: the educational system discriminates in favour of the more intelligent, although its contribution to worker productivity does not operate primarily via cognitive development.

Thus the education-related worker attributes that employers willingly pay for must be predominantly affective characteristics - personality traits, attitudes, modes of self-presentation and motivation. How affective traits that are rewarded in schools come to correspond to the needs of alienated production is revealed by direct inspection of the social relations of the classroom. First, students are rewarded in terms of grades for exhibiting the personality characteristics of good workers in bureaucratic work roles - proper subordinancy in relation to authority and the primacy of cognitive as opposed to affective and creative modes of social response - above and beyond any actual effect they may have on cognitive achievement. Second, the hierarchical structure of schooling itself mirrors the social relations of industrial production: students cede control over their learning activities to teachers in the classroom. Just as workers are alienated from both the process and the product of their work activities, and must be motivated by the external reward of pay and hierarchical status, so the student learns to operate efficiently through the external reward of grades and promotion, effectively alienated from the process of education (learning) and its product (knowledge). Just as the work process is stratified, and workers on different levels in the hierarchy of authority and status are required to display substantively distinct patterns of values, aspirations, personality traits, and modes of 'social presentation' (dress, manner of speech, personal identification, and loyalties to a particular social stratum), so the school system stratifies, tracks, and structures social interaction according to criteria of social class and relative scholastic success. The most effectively indoctrinated students are the most valuable to the economic enterprise or state bureaucracy, and also the most successfully integrated into a particular stratum within the hierarchical educational process.

Third, a large body of historical research indicates that the system of mass, formal, and compulsory education arose more or less directly out of changes in productive relations associated with the Industrial Revolution, in its role of supplying a properly socialised and stratified labour force.

The critical turning points in the history of American education have coincided with the perceived failure of the school system to fulfil its functional role in reproducing a properly socialised and stratified labour force, in the face of important qualitative or quantitative changes in the social relations of production. In these periods (e. g. , the emergence of the common school system) numerous options were open and openly discussed. The conflict of economic interests eventually culminated in the functional reorientation of the educational system to new labour needs of an altered capitalism.

In the mid- to late 19th century, this took the form of the economy's need to generate a labour force compatible with the factory system from a predominantly agricultural populace. Later, the crisis in education corresponded to the economy's need to import peasant European labour whose social relations of production and derivative culture were incompatible with industrial wage-labour. The resolution of this crisis was a hierarchical, centralised school system corresponding to the ascendance of corporate production. This resolution was not without its own contradictions. It is at this time that the modern school became the focus of tensions between work and play, between the culture of school and the culture of immigrant children, and between the notion of meritocracy and equality. Thus while Illich can describe the characteristics of contemporary education, his consumption orientation prevents him from understanding how the system came to be.

It seems clear that schools instill the values of docility, degrees of subordination corresponding to different levels in the hierarchy of production, and motivation according to external reward. It seems also true that they do not reward, but instead penalise, creative, self-initiated, cognitively flexible behaviour. By inhibiting the full development of individual capacities for meaningful individual activity, schools produce Illich's contended outcomes: the individual as passive receptor replaces the individual as active agent. But the articulation with the larger society is production rather than consumption.

If the sources of social problems lay in consumer manipulation of which schooling is both an exemplary instance and a crucial preparation for future manipulation, then a political movement for de-schooling might be, as Illich says, 'at the root of any movement for human liberation'. But if schooling is both itself an activity context and preparation for the more important activity context of work then personal consciousness arises not from the elimination of outside manipulation, but from the experience of solidarity and struggles in remolding a mode of social existence. Such consciousness represents not a 'return' to the self (essential human nature) but a restructuring of the self through new modes of social participation; this prepares the individual for itself.

Of course this evaluation need not be unidirectional from work to education. Indeed, one of the fundamental bases for assessing the value of an alternative structure of control in production is its compatibility with intrinsically desirable individual development through education. In so far as Illich's left-convivial concept is desirable in any ultimate

sense, a reorganisation of production should be sought conformable to it. This might involve the development of a vital craft/artistic/technical/ service sector in production organised along master-apprentice or group-control lines open to all individuals. The development of unalienated work technologies might then articulate harmoniously with learning-web forms in the sphere of education.

But a reorganisation of production has other goals as well. For example, any foreseeable future involves a good deal of socially necessary and on balance personally unrewarding labour. However this work may be reorganised, its accomplishment must be based on individual values, attitudes, personality traits, and patterns of motivation adequate to its execution. If equality in social participation is a 'revolutionary ideal', this dictates that all contribute equally toward the staffing of the socially necessary work roles. This is possible only if the hierarchical (as opposed to social) division of labour is abolished in favour of the solidary cooperation and participation of workers in control of production. Illich's anarchistic notion of learning webs does not seem conducive to the development of personal characteristics for this type of social solidarity. [3]

The second setting for a politics of education is the transitional society - one which bears the technological and cultural heritage of the capitalist class/ caste system, but whose social institutions and patterns of social consciousness are geared toward the progressive realisation of 'ideal forms' (i. e. revolutionary goals). In this setting, the social relations of education will themselves be transitional in nature, mirroring the transformation process of social relations of production. For instance, the elimination of boring, unhealthy, fragmented, uncreative, constraining, and otherwise alienated but socially necessary labour requires an extended process of technological change in a transitional phase. As we have observed, the repressive application of technology toward the formation of occupational roles is not due to the intrinsic nature of physical science nor to the requisites of productive efficiency, but to the political imperative of stable control from the top in an enterprise. Nevertheless the shift to automated, decentralised, and worker-controlled technologies requires the continuous supervision and cooperation of workers themselves. Any form this takes in a transitional society will include a constant struggle among three groups: managers concerned with the development of the enterprise, technicians concerned with the scientific rationality of production, and workers concerned with the impact of innovation and management on job satisfaction. The present educational system does not develop in the individual the capacities for cooperation, struggle, autonomy, and judgment appropriate to this task. But neither does Illich's alternative which avoids the affective aspects of work socialisation totally, and takes technology out of the heads of learners.

In a transitional setting, liberating technologies cannot arise in education, any more than in production, spontaneously or by imposition from above. The social relations of unalienated education must evolve from conscious cooperation and struggle among educational administrators (managers), teachers (technicians), and students (workers), although admittedly in a context of radically redistributed power among the three. The outcome of such a struggle is not only the positive development of education but the fostering of work-capacities in individuals adequate to the task of social transition in work and community life as well.

The inadequacy of Illich's conception of education in transitional societies is striking in his treatment of China and Cuba. It is quite evident that these countries are following new and historically unprecedented directions of social development. But Illich argues the necessity of their failure from the simple fact that they have not deschooled. That they were essentially 'deschooled' before the revolution (with no appreciable social benefits) does not faze him. While we may welcome and embrace Illich's emphasis on the social relations of education as a crucial variable in their internal development toward new social forms, his own criterion is without practical application.

The third setting in which the politics of education must be assessed - and the one which would most closely represent the American reality - is that of capitalist society itself. Here the correspondence principle implies that educational reform requires an internal failure in the stable reproduction of the economic relations of production. That is, the idea of liberating education does not arise spontaneously, but is made possible by emerging contradictions in the larger society. Nor does its aim succeed or fail according as its ethical value is greater or less. Rather, success of the aim presupposes a correct understanding of its basis in the contradictions in social life, and the political strategies adopted as the basis of this understanding.

The immediate strategies of a movement for educational reform, then, are political: (a) understanding the concrete contradictions in economic life and the way they are reflected in the educational system: (b) fighting to insure that consciousness of these contradictions persists by thwarting attempts of ruling elites to attenuate them by co-optation: and (c) using the persistence of contradictions in society at large to expand the political base and power of a revolutionary movement, that is, a movement for educational reform must understand the social conditions of its emergence and development in the concrete conditions of social life. Unless we achieve such an understanding and use it as the basis of political action, a functional reorientation will occur vis-à-vis the present crisis in education, as it did in earlier critical moments in the history of American education.

In the present period, the relevant contradiction involves: (a) Blacks moved from rural independent agriculture and seasonal farm wage-labour to the urban-industrial wage-labour system; (b) middle-class youth with values attuned to economic participation as entrepreneurs, elite white-collar and professional and technical labour, faced with the elimination of entrepreneurship, the corporatisation of production, and the proletarianisation of white-collar work; and (c) women, the major sufferers of ascriptive discrimination in production (including household production) in an era where capitalist relations of production are increasingly legitimised by their sole reliance on achievement (non-ascriptive) norms.

This inventory is partial, incomplete, and insufficiently analysed. But only on a basis of its completion can a successful educational strategy be forged. In the realm of contradictions, the correspondence principle must yet provide the method of analysis and action. We must assess political strategies in education on the basis of the single -

but distressingly complex - question: will they lead to the transitional society?

I have already argued that deschooling will inevitably lead to a situation of social chaos, but probably not to a serious mass movement toward constructive social change. In this case the correspondence principle simply fails to hold, producing at best a temporary (in case the ruling elites can find an alternative mode of worker socialisation) or ultimately fatal (in case they cannot) breakdown in the social fabric. But only if we posit some essential pre-social human nature on which individuals draw when normal paths of individual development are abolished, might this lead in itself to liberating alternatives.

But the argument over the sufficiency of deschooling is nearly irrelevant. For schools are so important to the reproduction of capitalist society that they are unlikely to crumble under any but the most massive political onslaughts. 'Each of us', says Illich, 'is personally responsible for his or her own deschooling, and only we have the power to do it.' This is not true. Schooling is legally obligatory, and is the major means of access to welfare-relevant activity contexts. The political consciousness behind a frontal attack on institutionalised education would necessarily spill over to attacks on other major institutions. 'The risks of a revolt against school,' says Illich,

> ... are unforeseeable, but they are not as horrible as those of a revolution starting in any other major institution. School is not yet organized for self-protection as effectively as a nation-state, or even a large corporation. Liberation from the grip of schools could be bloodless. ('DS', p. 49)

This is no more than whistling in the dark.

The only presently viable political strategy in education - and the precise negation of Illich's recommendations - is what Rudi Dutschke terms 'the long march through the institutions', involving localised struggles for what André Gorz calls 'non-reformist reforms', i. e., reforms which effectively strengthen the power of teachers vis-à-vis administrators, and of students vis-à-vis teachers.

Still, although schools neither can nor should be eliminated, the social relations of education can be altered through genuine struggle. Moreover, the experience of both struggle and control prepares the student for a future of political activity in factory and office.

In other words, the correct immediate political goal is the nurturing of individuals both liberated (i. e., demanding control over their lives and outlets for their creative activities and relationships) and politically aware of the true nature of their misalignment with the larger society. There may indeed be a bloodless solution to the problem of revolution, but certainly none more simple than this.

Conclusion

Illich recognises that the problems of advanced industrial societies are institutional, and that their solutions lie deep in the social core. Therefore, he consciously rejects a partial or affirmative analysis which would accept society's dominant ideological forms and direct its innovative contributions toward marginal changes in assumptions and boundary conditions.

Instead, he employs a methodology of total critique and negation, and his successes, such as they are, stem from that choice. Ultimately, however, his analysis is incomplete.

Dialectical analysis begins with society as is (thesis), entertains its negation (antithesis), and overcomes both in a radical reconceptualisation (synthesis). Negation is a form of demystification - a drawing away from the immediately given by viewing it as a 'negative totality'. But negation is not without presuppositions, is not itself a form of liberation. It cannot 'wipe clean the slate' of ideological representation of the world or one's objective position in it. The son/daughter who acts on the negation of parental and societal values is not free - he/she is merely the constrained negative image of that which he/she rejects (e. g. , the negation of work, consumption order, and rationality is not liberation but negative un-freedom). The negation of male dominance is not women's liberation by the (negative) affirmation of 'female masculinity'. Women's liberation in dialectical terms can be conceived of as the overcoming (synthesis) of male dominance (thesis) and female masculinity (antithesis) in a new totality which rejects/embodies both. It is this act of overcoming (synthesis, consciousness) which is the critical and liberating aspect of dialectical thought. Action lies not in the act of negation (antithesis, demystification) but in the act of overcoming (synthesis/consciousness).

The strengths of Illich's analysis lie in his consistent and pervasive methodology of negation. The essential elements in the liberal conceptions of the Good Life - consumption and education, the welfare state and corporate manipulation - are demystified and laid bare in the light of critical, negative thought. Illich's failures can be consistently traced to his refusal to pass beyond negations - beyond a total rejection of the appearances of life in advanced industrial societies - to a higher synthesis. While Illich should not be criticised for failing to achieve such a synthesis, nevertheless he must be taken seriously to task for mystifying the nature of his own contribution and refusing to step - however tentatively - beyond it. Work is alienating - Illich rejects work; consumption is unfulfilling - Illich rejects consumption; institutions are manipulative - Illich places 'nonaddictiveness' at the centre of his conception of human institutions; production is bureaucratic - Illich glorifies the entrepreneurial and small-scale enterprise; schools are dehumanising - Illich rejects schools; political life is oppressive and ideologically totalitarian - Illich rejects politics in favour of individual liberation. Only in one sphere does he go beyond negation, and this defines his major contribution. While technology is in fact dehumanising (thesis), he does not reject technology (antithesis). Rather he goes beyond technology and its negation towards a schema of liberating technological forms in education.

The cost of his failure to pass beyond negation in the sphere of social relations in general, curiously enough, is an implicit affirmation of the deepest characteristics of the existing order. In rejecting work, Illich affirms that it necessarily is alienating - reinforcing a fundamental pessimism on which the acceptance of capitalism is based; in rejecting consumption, he affirms either that it is inherently unfulfilling (the Protestant ethic), or would be fulfilling if unmanipulated; in rejecting manipulative and bureaucratic 'delivery systems', he affirms the laissez-faire capitalist model and its core institutions; in rejecting schools, Illich embraces a commodity-fetishist cafeteria-smorgasbord ideal in education; and in rejecting political action, he affirms a utilitarian individualistic conception of humanity. In all cases, Illich's analysis fails to pass beyond the given (in both its positive and negative totalities), and hence affirms it.

The most serious lapse in Illich's analysis is his implicit postulation of a human 'essence' in all of us, preceding all social experience - potentially blossoming but repressed by manipulative institutions. Indeed, Illich is locigally compelled to accept such a conception by the very nature of his methodology of negation. The given is capitalist (or state socialist) socialisation - repressive and dehumanising. The antithesis is no socialisation at all - individuals seeking independently and detached from any mode of social integration their personal paths of development. Such a view of personal growth becomes meaningful in human terms only when anchored in some absolute human standard within the individual and anterior to the social experience that it generates.

In such a conception of individual 'essence', critical judgment enters, I have emphasised, precisely at the level of sensing and interpreting one's pre-social psyche. This ability requires only demystification (negation); hence a methodology of negation is raised to a sufficient condition of a liberating social science. Dialectical analysis, on the other hand, takes negation (demystification) as the major precondition of liberation, but not its sufficient condition. Even the most liberating historical periods (e. g. , the Reformation, the French and American Revolutions), despite their florid and passionately idealistic rhetoric, in fact responded to historically specific potentials and to limited but crucial facets of human deprivation. Dialectical analysis would view our present situation as analogous and, rejecting 'human essence' as a pre-social driving force in social change, would see the central struggles of our era as specific negations and their overcoming in localisable areas of human concern - while embracing the ideologies that support these struggles.

The place of critical judgment (reason) in this analysis model lies in a realistic-visionary annihilation of both existing society and its negation-in-thought in a new, yet historically limited, synthesis. I have argued that this task requires as its point of departure the core economic institutions regulating social life - first in coming to understand their operation and the way in which they produce the outcomes of alienating work, fragmented community, environmental destruction, commodity fetishism, and other estranged cultural forms (thesis), and then in entertaining how we might negate and overcome them through political action and personal consciousness. Illich in his next book, might leave the security and comfort of negation, and apply his creative vitality to this most demanding of tasks.

6

PAUL GOODMAN

Mini-schools: a prescription for the reading problem

Source: Article in the <u>New York Review of Books</u>,
   4 January 1968.

* *

This piece shows Paul Goodman striking home with shafts that appear satirical as well as sharp. I had assumed that the section on teaching children to speak was a fantasy but I have been assured that there are some schools in the USA which attempt to do this. Much of my own experience confirms many of Goodman's assertions. Many teachers, teacher-trainers, and curriculum developers put the premium on teaching rather than learning. It is a general schoolman characteristic to try to create a curriculum which is linear, sequential, and graded, whether or not the model is appropriate to the nature of the thing to be learned, the learning, or the learner. In his other works Goodman takes the model of learning the native tongue too far. It may be that a feeling for the structure of language is within us, as Tolstoy intuitively asserted and Chomsky argues, but the implications of this for <u>second</u> language learning have still to be fully worked out and, of more general significance, it is doubtful whether this model applies to learning in other fields like political economy or natural sciences or mathematics. See also Reading 22 - David A. Reibel: Language learning analysis, where the argument is made that language learning is 'more exponential than linear'.

* *

What follows is a statement I recently made when asked to testify on teaching reading, before the Borough President of Manhattan:

A chief obstacle to children's learning to read is the present school setting in which they have to pick it up. For any learning to be skillful and lasting, it must be or become self-motivated, second nature; for this, the schooling is too impersonal, standardised, and academic. If we tried to teach children to speak, by academic methods in a school-like environment, many would fail and most would stammer.

Although the analogy between learning to speak and learning to read is not exact, it is instructive to pursue it, since speaking is much harder. Learning to speak is a stupendous intellectual achievement. It involves learning to use signs, acquiring a vocabulary, and also mastering an extraordinary kind of algebra - syntax - with almost infinite variables in a large number of sentence forms. We do not know scienti-

fically how infants learn to speak, but almost all succeed equally well, no matter what their class or culture. Every child picks up a dialect, whether 'correct' or 'incorrect', that is adequate to express the thoughts and needs of his milieu.

We can describe some of the indispensable conditions for learning to speak,

1. The child is constantly exposed to speech related to interesting behaviour in which he often shares. ('Now where's your coat? Now we're going to the supermarket, etc. ')

2. The speakers are persons important to the child, who often single him out to speak to him or about him.

3. The child plays with the sounds, freely imitates what he hears, and tries to approximate it without interference or correction. He is rewarded by attention and other useful results when he succeeds.

4. Later, the child consolidates by his own act what he has learned. From age three to five he acquires style, accent, and fluency by speaking with his peers, adopting their uniform but also asserting his own tone, rhythm, and mannerisms. He speaks peer speech but is uniquely recognizable as speaking in his own way.

Suppose, by contrast, that we tried to teach speaking academically in a school-like setting:

1. Speaking would be a curricular subject abstracted from the web of activity and reserved for special hours punctuated by bells.

2. It would be a tool subject rather than a way of being in the world.

3. It would not spring from his needs in immediate situations but would be taught according to the teacher's idea of his future advantage, importantly aiming at his getting a job sixteen years later.

4. Therefore the child would have to be 'motivated', the exercises would have to be 'fun', etc.

5. The lessons would be arranged in a graded series from simple to complex, for instance on a false theory that monosyllables precede polysyllables, or words precede sentences, or sentences precede words.

6. The teacher's relation to the infant would be further depersonalised by the need to speak or listen to only what fits two dozen other children as well.

7. Being continually called on, corrected, tested, and evaluated to meet a standard in a group, some children would become stutterers; others would devise a phony system of apparently speaking in order to get by, although the speech meant nothing; others would balk at being processed and would purposely become 'stupid'.

8. Since there is a predetermined range of what can be spoken and how it must be spoken, everybody's speech would be pedantic and standard, without truth to the child's own experience or feeling.

Turn now to teaching reading. These eight disastrous defects are not an unfair caricature of what we do. Reading is treated as abstract, irrelevant to actual needs, instrumental, extrinsically motivated, impersonal, pedantic, not expressive of truth or art. The teaching often produces awkwardness, faking or balking. Let me also make four further points specific to learning reading:

1. Most people who have learned to read and write fluently have done so on their own, with their own material, whether library books, newspapers, comic books, or street signs. They may have picked up the ABCs in school, but they acquired skill, preserved what they had learned, on their own. This self-learning is an important point, since it is not at the mechanical level of the ABCs that reading retardation drastically occurs, but in the subsequent years when the good readers are going it alone.

2. On neurological grounds, an emotionally normal child in middle-class urban and suburban surroundings, constantly exposed to written code, should spontaneously learn to read by age nine just as he learned to speak by age two or three. (This is the conclusion of Walla Nauta of the National Institute of Mental Health.) It is impossible for such a child not to pick up the code unless he is systematically interrupted and discouraged, for instance by trying to teach him.

But of course our problem has to do with children in the culture of poverty, which does not have the ordinary middle-class need for literacy and the premium put on it. Such children are not exposed to reading and writing in important relations with their parents and peers; the code does not constantly occur in every kind of sequence of behaviour. Thus there is an essential need for the right kind of schooling, to point to the written words and read them aloud, in use.

3. Historically, in all modern countries, school methods of lessons, copying, and textbooks, have been used, apparently successfully, to teach children to read. But this evidence is deceptive. A high level and continuing competence were required of very few - e.g. , in 1900 in the United States only 6 per cent graduated from high school. Little effort was made with children of the working class, and none at all with those in the culture of poverty. It is inherently unlikely that the same institutional procedures could apply with such a change of scale and population. Where a dramatic effort has been made to teach adults to read, as in Cuba, the method has been 'each one teach one', informally.

4. Also, with the present expansion of higher education, teachers of freshman English uniformly complain that the majority of middle-class students cannot really read and write, though they have put on a performance that got them through high school. As John Holt has carefully described, their real life need was not reading or writing but getting by. (This is analogous to the large group among Puerto Rican children in New York who apparently speak English well, but who in fact cannot say anything that they need or mean, that is not really simply parroted.)

I trust that the aim of the Borough President's hearings is how to learn reading as truth and art and not just to fake and get by. Further, since poor children do not have the continual incentives and subtle pressures of middle-class life, it is much harder for them to learn even just to fake and get by. And even if they do get by, it will not pay off for them in the end, since they do not have money and connections. To make good, they must really be competent.

The question is, is it possible and feasible to teach reading somewhat in the way children learn to speak, by intrinsic interest, with personal attention, and relating to the whole environment of activity? Pedagogically it is possible and feasible. There are known methods and available teachers, and I will

suggest an appropriate school setting. Economically it is feasible, since methods, staff, and setting do not cost more than the $850 per child that we now spend in the public schools. (This was demonstrated for two years by the First Street School on the Lower East Side, and it is in line with the budget of Erik Mann's new school for Negro children in Newark which uses similar principles.) Politically, however, my present proposal is impossible and unfeasible, since it threatens both vested interests and popular prejudices, as will be evident.

For ages six to eleven, I propose a system of tiny schools, radically decentralised. As one who for twenty years has urged democratic decentralisation in many fields, including the schools, I am of course interested in the Bundy recommendation to cut up the New York system into sixty fairly autonomous districts. This would restore some relevance of the culture (and the staff) of the school to the culture of the community. But however valuable politically, it is an administrative arrangement; it does not get down to the actual pedagogical operation. And it certainly is not child-centred; both poor and middle-class communities have their own ways of not paying attention to children, according to their own prejudices and distant expectations. By 'tiny school', therefore, I here mean twenty-eight children... with four teachers (one grown-up to seven children), and each tiny school to be largely administered by its own staff and parents, with considerable say also for the children, as in Summerhill. The four teachers are:

A teacher regularly licensed and salaried. Since the present average class size is twenty-eight, these are available.

A graduate from the senior class of a New York college, perhaps just embarking on graduate study. Salary $2000. There is no lack of candidates to do something interesting and useful in a free setting.

A literate housewife and mother, who can also prepare lunch. Salary $4000. No lack of candidates.

A literate, willing, and intelligent high-school graduate. Salary $2000. No lack of candidates.

Such a staff can easily be racially and ethnically mixed. And it is also the case, as demonstrated by the First Street School, that in such a small setting, with individual attention paid to the children, it is easy to get racially and ethnically mixed classes; there is less middle-class withdrawal when the parents do not fear that their children will be swamped and retarded. (We have failed to achieve 'integration' by trying to impose it from above, but it can be achieved from below, in schools entirely locally controlled, if we can show parents that it is for their children's best future.)

For setting, the tiny school would occupy two, three, or four rooms in existing school buildings, church basements, settlement houses otherwise empty during school hours, rooms set aside in housing projects, store-fronts. The setting is especially indifferent since a major part of activity occurs outside the school place. The setting should be able to be transformed into a clubhouse, decorated and equipped according to the group's own decision. There might be one school on every street, but it is also advisable to locate many in racial and ethnic border areas, to increase intermixture. For purposes of assembly, health services, and some games, ten tiny schools could use the present public school facilities.

The cost saving in such a setup is the almost total elimination of top-down administration and the kind of special services that are required precisely because of excessive size and rigidity. The chief uses of central administration would be licensing, funding, choosing sites, and some inspection. There would be no principals and assistants, secretaries and assistants. Curriculum, texts, equipment would be determined as needed - and despite the present putative economies of scale, they would be cheaper; much less would be pointless or wasted. Record-keeping would be at a minimum. There is no need for truant officers when the teacher-and-seven can call at the absentee's home and inquire. There is little need for remedial personnel since the staff and parents are always in contact, and the whole enterprise can be regarded as remedial. Organisational studies of large top-down directed enterprises show that the total cost is invariably at least 300 per cent above the cost of the immediate function, in this case the interaction of teachers and children. I would put this 300 per cent into increasing the number of adults and diversifying the possibilities of instruction. Further, in the conditions of New York real estate, there is great advantage in ceasing to build four-million-dollar school buildings, and rather fitting tiny schools into available niches.

Pedagogically, this model is appropriate for natural learning of reading:

1. It allows exposure to the activities of the city. A teacher-and-seven can spend half the time on the streets, visiting a business office, in a playground, at a museum, watching television, chatting with the corner druggist, riding the buses and subways, visiting rich and poor neighbourhoods and, if possible, homes. All these experiences can be saturated with speaking, reading, and writing. For instance, a group might choose to spend several weeks at the Museum of Natural History, and the problem would be to re-label the exhibits for their own level of comprehension.

2. It allows flexibility to approach each child according to his own style and interests, for instance in choice of reading matter. Given so many contexts, the teacher can easily strike when the iron is hot, whether reading the destination of a bus or the label on a can of soup. When some children catch on quickly and forge ahead on their own, the teacher need not waste their time and can concentrate on those who are more confused. The setting does not prejudge as to formal or informal techniques, phonics, Montessori, rote drill, Moore's typewriter, labelling the furniture, Herbert Kohl's creative writing, or any other method.

3. For instance, as a writer I like Sylvia Ashton-Warner's way of teaching little Maoris. Each day she tries to catch the most passionate concern of each child and to give him a card with that key word: usually these are words of fear, anger, hunger, loneliness, or sexual desire. Soon a child has a large ineradicable but very peculiar reading list, not at all like Dick and Jane. He then easily progresses to read and write anything. From the beginning, in this method, reading and writing are gut-meaningful,

they convey truth and feeling. This method could be used in our tiny school.

4. The ragged administration by children, staff, and parents is pedagogically a virtue, since this too, which is real, can be saturated with reading and writing, writing down the arguments, the rules, the penalties. Socially and politically, of course, it has the advantage of engaging the parents and giving them power.

I am assuming that for the first five school years, there is no merit in the standard curriculum. For a small child everything in the environment is educative, if he attends to it with guidance. Normal children can learn the first eight years' curriculum in four months anyway, at age twelve.

Further, I see little merit, for teaching this age, in the usual teacher-training. Any literate and well-intentioned grown-up or late teen-ager knows enough to teach a small child a lot. Teaching small children is a difficult art, but we do not know how to train the improvisational genius it requires, and the untrained seem to have it equally: compare one mother with another, or one big sister or brother with another. Since at this age one teaches the child, not the subject, the relevant art is psychotherapy, and the most useful course for a teachers' college is probably group therapy. The chief criterion for selection is the one I have mentioned: liking to be attentive to children. Given this setting, many young people would be introduced to teaching and would continue with it as a profession; whereas in the New York system the annual turnover approaches 20 per cent, after years of wasted training.

As I have said, however, there are fatal political and administrative objections to this proposal. First, the Public School administration does not intend to go largely out of business. Given its mentality, it must see any radical decentralisation as impossible to administer and dangerous, for everything cannot be controlled. Some child is bound to break a leg and the insurance companies will not cover: some teen-ager is bound to be indiscreet and the Daily News will explode in headlines.

The United Federation of Teachers will find the proposal to be anathema because it devalues professional perquisites and floods the schools with the unlicensed. Being mainly broken to the public school harness, most experienced teachers consider free and inventive teaching to be impossible.

Most fatally, poor parents, who aspire for their children, tend to regard unrigidly structured education as downgrading, not taking the children seriously, and also as vaguely immoral. In the present Black Power temper of Harlem, also, the possible easy intermixing is itself not desired. (Incidentally, I am rather sympathetic to black separatism as a means of consolidating the power of black communities. But children, as Kant said, must be educated for the future better society which cannot be separated.)

In spite of these fatal objections, I recommend that, instead of building the next new school building, we try out this scheme with 1200 children.

7

HARTMUT VON HENTIG
Deschooling the school

Source: Extract from Hartmut von Hentig:
<u>Cuernavaca oder: Alternativen zur Schule?</u>
(Klett/Kösel, 1971).

* *

Hartmut von Hentig is one of West Germany's leading reformers. He was a secondary teacher; became a professor at the University of Göttingen; and is at present Professor of Education at the new University of Bielefeld, where he is pioneering an experiment consisting of a laboratory school and an upper-school. His book, which is a combination of an exposition and a critique of deschooling, is based partly on a visit to Illich's centre in Mexico. Here he puts the case for deschooling the school, and lays down general guide-lines as to how it might be done. In particular, he tries to reconcile arguments about experience and learning. The practical dimension of his work in Bielefeld is only just beginning to be put into operation, after some years of discussion and planning. It remains to be seen whether it will be an isolated experiment, or whether it will influence the general system in West Germany, where schools, as in many other countries, tend to be 'ready made institutions'. See also Hartmut von Hentig et al., <u>Die Bielefelder Laborschule</u>, and Hartmut von Hentig et al., <u>Das Bielefelder Oberstufen-Kolleg</u>, both Klett Verlag, 1971.

* *

My view is that we should deschool the school. This position has three dimensions: it is founded on a critique of schools as they now are; a critique of the schools' critics; and a practical plan which will be put into operation at the University of Bielefeld. This plan is based on certain axiomatic propositions which have become visible and important only by considering the various proposed alternatives:

1. Alternatives do not exist. We have to create alternatives. In order to do this we have to think and use our imagination in conditions which need to be artificially 'liberated'. It would also involve protracted research and a specific political struggle.

2. Any alternative would need to be accepted and desired by those who had to live with it. Their understanding of it, and willingness to support it, would depend on whether they had ever seen the new idea in operation, and had been able to relate it to their own situation, problems, and opportunities. We would, therefore, need to create a model (in the sense of an architect's or an engineer's model) first.

3. Before we can deschool society, and abolish schools, we must first make society itself educative. Society has to be trained, as it were, in the use of networks, voucher-systems, street schools, etc. This would be possible only through deschooled

schools. The young people of the coming generation, who will be able and who ought to change the world, should have had some experience of what it means 'to be free from duress within a framework of necessities', and how to make use of that freedom. The older generation, who determine the present system, should realise from the model the opportunities for learning and experience denied to them and their children - in badly planned cities, in mass-produced blocks of flats, in barrack-like schools, in the kind of playgrounds that kill creativity, with pre-planned careers, and the artificiality of the whole educational system.

4. A society in which there is only one path to possessions, rights and opportunities is not an open society. Dropouts, for instance, who cannot or do not want to take this path, have only one possibility in our society - to return to the abandoned path. An educational system that does not provide alternatives, for these people and for others, is not only being unjust to the young, but it also lacks criteria for criticising and reforming itself.

5. 'Rolling-reform' can be a cover-up for failing to subject a system to evaluation and assessment. It can also be used as a pretext for educational theory to concern itself constantly with educational theory, instead of with children. If a critique and a reform of schools is to continue, and at the same time a system which constantly concerns itself with itself is to be avoided, then (a) the school itself needs to be developed and provided with the means to enable it to investigate and evaluate its own work; (b) the schools need to be enabled and authorised to deal in politics; (c) the school should be directed by statute continuously to return educational tasks and opportunities to society, by showing society how and what to do.

6. The new curricula constantly need to be related to the changing life of the child, and must not simply stem from the academic viewpoint of the teacher or the aims of the school. We have not yet exhausted, nor even foreseen, all the possibilities of experiences, insights and actions, which could be open and examinable, and to which the changed school could expose the children in order to help them in the process of growing up. Up to now the school has always converted anything it took in from the outside world into elements of the curriculum which would somehow fit in with the established order. The kind of 'meaningful learning' that Illich hopes to achieve through service-agencies operating in a free market can, in my opinion, be achieved only by sensible teachers, making full use of scientific aids and research findings, in open schools and free conditions. What is 'optimal' could be determined by research only under certain fixed conditions, or might be stated only in a very general way. Therefore, teachers and schools must be able to operate on their own. Whatever form the curriculum takes, it must not be regarded as a cassette that only needs to be inserted and played: nor can it be regarded as a 'correct' curriculum because it was produced and examined by scholars.

7. Schools need reforming not for their own sake but because new problems in society demand new kinds of preparation. The part that the school can play in changing society can be only a limited and indirect one. It is more a matter of adults consciously changing things in order to save children from the wrong problems and from false ideals. The major part of school reform, therefore, lies in reforming

the education of teachers, and directing it towards a conscious change in the tasks of the school.

These propositions which I have listed reflect my doubts about the possibility of perfecting the schools we have now, or of abolishing them altogether. In the first case my concern is caused by the threats of technocracy and manipulation in an educational system which is highly institutionalised, dependent on short-lived parliamentary governments, a permanent civil service, and the established knowledge-system. These threats become stronger if, through growing professionalism, the school makes itself more opaque and isolated from society, so that society itself loses sight of its own educational functions. In the second case I am concerned that the abolition of our present educational institutions could lead to an uncontrolled and uncontrollable education industry whose 'hidden curriculum' would be more hidden, and insidious, than that of our present schools, or that a period of confusion might lead back to a system more strict and centralised than the one we had before. The abolition of the common compulsory school might soon show that a free market in learning would be like a free market in consumer goods - it would favour the stronger producers, and increase social inequalities. The 'natural desire to learn' would not suffice as a regulating instrument, for - as we have known for a long time - the desire to learn, rather than being innate, is something which develops under favourable conditions and is encouraged by systematic efforts.

My doubts are based not only on those predictions but mainly, and more importantly, on my different view of the school's functions in general. In my opinion both of the following two assertions fail to identify the essence of the present crisis:

1. The school is failing because it does not achieve its own aims (those very general aims found in educational theory, recommendations from Ministries, and preambles in official reports - such as developing intellectual maturity, political literacy and awareness, and a concern for culture, humanity and reason).

2. The school is failing because it does not fulfil society's expectations (vocational training, social selection, providing a haven for children and young people; protecting the production-system, the administration, and political life from still 'unsocialised' trouble-makers; ensuring that the country should be able to compete on the world market, etc.).

You could find reasons for the first assertion at practically any time in history, but it would not have caused a crisis. The second assertion is probably not even correct. Society in the main wants this kind of school, and this kind of school has served society quite well. In my opinion the essence of the crisis is that our society has an objective and long-term need for a kind of school which is quite different from the one it has now. It needs a school which provides more than vocational training and which does more than adapt its pupils to society. Society needs an institution which would facilitate the dialectic of change and enable society to get beyond its own systems' constraints. This function was once carried out by the church, and then later by independent universities. In our society, though, the high degree of division of labour and extreme level of specialisation gives a man great potential power over others, and it is not enough to give freedom to monks and academics or to equip only certain positions and functions in society with the means to be critical and free: instead - in Rousseau's words - everybody must be 'forced to be free'. This necessary freedom lies in the possibility of self-determination within the framework of a Social Contract and can be achieved only by common agreement, through education.

The deschooled school can enable us to reach this goal. The characteristics of such a school would include:

1. It would restore genuine and open experience (i. e. it would not be artificially cut off from life).

2. It would restore the instrumental function of knowledge.

3. It would restore the dialectical relationship between knowledge and experience.

4. Learning would be organised in such a way as to provide opportunities for 'teachers' and 'educators' to act as helpers and mediators, and together to decide their own aims and methods. In this way they could become a model of what they themselves would like their students to be - enquiring, political, self-reliant people. Then the explicit curriculum would no longer be contradicted by the 'hidden curriculum'.

5. It would enquire into major common problems so that the growing diversity and lack of immediacy in our society would not make us lose the capacity for working together and understanding each other. (Attendance at such a 'compulsory school' could in the end be limited to a few months in the year.)

6. Around this common core of learning and experience it would offer a large range of choice, and in so doing it would provide a mechanism for criticising the educational system which was built into the system itself.

7. It would create a strategy for the transition from our present closed and almost total institutions to a system characterised by its openness, and its truly public systems of communication and cooperation.

If my diagnosis of the essence of the present crisis in education is correct, then deschooling the school must be the central feature of any policy aimed to get us beyond that crisis.

8

JOHN HOLT

Schools are bad places for kids

Source: Originally in the Saturday Evening Post,
8 February 1969, and reprinted in Holt's book
The Underachieving School.

* *

An example of Holt at his polemical best, arguing
that 'school is a long lesson in How To Turn Yourself
Off'. See also the Introduction, and the Quotational
Bibliography - HOLT, John.

* *

Of course, not all schools are alike. Some that I
know of are very good. Of those that are not so good,
some are much better than others, and many are
getting better. Moreover, I have talked to enough
school people, teachers, planners, administrators at
all levels, to know that many of them are very unhappy about our schools as they are, and would like
to make them much better places for kids, if they
knew how, or dared.

Still, most of our schools remain about what they
have always been, bad places for children, or, for
that matter, anyone to be in, to live in, to learn in.
In the first place, there is still a lot of cruelty in
them. The story that Jonathan Kozol told about the
schools of Boston could be told about almost any
other big city, as many people who have grown up or
taught in other cities have told me. A professor of
psychology, at a college where many of the students
do practice teaching in a nearby medium-sized city,
told me not long ago that one of them, when she went
to a school to teach, was handed a stick by the principal and told, 'I don't care whether you teach them
anything or not, just keep them quiet'. Needless to
say, the children were poor; rich parents generally
don't put up with this. The incident was not unusual,
but common. Many of this man's students, still hopeful and idealistic about children and education, came
back from their practice teaching in tears, saying
'I don't want to beat kids'. But in too many schools
this is still the name of the game.

I read once that in this country, and Great
Britain too, the societies for the prevention of cruelty
to animals have far more members and money than
the societies for the prevention of cruelty to children.
Interesting.

But few people in education will openly defend
cruelty to children, except perhaps a few of our right-
wing screwballs, so there is not much point in attacking it. Anyway, children can often resist cruelty.
It is at least direct and open. When someone is hitting you with a stick, or deliberately making you feel
like a fool in front of a class, you know what is being
done to you and who is doing it. You know who your
enemy is. But most of the harm that is done to children in schools they can't and don't resist, because

they don't know what is being done to them or who is
doing it, or because if they do know, they think it is
being done by kindly people for their own good.

Almost every child, on the first day he sets foot
in a school building, is smarter, more curious, less
afraid of what he doesn't know, better at finding and
figuring things out, more confident, resourceful, persistent, and independent, than he will ever again be in
his schooling or, unless he is very unusual and lucky,
for the rest of his life. Already, by paying close
attention to and interacting with the world and people
around him, and without any school-type formal instruction, he has done a task far more difficult, complicated, and abstract than anything he will be asked
to do in school or than any of his teachers has done
for years. He has solved the mystery of language.
He has discovered it - babies don't even know that
language exists - and he has found out how it works
and learned to use it. He has done it, as I described
in my book How Children Learn, by exploring, by
experimenting, by developing his own model of the
grammar of language, by trying it out and seeing
whether it works, by gradually changing it and re-
fining it until it does work. And while he has been
doing this, he has been learning a great many other
things as well, including a great many of the 'concepts' that the schools think only they can teach him,
and many that are more complicated than the ones
they do try to teach him.

In he comes, this curious, patient, determined,
energetic, skilful learner. We sit him down at a
desk, and what do we teach him? Many things.
First, that learning is separate from living. 'You
come to school to learn', we say, as if the child
hadn't been learning before, as if living were out
there and learning were in here and there were no
connection between the two. Secondly, that he cannot
be trusted to learn and is no good at it. Everything
we do about reading, a task far simpler than what
the child has already mastered, says to him, 'If we
don't make you read, you won't, and if you don't do
it exactly the way we tell you, you can't. ' In short,
he comes to feel that learning is a passive process,
something that someone else does to you, instead of
something you do for yourself.

In a great many other ways he learns that he is
worthless, untrustworthy, fit only to take other
people's orders, a blank sheet for other people to
write on. Oh, we make a lot of nice noises in school
about respect for the child and individual differences
and the like. But our acts, as opposed to our talk,
say to the child, 'Your experience, your concerns,
your curiosities, your needs, what you know, what
you want, what you wonder about, what you hope for,
what you fear, what you like and dislike, what you
are good at or not so good at - all this is of not the
slightest importance, it counts for nothing. What
counts here and the only thing that counts, is what
we know, what we think is important, what we want
you to do, think, and be. ' The child soon learns not
to ask questions: the teacher isn't there to satisfy
his curiosity. Having learned to hide his curiosity,
he later learns to be ashamed of it. Given no chance
to find out who he is, and to develop that person, who-
ever it is, he soon comes to accept the adults' evaluation of him. Like some highly advantaged eighth
graders I once talked with in a high-powered private
school, he thinks of himself, 'I am nothing, or if
something, something bad; I have no interests or
concerns except trivial ones, nothing that I like is
any good, for me or anyone else; any choices or
decisions I make will be stupid; my only hope of

surviving in this world is to cling to some authority and do what he says. '

He learns many other things. He learns that to be wrong, uncertain, confused, is a crime. Right Answers are what the school wants, and he learns, as I described in How Children Fail, countless strategies for prying these answers out of the teacher, for conning her into thinking he knows he doesn't know. He learns to dodge, bluff, fake, cheat. He learns to be lazy. Before he came to school, he would work for hours on end, on his own, with no thought of reward, at the business of making sense of the world and gaining competence in it. In school, he learns, like every buck private or conscript labourer, to goldbrick, how not to work when the boss isn't looking, how to know when he is looking, how to make him think you are working when you know he is looking. He learns that in real life you don't do anything unless you are bribed, bullied, or conned into doing it, that nothing is worth doing for its own sake, or that if it is, you can't do it in school. He learns to be bored, to work with a small part of his mind, to escape from the reality around him into day-dreams and fantasies - but not fantasies like those of his pre-school years, in which he played a very active part.

There is much fine talk in schools about Teaching Democratic Values. What the children really learn is Practical Slavery. How to suck up the boss. How to keep out of trouble, and get other people in. 'Teacher, Billy is...' Set into mean-spirited competition against other children, he learns that every man is the natural enemy of every other man. Life, as the strategists say, is a zero-sum game: what one wins, another must lose, for every winner there must be a loser. (Actually, our educators, above all our so-called and self-styled prestige universities, have turned education into a game in which for every winner there are about twenty losers.) He may be allowed to work on 'committees' with other children, but always for some trivial purpose. When important work is being done - important to the school - then to help anyone else, or get help, is called 'cheating'.

He learns, not only to be hostile, but to be indifferent - like the thirty-eight people who, over a half-hour period, saw Kitty Genovese attacked and murdered without offering help or even calling for help. He comes to school curious about other people, particularly other children. The most interesting thing in the classroom - often the only interesting thing in it - is the other children. But he has to act as if these other children, all about him, only a few feet away, were not really there. He cannot interact with them, talk with them, smile at them, often even look at them. In many schools he can't talk to other children in the halls between classes; in more than a few, and some of these in stylish suburbs, he can't even talk to them at lunch. Splendid training for a world in which, when you're not studying the other person to figure out how to do him in, you pay no attention to him.

In fact, he learns how to live without paying attention to anything going on around him. You might say that school is a long lesson in How To Turn Yourself Off, which may be one reason why so many young people, seeking the awareness of the world and responsiveness to it they had when they were little, think they can only find it in drugs. Aside from being boring, the school is almost always ugly, cold, and inhuman, even the most stylish, glass-windowed, $20-a-square-foot schools. I have by now been in a good many school buildings - hundreds, many of them

very new, but I can count on the fingers on two hands those in which the halls were made more alive and human by art or decoration, of the children or anyone else - pictures, murals, sculpture. Usually, the only thing that may be legitimately put up on the walls is a sign saying 'Beat Jonesville' or 'Go You Vampires' or the like.

Sit still! Be quiet! These are the great watch-words of school. If an enemy spy from outer space were planning to take over earth, and if his strategy were to prepare mankind for this takeover by making men's children as stupid as possible, he could find no better way to do it than to require them, for many hours a day, to be still and quiet. It is absolutely guaranteed to work. Children live all of a piece. Their bodies, their muscles, their voices, and their brains are all hooked together. Turn off a part of them, and you turn them off altogether.

Not long ago I visited a wonderful and radical school, founded and run by young people just out of college or still in college - the Children's Community in Ann Arbor, Michigan. [This school, in the prosperous home town of one of our largest and most highly regarded universities, has had to close, temporarily and perhaps permanently, for lack of money.] That year the school had been given the use of two rooms in the Friends' Meeting House, one quite small, the other average classroom size. The children had suggested and demanded that the smaller room be set aside for quiet activities - reading, story-telling, thinking, painting, work with numbers, talking, Cuisenaire rods, puzzles, and so on, leaving the larger room free for all kinds of active and noisy work and play. Active and noisy it certainly was. About half of the children were black and most were poor - what we now call 'disadvantaged', to hide the awkward fact that what poor people lack and need is mostly money. These children spent a lot of their time playing, much more noisily and actively than even so-called 'progressive' schools would allow. And as they played, they talked, to teachers and each other, loudly and excitedly, yes, but also fluently and expressively. They seemed not to have heard the news that poor kids, especially poor black kids, have no vocabulary and talk only in grunts and monosyllables.

Again, late last summer, in Santa Fe, New Mexico, I watched about a half dozen little boys, poor, of Spanish-speaking families - the disadvantaged of the Southwest - playing tackle football with a wonderful young man from the city recreation department. Thanks to miraculous tact and skill, he was able to play with them without hurting or even scaring them, but without condescending to them either. Somehow he managed to make them feel he was serious but not dangerous. The little boys, the oldest hardly eight, played with great energy and surprising skill. As they played, they kept up a running fire of chatter - fluent, pertinent, very often funny. One boy, a bit dizzy and shaken up after a head-on tackle, sat down at the sideline and said, 'Give me two minutes time out. ' One of the boys on the other team, cheerfully but not very sympathetically, said, 'OK. One two. ' And so on. Yet it is almost certain that the teacher of these boys, in their still and silent classrooms, see none of this intelligence, vivacity, and wit, and consider these children stupid and unteachable.

Children have a priority of needs. For some children, some of the time, this priority is not critical. That is, if a child can't do the thing he most wants and needs to do, there may be something else, or many other things, that he can do with almost as much pleasure and satisfaction. But at other times, and particularly if or when a child is troubled, the priority may be very critical. If he can't do the thing he most wants and needs to do, he can't do anything else; he is blocked, stopped. Turn off the number one switch and all the other switches go off. What I saw at the Children's Community, and have seen in other places since, makes me feel that many children have a strong and critical need, much stronger than I had ever suspected, for violent action, physical · and vocal, and for intense personal interaction. This personal interaction need not be fighting, though in most repressed classrooms, where children are held down until they become so frantic and angry that they cannot be held down any longer, this is what it usually comes to. Perhaps the best way to suggest what else it can be is to describe some of what the children at the Children's Community and elsewhere were doing.

One of the most popular toys in the Children's Community play and noise room was a group of old and beat-up tricycles. The game of the moment, when I was there, was the skid game. A little boy would stand up on the back step of the tricycle, get going as fast as he could by pushing with his other foot, and then throw the tricycle into a violent skid, usually leaving a long black tyre mark on the floor. The aim was to make the most daring skid and leave the longest mark. (These marks, by the way, had to be washed from the floor before each week-end, when the Friends themselves used the room.) One little girl, no more than five, spent at least an hour sawing into a chunk of wood. With exhausting effort, she made a rather wavy slot in it several inches deep. She was not making anything except a slot; she was just sawing, changing that piece of wood, leaving her mark on it. Other children were playing in a house made of a very heavy cardboard called Tri-Wall - a fine school material, by the way. Often some children outside would be trying to get in while others were trying to keep them out. This caused much excitement. Later a boy, or some boys, got inside another Tri-Wall box, with somewhat lower walls, and discovered that since the corners were hinged they could change its shape into a diamond. Soon they had made it into a very narrow and pointed diamond and were moving it around on the floor, pretending that it was a monster. Naturally this monster pursued other children, who fled from it, or pushed back against it. Either way, more excitement. Later some of the children and teachers got into, or fell into, a game in which the object was to hit someone else with a scarf and then run away or hide before he could hit you.

The need of poor children for this kind of play, noise, excitement, personal encounter, may be stronger than that of most children, but all children need it and love it. Some of the best children's games I have ever seen took place at the Walden Community School in Berkeley, California. This is a private elementary school, whose building costs, by the way, were cut by about one third by using the volunteer labour of parents and friends. The children there are mostly white, and mostly middle-class, not rich, but a good deal richer than most of the children at the Children's Community. The school day is wisely broken up by a number of free or recess periods, and during these periods many children of all ages rush to a big, largely unfurnished room that is used for many things, including dancing, sports, movies, school meetings, and so on. Usually the children put a rock record on the record player, turn up the volume good and loud, and begin to run and jump about.

One day they had taken from the closet a number of surplus parachutes - another good school material, not very expensive. Soon a game developed, in which the object was to throw part of the parachute over another child, or wrap or tangle it around him, and then drag and slide him over the floor to a pile of mattresses in the corner, all the while whirling the parachutes about. A kind of rotary tug of war, but disorganized, with the patterns continually changing. On another day a very different game developed. It started with a few children jumping from the top of a movable storage cabinet, about eight or nine feet high, onto a pile of mattresses on the floor. This took a good deal of courage, too much for some. Other children joined in, someone got out a parachute, and before long this was happening: the children, spaced around the edge of the parachute in a big, room-filling circle, would shout, 'One, two, three!' which later turned into 'Uno, dos, tres!' At 'three' or 'tres' they would all lift up the parachute quickly into the air. The parachute would billow up, higher than their heads, and while it hung there in the air, some child would leap or even dive from the top of the storage cabinet into the middle of the parachute, and then onto the mattresses on the floor beneath. Even when they missed the mattress, as sometimes happened, the parachute held by all the children acted like a fireman's net and broke their fall. The children holding the parachute moved around each time, so that everyone got his turn to jump. Some skipped their turn with nothing said. The teachers said that, until that day, that game had never been played before. How many such games have those children invented?

Young children, of any age and background, have a great and unmet need to be touched, held, jostled, tumbled, picked up, swung about. I think again of my first visit to the Children's Community. Bill Ayers, the founder and head of the school, had brought me over from the University of Michigan, where I had given a talk. We went into the big room, Bill in his old clothes, I in my dark blue speech suit. The children paid no attention to me, but clustered around him, each with something to ask or say, all shouting, 'Bill, Bill!' One little boy said, 'Pick me up. ' Bill picked him up. More clamour: 'Pick me up, pick me up!' Bill said, 'I can't pick up two at once. ' For some reason, with no plan in mind, I said, 'I can. ' For the first time they looked at me, now paying close attention. 'No,' they all said. 'Yes, I can,' I said. 'I'll show you. ' Two boys approached, cautiously. I squatted down, got one in the crook of each arm, and stood up. Great excitement. They all gathered round to look and exclaim. I was an instant celebrity. Then, finding that with a boy in each arm I still had both hands free, I said, 'What's more, I can pick up three at once. ' A louder chorus of 'No-o-o!' I insisted, and a third volunteer came up. I squatted down, got a good grip with my hands, and stood up holding all three of them. Sensation! From then on, there was almost always one of the children hanging onto me, or riding on my shoulders, or trying to chin himself on my forearm, another good though (for me) tiring game.

On another occasion I was at a summer camp for poor boys, white and black, labelled 'emotionally disturbed', from a nearby big city. At one point I went into a small room where one of the camp staff, a very sensitive and gifted worker with children, and three of the boys were talking into a tape recorder. They

41

were shy and reticent, and he, with great skill and
tact, was teasing and encouraging them to talk. I
sat on the floor near them, said nothing, but listened.
None of the boys even so much as looked at me. But
after a few minutes, one of them, to my surprise,
shifted his position so that he was partly leaning
against my knee. Shortly after, another moved around
so that he was in contact with me. Neither of them
spoke to me, looked at me, or acknowledged my presence in any other way. Not until after many minutes
of this silent contact did they begin to exchange glances
with me, and some time later to ask rather gruffly
who I was. The touch came first, and if, like most
teachers, I had withdrawn or even flinched from this
touch, that would probably have ended the possibility
of further contact.

But in most schools there is no contact, either
with the real world, or real things, or real people.

In these dull, ugly, and inhuman places, where
nobody ever says anything either very true or truth-
ful, where everybody is playing a kind of role, as in
a charade, where the teachers are no more free to
respond openly and honestly to the students than the
students are free to respond to the teachers or each
other, where the air practically vibrates with sus-
picions and anxiety, the child learns to live in a kind
of daze, saving his energies for those small parts of
his life that are too trivial for the adults to bother
with and thus remain his. Even the students who
learn to beat the system, one might say especially
those who beat it, despise it, and often despise themselves for giving in to it. It is a rare child indeed
who can come through his schooling with much left
of his curiosity, his independence, or his sense of
his own dignity, competence, and worth.

So much for complaints. There is much more to
be said - many others have said it - but this is
enough. More than enough.

What do we need to do? Many things. Some are
easy; we can do them right away. Some are hard,
and may take some time. Take a hard one first. We
should abolish compulsory school attendance. At the
very least, we should modify it, perhaps by giving
children every year a large number - fifty or sixty -
of authorized absences. Our compulsory school
attendance laws once served a humane and useful
purpose. They protected children's rights to some
schooling, against those adults who would otherwise
have denied it to them in order to exploit their
labour, in farm, shop, store, mine, or factory.
Today, the laws help nobody, not the schools, not the
teachers, not the children. To keep kids in school
who would rather not be there costs the schools an
enormous amount of time and trouble, to say nothing
of what it costs to repair the damage that these angry
and resentful prisoners do whenever they get the
chance. Every teacher knows that any kid in class
who, for whatever reason, would rather not be there,
not only doesn't learn anything himself but makes
learning harder for anyone else. As for protecting
the children from exploitation, the chief and indeed
only exploiters of children these days are the schools.
Kids caught in the college rush more often than not
work seventy hours or more a week, most of it on
paper busywork. For many other kids, not going to
college, school is just a useless time-wasting obstacle preventing them from earning needed money or
doing some useful work, or even doing some true
learning.

Objections: 'If kids didn't have to go to school
they'd all be out in the streets.' No, they wouldn't.

In the first place, even if schools stayed just the way
they are, children would spend at least some time
there because that's where they'd be likely to find
friends; it's a natural meeting place for children. In
the second place, schools wouldn't stay the way they
are, they'd get better, because we would have to start
making them what they ought to be right now - places
where children would want to be. In the third place,
those children who did not want to go to school could
find, particularly if we stirred up our brains and
gave them a little help, other things to do - the things
many children now do during their summers and
holidays.

Take something easier. We need to get kids out
of the school buildings and give them a chance to
learn about the world at first hand. It is a very
recent idea, and a crazy one, that the way to teach
our young people about the world they live in is to
take them out of it and shut them up in brick boxes.
It wouldn't have made a bit of sense even in a society
much simpler than ours. Fortunately, some educators are beginning to realize this. In Philadelphia
and Portland, Oregon, to pick only two places I have
happened to hear about, plans are being drawn up for
public schools that won't have any school buildings
at all, that will take students out into the city and
help them to use it and its people as a learning resource. Private schools in many cities are already
doing the same thing. It makes sense. We need
more of it.

As we help children get out into the world, to do
their learning there, we can get more of the world
into the schools. Apart from their parents, most
children never have any close contact with adults
except people whose sole business is children. No
wonder they have no idea what adult life or work is
like. We need to bring into the schools, and into contact with the children, a lot more people who are not
full-time teachers. I know of a school that has started to invite in artists and craftsmen in residence.
To a painter, or sculptor, or potter, or musician, or
whatever, they say, 'Come into our school for a few
weeks (or months). Use this as your workshop. Let
the kids watch you when you work, and if you feel like
it, answer some of their questions, if they feel like
asking any.' In New York City, under the Teachers
and Writers Collaborative, real writers, working
writers, novelists, poets, playwrights, come into the
schools, read their work, and talk to children - many
of them poor - about the problems of their craft. The
children eat it up. In another school I know of, every
month or so, a practising attorney, and a very successful one, from a nearby city comes in and talks to
several classes about the law. Not the law as it is
in books, but as he sees it and encounters it in his
cases, his problems, his work. And the children
love it. It is real, grown-up, true, not 'news'
prettied up for children, not 'My Weekly Reader',
not 'Social Studies', not lies and baloney.

Easier yet. Let children work together, help
each other, learn from each other and each other's
mistakes. We now know, from the experiences of
many schools, rich suburban and poor city, that children are often the best teachers of other children.
What is more important, we know that when a fifth
or sixth grader who has been having trouble with
reading starts helping a first grader, his own reading
sharply improves. A number of schools, some
rather tentatively and timidly, some more boldly,
are beginning to use what some call Paired Learning.
This means that you let children form partnerships
with other children, do their work, even including

their tests, together, and share whatever marks or results this work gets, just like the grown-ups in the real world. It seems to work. One teacher, teaching slow sections in which no students were very able, reported that when children were working in pairs the partnership did better work than either of the partners had done before. As we might expect. This could be a way of showing what is perhaps the hardest of all teacher's problems, getting children who have learned to protect their pride and self-esteem by the strategy of deliberate failure to give up that strategy and begin taking risks again.

Let the children learn to judge their own work. A child learning to talk does not learn by being corrected all the time; if corrected too much, he will stop talking. He compares, a thousand times a day, the difference between language as he uses it and as those around him use it. Bit by bit, he makes the necessary changes to make his language like other people's. In the same way, kids learning to do all the other things they learn without being taught - to walk, run, climb, whistle, ride a bike, skate, play games, jump rope - compare their own performances with what more skilled people do, and slowly make the needed changes. But in the school we never give a child a chance to detect his mistakes, let alone correct them. We do it all for him. We act as if we thought that he would never notice a mistake unless it was pointed out to him, or correct it unless he was made to. Soon he becomes dependent on the expert. Let him do it himself. Let him figure out, with the help of other children if he wants it, what this word says, what is the answer to that problem, whether this is a good way of saying or doing this or not. If right answers are involved, as in some math or science, give him the answer book. Let him correct his own papers. Why should we teachers waste time on such donkey work? Our job should be to help the kid when he tells us that he can't find the way to get the right answer. Let's get rid of all this nonsense of grades, exams, marks. We don't know how, and we never will know how to measure what another person knows or understands. We certainly can't find out by asking questions. All we find out is what he doesn't know - which is what our tests are for, anyway, traps designed to catch students. Throw it all out, and let the children learn what every educated person must some day learn, how to measure his own understanding, how to know what he knows or does not know.

Some harder reforms. Abolish the fixed, required curriculum. People remember only what is interesting and useful to them, what helps make sense of the world or helps them enjoy or get along in it. All else they quickly forget, if they ever learn it at all. The idea of the 'body of knowledge', to be picked up at school and used for the rest of one's life, is nonsense in a world as complicated and rapidly changing as ours. Anyway, the most important questions and problems of our time are not in the curriculum, not even in the hot-shot universities, let alone the schools. Check any university catalogue and see how many courses you can find on such questions as Peace, Poverty, Race, Environmental Pollution, and so on.

Children want, more than they want anything else, and even after many years of miseducation, to make sense of the world, themselves, and other human beings. Let them get at this job, with our help if they ask for it, in the way that makes most sense to them. Anxious parents and teachers say, 'But suppose they fail to learn something essential, something they will need to get on in the world?'

Don't worry; if it is essential in the world, they will find it and learn it out there. The adults say, 'Suppose they don't learn something they will need later?' The time to learn something is when you need it; no one can know what he will need to learn in the future; much of the knowledge we will need twenty years from now may not even exist today. The adults say, 'If you let children make choices they will make bad ones.' Of course, they will make some horrible ones. But how can a person learn to make good choices, except by making them, and living with them? What is more important, how can a person learn to recognize and change his bad choices, to correct mistakes, if he never has a chance to make any mistakes, or if all his mistakes are corrected for him? Most important of all, how is a child who is never given real choices to make going to think of himself as a person who is capable of making choices and decisions? If he thinks he cannot be trusted to manage his own life, to whom is he going to turn to manage it for him?

What this all boils down to is, are we trying to raise sheep - timid, docile, easily driven or led - or free men? If what we want is sheep, our schools are perfect as they are. If what we want is free men, we'd better start making some big changes.

9

JOHN HOLT

Reformulations: a letter written after two weeks in Cuernavaca

Source: Document of the Centro Intercultural de Documentacion, Cuernavaca, Mexico.

* *

John Holt, a leading school reformer in the USA, changes his mind. 'I have been saying that perhaps one way to bring about the repeal of compulsory school attendance laws was to so broaden the definition of school attendance that after a while it would be almost impossible to say who was "in school" and who was not...I now suspect that this is a mistaken way of looking at things...For the last year I have been completely convinced of the necessity for de-schooling society.'

* *

Dear Ivan, Everett, Dennis and all my friends and colleagues at CIDOC,

Once again I find myself back in Boston after two of the most pleasant, stimulating, and thought-stretching weeks of my life. I can't thank you enough for having helped make this stay in Cuernavaca what it was for me, and I want to share with you some of the thoughts that it has already generated in my mind on the way back to Boston.

One way of saying what has happened is that I have been helped to resolve, or at least reformulate, what had been for me a very difficult tension. For the last year I have been completely convinced of the necessity for deschooling society, for all the reasons that you very well know. On the other hand, I was very much involved in and committed to the whole notion of school reform, partly because this was something that I was very much interested in, partly because I had made a great many close friendships and connections with people who are working hard to reform the schools. My problem was how to resolve this apparent contradiction: how could reforming schools, making them more interesting, less punitive, less coercive, less inhuman, be reconciled with the larger problem of deschooling society? I attempted to find a solution to this through a metaphor, with which some of you are familiar - the idea that by pushing out or punching holes in the walls of the school, by letting the people in them out and more and more of the people outside them in, we might, so to speak, dissolve schools back into society. But my conversations with many of you have altogether convinced me that this is not a useful way of looking at the matter, for reasons, some of which, I may be able to make plainer with a specific example.

Thus, I have been saying that perhaps one way to bring about the repeal of compulsory school attendance laws was to so broaden the definition of school attendance that after a while it would be almost impossible to say who was 'in school' and who was not. I used the well known Parkway Project in Philadelphia, where hundreds of high school students use the entire city, its institutions, courts, businesses, libraries, laboratories, etc. as their learning resources. It seemed to me that if we could get enough schools to undertake similar projects, it would after a while no longer make any sense to speak of someone being 'in school', and we might get the attendance laws more easily done away with.

I now suspect that this is a mistaken way of looking at things, for at least a couple of reasons. One, as Dennis pointed out to me, is this - that we are in effect saying to the schools that they can take away from us a world which rightly belongs to us and then under some circumstances give it back. Why should we require the permission of schools to learn from agencies that we ought all to be learning from in any case. Now there is a very practical danger here and I'm sure that it exists at this minute. Thus we can imagine a group of students from the Parkway Project coming in, say, to a court in Philadelphia to see how it works. But suppose three or four other young people, hearing of this, but not in the Project, decided to do the same thing. I have no doubt at all that they would be asked for their credentials at the door, and if they could not show that they were part of the project, would be told that they could not stay, and might indeed get in trouble for not 'being in school'. In other words these learning resources, which ought to be open, would in fact be captured or preempted by certain prestige school projects. Indeed, as the popularity of the Parkway increases, I think that we will see more and more of the prestige schools starting such projects until we will soon be at a time when the 'good students' - the high-income students, will be treated to all such experi-

ences while the low-income kids will remain shut up in school rooms. In short, once the high prestige schools are convinced that learning out in the world is best for their students, they will gobble up most of the available resources. After all, who wouldn't rather have the son of a $50,000 a year suburban businessman working as an apprentice with him than some poor kid from the ghetto?

In other words, to put this a little differently, what now seems like a very great widening of the choices available to students could, in a very short time, become a new, high-priced, high-powered curriculum, available only to the most successful students. What's really important is that nobody ought to have to prove that he has a right to see how the institutions of his government, society and economy work.

My thinking has advanced in another direction. I have been ignorant about the history of schools. Being ignorant, I have assumed that, like our country in general they have fallen from some original state of grace, and that their current practices are in effect perversions of once noble and admirable ideals. I assumed that many people, indeed most people who push for universal and compulsory schooling, shared Jefferson's idea that through schooling a man might learn what he needed to know in order to understand the world about him, other men than himself, and what he must do to preserve his liberty and gain greater control of his own life in society. Or, to use Dennison's words, that the schools at least originally meant 'to empower people to think and do for themselves.' From what I have read of the recollections of Jordan Bishop and the book of Joel Spring, which I do recommend to all, I see that this was simply not true, and never even close to true. The people who forced universal and compulsory schooling on humanity had a clear enough idea, and one idea, but it was the very opposite of Jefferson's. They were all alike in seeing society as a machine - in this connection the writings of Lewis Mumford are most pertinent - a large, powerful, smoothly running machine, whose parts happen to be made of human beings, and they saw schools as the mechanism that would select and train and prepare people to be the part in which they could function most efficiently. There was never the slightest intention, even on the part of the progressives like Dewey, to make men capable of shaping their own society, or to give them the idea that they could or ought to. Indeed, it now seems to me clear that with respect to this question that there is absolutely no difference whatever between the thinking of John Dewey and Max Rafferty, or between the thinking of either or both of them and any educational or political leader you might find in any other country, however totalitarian. Indeed, if you read the early parts of Joel Spring's book, and look at some of the rhetoric of the people who were the founders of our immense school system, I think you will agree that you could not possibly distinguish it from the kinds of things that might be said on these issues in Hitler's Germany, or in Russia, or in whatever country you want to name. Man is for the state, and the function and business and duty of schools is to prepare him to fit into and serve the state as efficiently as his nature and talents will allow. And everything that was said in education about individual differences meant only that not all men would be the same parts, but that some would be gears, some nuts, some bolts, some bearings, some piston rods, some cotter pins etc.

I am a little rueful about having been so naïve about this. Our schools were never dedicated to the idea of human growth, or freedom or autonomy, or dignity, or self-actualization, or freedom, or whatever word or words you want to apply to these ideals. What I see more clearly than before is that they were designed to do what they are doing and it is really nonsense to think that they may be modified or altered or reformed or redesigned into doing the opposite. They are simply not suited to the task. Two foolish metaphors come into my mind. To talk about reforming the schools to make them places where human freedom and growth will be paramount is a little like talking about redesigning a camel to make it into an effective bird, or perhaps modifying a submarine to make an effective airplane. The job can't be done. The principles of construction are all wrong, so to speak. There really is no gradual process, adding a little here, taking a little away there, by which a submarine could be made to fly. We really have to start from somewhere else.

Oddly enough, this rather bleak way of looking at the matter makes it easier and not harder for me to relate to the many people who are now in schools and in varying degrees seem to look to me and people like me for different kinds of advice, guidance, hope or whatever. In this connection one of the most important documents that I saw at CIDOC is the small reprint on the very back of the pamphlet containing Ivan's address to that meeting of educational researchers - the one he talked about in his first CICLO. This particular statement is entitled or begins, LOOK OUT PRACTITIONERS - 'practitioners' being the paraphrase for what we would call teachers. You should really make a point of reading that back page. I am going to read considerable parts of it aloud to every group of teachers with whom I come in contact in the future. What it says to me is very plain. Just as I have said, to teachers or would-be teachers who are committed to ideals of human growth, development, freedom, choice, and self-control, that with the best will in the world they cannot make schools or schooling into institutions which will promote these ideas, so this document says to teachers who <u>are</u> committed to the traditional goals of schools, to the shaping and conditioning of people to function smoothly in a machined society that other people are going to take even this demeaning task away from them because they can do it so much better. In short, we really have excellent warrant for saying that schools, as educational institutions, are quite literally finished, to the extent that they are only programmers and conditioners, we can find vastly more effective ways of doing this kind of programming and conditioning. Our behaviourists have invented and will continue to invent very much better ways of controlling people's behaviour and softening and shaping human will, to the degree that the old-fashioned classroom teacher standing in front of a room with a textbook and assignment sheet is simply going to be obsolete, out of a job. I really am going to say most emphatically to teachers and school people who have seen themselves in this position, as 'getting children ready' for the real world of society that they're going to be technologically obsolete in a very short time.

The schools are out of business of true education because they never were in it and cannot be in it. They're out, or will be out soon, of the business of false education because other people and techniques can do it better. This is the message in a nutshell.

But what, then, of the many people, children and adults, who are in various ways and for various reasons enmeshed in the dying organism. The children are locked in there by law and custom and even more

imprisoned in their imaginations than anywhere else. Many adults are locked in simply because they need a job and this is the only kind of job they know how to do. Others have invested so much of their lives in education, or even in educational reform, in attempts to do their work in an intelligent and humane and life-enhancing way, that it is almost literally impossible for them to imagine turning around and starting somewhere else. If I can no longer speak to such people, as indeed I cannot, about reforming this organization, what can I say? Here again a metaphor seems to help me out. It is of a sinking ship, a kind of institutional Titanic. Maybe it was singing the song about the Titanic with Dennis and Jordan that put this in my mind. At any rate, I think we can see all these people, children, teachers, enlightened administrators, teachers of teachers, as trapped on a huge vessel which is sinking beneath them. Not so much because like the literal Titanic it struck an iceberg as because it was badly designed from the beginning and is simply falling apart under them. What can we do?

I think we have to keep the pump going as hard as we can, patch up a few of the leaks in the hull, or those we can reach, at least long enough until we can get the rescue vessels to the scene and get all the passengers of that sinking hulk - because they don't even have any life boats or life rafts. I think we can justify attempts to make existing schools less oppressive, and stupid and boring and inhuman, or attempts to create alternative schools, not as steps towards making the institutions we need, but simply as rescue operations while these new institutions are being built. What is important is that we not fool ourselves about what we are doing. We cannot convert that jerry-built and leaking hulk into a sea-worthy vessel. We can only help some of the people, who, as I say, are trapped in it, while we rush to make other alternatives. These reasons, or with this kind of thinking as a background, working as paid employees of presently existing school is preposterous. It is one thing, as I say, for people who are locked into this, or who have invested very large amounts of their life in it, but it seems to me an awfully foolish place to start off. Earlier in the letter I now see glaring inconsistencies in the position I tried to hold during most of this last year, and it may be that in the near future I will see, or some of you may point out glaring inconsistencies in the position I have just roughly outlined. But for the time being it gives me a feeling of having a place on which to stand and from which to work, and in the thought that this might be of interest to you I send it along. Once again, thanks so much for a most important two weeks. I would like to say to all of you what I said to a few, that I feel very much at home at CIDOC as at any place I know in the world, and I am grateful and happy for whatever has enabled me to be a part of this venture. Good luck and peace.

PS A final word about networks. I think some of us may already be getting hung up on this metaphor taking it too literally, which is always a danger with metaphors. Another way of looking at it is to say that the opposite of a network society is a monopolistic one, which is what we have. What happens now is that as fast as we can discover or become aware of some human need, some group of people rushes to 'package' it in such a way that they have a monopoly over the package and can thus profit from a situation in which there is not enough of whatever is needed to go around - whether in education, transportation, law, medicine or housing or whatever. What we want to do, again to use Dennison's phrase, is to 'empower people to think and do for themselves. To move as independently, directly freely and economically as possible to satisfy their needs as they perceive them, without having to go through the intermediary of various funnel-type institutions. Thus an educational TV programme is better than a school, because you don't have to get permission to watch it and nobody makes you watch it; but it would be still better to have the kinds of small local TV stations that Paul Goodman has talked about for years and that cable TV might make it much easier if we wanted to move in that direction; it would be better still to have the kind of genuinely free press, that is, free access to ways of printing and distributing printed matter, that would make it possible for every man to be his own publisher and editor. What is important in determining whether or not a human arrangement can be considered as a network is the matter of openness and accessibility. This does not mean that services must be provided free; indeed, I personally feel that it is of some importance that people using a service pay the cost of it. That is to say that the expensiveness of services shall not be inflated by those who are only seeking to make a profit out of it, but that on the contrary every effort would be made to meet human needs as cheaply and efficiently as possible.

10

MICHAEL HUBERMAN
Learning, democratizing and deschooling

Source: Specially commissioned for this volume.

* *

Michael Huberman, when an employee of UNESCO, produced a paper on Reflections on Democratization of Secondary and Higher Education which was published as part of the International Education Year 1970 and which, at that time, had 'Reproduction authorized' printed on it. The paper radically challenged a lot of orthodox thinking about the expansion of school systems, and a lot of UNESCO work up to that time. UNESCO refused us permission to reproduce that paper in this volume - a version of it is available in The Times Educational Supplement of 21 August, 1970 - so we commissioned this special contribution from Michael Huberman. While UNESCO accommodated some of Huberman's arguments in Learning to Be (UNESCO/Harrap, 1972) and published a tedious work called Present Problems in the Democratization of Secondary and Higher Education (UNESCO, 1973) which tamely concluded 'democratization still has to be achieved' it has continued to evade the central political question about democratisation: that is, that ruling groups do not move over just because someone points out that they are there, or because other people have collected more certificates. Educational systems may legitimise inequality but they alone cannot create the conditions for democratisation - indeed alone they serve as an alibi to divert attention away from questions of access to housing, jobs, transportation and health services. Huberman's contribution which we publish here is still radical about traditional systems but it is also critical of deschooling theory: it takes the argument on, and proposes a new approach to democratisation. The author is now Professor of Pedagogy at the University of Geneva. See also - Quotational Bibliography - HUBERMAN, Michael.

* *

Introduction

This paper deals with the concept of equal opportunity in education, relation to schools, to research on teaching and learning and to current proposals of deschooling. I should like to take up and elaborate on some of the points I made in an earlier paper on Democratization in Secondary and Higher Education, written early in 1970 at UNESCO. That paper has had a chequered career. Distributed in a number of countries in April, it was hurriedly taken out of circulation in May, and was subsequently shredded. The text was then censored and, some months later, a shorter, toothless version was released.

There were two sections in the paper which annoyed the Director-General of UNESCO. In one section, I criticised the indiscriminate transfer of educational policies from highly industrialised to Third World countries, in particular the policy of investing all available resources to attain full enrolment in primary education. My argument was that such a policy is based on a blind belief in the correlation between years of schooling and economic growth, that Third World countries were thereby using up all their resources in one sector at the expense of others (such as adult education and technical education) and, finally, that given the staggering drop-out rates in primary education throughout the Third World, this policy involved pumping more formal education into institutions with huge leaks. Having held and marketed that very policy for the past decade, UNESCO was not prepared at the time to have it criticised from within. However, anyone who has read Learning to Be (UNESCO, 1972) can observe that UNESCO is beginning to change its mind.

The first section, which I shall take up in more detail, put forth some of the tenets which were then coming to be known as 'deschooling'. My basic point was that education is simply a set of planned experiences which have been institutionalised in schools. We could surely imagine a number of alternative structures or arrangements which would attain the same objectives more effectively, all in reducing a number of fundamental injustices.

In the intervening years, I have spent a good deal of time trying to solve some of the problems raised in that initial paper. I think now - and will develop these thoughts in the following pages - that deschooling will not democratise education, although it can help to reconstitute the economic formula for costing in education and provide a model for school reform - a model which is already being acted on in several countries.

I   An analysis of the problem

1. EQUAL EDUCATIONAL OPPORTUNITY VS. DIFFERENTIATED OPPORTUNITY

When we refer to 'democratisation' in education, we are citing a political slogan, an educational policy found in most national statutes and, according to the UN Charter, a human right. The most common definition suggests simply the wider distribution of educational resources among the population at large - providing a higher proportion of each age group with schooling for more years. Democratisation also means equalising the real opportunity of all persons to gain access to education ('regardless of race, social and economic origin and sex') or, in more operational terms, attaining a distribution between social classes in schools which mirrors the distribution in society at large.

The UN Declaration of Human Rights is a good barometer of how far countries are prepared to go at present towards achieving that goal. Primary education is designed as a 'fundamental human right'. Secondary education should be 'available to all' and higher education should be 'accessible to all on the basis of merit'. (Merit is a deliberately ambiguous term and means what educational officials want it to mean. When backed against the wall, they tend to define merit as tested aptitude and, as we know, aptitude is what aptitude tests test...)

Here then we find the familiar educational pyramid, with limited access to higher education on the grounds that the supply of education should diminish as its level rises. A typical justification of that position reads: 'Some can learn more than others, and the higher skills need not be as plentiful as the lower. High-level people are needed but few have the potentials, so we concentrate resources on the talented.'[1] We shall sink our teeth into this quotation later on.

We can easily justify the counter-argument that a university should have no different criteria as to who is admitted than any other public service, such as a hospital, a railroad station or a canteen. Unfortunately, that argument is not yet compelling in even the most messianic socialist societies. Let us review briefly some of the reasons for this state of affairs.

The very notion of equal educational opportunity is a recent one. State-supported, compulsory (primary) schooling came into effect in Europe between 1830 and 1880, but it was only in the period 1930-45 that all school children followed the same stream in primary school. (The global primary school was instituted in the USA in 1890 and in the Soviet Union in 1923.) In the USA, secondary schooling was free by 1890, but only 7 per cent of the age group was enrolled. In France, on the other hand, the 'lycées' were still fee-paying institutions up to 1930. We can estimate roughly that the same proportion of the population is now enrolled in higher education as was enrolled in secondary education in 1900 and in primary education in 1850. Western European universities take in about 15-20% of the age group with a notorious disequilibrium between the various social classes.

In retrospect, it seems to have taken a long time

for state-supported education to come into effect. Aside from the traditional social resistances, it was probably hard to get used to the idea that one man's money be used to educate other men's children. With the industrial revolution, however, the training which a child received came to be of interest to all in the community, in particular to potential employers seeking apprentices who, as primary school graduates, could read instructions on machinery, make simple calculations, show disciplined work habits, respect private property, fear eternal damnation, do unpleasant tasks not of their own choosing and take orders from adults who were not part of the apprentices' immediate family.

Public education was also instituted for two further reasons: (1) in an effort to stop child labour in mines and factories; and (2) as Coleman points out because 'as men came to employ their own labour outside the family in the new factories, their families became less useful as economic training grounds for their children... Families needed a context within which their children could learn some general skills which would be useful for gaining work outside the family; and men of influence in the community began to be interested in the potential productivity of other men's children.'[2]

Coleman also shows that in England, by contrast with the USA, the idea of equality of educational opportunity was not even considered in the nineteenth century. The intention was to provide differentiated educational opportunity appropriate to one's station in life. In so doing, the community met its collective need for a trained labour force in one stream, while the middle class could use tuitions and, later, state grants to provide, in another stream, a better education for its children than was available in the family or with private tutors.

The differentiated system also served another need; that of maintaining the existing social order: 'a system of stratification that was a step removed from a feudal system of fixed estates, but designed to prevent a wholesale challenge by children of the working class to the positions held for children of the middle classes.'[3] The state schools thereby made legitimate and durable the separation of children along social class lines, while ensuring easier access to the better jobs for children of wealthier families.[4]

This distinction between equal and differentiated opportunity calls to mind Turner's discussion of 'contest mobility' and 'sponsored mobility'.[5] Contest mobility, as illustrated in the USA, resembles a sporting event, in which many compete for few prizes - those of high status and high paying professions. Elite status can be attained by competing in the schools, with each child presumably having an equal opportunity to succeed. In order to enhance everyone's chances, the educational system avoids early judgements or eliminations and tries not to give special advantage to those who are ahead in the race.

England is seen as an example of 'sponsored mobility'. Elite recruits are 'called' or chosen by established elites or their agents; that is, they are not weeded out after competition. The choice is made early in order to prepare the recruits for their induction into the recognised elite hierarchy. Their training is carried on in separate schools, which are inaccessible to anyone not having the proper credentials at the outset. At no point is there a contest for the better education or better jobs between children of different backgrounds.

Turner also deals with the problem of how a given society ensures loyalty towards the educational system on the part of the disadvantaged who systematically receive less than their share of society's goods. Under 'contest mobility', the pupil is encouraged to see himself as competing for an elite position, so that he becomes too committed to the system to change radically when he is obliged to drop out. Thus, there is never a collective threat to the school system. This is the process known as 'cooling' out. If schools failed outright large numbers of children, the rejects would feel that their ambitions had been blocked by a particular, identifiable group, and their parents might mobilise politically to alter the system. To avoid this, selection must be carried out in a low key, giving the child the impression of having made his own choices. When he is eliminated, he gets the impression that he has left the school system voluntarily, or, rather, that his elimination is due to his own inadequacy and not to any unfairness in the schools.

Under 'sponsored mobility', lower-class children are trained very early to see themselves as incompetent to manage a society from a position of public authority or expertise. Rather, they are taught to be 'realistic' in the light of their background and/or test results and to accept a more humble status. The notion here, implicit in the quotation from Anderson cited earlier, is that it is a better policy to discourage some children early from university preparatory streams so that we can give more public resources to 'those who can benefit most from them'.

So much is certain: public resources for education do tend to be used up disproportionately by the children of already wealthy and well-educated parents. UNESCO and OECD statistics for Western Europe show students from working-class families making up about 15 per cent of the upper secondary school enrolment and 10 per cent of the university enrolment, while their parents account for 40 per cent of the active population. Professional families, comprising 5-7 per cent of the population, make up some 30-40 per cent of the university population. Universities, of course, cost far more per student than do primary schools. Mishan[6] estimates that in order for the marginal tax per family paid for a given British pound's worth of higher education to be proportional to gross earnings, middle-class families should be paying about nine times the increment of tax paid by the average working-class family. It would be a safe estimate that in the majority of countries in the world, the wealthiest 10 per cent of the population receives ten times as much public funding for education, per capita, as the poorest 10 per cent. Under the present system, the poor man appears to be subsidising the higher education of the children of the affluent.

In Europe, we have moved progressively from sponsored mobility to contest mobility, (a) as the European economy was able to keep a greater proportion of children and youth out of the labour market, (b) as higher levels of training in various forms of reading, writing or calculating have been required and (c) as more middle-level and higher-level jobs have been created by changes in work requirements or by the creation of new kinds of work. When upper- or middle-class parents did not have enough children to fill all the middle and higher status positions, there was easier access from below. Gradually, there has been more open competition for places in schools leading to the best paying and most prestigious jobs, and we come to speak of a 'meritocracy', i. e. an elite of talent rather than of birth. Also the children of poor or ill-educated parents, profiting from a higher standard of living and internalising the values of the middle classes, got better at competing.

This 'open competition', however, is still more apparent than real. In industrial democracies there is enough fluidity to allow some able and industrious children to move to a higher level of schooling than their parents, but there is also enough stability to ensure that higher status parents can pass their advantages on to their children. This may seem surprising in the face of statistics showing a massive absolute growth in secondary school enrolments since World War II and giving the impression of greater participation in secondary and higher education among children whose parents had not finished primary school. But an analysis of these statistics shows that, despite quantitative increases, the proportion of lower-class children enrolled has remained practically stable. It is the middle class in particular - children of senior clerks and shop-owners - which accounts for the bulk of the increased participation. There is a tendency for limited participation among lower class families to continue until the other social classes have reached saturation, that is, something approaching 100 per cent in their participation.

2. THE INEQUALITY OF EQUAL OPPORTUNITY

The basic premise of the educational pyramid is that there is not enough schooling to go around, so what there is must be distributed unevenly among all the contestants. The argument goes as follows: For the general social good we need a balanced supply of people with different skills and aptitudes, and we must be careful to train people for these jobs at the least waste of public money and effort. Those who justify the greatest expenditures are the scientists and doctors, senior technicians and administrative cadres, since their jobs are more complex and their mistakes are more costly than those of foremen and clerks. Therefore, we must find the most talented people as early as possible and concentrate our resources on them, at the same time as meeting our basic obligations at the elementary level for the mass of children.

Since this 'scarcity model' postulates that one cannot give an equal amount of education to everyone, priority should go to those who will profit most from the training and thereby justify the cost incurred for their schooling. These children can best be identified by comparative testing in a group of their peers.

The key point here is that schools do not undertake to equalise the chances of success of children from different backgrounds. Rather, their functioning allows the initial advantage of children from well-educated families to be maintained, even increased, while the competition for places in secondary and higher education is going on. When children are tested at their entry into primary school, we already find significant differences between them on the same kind of measures used to stream them a few years later. In short, schools treat unequal children as if they were equal. Some of these children have had a particular physical and social environment - a special kind of extra-scholastic education -

in the years preceding their entrance in primary school, and that very environment will become the basis of the scholastic education given to all children. Less favoured children thus begin school with a major handicap and, moreover, must begin to learn virtually an entirely new culture. Clearly, a school system tied to the prevalent cultural and social values of one part of the population and excluding other criteria of quality is not likely to help young people from other backgrounds toward scholastic success. The situation calls for compensatory opportunities, that is, helping the needier rather than treating both alike.

It is important to emphasise here that the role of the school system has been consistently passive. It was assumed that once primary education was free of cost and all children went through the same curriculum, one could no longer speak of inequality of opportunity. To be sure, richer or brighter children were being given no advantages in terms of materials, teaching personnel or hours of instruction.

The insinuation, then, was that the pupils differed in the use they made of the opportunities provided for all. The sleight of hand here is that if the child failed, the school was not to be held responsible. And, of course, generation after generation the children from certain cultural backgrounds came out on the lower end of the normal curve.

3. THE NATURE AND CONSEQUENCES OF TESTING

We shall be looking more closely into the nature of the handicap from which lower-class children suffer upon entry to school, and into what is being done to 'compensate' for these handicaps. First, however, the part of evaluation must be added to the mosaic of educational opportunity. Children are selected and sorted out with respect to tested ability or aptitude; those with higher scores are kept in school for a longer period. There are four dimensions of the testing process which affect equal opportunity.

3.1 Construction and scoring of tests. Achievements and aptitude tests, which form the basic repertoire of school-level evaluation, are constructed so as to ensure that test items yield a good discrimination on each item, i.e. some 25 per cent will perform particularly well, 50 per cent average and 25 per cent poorly. The usual procedure in determining who succeeds and fails is to establish a cut-off point at some percentile rank for an average score on all items.

This kind of comparative testing means that there are no absolute performances but only scores relative to the performances of others taking the test. Theoretically, everyone could do very well on the test, but the lower 10 per cent or so would still be failed (unless national norms are available). Also, a child who makes considerable progress from one test session to another but still falls below the cut-off point could be failed or eliminated, although his own performance had improved steadily.

Note that there is no compelling reason to fail a fixed percentage on any test, unless the test has the specific function of selecting a given proportion of pupils from the whole group. One could easily establish a level of performance judged to be sufficient to pass and then let pupils take the time necessary to arrive at that level.

The point is that these tests have been based on the premise of fixed or inherited intelligence. Since a given percentage of children are supposed to be innately inferior and others superior, only a small percentage could learn effectively what the schools have to teach. The tests, constructed on that theory, consistently have supported it by yielding results on a normal curve which is meant to show that intelligence is distributed unevenly among the population in the same way as height and weight.

There is now evidence to show that this premise is false, and that test construction itself has made for a self-fulfilling prophecy. We also know that 90 per cent of school-age pupils can master all the elements of a primary and secondary curriculum, provided they are given the time. That is to say, pupils differ in the rate at which they learn, not in their basic capacity to learn.[7] Children from culturally deprived homes could probably match the results of middle-class children if given the necessary time and learning conditions to make up for their initial handicaps. As most tests are age-grouped, this means basically that those who are 'ahead' at the time of the evaluation are judged more able and apt.

3.2 The nature of school tests. There are two dimensions to this problem. First, school tests supposedly are given to predict children's aptitude to do non-school tasks. We test children's reasoning ability and calculation skills on the premise that the results will tell us whether or not they will reason and calculate well at work and at home when they take on adult responsibilities. In fact, we tend often to forget that the objective of schools should be to enable its graduates to succeed in their endeavours once out of school, not simply to produce good students per se. And there is evidence to show that years of schooling or school grades do not predict proven talent as a scientist, administrator or entrepreneur. Superior achievement as an adult is not related directly to academic aptitude or scholastic achievement, but rather to such non-cognitive traits as perseverance, concentration, willingness to take moderate risks and need for personal achievement.[8] We suggest here that there may then be other ways of seeking and identifying talent than via the criteria and testing procedures presently used in the school system. This in turn would mean that we could justify using other ways of distributing our educational resources among the young that in function of their performance on comparative tests.

Next, the tests themselves can be called into question. Aptitude and achievement tests are usually in written form, thereby giving advantage to children who can read instructions and questions rapidly and can verbalise well. As we shall see, lower-class homes are not good models of the kind of language usage tested in schools. Moreover, poor language development tends to retard or block the development of general intelligence as tested by the type of IQ tests given in school and influential in procedures of selection and streaming. Significantly, children from poorly-educated families do better on the non-verbal or mathematical parts of tests than on the parts requiring more reading and writing.

Another element in these tests which favours children from wealthier and better-educated families is the great number of questions meant to reveal the child's general knowledge about the world (making distinctions and comparing objects and ideas). The presence of books, pictures, informative conversation and travel in some homes represents a hidden curriculum which supplements the material given and tested at school.

These tests also stress logical reasoning and problem-solving. Here, many of the items are non-verbal, but they cannot be said to be culture-free. The ability to solve theoretical problems, think clearly about a variety of issues and to deal with abstractions is taught to all children in school, but it is also developed out of school in the very fabric of day-to-day life in well-educated families. There, children are encouraged to think clearly and logically, are reasoned with in cases of disagreement with their parents and are included in conversations with adults about them.

Logical reasoning and problem-solving are critical skills. They form the crux of professional, technical and administrative work in advanced industrial societies, where calculations, decisions and operations have to be made rapidly on the basis of insufficient or complex evidence. Naturally, professional families encourage the development of these skills in their children and exercise them as often at home as at work. Factory workers or filing clerks do not get to exercise these skills very often at work - in fact, they are not encouraged to think independently, but rather to follow instructions and repeat accurately a number of uniform operations. At home, they look understandably for quiet and escape, and can be impatient with the intellectual games their children bring home from the classroom. And they are statistically very realistic in assuming that their children will not get much benefit from exercising the type of conceptual skills needed for success in higher education and in professional work since they will probably be manipulating things rather than ideas.

To resume these arguments, the point is not that aptitude or achievement tests in school are irrelevant, but rather that they further accentuate cultural differences between social classes all in claiming to be objective instruments of judgement between children. We know that human beings can learn their culture only from other human beings who already know and exhibit that culture. School experience and school tests are founded on a particular culture, on one kind of learning environment, a unique system of communication and certain rules of behaviour which are natural to some people in society and foreign to others. The tests determining which children will receive more education and eventually better jobs and higher salaries are designed to measure the ease and understanding of children in that particular learning environment. This gives an overwhelming advantage to some children at the expense of others.

Moreover, test items either do not measure the kinds of things which children from poor homes can do well, or else these skills are measured in such a way that these children cannot display their abilities on them. For example, children from poor families tend often to be independent, resourceful and to have a great amount of factual knowledge built around neighbourhood life. These attributes, however, do not show up on aptitude tests, where other types of resourcefulness and factual knowledge are solicited and which are foreign - or simply irrelevant - to their experience. Even mechanical aptitude tests do a disservice to the special skills of poor children. Other qualities such as physical dexterity, loyalty, emotional openness or facility in group work - which are more prominent in many children from poor backgrounds than in middle-class children - are not included in test batteries, although they are as important for adult success as some of the other items and

more important than some of the other criteria of selection, for example, handwriting or size of vocabulary.

3.3 <u>Non-academic evaluations</u>. Schools also exist to 'build character', to make certain that by the end of compulsory schooling, children will have learned to be punctual, clean, obedient to adults, sexually modest, decorous, respectful of private and public property and willing to work for long-term aims. If we study the events of the school day, in fact, we could conclude that the primary role of schools is to socialise children, with instruction in reading, writing and calculating as a secondary goal. Here again, we are talking of behaviours taught early in middle-class homes, with the result that most of the transgressions come from children from poorer families.

There are several consequences. First, grades for good conduct and good citizenship, for character, self-discipline and 'cooperation', count towards promotion and selection. Secondly, children from lower-class families may be disruptive because they do not understand the language of the teacher, nor the sense of sitting still for hours, working separately even though another child is doing the same task in the next seat, or waiting for long periods of time to be noticed. Alternatively, they may not place great value on school experience, nor share the cultural values of the middle class towards intellectual achievement. [9]

Finally, teachers themselves are more impatient with violations of school rules or codes than with intellectual deficiencies, and they are ready to punish any child who threatens to upset the teacher's precarious control over other children in a classroom. Those children most frequently punished tend not to advance very far in schools, irrespective of their intelligence or aptitude scores. The system of informal sanctions and formal evaluations of 'character' is often the vehicle used by the school system to scapegoat those with whom it is having the greatest difficulty.

3.4 <u>The consequences of testing</u>. Here we focus less on those who are chosen than on those who are eliminated. Studies of drop-outs from school often show them to feel alienated from most social institutions and to feel themselves to be inadequate, worthless, frustrated or incapable of being successful in any endeavour they make. Spend a week in school and you will see the same children reminded day after day that they are not much good. Testing is one of the most frequent activities at school and, after a number of unsuccessful experiences in class, children come naturally to see themselves as inadequate persons if their behaviour is consistently judged inadequate.

Given the collective nature of the classroom, these reminders of inadequacy are carried out in public. Everyone watches everyone else being tested by the teacher. Moreover, other children are often invited to evaluate their peers. Adults would never allow themselves to be put in this kind of situation if they could avoid it, but children cannot, inasmuch as there is no privacy in schools, nor, of course, the option to stay away. Thus the child is bombarded with messages telling him how well he has done by comparison with other children of the same age and the same general circumstances. [10] These comparisons can be very damaging to the child's image of himself.

The duration and intensity of this kind of evaluation goes beyond any other institutional initiation rite to which most children or youth will be subjected. We are not surprised to find evidence that failure at school can carry over to adult performance, by making the individual feel that he cannot deal effectively with his environment. School failures, having a view of themselves which is negative or at least defensive, tend to spend more time indulging in compensating fantasies or in passive entertainment (television, music, cinema) than do successful pupils. More seriously, they are far less likely to expose themselves to further education of any kind.

In this way schools render a lasting disservice to those who do not prosper in its special culture, most of whom come from poor and ill-educated families. Without school certificates, they are unable to get meaningful work. Having been judged inadequate at school, they judge themselves inadequate to succeed by another path. Placed in jobs menaced by automation or conversion, they are loath to enrol in retraining programmes for fear of further humiliation in a classroom and testing situation.

4. THE ORIGINS OF INEQUALITY

Anthropologists have studied closely the attempts of immigrants to establish themselves and prosper in an alien culture. They are most successful when the culture has values which are relevant to their own and, more specifically, when there are many of the same codes of communication and rules of conduct. Any given society is a complex constellation of shared beliefs and rituals; that is to say, it is a figment of the imagination for the member of another society or for an observer from another planet. One of the principal roles of the school is to operate on and reinforce those beliefs and rituals which are dominant in a given society.

This point helps us to appreciate that when children from one social class succeed disproportionately well at school by comparison with other children, it is not an intentional policy on the part of most school systems, but results primarily from the cultural differences between social classes. By 'social class' we generally mean a given stratum in accordance with one's income, occupation, type of dwelling and area of residence. But there is also a more qualitative dimension of belonging to something larger than oneself: of coming principally into contact with certain types of people, of identifying one's own status in relation to others, of considering certain values and behaviours to be important or right. These conditions in turn serve to define and systematise different learning environments for children of different families and neighbourhoods. Here a child learns ways of acting and definitions of action, and these account for much of his personality.

In a modern industrial and urban society, some of these values and behaviours are more important than others. In particular, work requiring higher levels of education calls for special attributes: manipulating language and other symbols, solving problems by means of abstract reasoning, working for long-term rewards, relating smoothly to strangers, putting up with uncertainties, having the desire to achieve, master and persevere, etc. Schools require these capacities when making selections for access to education beyond obligatory schooling. Some home environments are a natural training ground for these attributes before and during schooling: the parents have these attributes themselves; they exercise them and try to develop them in children as soon

as possible. They are also aware of the nature of the school's demands on their children. Other parents are less successful models in this respect, and are less ambitious (or more realistic) for their children. They are also less school-wise.

Put bluntly, when the patterns at home are not the same as those leading to success at school, we tend to look at children from these families as 'handicapped', 'disadvantaged' or 'culturally deprived'. The implication is that any cultural behaviours deviating from the norms behind school achievement are deficits.

Here is a brief catalogue of these 'deficits', with a mention of some attendant causes:

4.1 <u>Perception and cognition.</u> Compared with middle-class children, those from poor and ill-educated families do not discriminate well between different sounds or objects. This is not due to physical defects, but to less well-trained or different habits of hearing, seeing and thinking. It has obvious consequences for social learning based on decoding the teacher's instructions, reading aloud and identifying similarities and differences between objects and shapes. These children depend less on verbal and written language for cues and concentrate and persist less on tasks of perception and cognition than do middle-class children. They tend to work and think more slowly on tasks having to do with symbols (words, numbers, designs) which represent objects not directly in front of them. Their scores of IQ and academic aptitude tests are often below national norms.

Numerous explanations have been forthcoming. Lower-class families are said to lack books and other self-instructional devices, to have insufficient communication between children and adults, to be less ideational then middle-class families, to punish by rule rather than by reasoning, to make less use of conventional verbal symbols in order to represent and interpret feelings and objects around them. There is presumably less constructive stimulation in the early years; the child encounters fewer objects, cannot use furnishings as toys, has less space to move about without getting in the way of adults. Good behaviour in these families can often mean doing nothing and saying little.

4.2 <u>Language and reading skills.</u> Language and words make up a system of symbols which increase the efficiency of abstract thought - dealing with objects or situations which are not immediately present - in such a way that the ability to manipulate verbal symbols seems to play an important part in the process of thinking and problem-solving. The more language skills available to children at an early age, the more rapid their ability to perform mental operations requiring the use of symbols. Children with speech disturbances, for example, are often retarded in this respect. Even their scores on non-verbal tests of intelligence are depressed. Language allows the child to categorise and integrate his experience, and to differentiate himself from others.

Children from poor families tend to depend more on concrete than on symbolic experiences. They have trouble being deductive, making accurate generalisations and using concepts stored in their heads in new situations. They use language to meet their material needs, but less so to obtain or transmit information or to monitor their own behaviour. Their vocabulary is limited - approximately one-third that of the vocabulary of middle-class children at age 9 - with few mature sentence types or complex sentence constructions. As Bernstein has shown in his research, working-class children use short, simple and concretely descriptive sentences. They use few adjectives and adverbs or impersonal pronouns. They have a very reduced symbolic vocabulary to express the complex connections between persons, objects, time and situations.

A highly technical society depends on the symbolic mode of conceptualisation used by middle-class mothers with their children and by teachers with their pupils. One of the most important features of the school is that it is abstract and cut off from the places or experiences treated in classrooms. With all its limitations, this system does allow children to symbolise reality. The language used in lower-class homes - and, incidentally, in rural families as well - is apparently more concrete and primitive, and there is evidence to suggest that exercising more complex syntax and richer lexical options has an accelerating effect on the ability to deal with complex problems.

But there is also some evidence that many lower-class families have a powerful capacity for solving their kinds of problems and a very sophisticated dialect for self-expression, and these qualities will appear when tested on terms other than by reference to middle-class cultural norms. There may well be other rather than fewer cognitive abilities at work here. [11]

4.3 Norms and attitudes, including attitudes towards education. Consistent with their own professional success and with their concern for turning out equally successful children, well-educated families have higher expectations and make more demands on their children's performance at school. They take a great interest in that performance and are, of course, well equipped to help out. They also enforce the norms which characterise 'middle-class' society and lead to success in the performances required at school: ambition, self-improvement through work, individual responsibility, the desire to attain excellence in everything one undertakes, postponement of immediate satisfactions, control of aggression, constructive use of leisure time, respect for authority, cultivation of courtesy and respect for property.

We note here three cultural overtones: activism (the belief that one can manipulate the physical and social environment to one's own advantage), individualism (the belief that an individual need not subordinate his needs to the family or group) and an orientation toward the future (to forego short-term rewards in the interest of long-term gains). To be sure, these attitudes make for success at school and afterward. But they are also luxuries which parents and children from poorer families cannot usually afford or may never have known. If the aspirations of these families towards school and success in professional life are lower than in wealthier homes, they may well be an accurate perception of the opportunities and rewards available to them. [12]

II Some solutions to the problem

5. THE NOTION OF COMPENSATORY EDUCATION

As we saw earlier, a child is 'culturally deprived' when his own culture deprives him of the pre-school experiences contingent on success at school. That culture, incidentally, is almost always described in negative terms because it provides experiences which are inappropriate to school and professional achievement. The objective of compensatory education is to compensate for those deficits by providing more of the learning experiences and advantages from which middle-class children already benefit.

The idea is open to criticism, but it does go far beyond the delusion that providing equal treatment to all children will equalise their opportunities to succeed at school. We have now the first indications that (a) proportionately more resources are being given to those starting school with an initial disadvantage, (b) the school system is beginning to take some responsibility for academic failure on the part of children, and (c) the new objective may become equality of educational achievement for all, rather than equality of educational opportunity.

There is another important premise: that intelligence is not fixed but can be modified by changing the environment of a child or his parents. There is convincing evidence of this fact from studies of migration, acculturation and adoption from orphanages, where children's scores on intelligence and aptitude have increased markedly as their environments were enriched. But more orthodox geneticists have resisted, and are still resisting as to the degree of improvement which is possible.

For some time schools have been providing limited remedial services for children with learning handicaps, but with little success. The problem has been both that the services have been insufficient and that they have come too late to make up the cumulative deficit. 'Too late' may well mean the age of 6 or 7. Comparing the results of the longitudinal studies on children carried out in England, Germany and Sweden, in particular the data on general achievement, reading comprehension and vocabulary development, we can concur in general with Bloom's commentary on the American data: by age 9 (grade 4), at least 50 per cent of the general achievement pattern at age 18 (grade 12) has been developed. About one-third has been developed by the time the child enters school, and about 17 per cent between ages 4 and 6. [13]

The implication is that the pre-school and early primary school years are crucial periods for the development of the language, reading and reasoning skills used at school. There is also evidence to show that the early years are the most critical period in the development of all cognitive and affective characteristics, school-related or not. This is true for a number of reasons. The early years constitute the phase of most rapid growth of many mental and emotional characteristics. The sequential nature of much of human development means that growth occurs in stages or layers; developments at a later period are in part determined by earlier developments, on which they are built. The learning which takes place before the development of a language capacity may be more decisive than that in later stages because it is inaccessible to conscious memory. Finally, there are indications that certain abilities are never or poorly acquired if they are not learned by a certain age or during a particularly critical period. [14]

If it is crucial to intervene early in the child's life, it is also more efficient, if we agree with Bloom and a number of learning theorists that it is easier to learn something new than to eliminate a number of learned behaviours and replace them by a new set. It is, however, harder to gain access to a child before

52

his entry into school, and very difficult to find the right combination of social welfare services willing and able to intervene together. Parents have exclusive rights over their children up to the age of compulsory schooling, and they are hesitant to believe that their parenthood is in any way insufficient. They suspect, with some justification, that their children are only handicapped in terms of an arbitrary scale of sufficiency of which they are the victims. Finally, they fear that as a result of pre-school enrichment programmes, their relationship with their children will be modified.

This fear is often countered by associating parents at the outset with the compensatory education programmes and even, in a few American communities, by giving the funds directly to the parents so that they can hire their own experts. Unless parents are brought in, there tends to be resistance to these projects as well as inferior results, since the child still spends most of his time at home.

The basis of these programmes is to allow the very young child to encounter different kinds of situations and to manipulate objects of different sizes and shapes in order to develop his capacity to understand and organise his physical world. A shild's notions of space, time, matter and causality come through the transactions he makes with his environment. Put very simply, he experiments as he plays. Balancing a see-saw, building a block tower, floating play toys, putting away play toys by categories (large and small, round and square), and pouring juice into containers of different sizes are examples of play activities which allow the child to build on the previous transactions he has made and at the same time adapt himself to a more complex idea of how the world is organised. [15]

Later, the accent is put on language development. Language skills are to be built up from the images which the child has retained from his encounters with these objects and events. These images become the referents for the spoken symbols required in the phonemic combinations of spoken or written language. In its simplest form, the process involves having the child do something or see something and helping him abstract these operations into language.

The principal problem is to individualise the interactions with various children who have different kinds of handicaps - to diagnose correctly the nature of the learning deficit in order to prescribe materials and models which match up with what the child already has in his storage. Otherwise, the enriched stimulation he gets in these compensatory programmes will not be integrated into his behaviour.

Some pre-school and primary-level projects go beyond the exercise of purely cognitive skills. There is often an attempt to develop in children and their parents positive attitudes towards achievement in school-type activities, and an effort to bolster the child's image of himself in the school setting. Work habits (concentration, persistence, initiative) are improved through positive reinforcement (rewarding the child when he shows these behaviours and ignoring dysfunctional behaviours) and modelling (showing films of other children concentrating, persisting and initiating with great pleasure). We should also mention a number of structural changes in the schools: introducing a more individualised or programmed curriculum, training teachers for work with disadvantaged learners, team-teaching, using the school after hours for additional work with children or in-struction to parents, hiring parents or other teacher aides to help in classroom activities and the like.

These programmes have been criticised on several levels. For our purposes, there are two comments to make. First, compensatory education has not been effective without continual help throughout the primary school years. When remedial work is discontinued earlier, initial gains in IQ and achievement scores are lost quickly. As work is on an individual basis, the operation becomes prohibitively expensive for large numbers of children - on the order of 1200 US dollars per child per year from ages 3 to 6.

Secondly, this help has come almost entirely after school hours. That is, classrooms have not been modified by any of the problems raised or lessons learned by compensatory education. These pre-school or remedial projects, in turn, make no effort to change the school programme as their proper setting. The idea is simply to ready the disadvantaged child to cope with traditional school requirements - to extend formal schooling down into the pre-school years. The money and energy which could be used to restructure the school system or create viable alternatives is being used to reduce the deviant or dysfunctional elements in the traditional classroom. Here again, the hidden premise is that there is something inherently wrong with the people who do not succeed in the system rather than with the institutions which are unable to avoid creating a great number of failures.

6. SOME ALTERNATIVES FOR EQUALISING OPPORTUNITIES

There is as yet no evidence and little likelihood that compensatory education will change the statistics on equal opportunity at the upper secondary and higher educational levels. A small number of children who might otherwise have dropped out earlier will stay in longer and compete better for selective entry to university. But the overall proportions of children in school beyond the age of compulsory education from different social classes will probably stay the same.

This brings us to some brutal conclusions. First, the school itself in its present mode of functioning does not seem able or willing to eliminate the inequalities between children which exist before entry to school. Schools seem to be part of the problem, not part of the solution. Or, as Pestalozzi wrote long ago, education is the staircase in the house of injustice. This suggests the obvious: that the school is essentially a social microcosm which will reproduce the qualities and inequalities of the surrounding social environment. Schools tend to bring little influence to bear on a child's achievement that is independent of his social background. Or, put differently, we should not expect the schools to carry the burden of redressing inequalities which result from unemployment, malnutrition, poor housing conditions and an unequal distribution of income among different social groups.

If our objective is to democratise - in the sense of equalising the proposition of participation in all levels of education in accordance with that proportion in society at large - we have two options. If we choose to stay with the current organisation of schooling, we can simply discriminate in reverse, so that the number of upper secondary and university places corresponds to the social class distribution in the country. Rather than lavish resources on the already privileged, we lavish them on those who have had the fewest, until a more equitable distribution is attained. Assuming that intelligence or ability is not genetically fixed but that stimulating environments can uncover and create talent, there is every reason to believe that a university population of 40 per cent working-class youth will be as talented as was the preceding cohort under the system of traditional selection. We may, in fact, be able thereby to make changes in content and examinations which would reveal and validate new abilities.

This is the solution adopted in many socialist countries in Eastern Europe and it has, on the whole, met its objectives.[16] It is unlikely, however, that free enterprise countries would set voluntarily such Draconian social controls on themselves, if only because the children of those planning and executing those controls would be among the first victims. What, then, are the alternatives?

6.1 Change the mode of functioning in primary and secondary schools. The basic idea would be that all children succeed in finishing compulsory schooling and, eventually, in gaining access to higher education. This is far less utopian than it appears, and has already been fairly well researched. To recall the thesis that aptitude is a function of rate of learning rather than quality of learning, it follows that all children, given the time and proper conditions, could master the primary and secondary school curriculum. This is impossible at present because of the industrial model of school organisation the school functions in standardised instructional periods for whole groups of children using uniform materials and methods. This structure, plus the small number of adults per group, makes it impossible to work individually and remedially with children in the same way as is done in the pre-school projects, and explains in part why initial gains in IQ and achievement scores have been lost in the course of primary school. This model is serviced further by the testing procedures, i.e., measuring children by reference to class norms and eliminating a fixed percentage irrespective of the fluctuations in their absolute performances. The tests favour the fastest workers in the group - those who 'produce' the most in the shortest space of time - who are rewarded more often and promoted to the fewer available posts in upper secondary and higher education. And the fastest workers, in turn, are the children whose non-school environment trains best for performance in the school environment.

The alternative, then, consists in specifying the criteria of success at various scholastic levels and aiding each child to attain those criteria at his own pace. In principle, fewer staff would be required for the faster children and more teachers would be available for the slower learners. Teacher aides could be used to improve the adult-child ratio. In a primitive form, current experiments with ability grouping, team teaching, teacher aides and use of programmed instruction for remedial work all tend in this direction. Testing devices would be criterion-referenced rather than norm-referenced, i.e., the curve of progression for each child towards the criteria of success or graduation would be used to determine the type of test needed, rather than testing and monitoring his performance relative to the other children in the group.

Assuming that the economy of a given country cannot enrol the active school-age population at the same time in upper-secondary school and in univer-

sities, there may well be a waiting list or, more practically, the possibility of using that time and those educational resources later in one's life. There are a number of additional problems having to do with extreme age mixtures and the nature of learning activities for faster learners. For at first sight the implication seems to be that, although instructional time periods are no longer fixed, every child is still going through the same programme, but some are doing it faster than others. That is, there is equal achievement but there is also uniform achievement. Here again, the problem is soluble if certifying agencies would accept that children and youth be able to use different ways of attaining the criteria of graduation or final certification.

6.2 Equalise the resources available to those who drop out as well as to those who continue on to higher education. We saw that upper secondary and higher education are far more expensive than primary education and that middle-class children occupy a disproportionate number of the available places. What is more, those who leave school or are eliminated in selective tests get no further resources. In fact, very soon they and their parents are paying taxes to help support other young people staying on at school. Those who do not attend upper secondary school or university could justifiably lay claim to an amount of national subsidy equal to the public cost, for example, of each university student.

This subsidy could be used as a direct grant to be spent as one pleases, but preferably to buy materials for apprenticeships or even to buy into small businesses. The allotment could also be used as an educational grant, to be spent on continuing education in any form available: private commercial or trade schools, travel to visit other shops or factories, self-instructional courses, time hired for tutoring by an expert, and the like. The young school leaver or graduate is then buying his education in the market-place as he would buy any service. Note, however, that the school system is left untouched and that the better jobs still go to those who continue in formal education beyond the minimal school-leaving age. What has changed is basically that the public school system is no longer using up all the funds for educational services in a given country.

6.3 Deschool society. Illich's point is well taken that to equate equal educational opportunity with obligatory schooling is to confuse salvation with the Church. With this third alternative, compulsory public schooling would be abolished. All the funds earmarked for formal education would be channelled directly to parents by means of an educational account until the children were able to choose wisely for themselves among the various facilities for learning which would spring up. Presumably, each child would receive the same amount. He would use up his credits or vouchers in accredited institutions or with certified tutors. Schools as we know them would disappear into a host of private institutions competing for the vouchers by offering more specialised services. 'Schools would stand, adjust or fail according to the satisfaction they gave their clients. Other educational institutions would develop in accordance with their ability to satisfy client needs. Learners would choose between learning on the job and full-time learning, among the skills they wanted to learn, at what age they wanted to use their educational resources, and how.'[17] As Illich has suggested, a central computerised reference service could match those seeking skills or services with those offering them.

This would send teachers, along with other certified specialists or professionals, into the educational marketplace. Theoretically, teachers could advertise their special training and skill at adapting learning tasks to different ages and abilities - a specific training to teach which neither a foreman nor an interpreter, for example, has - although some research suggests that untrained housewives can teach many school-related tasks as well as trained teachers.

7. SOME PROBLEMS TO BE SOLVED

In the case of the first alternative, there are a few examples of institutional reform to indicate that schools are becoming more accountable for the success and failure of their pupils. More particularly, school officials are ready - but certainly not impatient - to try out more flexible ways of organising instructional time, space and groupings of pupils. The second alternative is frequently discussed by apprentices and their unions or at university seminars, but has produced little social legislation. The notion of paid educational leaves of absence has been implemented in several countries, but principally for adults having already worked a number of years.

The third alternative is generating a good deal of heat. It puts forward the thesis that if our objectives are more efficient learning and more self-motivated learners, the schools are inefficient institutions for attaining those objectives. For once, we lay schools open to the same kind of dispassionate analysis which we would use to gauge the efficiency of an industrial enterprise. Unfortunately there is evidence
- that schools are still semi-religious institutions in most countries which cannot be disassembled and rearranged in the same sense as factories or new commercial products;
- that children are too precious a property for dispassionate discussions about their welfare to take place;
- that few children are self-motivated when they first come to school;
- that schools serve a multiplicity of social and economic functions, of which teaching children to read, write and count may be among the least important.

Let us go over briefly our own catalogue of the problems raised by deschooling.

7.1 <u>Societies do not voluntarily give parents full control over the development of children up to the age of puberty</u>. This is the famous 'socialisation' question. Schools are compulsory because societies want to be certain that all children will behave in a number of predictable ways by the time they acquire adult rights and responsibilities. The less close-knit the community, as is the case in industrialised countries, the less able are the community leaders to monitor what is going on inside local families, and the greater the insistance that parents turn their children over at an early age to certified social agents. These agents will see to it that children learn the requisite social behaviours mentioned earlier: to respect adult authority, to carry out work not of their own choosing, to be punctual and orderly, to work for longer-term rewards, to repress hostility in public, etc. In addition, the basic skills of literacy and numeracy are certain to be acquired by all children. These skills in turn are taught by means of a content which further encourages children to comprehend the local economy and history,

to revere national laws and national leaders and to have a vision of the world lying outside their immediate neighbourhood.

This means that teachers are value-bearers as well as instructors. Their task is to pass on, by example and training, certain moral values and standards of conduct - to enculturate as well as to educate. One of their chief functions is to narrow the child's perceptual field, to put out of his mind ideas and behaviours not selected for his perceptions by the dominant culture. The teacher helps to ensure the stable functioning of society by making certain that there are a number of shared behaviours in all future members.

In order to carry out this regulatory training, the teacher is accorded wide influence over children. He has almost limitless powers to reward or punish children for what he considers correct or incorrect actions. At the same time, children are enormously plastic at this age; their minds and bodies can be durably conditioned by what they are exposed to. These exposures are very frequent (approximately 7000 hours up to the end of primary school) and they take place in a setting where children depend entirely on a single adult for their physical and mental needs. Finally, parents give children to understand that going to school is the most important thing they will do until the age of 12 or 14.

In brief, the school is used to provide the transition from family life to public life by cutting down variations in the behaviours which are important to the society and economy. Freire is correct to argue that the effect of the schools' transmission of 'dead knowledge' is to domesticate rather than educate. But he does not seem to realise that this is intentional, just as the effort to make children depend on teachers and approved institutions for their learning is intentional. The so-called 'de-humanisation' or stereotyped uniformity of the classroom is also intentional, the idea being that children learn to see themselves as identical to others, as having none of the special rights they can claim in their own families.

Thus some of the apparent deficits of the primary school - dependence on external motivation, lack of independence, uniformity, arbitrary use of authority - are actually part of its objectives and serve a deliberate purpose. This is why there will continue to be a kind of unidentified but powerful resistance to deschooling up to the age of 12 or 14.

7.2 <u>The problem of motivation</u>. With an end to compulsory schooling all learning becomes self-motivated. One of the most emphatic arguments of deschooling theorists is that children's intrinsic motivation for learning is erased at school, where all instruction is mediated by extrinsic rewards and punishments. The implication is that, were schools removed, the child's natural curiosity would ensure his learning the basic repertoire of skills and knowledge.

The problem is more complex than either side is willing to admit. Doubtless, schools and educational psychologists have underestimated the power of discovery learning, of the child's natural tendency to explore and reconstruct his environment, of his need and capacity to organise his own learning experiences. As Piaget has written often, every time we teach a child something, we keep him from inventing it himself, which is the only way in which significant learning goes on. On the other hand, there are some considerations which complicate the problem:
- Little will be learned if the environment does

not contain the objects and situations necessary for learning. Schools ensure the presence of such a minimal environment; families and voluntary services do not.

- Children have come to depend on extrinsic motivations in their families before they go to school. Parents mete out rewards and punishments very often as a way of training their children at home, particularly in lower-class families.

- There is evidence that no significant learning goes on unless the environment is slightly more complex and more uncertain than what the child is used to. Many children and youth do not spontaneously seek out these environments. Some avoid any experience where there is a risk of failure; some need more reassurance or structure on the part of adults than others. School allows for relatively safe environments for the child to carry on this kind of experimentation.

- Leaving much of the learning process to chance is a risky alternative. A good deal of organised practice and sequencing is required for many crucial skills and operations.

- The very notion of intrinsic motivation involves accepting the child for what he is, approving his acts even if they appear illogical to an adult or letting him act out his emotions. This is as much a cultural ideology as a theory of learning. And it is far more common in well-educated, psychologically sophisticated families than in poor homes where the child is often expected to conform very early to his parents' expectations of him. Most of the deschooling theorists come from privileged milieux and use that point of reference for their generalisations. The already disadvantaged might suffer the most in a free enterprise, self-motivated educational system.

7.3 Supervision, evaluation and bureaucracy. Who will supervise and certify the educational network or 'learning web'? How do we know whether privately controlled schools and teachers are performing any better than those which submit to public control? If clearing houses, guidance and orientation centres, supervisory and evaluation offices are required to make the system work, will we have a more mammoth educational bureaucracy than we already have?

7.4 A new primitivism? Deschooling theorists often refer to primitive or pre-industrial epochs when all children were educated sufficiently without schools. This initiation into adulthood, however, was carefully structured, ritualised and supervised; there was nothing incidental or elective about it. Nor did people entrust their children to adults who were not relatives or at least village elders, and there is evidence in this connection that less privileged families in modern times have a similar mentality. In short, we may be technologically ready, but we are not yet psychologically or socially ready in most countries for the 'global village' laid out by McLuhan and Illich.

7.5 The temptation to escape current problems. Some of the debate over deschooling resembles the current debates over the usefulness of literacy in future societies which will depend less on written language. That is, a convenient way of escaping from the complex and persistent problems faced in schools is to speculate on their disappearance.[18] That disappearance is very unlikely in the short term, no matter how convincing or militant its partisans may be. Until very recently, in fact, little time, effort and money went into improving schools. Most of the resources went into extending its services. As

for the possibility of rapid or radical change, we have tried to show elsewhere[19] that innovation in education is in its very nature conservative, in that its primary function is to make the unfamiliar into the familiar, to graft the new onto the old. Social institutions are made up less of machinery than of people, attitudes and well ingrained habits. All these things change slowly when they change at all. Radical changes are seldom possible and are only effective when the new behaviours required for them are controlled and reinforced over a fairly long period of time, as has been the case in Cuba, Albania or the USSR. Otherwise, people tend to reproduce the old behaviours in the new environment. Given the lack of social controls under deschooling, this constitutes a real problem.

7.6 Deschooling may not equalise opportunities. If we distribute equally the sum of public funds available for education among families, this does not prevent wealthier parents from buying more and better services for their children. Presumably, the better paying and more responsible jobs will still be given to those having the right certificates or the highest grades in competitive examinations. Preparation for these certificates and exams will be sold in the marketplace at various prices and in various forms. In addition, wealthy and well-educated homes will still constitute a privileged training ground for access to selective professions, unless the requirements for certification are changed radically.

7.7 The dangers of parochialism. In an extreme form, the danger of abolishing compulsory schooling without making any other major social changes is that children and youth might be exploited as cheap labour by parents or employers who would lay claim to the time formerly allotted for formal schooling.

In all likelihood, this problem would be faced and solved rapidly in a deschooled society. But it does pose the question of how one separates the child from his immediate family and local environment. This is one important service which schools render in more rural or backward areas of the country, notably in the Third World. Schools help to nationalise children, to take them out of their ethnic, religious or geographic parishes and expose them to a more cosmopolitan world than they might have known at home. Much of this has changed with the advent of mass media, but less so than we might have expected. There are a number of studies comparing school graduates with those who have not completed compulsory schooling, and the differences can be dramatic, even among children from families with the same social background. The school graduates tend to feel that they have more personal control over their lives, that they will follow a different career from that of their parents and will raise their own children differently from the way they were brought up. They are more open to social change and the use of modern technology, more likely to seek further education, better informed of national and international affairs and more able to think about and solve problems relating to objects or situations not immediately in front of them.

A second dimension, implicit in these research data, is the role of school in weaning the child from his family. He learns at school to establish and sever close relationships with adults and peers who are not relatives. It is principally at school that the child widens his circle of acquaintances, learns to be a member of several groups and still maintain his identity and slowly gains independence from his mother by forming shorter attachments to adults who are not his mother.

Here again, the poorest and least cosmopolitan families, in which contact with non-relatives or non-neighbours is usually limited, may gain far more from compulsory schooling than from voluntary educational services. In fact, the already privileged may profit the most from deschooling. Well-educated parents need no longer send their children to school where they will be bored by material already partially covered at home, or slowed down by children of less educated families. They can retrieve their share of taxes for public schooling in order to hire more specialised tutors whom they themselves can select. They will have the leisure and sophistication to be best informed of the offerings listed in the directories of educational resources, and will be more expert in diagnosing the skills of these people and services as teachers of their children. Finally, they are as certain as under the former system to bring their children to the point of competence needed for certification at the higher professional levels.

8. TOWARD A NEW MODEL OF DEMOCRATISATION

As inefficient or inequitable as the schools are, they may be a better social investment, at least for ages 5-12, than any of the alternatives proposed. Given their industrial mode of functioning, schools are relatively cheap, rational enterprises which process large numbers of units with the help of few executives or administrators at a very low per capita cost. They hire trained professionals at low wages; they are centrally located; they serve a custodial or baby-sitting function which enables parents to work. In addition, schools teach the basic rules of conduct and basic social behaviours, rehabilitate social deviants, wean children from their parents and widen parochial horizons. They teach basic skills of literacy and numeracy and provide instruction in health and hygiene, human relations, cooking and sewing, local and national history and legislation. They identify and cream off the élite for senior professional posts and control the numbers of applicants entering the labour market at different levels. They provide an environment in which a child's effort counts for something and where most tasks are adjusted to his level of mental and physical functioning. And they are already in operation...

From ages 12 to 17, however, the situation is different. The separation between scholastic and real life is too great. Facts and theories are abstracted from ongoing professions and social institutions, and these ideas are again thinned out and processed to be imported in secondary school classrooms and taught as the curriculum. Most school graduates are receiving an education abstracted from work in a given field and then given certificates obliging them to go into that field and relearn everything in terms of the actual work. That is, few concepts are taught in relation to the experiences that correspond to them and, as a result, go unheeded.

Secondary schools are ill-prepared to teach vocational skills, and they have not been markedly successful in mixing an academic programme with a specialised occupational training within a single institution. Rather than increase their scope and services, they would do well to contract out all their non-intellectual work to offices, laboratories, community agencies and actual work experiences for youth. Adolescents should be spending far less time in school, first because they have more to learn at this age outside school and are equipped to get much of that instruction by themselves. Also, secondary schools are highly unnatural places for adolescents to spend time and there is no overriding reason to continue their socialisation to unnatural but socially useful habits beyond the age of puberty. Adolescents need an environment which runs counter to the industrial organisation of schooling: some privacy and independence, some space to move around, a more nurturant emotional climate, a chance to test themselves in concrete rather than contrived situations, a place where they are treated as unique persons, and some contact with adults who are not cerebral. Here, the deschooling model is highly appropriate and its implementation is overdue. Many secondary schools in Western Europe and North America are already having to be wildly imaginative or repressively authoritarian in order to keep the lid on. These schools are increasingly like hospitals without sick patients, places where few persons - be it pupils, teachers or administrators - are comfortable or have the impression of being productive.

In the long run we shall come around to the sensible principle that a young man of 15 or 16 has as much right to work as to study, and the adult as much right to study as to work. This will be less a gesture of social democratisation than a revision of the unintelligent way in which we space events in our life cycle. For the practice of squeezing into the age period 15-30 years the terminal stages of education, the most energy for vocational promotion, marriage and family formation dates from an historical context in which life expectancy was 40 to 50 years. We continue to divert still more public resources for education into the extension of public schooling for those young people who need, above all, experiences of adult life to which they can relate what they have learned. We should have long since outgrown the theory that one can only learn before one becomes an adult and admit that one learns certain things best as an adult.

A number of secondary schools have begun reforms in this direction. They are also getting used to the idea of young people leaving and re-entering the school system and completing their schooling at their own pace. The procedure should become one where educational officials make public the skills, knowledge and experiences which pupils must have acquired by the time they are ready to leave formal schooling. The secondary schools would then no longer monopolise all the places, time, materials and people who can provide these competencies; rather, schools will give services connected with more intellectual or speculative skills. The objective will be to bring all young people to final certification by allowing them various learning routes in accordance with their own individual schedule, strategy and, when possible, their own choice of teachers.

This creates a very new perspective of education as a more individual ideosyncratic act, rather than a collective operation. It also involves separating cognitive learning and child-care activities from socialisation. We shall have to learn that equal opportunity does not mean identity of opportunity and treatment, but rather the provision of learning resources which match the competencies and level of development of different learners with the requirements of the task to be learned. Since schools have seldom done this, we know very little about how it is to be done, except that it is a very complex business.

Even if everyone has equal access to these educational resources, it will be the match between learner and task which matters, rather than the sheer number of services available. We shall attain equal opportunity in education not when we have sufficient money and facilities for all, but when we have individual mixtures of people, materials and environment for each.

11

ROBERT M. HUTCHINS
Toward a learning society

Source: The Center Magazine, Vol. IV, No. 4 (July/August 1971).

* *

Robert M. Hutchins, the former Chancellor of the University of Chicago, is the person who created the phrase 'the learning society'. An optimist, he saw the positive possibilities of the abolition of repetitive work: in 1963 he looked forward to the coming of 'a wantless, workless world' in which the machines would do the work and wrote: 'One who has faith that man is in some degree rational... must believe that sooner or later the light will shine through the murk. Sometime we shall understand that what we are after is wisdom, and we shall try to reform our educational system in order to get it.' (The University of Utopia, University of Chicago Press, 1953 and 1964.) In this piece Hutchins stresses that education must be man-centred, not economy-centred ('manhood, not manpower') and puts his case for the provision of lifelong learning opportunity, the preconditions for which, he argues, include 'an immense decentralisation, debureaucratisation, and deinstitutionalisation' and an increased use of the new media of communication. See also Quotational Bibliography - HUTCHINS, Robert M. and WRIGHT, Douglas.

* *

We do not ask what a graduate knows but whether he has his diploma.

We did not talk much about the prospects for a learning society in the old days at the University of Chicago. We were having enough trouble trying to make sense of what we were doing already. And we could not really imagine a learning society. We knew about technology and knew that technological change would make idiots of those who thought people should be trained to acquire technical skill. We knew that because John Dewey had told us so when he was a member of the Chicago community in 1897. We saw that the aim of education must be manhood and not manpower. We could not foresee a day in which everybody, by virtue of technology, would have free time and the question would be what in the world he would do with himself. We believed that everybody could learn, a conviction since confirmed by the scientific work of Bruner and others. We believed he could learn all his life long; we considered that

the efforts of the University of Chicago since Mr Harper's day proved that. We could see that American education was enormously wasteful of time and money, that the lockstep did not accommodate individual differences, that a system based on time served and credits accumulated could only by accident provide an education, and that by wiping out this system, which we did, we could make it possible for people to proceed at their own pace, to drop in and drop out, and to continue to use their minds as long as they lived. But we thought there would not be many.

Except for radio (the University of Chicago had the oldest programme on the air) and films (with which we began to experiment around 1940) we had available as a means of distributing only that which had originated with Gutenberg. The trouble with radio was that it was in the hands of the oligopoly that controls it today. The University of Chicago Roundtable suffered a fatal blow when NBC moved it to an impossible hour. The 7-Up Company had bought the half-hour next to the Roundtable's traditional time and demanded that the Roundtable be moved on the ground that it was not a 'good adjacency'. The trouble with films was that the so-called portable equipment used in the classroom had to be moved by a truck and operated by a graduate of MIT.

Thomas Jefferson thought that some were destined to rule the commonwealth; the others were destined for labour. We do not believe in this kind of natural selection any more. Samuel Johnson held that all intellectual improvement came from leisure and that all leisure came from one working for another. We know now that leisure can come from technology: machines can do for us what slaves did for the Athenians. Tocqueville found that it was as impossible to have everybody educated as it was to have everybody rich. Now we do not think it idle to talk about the abolition of poverty. We are no longer bothered by these ancient prejudices. Our trouble now is that we are confused about the purpose and meaning of education and that we suffer from what may be called the Institutional Illusion.

A president of Harvard once said that he did not want to discuss what education was. As far as he was concerned he was prepared to call education anything that was going on in an institution that called itself educational. So a president of Sarah Lawrence said that every student should plan his own curriculum, which is the same as saying that education is anything that is going on in anybody that calls himself a student. What goes on in most institutions that call themselves educational is some education, some child care, some training, some vocational certification that calls itself training or education but is not, and, at the higher levels, some research. As for students, the Special Task Force that reported to the Department of Health, Education, and Welfare the other day said, 'Most students entering higher education today are not academically oriented.' If then they were to plan their own courses of collegiate study, such academic institutions as we possess would rapidly pass out of existence.

There is a fundamental, though not always sharp and clear, distinction between a learning society and a society in training. Learning, as I am using the word, aims at understanding, which is good in itself, and hence at nothing beyond itself. Training is instrumental; it may not require or lead to any understanding at all; it aims at the performance of prescribed tasks by prescribed methods.

This distinction does not depreciate specialised, technical training. Any society, certainly any industrial one, has to have it. A rapidly changing cybernated society will have a tremendous job of continual retraining on its hands. The only question about such training is how to give it effectively. There is no apparent reason why industries, occupations, and professions that want trained hands should not train them themselves. Including training in educational programmes or institutions simply means that they work at cross-purposes.

Training, which is simple, direct, with an easily definable and defensible object, is also quite readily measurable. It may involve no higher mental faculty than memory. Learning, or education, on the other hand, is infinitely complicated, frequently unappealing, and not readily accessible to quantitative assessment. Hence the attraction of training to a man like the new United States Commissioner of Education, who proposes to chloroform whatever there is of general education in the schools and replace it with something real, vital, and interesting, namely vocational training. In an effort to make this more palatable he adds to the confusion by officially renaming vocational training: he calls it 'career education'.

Training will always be seductive, if only because it puts little strain on the mind of the teacher or the student. The trouble is, as John Dewey pointed out, it is always obsolescent. And the rate of obsolescence is higher now than at any time in history. René Dubos has remarked that the more technical a society is the less technical its education has to be.

Yet most programmes in most institutions called educational are now largely technical. And the remarkable fact is that all pretense that the curriculum has any relation to technical skill or that the diploma or degree awarded on the completion of the programme denotes possession of technical skill has been abandoned. We do not ask what a high-school college, or university graduate knows or what he can do. We merely inquire whether he has graduated. Educational credentials are helpful to married personnel managers, who simply announce that persons not having the requisite credentials, though capable of doing the work, will not be employed.

Learning, or education, cannot be defended as a means to anything beyond itself. It has no predictable effect on the prosperity of states or individuals. We cannot say whether the United States is rich and powerful because of its educational system or in spite of it. As for the developing nations, we know that as countries develop, their educational systems and expenditures expand. We do not know whether this expansion is a cause or a result of economic development.

It cannot even be shown that literacy is always indispensable to economic development. A big biscuit factory in Hanover in West Germany, which is fully automated, is staffed largely by illiterate Spanish women who cannot speak a word of German.

We should ponder, too, the report made in 1948 to the American Association on Mental Deficiency by an eminent sociologist. She showed that the typical male moron earned as much as $3.50 a week more than the average industrial wage and that the female moron uniformly made more money than the normal woman industrial worker.

A cybernated world is likely to be one in which a few highly trained experts and a small labour force, whose qualifications are that they can see a red light or hear a whistle, can operate an industrial plant. We need education in science and technology in a scientific age not to train us for the work we have to do but rather to understand the world we are living in.

The report of the Task Force to which I have referred ends with an absurd question: 'How can students be freed from the infatuation of American society with the form rather than the substance of learning?' The students cannot be freed from this infatuation until the form rather than the substance of learning ceases to satisfy those upon whom their educational, economic, and social future depends.

The real question is, why is American society infatuated with the form rather than the substance of learning? The answer must be that if you don't know what the substance is you have to be content with the form. Or if you are confused about the substance you can at least identify and seek the form. You may not be able to tell whether a person is educated, but you can always count his credits, grades, and diplomas and the number of years he has been in school. Since the Second World War we have said two things: first, that education promotes the power and prosperity of states and individuals, which cannot be proved, and second, that the status of persons rises in proportion to the time they have spent in educational institutions and the number of diplomas they have, which may be true but which makes no sense.

We shall not have a learning society until we get over our infatuation with form rather than substance. I see no hope of this until the cost of confusion resulting from a preoccupation with form becomes so obvious and overwhelming as to bring us to the realisation that form without substance is as wasteful as it is meaningless. Think of the prospects of a learning society if we were to do what I have proposed many times before, if we were to confer the bachelor's degree on every American citizen at birth.

* * *

This brings us to the Institutional Illusion. Institutions calling themselves educational are the only culturally accredited instruments of education. Their forms are the only ones that count. In the advanced countries they are largely custodial: they take up the time of the young until we are ready to have them go to work. Everywhere in the world the length of time one spends in educational institutions and the success one has in them are determined by one's socio-economic status and family background. This means that the power and prosperity presumably promoted by an educational system are conferred upon those who already have the most. The educational system, in short, is a means of maintaining the status quo.

We see this most clearly in the case of the developing countries. Many of them spend a third of their budgets on schools and universities. They all find the bulk of this money going to perpetuate the advantages of that tiny fraction of the population which is at the top of the social and economic pyramid. The overwhelming majority of the children never get beyond the first few grades. They not only fail to receive any benefits from the expenditures on education, but also suffer grave indignities that might not be visited upon them if the educational system did not exist. The graded curriculum degrades those who are unable to continue in it. These are uniformly the children of the poor. It is not that they are ineducable. The failure is that of the institution and its bureaucracy and the rigidities inherent in them.

As Ivan Illich has said, 'Educators appeal to the gambling instinct of the entire population when they raise money for schools. They advertise the jackpot without mentioning the odds.' The odds against the poor in the educational systems of every country are such as to intimidate the most hardened habitué of Las Vegas or Monte Carlo. The dice are loaded. We must look forward to an immense decentralisation, debureaucratisation, and deinstitutionalisation if we are to have a learning society.

Here technology can help us. The electronic devices now available can make every home a learning unit, for all the family. All the members of the family might be continuously engaged in learning. Teachers might function as visiting nurses do today - and as physicians used to do. The new electronic devices do not eliminate the need for face-to-face instruction or for schools, but they enable us to shift attention from the wrong question, which is how can we get everybody in schools and keep him there as long as possible, to the right one, which is how can we give everybody a chance to learn all his life? The new technology gives a flexibility that will encourage us to abandon the old self-imposed limitations. They are that education is a matter for part of life, part of the year, or part of the day, that it is open in all its richness only to those who need it least, and that it must be conducted formally, in buildings designed for the purpose, by people who have spent their lives in schools, in accordance with an incomprehensible programme, the chief aim of which is to separate the sheep from the goats.

The Open University in England, if it can hold off the Tories and avoid suffocation from its credits and degrees, gives us some intimation of what the educational future could look like. The Open University is nothing less than a national commitment to use all the intellectual and technological resources of the country in a coherent way to give every citizen, no matter what his background or academic qualifications, an opportunity to keep on learning throughout his life.

In this country the University Without Walls, which is just getting started under the sponsorship of nineteen colleges and universities, including the University of Chicago, appears to be contemplating the same thing.

The other day L. E. Dennis, provost of the Massachusetts State College System, responding to the question, 'What's at the other end of "Sesame Street"?' proposed a University of North America on the same lines.

Other technological possibilities are suggested by the agreement recently made between NASA (the space agency of the United States) and the government of India. It provides for educational broadcasting via satellite to some five thousand remote Indian villages. Brazil has shown interest in similar arrangements. The United Nations has set up a Working Group on Direct Broadcasting to promote and follow such experiments.

Then there are cables, cassettes, computers and videotape. It is reported that a cable system is now being built in San Jose, California, that will have forty-eight channels. It is hard to accept the proposition that all of these must be dedicated to the kind of triviality that is now the common fare on commercial television. The San Jose people would have to make a tremendous effort to avoid using some of these channels - and we are told that many more are technically possible - for cultural, artistic, and educational purposes, and in particular for the discussion of political, economic, and social issues.

Of course I know there is little in the record of the American people to suggest that we will use these new devices for our enlightenment. I remember running into E. M. Herr, president of Westinghouse, forty-five years ago. He said he had been at a big meeting in Washington with Mr Herbert Hoover, then Secretary of Commerce, which had been called to settle the future of radio. I said, 'Did you settle anything?' Mr Herr replied: 'We certainly did. We decided there should never be any advertising on the air.' Therefore I do not say we will use the new instruments technology has given us in order to create a learning society. I say only that we can create such a society.

* * *

We can have a learning society. Its object would be to raise every man and woman and every community to the highest cultural level attainable. The affluence of a world in which science creates wealth will make it impossible to plead poverty as an excuse for not trying to educate everybody. As for our pitiful record in the use of our free time, Arnold Toynbee, who has a long historical view, reassures us by saying that free time may be abused at first by people who have had no experience of it; but sooner or later we shall be able to salvage some of it for learning.

In such a society the role of educational institutions would be to provide for what is notably missing from them today, and that is the interaction of minds. Eventually these institutions would not be 'processing' anybody for anything or awarding diplomas or degrees. The search for what have been called sheepskins to cover our intellectual nakedness, which has been necessary to gain status in an industrial society, has held back learning.

In the coming age the university could be transformed into a contemporary version of the Platonic Academy. It could be a centre of independent thought and criticism, bringing the great intellectual disciplines together so that they might shed light on one another and on the major issues facing modern man.

So when Karl Jaspers proposed something new for Europe, a technical faculty in the university, he did not do so in order to turn out more engineers or to get ahead of Russia. He did it because he thought how to live with science and technology was the most urgent problem of humanity. It could be solved, if at all, only by forcing technology to wrestle with other disciplines and forcing them to face up to it. The place for such confrontation, if you will forgive the expression, is the university.

No doubt this would compel a change in the organisation and personnel of the university, which is now a collection of specialists who appear to grow more narrow as they become more numerous. The recent statement of Victor Ferkiss of the Department of Government at Georgetown University about what specialists in political science have done has the ring of truth. Mr Ferkiss said, 'The great issues of politics have been left untouched not so much because of a quasi-conspiracy in favour of the status quo as because of a trained incapacity to think in a creative, innovative, interdisciplinary way about social matters, an incapacity fostered by the entire process of professional socialisation, now beginning even at the undergraduate level. ' If a trained incapacity to think is the result of university study, we should perhaps re-examine its structure and its purposes.

To attain full humanity is to reach the level of critical consciousness. This means understanding reality and understanding that men can and should transform it. The university is the institution which should lead in the achievement of critical consciousness. It must use and contain within itself all the major modes of understanding and transforming reality. Thus the university would represent and constitute the circle of knowledge, in which everything is understood in the light of everything else.

Such a university could preside over the progress of the learning society.

12

IVAN ILLICH

The redistribution of educational tasks between schools and other organs of society

Source: Document of the Centro Intercultural de Documentacion, Cuernavaca, Mexico.

* *

This paper was delivered at a conference on educational planning co-sponsored by the University of Puerto Rico and the Puerto Rican Planning Board in July 1967.

In this early paper Illich argues that in modern society the school has accumulated tasks, many of which it cannot perform, and he raises the general question: 'Can the purpose of a school system established by any given society be continually and effectively renewed?' Illich himself writes of this document: 'To the best of my knowledge this paper has never been formally published. Please note: The paper was written specifically for the Conference... it was written as a contribution to the discussion during an intermission of the Conference; it is probably a good indication of the manner in which I struggled with some ideas in early 1967; it is in no way a well-rounded and final statement of my thinking on this problem'. The document is reproduced here not only for its historical importance but also for its clear formulation of several questions to which subsequent deschooling analysis attempted to reply. See also the Quotational Bibliography - BEREITER, Carl and CALLAWAY, Archibald for two pieces on a similar theme, and, of course, ILLICH, Ivan.

* *

The purpose of this paper is not to stimulate discussion on internal change within school systems. I would like to raise a different question: can the purpose of a school system established by any given society be continually and effectively renewed? If so, what are the necessary conditions for constant renewal?

Only a limited portion of the total educational process in any given nation is organised under formal bureaucratic control. The remainder is usually left to institutions over which the planner and programmer have little influence. If we look only at that part of the educational process under formal control, we discover that only a part of it is actually performed by institutions which society considers 'schools'. The rest is left to programmes which are not thought of as formal 'schooling'. This would include everything from in-service training to drivers' education or sex education.

At this moment we are beginning to analyse society's ability to reapportion education and to influence the growth and orientation of 'non-school' education. In this discussion I would like to set aside the concrete mechanics of renewal in the schooling process in order to examine the conditions necessary for a constant renewal of the school's goals.

First, I will identify the school system which I have observed, and with which I am the most familiar. Then I will list a series of conditions which I consider necessary in order for any school system to continually renew itself - and by renewal I mean: allowing new levels of humanism in teaching to be reached, revising educational technology, and eventually abandoning previous tasks to 'non-schools' so that the 'schools' can assume new tasks.

Catholic schools in Latin America

During the last few years I have spent a great deal of time analysing the effect of private schools on the over-all educational process in each of the Latin American nations. And in Latin America 'private school' means Catholic school. The latter have a double, stated purpose: they were established to inculcate an ideology which is often taken to be the Catholic Faith, and to offer educational services (i. e. alternate schooling, usually custodial child-care) for those whose parents or sponsors are of the moneyed classes.

At present traditional (Church) and new (private enterprise) ideologies keep private schools beyond the reach of the educational planners. Yet we can forecast a strong trend in the opposite direction: namely, that specialised instruction will be industrialised, and that public agencies will both license and contract the services of institutions dedicated to such instruction.

The disestablishment of a school system

We can consider the Catholic school system in Latin America as a model for the study of the dynamics of other school systems. We have pursued this line of research in Cuernavaca for the past six years. We have been privileged to act as self-appointed observers and promoters of the only case known to us of the disestablishment of an entire school system. Some of our observations might be relevant for other school systems and their eventual, partial disestablishment.

Church schools are by no means a negligible factor in Latin America. The Church spends from 60 to 80 per cent of her total budget in any country (except Cuba) for the building and maintenance of schools. From five to 20 per cent of the school-age population in any Latin American nation is studying in Catholic-controlled schools. The total enrollment in Latin American Catholic schools is greater than the total public school enrollment in all but three of the Latin American countries. Yet if present trends continue this percentage will have shrunk to almost nothing by 1980.

These trends are caused by factors beyond the control of Church administrators and constituencies: ever-rising costs, manpower crises, socio-political variables. And just as important in this trend toward the disestablishment of the Church from schooling is the conviction of a number of key church-men that Catholic schools constitute the major obstacle to the socio-educational relevance of the Church on this continent.

This surprising process (which I foresee) is of paradigmatic value for an often neglected relationship; namely, the relationship between educational intent and the choice of schools for the implementation of that intent. Since the Conquest the primary social function of the Latin American Church has been education. But now the Church finds herself entangled in her own school system and is trying to remove herself from school administration altogether. This trend will become surprisingly obvious by 1970. But if recognised now, policies can be created which will allow teachers to eventually accept the rethinking of education, the radical re-apportionment of educational functions or the charismatic renewal of an already functioning educational system.

Major points

1. Mechanisms can be built into school systems which accelerate their innovative capacity, but pressure for the renewal of a school system will usually come from outside that system. The preceding statement is a corollary of the knowledge that good schools are 'teacher proof'. That is, we have

evidence that teachers advocate more reform of their milieu than almost any other professional group, yet they are the least effective when it comes to actually effecting that reform. This is due to the fact that the teacher's main task is to formulate questions never asked, or even accepted, outside of the classroom. At the same time, he must preside over an academic life which is accepted outside the school only if it carries the academic 'label'. Indeed, the better a school can function despite its 'subversive' teachers who formulate questions not acceptable to non-academic society, the better teachers that school can afford to hire. The exercise of academic freedom can never be the source of the systematic improvement of the system itself. Indeed, the teacher's very job greatly dilutes his ability to change the educational system from within. His ideas will be generally ignored when he voices them beyond the walls of academia.

2. The school planner is the last person who can make fundamental innovations in the system. His employer has already told him exactly what special educational task the school must perform, and the school planner simply arranges the allocation of resources to accomplish that task. As soon as the school planner raises the question of a totally different apportionment of the task itself he moves out of his limited area of money allocation, and into the broadest type of social planning.

3. The definition of the school planner's task is ultimately based on a clear separation of: (a) the school system, and (b) overall educational planning.

The planner of the overall educational process, as opposed to the school planner, must decide which specific social tasks should be performed by formal schooling, as differentiated from educational tasks which must be left to the responsibility of others - from mothers in a community to driving instructors. Only if this decision is made outside of the school system, will the latter avoid becoming a 'state within a state' (like the Medieval Church), or a political football. If the school planner would attempt to formulate overall educational policies, he would reduce all education and instruction demanded by clients, economic planners or politicians to a form of formal schooling. On the other hand, if the overall educational planner cannot treat the school system as a service agency to which specific tasks may be assigned, he will never be able to demand effectiveness and efficiency from that system.

4. The demand for renewal will either take the form of a request to serve new clients, or will be a reaction to a model tried and proved successful elsewhere. The clients of a school system may demand that their system produce new results in a new manner which has proved successful elsewhere. 'Schools should produce...' 'Schools should serve...' - it is doubtful that such demands will be effective, since good school systems are not only 'teacher proof', but they are also vaccinated by constant disillusionment against utopian ideas coming from outside the system itself. Therefore, effective demands for renewal will usually take the form of a request that the system incorporate competitors. 'If the teachers there can do it, why can't our teachers do it? If another system can produce these results, why can't ours?'

5. A model is usually the agent utilised to effect change in a system. Politics aimed at polarising power for change in educational systems consistently utilise models to create issues. An effective educa-

tional model or experiment must have four facets. The model must prove the following:

(a) That something new is now possible, that the present behaviour of another can determine our own future. I would expand a bit on Jerome Bruner and say: 'Personal creativity produces an effective surprise concerning a present possibility. ' ('They did it! ')

(b) Something previously untried has proved itself effective, that it has produced education outside of the current school system. An effective educational result has, for the first time, been defined as a scholastic need. This need is a possible result of systematic teaching, and should now be adopted here. ('Our school should do it. ')

(c) The experiment raises a question. Can the educational system effectively allow the model to be reproduced? Must the reproduction of the model remain outside of the system? ('Should we do it? Is our system that "teacher-proof"? Let "them" organise it. It's none of our business. ')

(d) Is the present system willing to pay the price of adapting to the new process? Can the present system insure the continuation of the model through its institutionalisation? ('Maybe we had better let them continue to try it. ')

6. The last characteristic (d) puts the educational experiment into a class by itself. A school system cannot produce teachers, contrary to popular opinion. It can only create more or less ideal situations for teaching. In the strict sense, educational invention is personal and inimitable. Ideally, the individual teacher is a creator with a personal style which cannot be imitated by another. Individual teaching is the 'celebration' of an intimate experience which has no precedent. The charismatic and prophetic quality of a new style of teaching distinguishes it from invention of educational technology.

Since most teachers are uninventive, dull, or worse, the school system tends to make the teacher a part of the programme itself in order to guarantee that his presence in the system be worthwhile. He must 'follow the teaching programme' laid down by his superiors. This kind of thinking should be avoided. New teaching should not be a model for a process which will eventually be institutionalised. On the contrary, it is concrete proof of a possibility which might lead to the adoption and development of a methodological model within a school system.

Summary

This principle could very well be restated in a paradox: Nobody should be paid for the privilege of teaching. But effective and efficient instructors should be so well paid that they can have the privilege of becoming true teachers.

The effectiveness of planned change in a school system depends largely on the rational selection of scholastic goals within the overall educational process, formal and informal, which a society has defined for itself.

The Latin American public school systems are irrational, comprehensive, ecclectic combinations of educational goals which have sedimented over a period of 150 years and are glued together by an intensely formalised ideology. The levels and branches of these systems, even if they are somewhat updated, are still historical relics which have

ceased to be self-contained sub-systems or 'careers'. Now education is measured by the number of years one has 'passed' on successive levels of the 'educational supermarket'. The student moves from the First Grade 'supermarket' to the Second Grade 'supermarket', and eventually may move through 15 or 20 different 'supermarkets' and receive a university degree. This system will probably have to be replaced by measurement through statistically described sets of typical educational processes resulting from parallel educational services. In each of these processes almost any individual may obtain a qualitatively, narrowly defined 'schooling' at almost any moment in his life.

I propose that for the intent of the present discussion, the suggestions made here be seen against the background of history; in fact, I believe that only through the study of history will we be able to gain the sufficient freedom of imagination to envisage radically new re-distribution of educational tasks between formal schooling and other forms of education or celebration.

For this purpose, I suggest that we analyse the history of religious institutions through the centuries. They are the only major formally educational bodies who, in the past, had to grapple with the issues now faced by major school systems.

13

IVAN ILLICH

Schooling: the ritual of progress

Source: Document of the Centro Intercultural de Documentacion, Cuernavaca, Mexico.

* *

Illich himself writes: 'This essay went through several stages, and in each it was published: Conseil de la Culture (Aspen Meeting); New York Review of Books; Deschooling Society; Smithsonian Symposium on Alternatives for the Future. ' It is reproduced here as it embodies Illich's central challenge to the Western European idea of progress as it is reflected in the growth of school systems. It is discursive in style, uses associative arguments, treats schools as metaphysical categories, and is a curious counter-version of schoolman theology. It is also full of insights and provocations, and it initiated me into the myth of the unending consumption of Illich writings. See also Quotational Bibliography - BECKER, Howard S. ; GOFFMAN, Erving; ILLICH, Ivan; and REIMER, Everett.

* *

The university graduate has been schooled for selective service among the rich of the world. Whatever his or her claims of solidarity with the Third World, each American college graduate has had an education costing an amount five times greater than the median life income of half of humanity. A Latin American student is introduced to this exclusive fraternity by having at least 350 times as much public money spent on his education as on that of his fellow citizens of median income. With very rare exceptions, the university graduate from a poor country feels more comfortable with his North American and European colleagues than with his non-schooled compatriots, and all students are academically processed to be happy only in the company of fellow consumers of the products of the educational machine.

The modern university confers the privilege of dissent on those who have been tested and classified as potential money makers or power holders. No one is given tax funds for the leisure in which to educate himself or the right to educate others unless at the same time he can also be certified for achievement. Schools select for each successive level those who have, at earlier stages in the game, proved themselves good risks for the established order. Having a monopoly on both the resources for learning and the investiture of social roles, the university co-opts the discoverer and the potential dissenter. A degree always leaves its indelible price tag on the curriculum of its consumer. Certified college graduates fit only into a world which puts a price tag on their heads, thereby giving them the power to define the level of expectations in their society. In each country, the amount of consumption by the college graduate sets the standard for all others; if they would be civilised people on or off the job, they will aspire to the style of life of college graduates.

* * *

The university thus has the effect of imposing consumer standards at work and at home, and it does so in every part of the world and under every political system. The fewer university graduates there are in a country, the more their cultivated demands are taken as models by the rest of the population. The gap between the consumption of the university graduate and that of the average citizen is even wider in Russia, China, and Algeria than in the United States. Cars, airplane trips, and tape recorders confer more visible distinction in a socialist country where only a degree, and not just money, can procure them.

The ability of the university to fix consumer goals is something new. In many countries the university acquired this power only in the Sixties, as the delusion of equal access to public education began to spread. Before that the university protected an individual's freedom of speech, but did not automatically convert his knowledge into wealth. To be a scholar in the Middle Ages meant to be poor, even a beggar. By virtue of his calling, the medieval scholar learned Latin, became an outsider worthy of the scorn as well as the esteem of peasant and prince, burgher and cleric. To get ahead in the world, the scholastic first had to enter it by joining the civil service, preferably that of the Church. The old university was a liberated zone for discovery and the discussion of ideas both new and old. Masters and students gathered to read the texts of other masters, now long dead, and the living words of the dead masters gave new perspective to the fallacies of the present day. The university was then a community of academic quest and endemic unrest.

In the modern multiversity, this community has fled to the fringes, where it meets in a pad, a pro-

fessor's office, or the chaplain's quarters. The structural purpose of the modern university has little to do with the traditional quest. Since Gutenberg, the exchange of disciplined, critical inquiry has, for the most part, moved from the 'chair' into print. The modern university has forfeited its chance to provide a simple setting for encounters which are both autonomous and anarchic, focused yet unplanned and ebullient, and has chosen instead to manage the process by which so-called research and instruction are produced.

The American university, since Sputnik, has been trying to catch up with the body count of Soviet graduates. Now the Germans are abandoning their academic tradition and are building 'campuses' in order to catch up with the Americans. During the present decade they want to increase their expenditure for grammar and high schools from 14 to 59 billion DM, and more than triple expenditures for higher learning. The French propose by 1980 to raise to 10 per cent of their GNP the amount spent on schools, and the Ford Foundation has been pushing poor countries in Latin America to raise per capita expenses for 'respectable' graduates toward North American levels. Students see their studies as the investment with the highest monetary return, and nations see them as a key factor in development.

For the majority who primarily seek a college degree, the university has lost no prestige, but since 1968 it has visibly lost standing among its believers. Students refuse to prepare for war, pollution, and the perpetuation of prejudice. Teachers assist them in their challenge to the legitimacy of the government, its foreign policy, education, and the American way of life. More than a few reject degrees and prepare for a life in a counter-culture, outside the certified society. They seem to choose the way of medieval _fraticelli_ and _alumbrados_ of the Reformation, the hippies and dropouts of their day. Others recognise the monopoly of the schools over the resources which they need to build a counter-society. They seek support from each other to live with integrity while submitting to the academic ritual. They form - so to speak - hotbeds of heresy right within the hierarchy.

* * *

Large parts of the general population, however, regard the modern mystic and the modern heresiarch with alarm. They threaten the consumer economy, democratic privilege, and the self-image of America. But they cannot be wished away. Fewer and fewer can be reconverted by patience or co-opted by subtlety for instance, by appointing them to teach their heresy. Hence the search for means which would make it possible either to get rid of dissident individuals or to reduce the importance of the university which serves them as a base for protest.

The students and faculty who question the legitimacy of the university, and do so at high personal cost, certainly do not feel that they are setting consumer standards or abetting a production system. Those who have founded such groups as the Committee of Concerned Asian Scholars and the North American Congress on Latin America (NACLA) have been among the most effective in changing radically the perceptions of the realities of foreign countries for millions of young people. Still others have tried to formulate Marxian interpretations of American society or have been among those responsible for the flowering of communes. Their achievements add new strength to the argument that the existence of the university is necessary to guarantee continued social criticism.

There is no question that at present the university offers a unique combination of circumstances which allows some of its members to criticise the whole of society. It provides time, mobility, access to peers and information, and a certain impunity: privileges not equally available to other segments of the population. But the university provides this freedom only to those who have already been deeply initiated into the consumer society and into the need for some kind of obligatory public schooling.

* * *

The school system today performs the threefold function common to powerful churches throughout history. It is at the same time the repository of society's myth: the institutionalisation of that myth's contradictions: and the locus of the ritual which reproduces and veils the disparities between myth and reality. Today the school system, and especially the university, provides ample opportunity for criticism of the myth and for rebellion against its institutional perversions. But the ritual which demands tolerance of the fundamental contradictions between myth and institution still goes largely unchallenged, for neither ideological criticism nor social action can bring about a new society. Only disenchantment with and detachment from the central social ritual and reform of that ritual can bring about radical change.

The American university has become the final stage of the most all-encompassing initiation rite the world has ever known. No society in history has been able to survive without ritual or myth, but ours is the first which has needed such a dull, protracted, destructive, and expensive initiation into its myth. We cannot begin a reform of education unless we first understand that neither individual learning nor social equality can be enhanced by the ritual of schooling. We cannot go beyond the consumer society unless we first understand that obligatory public schools inevitably reproduce such a society, no matter what is taught in them.

The project of de-mythologising which I propose cannot be limited to the university alone. Any attempt to reform the university without attending to the system of which it is an integral part is like trying to do urban renewal in New York City from the twelfth story up. Most current college level reform looks like the building of high-rise slums. Only a generation which grows up without obligatory schools will be able to re-create the university.

The myth of institutionalised values

School initiates the Myth of Unending Consumption. This modern myth is grounded in the belief that process inevitably produces something of value and, therefore, production necessarily produces demand. School teaches us that instruction produces learning. The existence of schools produces the demand for schooling. Once we have learned to need school, all our activities tend to take the shape of client relationships to other specialised institutions. Once the self-taught man or woman has been discredited, all non-professional activity is rendered suspect. In school we are taught that valuable learning is the result of attendance; that the value of learning increases with the amount of input; and, finally, that this value can be measured and documented by grades and certificates.

In fact, learning is the human activity which least needs manipulation by others. Most learning is not the result of instruction. It is rather the result of unhampered participation in a meaningful setting. Most people learn best by being 'with it', yet school makes them identify their personal, cognitive growth with elaborate planning and manipulation.

Once a man or woman has accepted the need for school, he or she is easy prey for other institutions. Once young people have allowed their imaginations to be formed by curricular instruction, they are conditioned to institutional planning of every sort. 'Instruction' smothers the horizon of their imaginations. They cannot be betrayed, but only short-changed, because they have been taught to substitute expectations for hope. They will no longer be surprised for good or ill by other people, because they have been taught what to expect from every other person who has been taught as they were. This is true in the case of another person or in the case of a machine.

* * *

This transfer of responsibility from self to institution guarantees social regression, especially once it has been accepted as an obligation. I saw this illustrated when John Holt recently told me that the leaders of the Berkeley revolt against Alma Mater had later 'made' her faculty. His remark suggested the possibility of a new Oedipus story - Oedipus the Teacher, who 'makes' his mother in order to engender children with her. The man addicted to being taught seeks his security in compulsive teaching. The woman who experiences her knowledge as the result of a process wants to reproduce it in others.

The myth of measurement of values

The institutionalised values school instills are quantified ones. School initiates young people into a world where everything can be measured, including their imaginations, and, indeed, man himself.

But personal growth is not a measurable entity. It is growth in disciplined dissidence, which cannot be measured against any rod, or any curriculum, nor compared to someone else's achievement. In such learning one can emulate others only in imaginative endeavour, and follow in their footsteps rather than mimic their gait. The learning I prize is immeasurable re-creation.

School pretends to break learning up into subject 'matters', to build into the pupil a curriculum made of these prefabricated blocks, and to gauge the result on an international scale. Men and women who submit to the standard of others for the measure of their own personal growth soon apply the same ruler to themselves. They no longer have to be put in their place, but put themselves into their assigned slots, squeeze themselves into the niche which they have been taught to seek, and, in the very process, put their fellows into their places too, until everybody and everything fits.

Men and women who have been schooled down to size let unmeasured experience slip out of their hands. To them, what cannot be measured becomes secondary, threatening. They do not have to be robbed of their creativity. Under instruction, they have unlearned to 'do' their thing or 'be' themselves, and value only what has been made or could be made.

Once men and women have the idea schooled into them that values can be produced and measured, they tend to accept all kinds of rankings. There is a scale for the development of nations, another for the intelligence of babies, and even progress toward peace can be calculated according to body count. In a schooled world, the road to happiness is paved with a consumer's index.

The myth of packaging values

School sells curriculum - a bundle of goods made according to the same process and having the same structure as other merchandise. Curriculum production for most schools begins with allegedly scientific research, on whose basis educational engineers predict future demand and tools for the assembly line, within the limits set by budgets and taboos. The distributor-teacher delivers the finished product to the consumer-pupil, whose reactions are carefully studied and charted to provide research data for the preparation of the next model, which may be 'ungraded', 'student-designed', 'team-taught', 'visually-aided', or 'issue-centred'.

The result of the curriculum production process looks like any other modern staple. It is a bundle of planned meetings, a package of values, a commodity whose 'balanced appeal' makes it marketable to a sufficiently large number to justify the cost of production. Consumer-pupils are taught to make their desires conform to marketed values. Thus they do not behave according to the predictions of consumer research by getting the grades and certificates that will place them in the job category they have been led to expect.

Educators can justify more expensive curricula on the basis of their observation that learning difficulties rise proportionately with the cost of the curriculum. This is an application of Parkinson's Law that work expands with the resources available to do it. This law can be verified on all levels of school: for instance, reading difficulties have been a major issue in French schools only since their per capita expenditures have approached US levels of 1950 - when reading difficulties became a major issue in US schools.

In fact, healthy students often redouble their resistance to teaching as they find themselves more comprehensively manipulated. This resistance is not due to the authoritarian style of a public school or the seductive style of some free schools, but to the fundamental approach common to all schools - the idea that one person's judgement should determine what and when another person must learn.

The myth of self-perpetuating progress

Even when accompanied by declining returns in learning, paradoxically, rising per capita instructional costs increase the value of the pupil in his or her own eyes and on the market. At almost any cost, school pushes the pupil up to the level of competitive curricular consumption, into progress to ever higher levels. Expenditures to motivate the student to stay on in school skyrocket as he climbs the pyramid. On higher levels they are disguised as new football stadiums, chapels, or programmes called International Education. If it teaches nothing else, school teaches the value of escalation: the value of the American way of doing things.

The Vietnam war fits the logic of the moment. Its success has been measured by the numbers of persons effectively treated by cheap bullets delivered at immense cost, and this brutal calculus is unashamedly called 'body count'. Just as business is

business, the never ending accumulation of money, so war is killing - the never ending accumulation of dead bodies. In like manner, education is schooling, and this open-ended process is counted in pupil-hours. The various processes are irreversible and self-justifying. By economic standards, the country gets richer and richer. By death-accounting standards, the nation goes on winning its war forever. And by school standards, the population becomes increasingly educated.

School programmes hunger for progressive intake of instruction, but even if the hunger leads to steady absorption it never yields the joy of knowing something to one's satisfaction. Each subject comes packaged with the instruction to go on consuming one 'offering' after another, and last year's wrapping is always obsolete for this year's consumer. The textbook racket builds on this demand. Educational reformers promise each new generation the latest and the best, and the public is schooled into demanding what they offer. Both the dropout who is forever reminded of what he or she missed and the graduate who is made to feel inferior to the new breed of student know exactly where they stand in the ritual of rising deceptions and continue to support a society which euphemistically calls the widening frustration gap a 'revolution of rising expectations'.

But growth conceived as open-ended consumption, eternal progress - can never lead to maturity. Commitment to unlimited quantitative increase vitiates the possibility of organic development.

Ritual game and the new world religion

The school-leaving age in developed nations outpaces the rise in life expectancy. The two curves will intersect in a decade and create a problem for Jessica Mitford and professionals concerned with 'terminal education'. I am reminded of the late Middle Ages, when the demand for Church services outgrew a lifetime, and 'Purgatory' was created to purify souls under the Pope's control before they could enter eternal peace. Logically, this led first to a trade in indulgences and then to an attempt at Reformation. The Myth of Unending Consumption now takes the place of belief in life everlasting.

Arnold Toynbee has pointed out that the decadence of a great culture is usually accompanied by the rise of a new World Church which extends hope to the domestic proletariat while serving the needs of a new warrior class. School seems eminently suited to be the World Church of our decaying culture. No institution could better veil from its participants the deep discrepancy between social principles and social reality in today's world. Secular, scientific, and death-denying, it is of a piece with the modern mood. Its classical, critical veneer makes it appear pluralist if not antireligious. Its curriculum both defines science and is itself defined by so-called scientific research. No one completes school - yet. It never closes its doors on anyone without first offering him one more chance: at remedial, adult, and continuing education.

* * *

School serves as an effective creator and sustainer of social myth because of its structure as a ritual game of graded promotions. Introduction into this gambling ritual is much more important than what or how something is taught. It is the game itself that schools, that gets into the blood and becomes a habit. A whole society is initiated into the Myth of Unending

Consumption of services. This happens to the degree that token participation in the open-ended ritual is made compulsory and compulsive everywhere. School directs ritual rivalry into an international game which obliges competitors to blame the world's ills on those who cannot or will not play. School is a ritual of <u>initiation</u> which introduces the neophyte to the sacred race of progressive consumption, a ritual of <u>propitiation</u> whose academic priests mediate between the faithful and the gods of privilege and power, a ritual of <u>expiation</u> which sacrifices its dropouts, branding them as scapegoats of underdevelopment.

Even those who spend at best a few years in school - and this is the overwhelming majority in Latin America, Asia, and Africa - learn to feel guilty because of their underconsumption of schooling. In Mexico six grades of school are legally obligatory. Children born into the lower economic third have only two chances in three to make it into the first grade. If they make it, they have four chances in 100 to finish obligatory schooling by the sixth grade. If they are born into the middle third group, their chances increase to twelve out of 100. With these rules, Mexico is more successful than most of the other twenty-five Latin American republics in providing public education.

Everywhere, all children know that they were given a chance, albeit an unequal one, in an obligatory lottery, and the presumed equality of the international standard now compounds their original poverty with the self-inflicted discrimination accepted by the dropout. They have been schooled to the belief in rising expectations and can now rationalise their growing frustration outside school by accepting their rejection from scholastic grace. They are excluded from Heaven because, once baptised they did not go to church. Born in original sin, they are baptised into first grade, but go to Gehenna (which in Hebrew means 'slum') because of their personal faults. As Max Weber traced the social effects of the belief that salvation belonged to those who accumulated wealth, we can now observe that grace is reserved for those who accumulate years in school.

The coming kingdom: the universalisation of expectations

School combines the expectations of the consumer expressed in its claims with the beliefs of the producer expressed in its ritual. It is a liturgical expression of a world-wide 'cargo cult', reminiscent of the cults which swept Melanesia in the Forties, which injected cultists with the belief that, if they but put on a black tie over their naked torsos, Jesus would arrive in a steamer bearing an icebox, a pair of trousers, and a sewing machine for each believer.

School fuses the growth in humiliating dependence on a master with the growth in the futile sense of omnipotence that is so typical of the pupil who wants to go out and teach all nations to save themselves. The ritual is tailored to the stern work habits of the hardhats, and its purpose is to celebrate the myth of an earthly paradise of never ending consumption, which is the only hope for the wretched and dispossessed.

Epidemics of insatiable this-worldly expectations have occurred throughout history, especially among colonised and marginal groups in all cultures. Jews in the Roman Empire had their Essenes and Jewish messiahs, serfs in the Reformation their Thomas Münzer, dispossessed Indians from Paraguay to Dakota their infectious dancers. These sects were always led by a prophet, and limited their promises to a chosen few. The school-induced expectation of the kingdom, on the other hand, is impersonal rather than prophetic, and universal rather than local. Man has become the engineer of his own messiah and promises the unlimited rewards of science to those who submit to progressive engineering for his reign.

The new alienation

School is not only the New World Religion. It is also the world's fastest growing labour market. The engineering of consumers has become the economy's principal growth sector. As production costs decrease in rich nations, there is an increasing concentration of both capital and labour in the vast enterprise of equipping man for disciplined consumption. During the past decade, capital investments directly related to the school system rose. Disarmament would only accelerate the process by which the learning industry moves to the centre of the national economy. School gives unlimited opportunity for legitimated waste, so long as its desctructiveness goes unrecognised and the cost of palliatives goes up.

If we add those engaged in full-time teaching to those in full-time attendance, we realise that this so-called superstructure has become society's major employer. In the US sixty-two million people are in school and eighty million at work elsewhere. This is often forgotten by neo-Marxist analysts who say that the process of deschooling must be postponed or bracketed until other disorders, traditionally understood as more fundamental, are corrected by an economic and political revolution. Only if school is understood as an industry can revolutionary strategy be planned realistically. For Marx, the cost of producing demands for commodities was barely significant. Today, most human labour is engaged in the production of demands that can be satisfied by industry which makes intensive use of capital. Most of this is done in school.

Alienation, in the traditional scheme, was a direct consequence of work becoming wage-labour which deprived man of the opportunity to create and be re-created. Now young people are pre-alienated by schools that isolate them from the world of work and pleasure. School makes alienation preparatory to life, thus depriving education of reality and work of creativity. School prepares for the alienating institutionalisation of life by teaching the need to be taught. Once this lesson is learned, people lose their incentive to grow in independence; they no longer find relatedness attractive, and close themselves off to the surprises which life offers when it is not predetermined by institutional definition. And school directly or indirectly employs a major portion of the population. School either keeps men and women for life or makes sure that they will be kept by some institution.

The New World Church is the knowledge industry, both purveyor of opium and the workbench during an increasing number of the years of an individual's life. Deschooling is, therefore, at the root of any movement for human liberation.

The revolutionary potential of deschooling

Of course, school is not, by any means, the only modern institution which has as its primary purpose the shaping of man's vision of reality. Advertising, mass media, and the design components of engineered products play their part in the institutional manipulation of man's demands. But school enslaves more profoundly and more systematically, since only school is credited with the principal function of forming critical judgement and, paradoxically, tries to do so by making learning about oneself, about others, and about nature depend on a pre-packaged process. School touches us so intimately that none of us can expect to be liberated from it by something else.

Many self-styled revolutionaries are victims of school. They see even 'liberation' as the product of an institutional process. Only liberating oneself from school will dispel such illusions. The discovery that most learning requires no teaching can be neither manipulated nor planned. Each of us is personally responsible for his or her own deschooling, and only we have the power to do it. No one can be excused if he fails to liberate himself from schooling. People could not free themselves from the Crown until at least some of them had freed themselves from the established Church. They cannot free themselves from progressive consumption until they free themselves from obligatory school.

We are all involved in schooling from both the side of production and that of consumption. We are superstitiously convinced that good learning can and should be produced in us - and that we can produce it in others. Our attempt to withdraw from the concept of school will reveal the resistance we find in ourselves when we try to renounce limitless consumption and the pervasive presumption that others can be manipulated for their own good. No one is fully exempt from exploitation of others in the schooling process.

School is both the largest and the most anonymous employer of all. Indeed, the school is the best example of a new kind of enterprise, succeeding the guild, the factory, and the corporation. The multi-national corporations which have dominated the economy are now being complemented, and may one day be replaced, by supernationally planned service agencies. These enterprises present their services in ways that make all men feel obliged to consume them. They are internationally standardised, redefining the value of their services periodically and everywhere at approximately the same rhythm.

'Transportation' relying on new cars and superhighways serves the same institutionally packaged need for comfort, prestige, speed, and gadgetry, whether its components are produced by the state or not. The apparatus of 'medical care' defines a peculiar kind of health, whether the service is paid for by the state or by the individual. Graded promotion in order to obtain diplomas fits the student for a place on the same international pyramid of qualified manpower, no matter who directs the school.

In all these cases, employment is a hidden benefit; the driver of a private automobile, the patient who submits to hospitalisation, or the pupil in the schoolroom must now be seen as part of a new class of 'employees'. A liberation movement which starts in school, and yet is grounded in the awareness of teachers and pupils as simultaneously exploiters and exploited, could foreshadow the revolutionary strategies of the future; for a radical programme of deschooling could train youth in the new style of revolution needed to challenge a social system featuring obligatory 'health', 'wealth', and 'security'.

The risks of a revolt against school are unfore-

seeable, but they are not as horrible as those of a revolution starting in any other major institution. School is not yet organised for self-protection as effectively as a nation-state, or even a large corporation. Liberation from the grip of schools could be bloodless. The weapons of the truant officer and his allies in the courts and employment agencies might take very cruel measures against the individual offender, especially if he or she were poor, but they might turn out to be powerless against the surge of a mass movement.

* * *

School has become a social problem; it is being attacked on all sides, and citizens and their governments sponsor unconventional experiments all over the world. They resort to unusual statistical devices in order to keep faith and save face. The mood among some educators is much like the mood among Catholic bishops after the Vatican Council. The curricula of so-called 'free schools' resemble the liturgies of folk and rock masses. The demands of high-school students to have a say in choosing their teachers are as strident as those of parishioners demanding to select their pastors. But the stakes for society are much higher if a significant minority loses its faith in schooling. This would not only endanger the survival of the economic order built on the co-production of goods and demands, but equally the political order built on the nation-state into which students are delivered by the school.

Our options are clear enough. Either we continue to believe that institutionalised learning is a product which justifies unlimited investment, or we rediscover that legislation and planning and investment, if they have any place in formal education, should be used mostly to tear down the barriers that now impede opportunities for learning, which can only be a personal activity.

If we opt for more and better instruction, society will be increasingly dominated by sinister schools and totalitarian teachers. Doctors, generals, and policemen will continue to serve as secular arms for the educator. There will be no winners in this deadly game, but only exhausted frontrunners, a straining middle sector, and the mass of stragglers who must be bombed out of their fields into the rat race of urban life. Pedagogical therapists will drug their pupils more in order to teach them better, and students will drug themselves more to gain relief from the pressure of teachers and the race for certificates. Pedagogical warfare in the style of Vietnam will be increasingly justified as the only way of teaching people the value of unending progress.

Repression will be seen as a missionary effort to hasten the coming of the mechanical Messiah. More and more countries will resort to the pedagogical torture already implemented in Brazil and Greece. This pedagogical torture is not used to extract information or to satisfy the psychic needs of Hitlerian sadists. It relies on random terror to break the integrity of an entire population and make it plastic material for the teachings invented by technocrats. The totally destructive and constantly progressive nature of obligatory instruction will fulfil its ultimate logic unless we begin to liberate ourselves right now from our pedagogical hubris, our belief that man can do what God cannot, namely manipulate others for their own salvation.

Many people are just awakening to the inexorable destruction which present production trends imply for the environment, but individuals have only very limited power to change these trends. The manipulation of men and women begun in school has also reached a point of no return, and most people are still unaware of it. They still encourage school reform, as Henry Ford III proposes less poisonous automobiles.

Daniel Bell says that our epoch is characterised by an extreme disjunction between cultural and social structures, the one being devoted to apocalyptic attitudes, the other to technocratic decision making. This is certainly true for many educational reformers, who feel impelled to condemn almost everything which characterises modern schools - and at the same time propose new schools.

In his The Structure of Scientific Revolutions, Thomas Kuhn argues that such dissonance inevitably precedes the emergence of a new cognitive paradigm. The facts reported by those who observed free fall, by those who returned from the other side of the earth, and by those who used the new telescope did not fit the Ptolomaic world view. Quite suddenly, the Copernican paradigm was accepted. The dissonance which characterises many of the young today is not so much cognitive but a matter of attitudes - a feeling about what a tolerable society cannot be like. What is surprising about this dissonance is the ability of a very large number of people to tolerate it.

The capacity to pursue incongruous goals requires an explanation. According to Max Gluckman, all societies have procedures to hide such dissonances from their members. He suggests that this is the purpose of ritual. Rituals can hide from their participants even discrepancies and conflicts between social principle and social organisation. As long as an individual is not explicitly conscious of the ritual character of the process through which he was initiated to the forces which shape his cosmos, he cannot break the spell and shape a new cosmos. As long as we are not aware of the ritual through which school shapes the progressive consumer - the economy's major resource - we cannot break the spell of this economy and shape a new one.

14

IVAN ILLICH IN AUSTRALIA:

questions and answers

Source: Quality in Australian Education Conference, 1972 (Australian National Union of Students, 1972).

* *

This piece is as interesting for the questions as for the answers. One Questioner: 'I am curious as to your explanation of the practicality of deschooling in Australia... we don't particularly have major problems...' Another Questioner: 'in Victoria... our education system is collapsing.' The session took place at a conference at Melbourne in May 1972 and was attended by 2,000 people.

* *

Questioner: When did the accumulation of knowledge - the knowledge stock you have been talking of - become a commodity of exchange value, and when did this particular exchange value become a particular first necessity?

Dr Ivan Illich: Wait a moment. In this seminar we discussed the following hypothesis. We started out from an analysis not of Marxism, but from the first chapter of the Kapital, where Marx says 'that there are at least three ways in which a product can have use-value without having exchange value. And he mentions concretely fresh water and fresh air and virgin soil - which evidently at this time did still exist - as one category.

As another category, those things which you do not produce for exchange, but simply for somebody else's or your own consumption - or subsistence products to put it very simply. And thirdly, things which you want but to which society doesn't attribute any value, such as pleasure.

My hypothesis was that the following has happened: learning about the world, when it became a product of an institution, translated in the intake of teachings, became a commodity. And this is not necessary, because in most societies most of what people know does not yet have the quality of exchange value, but only of use-value. In most countries, for instance - I don't know about Australian women - the women know how to breast-feed their children; in the United States, they need 6 weeks of teaching inputs for that purpose!

The first thing which has therefore happened, and which I want to subject to analysis, is the transformation into fitness in the world, into something which can be acquired apart from the world, and then, in one way or another, so in everyday life.

Then something else happened. We decided that a democracy cannot exist without all the people having consumed at least a certain minimum of education. I mean Jefferson's statement that we need schools to create voters and rake a few geniuses from the ashes of the masses. This is a quotation.

At that very moment when we need schools in order to have a voter, education has not simply exchange value, but it is attributed the value of a first necessity, without which you do not enjoy your civil rights. Evidently we have gone much further. In the United States - in New York - you cannot be a street cleaner unless you have a high school diploma - which is difficult to believe, at least in South America.

And even more difficult to believe, but quite logical is the fact that this rule was set up by the labour unions.

Why, the military junta in Brazil, which is a very cruel one, and which is the only one in Latin America to use torture for pedagogical purposes: I mean, which picks people up, gives them electric treatment, then sends them back so that others find out what happens to people who have the intention of dissenting; has increased... (laughter).

I am not joking. I am dead serious. I am not joking. I am quite willing to make the statement in front of a court and prove it and give evidence for it. But, this is not the issue here.

You are sometimes perhaps not informed about what is going on with the United States' military technical assistance. The man who was shot in Uruguay a year and a half ago - Vitrioni - we published from CIDOC a year earlier the evidence, given by some of the escapees from the torture sessions, that he taught the Brazilians on his body how to torture more effectively. He was a USAID police specialist.

Forgive me, this is a parenthesis here.

In Brazil the junta raised compulsory schooling from 5 years to 8 years, thereby restricting participation in society of production - consumption to a very tiny group who can go through eight years. This inevitably can't be more than 12 or 15 per cent.

Does that explain what I mean by making education a commodity and then making it of a first necessity? Do you have any further questions on this?

Questioner: Some writers have distinguished between over-development as the opposite of under-development, and talking of over-development as a situation where we have lived in a society in which the conditions of living here could never feasibly be generalised to a whole world population. The world could not live as we live. Now, what I would like to ask you is: is school an institution of an over-developed society and, if it is, is it morally imperative that we look now for new ways of education?

Dr Ivan Illich: There are three things there. You speak about over-development and under-development. You speak about schools. And you still hold pretty tenaciously - to which you have full right - to the idea that people do need education.

Let me deal with the first two aspects. I doubt - you know - that school is an institution of over-developed countries. I rather would like to ask more colleagues and thinkers to take seriously the following hypothesis: that school has today, for the entire world, the function which sociologists, but even people like Toynbee, ascribe to world churches. People formerly were born in original sin and couldn't be Spanish citizens until they were baptised. They remained more or less outside it, and were not even allowed to pay tribute because anything could be taken from them if the King wanted.

Then, in the 16th or the 17th century, the 17th century really, we became much less concerned about people being born or not in what kind of sin, but all people were assumed to be born in original stupidity. And we needed new ritual in order to redeem them and incorporate them into society.

Now, the horrible thing, in my opinion, which has happened - I can speak only about Latin America - in 1963, UNESCO at its meeting in Santiago came to the conclusion that the main obstacle to development in Latin America was a lack of desire of these stupid people to send their children to school. Seven or eight years later, our entire society is hung up on the idea that through schooling - through this ritual - the better world will come. This is a cargo-cult. If we

put on a tie, then Jesus will come and bring an icebox. If we sit enough hours,...

A society therefore can be highly mentally schooled, hung up on this particular ritual, even though a majority of its citizens have no effective access to the second year of schooling. They - and this is the sad thing which we have linguistically verified in Mexico - instead of calling themselves 'poor people' (as we would have said ten years ago), now say, 'I am ignorant' - I'm unschooled.

So schooling is a ritual, an initiation ritual into a world of unlimited progress and production of learning, and consumption of learning, which hooks everybody; though it teaches to the majority that they do not - and cannot - reach the upper levels.

Now, when you spoke about over-development, I would have gone along with you a couple of years ago. I really think that we now are close to the point of speaking in a different way about what is happening to societies. I don't know. I don't know Australia. I do know Canada a little bit, and the United States and Mexico. I think we can say that if you want to develop a theory of development, it is not enough to speak about increasing GNP.

I would like to look a little bit deeper - again going back to Commenius and what I discussed about schools - and speak about what rich countries have succeeded in doing, as a progressive institutionalisation of values, until more and more values of everyday life, which people need, became the output of institutions and thereby people became less and less capable of doing things for themselves; and speak about under-development, human under-development, the breakage of the balance between man and his environment in a society in which institutions disable more men from doing their own thing, than they enable to do their own thing better.

Do I explain that properly? Now school and the idea - not only school - but any other alternative way of increasing the productivity of education is to teach people more and more to rely on institutional inputs.

Questioner: Dr Illich, I'm afraid that in the seminar we had today, far more questions came up than answers, and, if I might ask your indulgence, I have a couple.

Dr Ivan Illich: Good. Please do.

Questioner: Before I do, I'd like to make a point. I've forgotten the phrase you used... 'when education becomes a first necessity'. It seems to me that there is a very good example of this in Rhodesia at the present time, where the argument used by the White Rhodesian government for not giving Black Africans a vote is that they are not educated and not responsible. But you deprive them of the education which would allow them to have the vote.

I think that is a rather nice example of what you suggested, in action.

You might like to comment on that later. The main question I wish to ask is about the implications of what you are suggesting to all of us really. We have been influenced very heavily by the Puritan ethic. I can take two examples of that. The first one is that we have been taught that it is right and desirable to work.

The second one is that it is wrong and highly undesirable to accept charity.

Dr Ivan Illich: Yes.

Questioner: Now, you have openly threatened the role of doctors and implicitly threatened the role of teachers. I imagine that a very large proportion of the audience are in fact teachers, probably dedicated teachers. What can you say to them about this threat to their role, and what their role will be after such change?

Dr Ivan Illich: I can't predict the future. I think we are prophets when we describe what we see happening right now. Forgive me if I repeat again.

I'm referring to the conversation between Goodman and Friedenberg, both men whom I respect very highly, and whom I consider my teachers. Friedenberg said to Paul that you can't go on ridiculing the teaching profession, saying that it is not a legitimate profession, that it is the second oldest profession, and then do nothing in your life but pick up people, interfering with their intimacy, and teach them. There is a contradiction there.

And Goodman said there is a great difference between teaching on one's own responsibility, even promiscuously picking up people, but assuming the full responsibility for the damage you inevitably do when you interfere in someone else's intimacy - even though you might do a lot of good at the same time - and taking an assignment from the madam principal at what time to be in what room for what activities with whom, and shifting the responsibility of what happens to the curriculum, in that school, to the school.

I do therefore believe that the main problem at the moment is a very deep professionalisation which has become possible thanks largely to modern science. For the doctor, this is very clear.

I am certain that New Guinea might need a few biological specialists, but doesn't need a doctor. As long as you have one doctor there, there are cases which have to be referred to him. But I do also believe, as many people do already in Canada and the United States and some South American countries, that even underdeveloped countries would be better off if people knew that they can't refer anything to a higher authority for further fixing up life prolongation.

If a helpful environment, a healthy form of living, mutual care and very simple, but highly sophisticated tools were available to everyone...

Questioner: What you are suggesting seems to be rather similar to what they are trying to do in China?

Dr Ivan Illich: I do believe it is similar. I have much hope that it is similar.

I have unfortunately recently spoken to ten Yugoslav doctors who came back from China, and who told me that I am making illusions that the Chinese consider the barefooted doctor and the non-professional acupuncturist as intermediary technology, as a stop-gap until everybody is a doctor.

I can't believe that as yet. I hope you are right, but there is this white area on the map about which I don't know anything, and therefore can't make any statements.

You had a second question?

Questioner: I'd like you to comment on my remark about Rhodesia being an example...

Dr Ivan Illich: Much more eloquently, the example of Rhodesia was yesterday given in the case of England. Because yesterday we heard that there is nothing which can be done for England. You follow

me? This is intrinsic to life in a growth society, where you make the environment complex and non-transparent, and powerful and efficient to any desirable degree, and then you have to programme people: first to decide who gets to operate the tools, and then, who gets the privileges connected with it. No matter if you are in a capitalist or socialist society. What is done in Rhodesia, which I do not know, is simply openly saying what schools do here.

Questioner: You made some interesting comments today about the unique nature of Australian society for the three days that you have been here.

Dr Ivan Illich: I'm blushing, you know. But there are perhaps things which one may say when everyone knows that one has been only 24 hours in a country, which one may not say after a week. Because it is quite evidently superficial and flair.

Questioner: I am thinking particularly in terms of the Australian situation, that we don't particularly have major problems, like the race problems of the United States, the poverty problems of some South American countries. I am curious as to your explanation of the practicality of deschooling Australia?

Dr Ivan Illich: In that seminar - it was worthwhile for me coming to Australia for the half hour we had together at that particular time, because I saw something which I had never seen before - a group of people, not so very young, but responsible people - responsible in the sense of with certain institutional responsibilities, who realised that we were in the midst of the crisis of industrial society, not a crisis within industrial society - which is about the ownership of tools of distribution of products - but of industrial production, and who didn't have the way out to become activists, but had to face this crisis for which we were not prepared. Even though anguish becomes unbearable.

In the meantime, I wanted to take a rest. But I ran into a book by Ian Turner called The Australian Dream, and read a dozen passages of Australians of the last hundred years each speaking about the future of Australia. My head is spinning: I don't bear to say more.

You understand what we have discussed then?

I can't say - this is Australia - but I have never been with a group of twenty people who had no way out into an immediate political issue. Who couldn't go: stop the war in Vietnam, race integration, development. But who had to face: What does it mean that the world view with which we have lived for 200 years - namely that the world can and must necessarily evolve, industry must become more productive, and more things must be made for more people even if this means that fewer people can do things for themselves - this world view is breaking down.

Now I do personally believe, because you asked me about the future, that we are, I hope at least, very near a major crisis in consciousness. At the moment we still believe that if education doesn't work, that we can do something about it, and we can make it more efficient.

If people have too little money to go to doctors, we can give them more money. If doctors are too self-centred and egotistic, we can control them by law. We should not control them by law, we can better select them or something like that. Whatever the proposals are, we can solve the problem by producing better medicine. If transportation doesn't function, then we can simply order privately owned cars off the roads and have buses which run even faster.

We forget that inevitably we change the geography if we have fast tools. The study of which I spoke before will I hope be published by the end of this year, and it shows that in every society the cost of transportation in terms of time spent on it, increases with higher speed.

We believe that each one of these can be solved individually, and suddenly we will find out that only by accepting limits, which we politically determine, on certain basic tools, can we have a reasonable world in which our old ideals can be made a reality.

Questioner: This follows on from the statements you made this afternoon, in one of the seminars on the question of authority, where you said that one needs to be, as an individual, responsible for the feeling that others have about me or for that matter the action which others might take in relation to me.

I can accept that. I personally agree with that. But I have observed in group situations for instance that at least in the short-term, some people can dominate, and if that initial dominance in the short-term is crucial, then it can, in fact, have long-term connotations.

I really don't wish to actually cop out of this feeling of individual responsibility for what other people feel or do for me, but I am still sort of doubtful about this question of responsibility.

Could I ask you to comment on that?

Dr Ivan Illich: This is the question with which I really opened my remarks this evening.

There is something highly ambiguous in having as good acoustics as there are in a large room like this one - it is quite a technological achievement - but there is something very dangerous about it too. You don't fill up a hall like this one because people want to engage in a conversation, but because they ascribe to you the authority of performing an act.

Now, when I first landed in Australia, I was asked, 'Why do you refuse so strictly to go on television?' I said, 'I won't submit to the indignity of being shown to other people when I am in personal intercourse with you. Other people whom I don't know, somewhere else. ' Television is inevitably a demagogic tribune. It provides for a few the possibility - because of their role, not because of their true personality - to impress a majority.

Now, in a world in which institutions become powerful, beyond a certain point at which technology makes it possible for a few people to talk to millions or ten millions, you inevitably have a regression of a sense of personal contact.

For instance, it is the first time in a year and a half, I think, that I speak at a large meeting. Had I known that this was to be this large, I would have said no, because I do believe it is much more efficient if you think through what we have discussed along together, and discuss it with others, rather than have an expert in explaining his ideas, broadcast them.

Now, the basic question you wanted to raise... ?

Questioner: It is the question of responsibility which you raise. We were at the time discussing authority. I'm not sure that exactly answers what I'm thinking, because the question of authority swings on a concept of responsibility of the individual; that nobody is in fact an authority. But it swings on the idea of a person who...

Dr Ivan Illich: Nobody is really an authority. Both responsibility and authority mean something quite different when you say school is the place - as we heard yesterday - the teacher is the man who knows how to teach football really, but he can associate parents who perhaps don't know the right way of doing it - and I'm exaggerating, I'm caricaturing.

Authority means something entirely different than responsibility when you ascribe them to an institution, and when you take responsibility on your authority.

In the first case, the relationship of the person over whom you have authority is an impersonal relationship - what Jaceleu would call an institutionalised value. In the second case, it is a personal form of intercourse: relatedness between two neighbours.

In the first case, if you have an institution which is responsible for the education of a populace, you can be optimistic or pessimistic that it will do it. You have expectations. On the other hand, when I have a man or a woman who takes on responsibility for me - and therefore a certain authority - I don't have expectations; I have hope that he will care for me.

Unless we learn how to distinguish between institutionalised values, in relations to which we have expectations, from hopefulness and anomie and despair, the whole issue cannot be discussed.

My theory is that what generally has been called 'development', was the development of an expectant attitude towards satisfaction through institutional production, and it has become so overwhelming that most people now - you see it in language very clearly, use nouns rather than verbs.

Larry Grimes - a friend of mine, a linguist in Cuernavaca - has done some studies on this. He points out that over the last 25, even over the last 80 years, in all Western languages, there has been a quick transition from the use of verbs to the use of nouns. 'Do you have an education? How much education do you have?' rather than 'What do you know? Have you learned this?'

Now, in Western societies, people even have fun - have work - have sex... to such a point that the verb describing these activities is either unused or unpronounceable!

(Applause)

This is the issue which I wanted to raise. This leads then to people - no matter whether they get it in school or outside of school - expecting to get an education. I don't care if you find more efficient ways of doing it.

An education which is constituted of subjects. The concept of the subject matter is an absurd one. I find it always easier for this purpose to use an image rather than complex words. A brilliant description of this you find in Michael Fouco's book, where he uses a Latin American author to describe what he means by a heterotopia. In a Chinese encyclopaedia he found the following listing of animals - those which belong to the King, those which are dragons, those which are suckling pigs, those which have four legs, etc. , etc.

Fromm puts it in different terms: Bureaucrats divide humanity into those who have a college degree, those who are Jews, those who ride bicycles, and those who wear glasses. This is essentially what the institutional responsibility of schools is in relation to a society - to provide people with an education which comes as this and this and this.

And when you only think it through, it is a heterotopia. It becomes almost anguishing when you try to think what it means: somehow to see all these things in one space... but there is no space into which they all fit. Such irresponsibility can be taken on only by an institution or by a bureaucrat employed by the institution in order to assume it. This authority is quite evidently illegitimate.

Questioner: I don't know how to ask this question, because it is very hard for me to ask and I think very hard for you to answer, but, without asking it, I think that what we are doing is so much academic talking.

Most people agree that we have a hopelessness about the future. Most of us are students or teachers or educationists, and we keep doing what we are doing because we have some sort of hope that what we are going to produce are children who are critical, creative, compassionate; and that might do something. But mostly we don't believe that. That is a rationale we keep going.

We talk and think about a society in which people will learn to live by living, yet we all know that this cannot happen in this society we are in.

And no-one shied away from the word 'revolution'. Our society as it is cannot operate other than in the way it does. Or in some modified way like we heard last night; which is really no different, just the same except that it looks a bit nicer.

The question is: What do we do? Do we keep on doing the things we are doing in schools? What can we say, what can we do, what would you do if you were in Australia, if you were us - a teacher or a student?

I know it is a hard question, because you don't know the Australian context, but - what can we do? And without that, all we are doing is just talking.

Dr Ivan Illich: Your question is not unfair, but it is personal. It is personal at least on two different levels. You ask me a question which I say is particularly personal because I will give you an answer which will allow you immediately to say, 'You have it easy to give it'. I made up my mind 30 years ago that by becoming a Catholic priest - for whatever reasons, leave it alone - I would not procreate children. Therefore I am a 45 year old man who has no children, and therefore what I now say can be cruel. Perhaps this also helps me to see certain things which I probably could not face if I had my own children, because there is a relationship of flesh with one's own children which no amount of charity can overcome.

What I see is that children who are born today are children of a horrible period. One of the difficulties which you will probably have in sharing my vision about where the world is moving is that you want to have your child and place it into this world, and therefore you say that it cannot be as bad as the Club of Rome outlines: there must be something wrong with the computer.

So, I accept this challenge.

I do believe that at present our major institutions or tools are growing at a rate which is throwing the balance of the world off, not just in one, but in several directions. And irreversibly.

Let me mention six dimensions to you.

I do believe that the rate of growth of our transformation of nature into vulgar, durable junk will, unless checked in a very short time, throw out the physical balance between the human animal and his environment. This is a philosophical issue. You cannot transform nature into a culture product and not kill a man. A very good example is a recent editorial in the Bulletin for Atomic Scientists which takes issue with the people who say that we have to pass through a stationary state economy, and says that there is no evidence, for instance, that man could not survive as the only animal in the world as long as his intestinal bacteria remain intact. Imagine a world in which you continue to live with your intestinal bacteria!

There is a second unbalance which is just as critical, and which I would call the radical monopoly of tools over human energy. The one resource which is very basically, equally distributed over the world is human energy. Each man has a manpower. It is only by creating increasingly more powerful tools that fewer people become more effective or efficient or productive, and therefore earn more, and most people, in fact, become less effective and can do less things for themselves. Fewer people can work, fewer women can breast-feed, or recognise pneumonia, or deliver a baby.

This radical monopoly of tools over man's energy is a second, not yet fully recognised unbalance, just as serious as is the unbalance produced by pollution and depletion.

A third one is one which I would call the creation of a demand for increasing amounts of education, in the sense of which I have just spoken. As the world becomes more manmade, fewer people can learn just by living in it, and more people need more education in order to feel at home in it. And all over the world, in the last 20 years, the cost of education has risen faster than the cost of any other production.

Now a subsystem which grows faster than the system, soon becomes the system. It is silly to speak about education as a superstructure, or as one of the institutions of society.

Fourth, with the rate of obsolescence and renewal to which we are now committed - and you can't stop it overnight, I am just pointing out how serious the matter is - inevitably you polarise privileges more and more.

You might perhaps see it less in Australia than anywhere else - this is my first impression - because in a strange way you are very privileged, having a very privileged relation of resources to man, and so on.

The rich inevitably become richer, not only in capitalist countries, but also in socialist countries committed to higher production. Because even though you might equalise personal incomes, increasingly privileges go with the job, and only he who is considered a knowledge capitalist of high order - who holds the highest knowledge stock certificate - is given a secretary or the privileges which men in that society value.

Fifth, law. In the old, especially the Anglo-Saxon way, law becomes impossible as the rate of renewal of the tools of a society increases faster. Why? Because we believe that law, I mean common law, is a reasonable judgement of peers about how a man acts under ordinary circumstances. But how should somebody over 30 judge what is an ordinary circumstance for somebody under 30?

This is structural. And finally institutions become increasingly, not simply dysfunctional, but produce negative outputs, as we have seen in the case of education, health, transportation, and I could show you in many other areas.

In front of this almost inevitable trend to a catastrophic imbalance, what can you do?

I think that you should stop and not rush in and do something right away. And see clearer and clearer how anguishing this problem is. Do I make myself understood?

Then, I do believe, decide with a few friends what you personally can do without. There are many things which you can do without - not because you want to give them to somebody else - but simply because these things which you need increasingly make it impossible for you to do things in a way for yourself which is really human and which most people could share.

I am speaking of voluntary poverty as the only way to own the earth, on a personal level.

Third, begin to talk with people about the issue you have raised, but with the intention not of going and doing something but of seeing more clearly. I do believe that this is the only political inversion which you can do, because I do expect a major crisis to result from the convergence of the various institutional crises in which we are caught.

At the moment of that major crisis - as in every new crisis - a new opinion-finding leadership can emerge. It is most important that then not a new party emerge which wants power, but that lots of people who have thought through carefully and painfully what the reason for the crisis was - over-institutionalisation - be available to provide an explanation. And in a democracy - as this still hopes to be - a voting majority can form.

A voting majority in a democracy is not bound together by some kind of ideological programme; it is the result of many different interest groups, each one, for a very different reason, wanting the same law passed. For instance, a speed limit. Some people want it because they know it is rational not to have speeds above 20 miles an hour. It is enormously more than you have available for effective locomotion today, unless you take a plane.

I feel very guilty about taking planes. But, if I abandon taking planes, I would not be as immobile or as slow as my father or grand-father, but much closer to my great-great-grand-father of Clipper days.

Then, some other people don't want cars because they don't want inequality. Other people will not want cars because they don't want pollution. Others because they want a different pattern of urbanisation. So, for entirely different reasons, various groups must see clearly that for a fundamental reason, a speed limit on all transportation would not be unreasonable.

And you are just as qualified as the best engineer to think these very simple thoughts, and to take personal responsibility that some other people will come to see how evident they are.

Do I explain?

Questioner: You explain, but where I am doubting is whether we can do that. I think people have been trying to do things by personal example or by talking to people, for centuries. I don't think that they have got very far. It seems to me - and this is

the hopelessness we talked about - that the ruling power groups in our society hold sufficient cultural power over what people think that what we say is meaningless.

Now, if we wait for a crisis... I suppose that is all you can do...

Dr Ivan Illich: This is the only thing which I know that I can do. Perhaps I was wrong to say you should do this.

I am deeply convinced, and of this I am certain, that the necessity of limiting the power of certain tools - to use this very broad phrase - will become evident in the next two or three years, and a general theme for discussion. I fear very much that the limitation, the decision of what is speedy enough, will be made by technocrats - bureaucratic fascists - rather than being submitted to political decision.

And when the speeds will be set, they will be set on the maximum limit which is still tolerable for industry and provides industry and the producer with maximum income and power.

I do believe that it is at this moment very important to begin to speak about a popular vote for limits. Go into politics...

Questioner: Can I ask you just one last, yes-no question? Are you basically optimistic about the future? Do you think we will overcome the anguish or are you, like so many others of us, just hoping?

Dr Ivan Illich: I have made a distinction between expectation and hope. I am very pessimistic and hopeful.

Questioner: Following on from that question about awareness: I think perhaps that a lot of people would feel that it will take a long time before something like that will come about, and the whole concept of a deschooled society will probably take a while to be accepted. Within the educational sphere, do you see something like a community school or an open classroom as a stepping stone towards something like that, or would you prefer to wait and see it all break open?

Dr Ivan Illich: That would be terroristic, cruel and sadistic.

While in Sydney for two days, somebody showed me his little school for Aboriginals. That is what you call people here because you can't face the fact that they have... they are no more aboriginal than most people here - but they were black. I just checked where they came from.

Anyway - and since I am talking about and criticising a concrete situation in Australia, can I ask the reporters not to report this? - I saw eight children in a very simple room with five mothers taking care of them in pre-school education. The aboriginal mothers... talking in all this pseudo-educational language.

The room was filled up with seventh grade illustrations. Supposedly these people come from a tremendously art producing society. And yet I had to say how beautiful that these people take so seriously making the life of these children as good as they can.

The question of what do I do for this one person who is my neighbour and in front of me, is an entirely different question from would I advocate what I called before the dispersal and rooting of school in society as a solution to the present educational problem.

It's nonsense. You only prolong the agony of a society which has to educate its people for an absurd life. Because you can't lead an absurd life unless you are carefully programmed for it. A life of never ending expectations, which only knows what is better and never what is good. For politics, we are satisfied with priorities and not with saying where our limits lie. Imagine a country which couldn't decide where its limits lay. That's what Hitler stood for.

Do I answer your question?

Questioner: Yes. It is just that may be it will take a long, long time to come about. Do we just wait and hope.

Dr Ivan Illich: You take these kids: I wish yoú would take it as a promiscuous lover rather than as in the second oldest profession!

One recent example: a group of Mexican workers stuck somewhere in California invited me to talk with them for an evening. They took most of their children out of school years ago, and had decided that among the six families with 17 children in that group, each day one person would take the day off work and make himself responsible for the entire group of young people.

I was tremendously impressed when I found out that they had never together institutionally planned what Mrs Sanchez will do when she is responsible for the 17 children. You see, for simple people who have their heart and guts in the right place', things still function.

I would now ask the people who were at the meetings this afternoon to now give precedence in asking questions to those who are new this evening.

I used the first questions really in order to go on with my exposé. Since there are quite a few people who want to ask questions, I will be as quick as I can. I don't like quick answers, especially when you have my kind of character and brain, because one becomes easily flippant or offensive. So forgive me if I am quick in my answers, it is not meant to be offensive.

There is one more question which was asked by three people: how do we find out what is going on in Cuernavaca, Mexico where I am associated at CIDOC? I am in no way the founder, much less the director of it. We earn our economic independence by teaching, in an extremely rigorous and scholastic way, adults who want to learn Spanish, how to speak it in two months. This gives us economic independence for an international thinkery and publications centre and library. I won't speak about it, though many people ask me, because I don't know what is going on at a given moment. Anybody can take the initiative to offer a seminar or a course there, as long as he observes three rules.

The three rules are: The organisation or operation of violence against the Mexican Government institution is ruled out during class hours announced in the catalogue. Second, you may state your tuition fee - not more than $25 - but you may not collect it before you have submitted to a two-hour examination by your students. And third, you may not engage in classroom activities which our gardeners consider lewd... without closing the curtains.

Anybody who wants information should write to Cuernavaca in Mexico, post office box 479, and we automatically send you off a catalogue. There is no list of people to whom this is regularly sent; you have to write every four months.

Questioner: I am an economics student who faces this next term with the prospect of studying the economics of education, which fairly simply, is the role of human capital in the growth process.

I want to talk to you about the long run stationary state. As I see it, the problem stems from our desire for full employment. Because we are a capitalist society - though not only because of that - we measure our growth in terms of GNP, and growth is investment. We need increasing investment to maintain full employment. If we are going to stop growth, i. e. stop investment, then we are going to cause unemployment.

As I see it, where education comes in to it, is that we need to somehow eradicate or reject our concept or our need for full employment and, at the same time, destroy our concept of unemployment, and replace it, through the educative process, with full people with inner contentment, who don't want a new car every other year, and who are content to be themselves.

This is not incompatible with your idea of self-imposed poverty, but the reason I wouldn't recommend this as a policy is that if we act individually, then the process is, on the one hand, too slow and, secondly, that doesn't eradicate the need for full employment, for the government can step in with fiscal policies and someone else can come in and increase his consumption, thereby replacing ours.

I don't have so much a question, as a comment on that role.

Dr Ivan Illich: Let me make a comment back. Read Martin Karnoi from UCLA, Sam Bowles from Harvard, and Herman Bailey. If you will write to me for them, I will send them to you. I do think there is a major breakthrough by these young educational economists which you should be aware of.

I met two professors from La Trobe University, who are aware of this.

Questioner: What you have been proposing seems very appealing to us in our kind of society. I might make an observation about our kind of society, and that is, that education as a commodity, is becoming redundant. PhDs and graduates are finding it difficult to be employed, and most of us who are concerned are in this category.

The expectations that we have had are not capable now of being fulfilled. So, consequently, I understand what we have been talking about today and what you have been talking about tonight. This wouldn't have been as easy for me to understand, it wouldn't have been as interesting to this large number of people even two years ago, which indicates the rapidity of the change.

This seems understandable and desirable in our kind of society, but we have, as a result of our technology which has caused this in part, lots of goods which we enjoy, which we could choose to retain, which we can give up if we don't think they are important.

The question then is: is it an elitist position for us in this privileged position to urge this sort of a solution on underdeveloped countries who are not able to choose?.

Dr Ivan Illich: I am grateful that you bring up this objection, which is made by the rich university graduates from under-developed countries all over the world, from the people who want to play up to them - students in rich countries - and by the leaders from the slums.

To this I can say only two things. You raise a question which is emotion-loaded in a very quiet and beautiful way.

My normal answer to this, because others want to raise it much more belligerently, is: I will not have my past privileges thrown in my face as rendering me incompetent for speaking the truth.

Secondly, I do recognise that education is the most evil form of riches because once a man has been certified a knowledge capitalist - nothing, not even a concentration camp, can wash from him his status as a more precious person than others.

Third, I do want to belong to an elite which is dissident from the one legitimate elite at this moment - the scholastic elite - the school-certified elite - because I do know that true revolutionary changes happen always at least with the leadership and collaboration of a dissident group in the elite.

And finally, I can assure you that most of these ideas which, according to you, two years ago you could not have discussed with the majority of people assembled here, 2 years ago, 5 years ago, 20 years ago, if you had discussed them in these terms, you could have easily discussed them on every plaza of a Mexican village.

Let me again take speed as an example. I do feel that the idea which I suggested of a 20 miles per hour speed limit on transportation in Australia, seems some kind of a crazy implausible suggestion to the majority of people who have heard me talk about it. They will probably write it off. On the other hand, I also know that 99% of the world's population outside of a few rich countries, last year did not move even once over a distance of 15 miles in the period of an hour. For them such a speed limit is irrelevant.

Let us have the guts to figure out that some of us perhaps speak about very simple things in very normal terms, even though we have consumed education.

Questioner: Just one thing; I think it is a yes-no answer.

You are then against the current view of most under-developed countries that compulsory education is their salvation?

Dr Ivan Illich: Of course.

Questioner: I would just like to ask: within the framework of our absurd society, what do you think is the best environment to bring up children so that when the crisis really comes to the crunch, they can think clearly for themselves? I mean in practical forms, in terms of us in Australia.

Dr Ivan Illich: That is a very personal question which you should ask your girl.

Questioner: Yes, but in Australia people are still going to go on teaching, they're not going to abandon the Education Department tomorrow.

Dr Ivan Illich: I can answer only with a sentence which someone didn't quote quite correctly.

Jean-Paul Sartre said that everybody is forever responsible for what has been done to him, even though perhaps he has nothing else - no other choice is open to him, and he can't do anything else but accept this responsibility.

Questioner: I wish to return to the question of what we should do, which I feel has been the most disturbing question we have discussed today.

You have discussed brilliantly the problems in education, the problems in society which, implicitly, are caused by society and a world based on privilege and the ownership of society in the hands of a few, and the subjugation of the many to that few.

Now, what has come across to me - and this may well not be what was in your mind - is that the line of development then follows this way: the sort of changes in education and the ideas that you advocate cannot take place if they are going - in the society and world as it is - to contravene the privileges of the few who have them. Therefore, these changes will only be able to occur in a crisis. The nature of the system is such that a crisis is inevitable. Therefore, wait for the crisis and be prepared to act. Now...

Dr Ivan Illich: To think and speak clearly, to understand; I didn't go so far as to say to act.

Questioner: Now, it seems to me that there is a point that you have left out - you have included one point after this - that the crisis may be disastrous to human life on this planet. That after this crisis - or in the process of it - there may be no human at the end of it.

The point that you have left out is that the growth process of this crisis that we are already experiencing in the developed countries - or the over-developing countries - is being experienced far more painfully in the under-developed, or under-developing countries. Vietnam and Latin America are victims of our growth crisis.

Now, the question is whether it is enough to stand by, concerned with the crisis developing at home, whilst this inordinately more painful crisis is being experienced in the under-developing countries. Or whether we should try to force a crisis here which will solve the problems before the inevitable consumer/technological crisis comes upon us.

The question is: how can your educational reform ideas be integrated as part of a weapon needed to shatter the structure of the society, to shatter the privileged structure sufficiently in order to, first of all, stop the exploitation of the under-developed countries, and, secondly, to stop the developing crisis which is going to come here very soon?

Dr Ivan Illich: This is a brilliant exposition of a basic question.

To direct this question to the entire audience is in itself to make this whole seminar a success. I am a man who stands with one foot in one world and another in another world, and I question one of your expressions and one of your concepts, only.

The expression which I question is 'the approach of a crisis' and the 'first forewarnings of a crisis', because if the crisis is useful, then it will be a sudden crisis. A sudden shattering crisis of consciousness such as the French Revolution. Such sudden changes have happened before.

Second, I doubt very much that one can force the crisis, through anything else but developing an increasingly acute awareness of what is already happening.

And now I come to the substantive point.

I doubt very much that we are still in the early 60s, when the difference between what the developed rich countries produced and the poor was then more painfully felt in the poor than in the rich. I do believe that places like New York or Chicago are really good demonstration models of the crisis now. The crisis which is developing now of over-institutionalisation of values, is much more painful for the people who live at $6000 on the poverty line than for the people whom I know in South America who most of the time, in most circumstances of life, know how to learn, how to feed their babies, how to cook for themselves, how to move, how to house themselves, who still use verbs and not nouns.

Questioner: But the point which I wish to elicit from you, and I think you have half-answered it, is, first of all, I agree with you that there are people here now who are suffering more than those in South America, but, secondly, the people in South Vietnam are suffering more than that.

The point I wish to take from that is, when you talk about Chicago and New York, I think one also has to talk about the things that people are doing now in order to raise people's consciousness of the crisis that is impending, not just talking amongst each other, but actually trying to highlight it in sometimes extremely violent or provocative forms of action.

Such things as demonstrations outside the Democratic convention, such things as...

Dr Ivan Illich: There is no question that show processes can change a subjection to the draft, to school, to the hospital, to a mental asylum, to a corrective prison, to whatever you want. Can change a subjection to a participation in the process of society which is supposed to produce value.

Demonstration, public testimony are at extreme personal costs. It is much more costly to abstain from compulsory transportation in Melbourne and therefore to have to take a street-cleaner's job next door, than to go to prison. And make people understand why.

I do think that when the crisis comes upon us, a few hundred people who did the right thing very lucidly and clearly can give more orientation than the largest, most powerful means of public communication.

Questioner: I think you would agree though that the two would have to be integrated?

Dr Ivan Illich: OK. Agreed. Let's be realistic.

Let me put one other thing. One of the most powerful things we can do - you and I and all of us - is to lose faith in the claimed effectiveness of our institutions. A teacher who gives not a damn about school, and yet who goes there because he wants to meet Johnny and Mary and he tells the others that he really isn't interested in them, might be a more important man than one who tries to produce a new curriculum for the entire country.

Questioner: The question I asked at the end has again been half-answered: can your ideas be used by people involved in the educational scene at the moment to try and highlight and shock the system to be taking action now to force people's understanding up.

Dr Ivan Illich: For theoretical reasons, I cannot answer the question, because this is a question which must be tested in practice.

Questioner: I find a lot of the things that have been said here tonight very interesting and stimulating. One thing that is very strong in my mind is that I have recently been to China with a group of teachers for the main purpose of looking at education in China.

It is very clear that the education system in China serves the interests of a different class than the education system in Australia. This is becoming recognised by teachers, especially in Victoria, because our education system is collapsing.

We can see clearly that it is the children of the working class that get the worst end of the stick all around. That is the main thing.

The second point I would like to make is that it seems somehow wrong to go from where we are to a position of idealism, where we are doing the right thing in individual terms, without looking at what the main problem is to do next, and how to do it.

Again, in China, their education system is not in a fixed form; it is changing all the time at all levels. The children, the teachers and the workers in China form the revolutionary committee at each school, and together they decide how to go forward.

Now, it seems surely that we should tackle problems one step at a time, summing up from as wide a source of information as we can. What is the main step to take?

I believe that you haven't been to China. Do you - as a man with your obvious intellect - intend to go to China? We would really like to hear you after you have been.

Dr Ivan Illich: The real change in China is the limiting of most government functions to the size of a commune, that is a scaling down of society where it really counts. The type of education system is a consequence of such a voluntary accepted limitation. But the real decision making - within the limits set by central planning - goes on in the commune level.

This is a political revolution of extraordinary extent. This makes a society reasonable, and in it you can experiment a hundred different ways to prepare people or to help people grow into it.

It is essentially a political question.

Questioner: Do you know when you are going to China? Do you have any idea?

Dr Ivan Illich: I have an invitation for next year.

Questioner: Could I urge you to go anyway?

Questioner: Dr Illich, we have been conditioned to expect institutional authority - I think by and large in the Western communities anyway - and this leads us to questions of you on the future, and to ask you to answer, to the best of your ability, what can be done: I don't want to ask you a question so much as to ask you to comment.

We have a sort of two-dimensional attitude towards survival, I think. If there is a crisis we tend to think of how many dollars we can spend or how much schooling we can give people to cure it. In effect, we are changing our tails.

On your point about political survival, we can look to the north of us and say there is Indonesia with a hundred million people and there are elites which are favourable to us at the moment, so we must help them in order to ensure that nobody else takes over the country. And in doing that we would, of course, separate the elite further from the people.

There are more basic things happening in our Western societies: to coin a phrase, it is a psychic threat to our psychic survival. People are going mad in vacuums. They are so far removed from the basic things like breast-feeding...

Dr Ivan Illich: I'll give a good example of this.

The US State Department is distributing a pamphlet in Latin America which describes the great privileges which democracy has produced for United States' citizens. One of these privileges listed is that eighteen point something per cent of all Americans can receive mental care! I am not joking.

Questioner: You were talking about different groups wanting the same thing for different reasons. It occurred to me that there would conceivably be lots of different groups which want different things, and their demands may not be reconcilable in the terms of a majority...

Dr Ivan Illich: Wouldn't they polarise? It would become an issue, and on each side of the issue is an otherwise crazy ideological assembly, but they stand on two sides of this concrete issue.

Questioner: This sort of tied in with what my group was talking about in the seminar today on curriculum. What I was going to ask you was: must there be a structure after the crisis?

Dr Ivan Illich: Let me answer in a broader way. I do not want to be taken for a romanticist simply because I say that there is such a thing as natural limits, for humanity. I don't want to be taken for a Luddite - people who destroyed machines - simply because I say we can use science in order to... we can put penicillin, a very powerful tool, into the hands of most people.

I think I told you today of the black girl who was in Cuernavaca for six months. Half a year later, she rang me up from America in need of a lawyer. She was arrested for possession of drugs and unfair competition with the testing lab. Her lawyer got witnesses in who showed that no public health service in all of the United States succeeded in retesting all those treated after 5-6 weeks, as she did.

I don't want to be taken for a Luddite because I speak against use of science or the increasing institutional output. In the same way, I don't want to be taken for somebody who doesn't believe in the necessity of institution of law for human beings to be free.

I am inclined in a deep sense, as a Christian and as a human being, for anarchy. But an anarchist is a person who recognises that we need a few very stringent 'don'ts', and as little 'do's' as possible.

Questioner: Could I raise a kind of practical problem about the planning of education policies in an affluent country such as Australia. Now, in a city like Melbourne, generally speaking, the poor live in the north and the west and the rich live in the east and the south. For a long time, all the people who went to university came from the privileged private schools. Since the Second World War, there has been a movement for public high schools and for more children from lower and middle-class homes to go to university.

Now, the present emphasis by political parties is to attempt compensatory education to advantage the poor so that they, in a sense, can climb up that ladder, or go through the funnel, as you have been saying.

Now, I can quite see the beauty and simplicity and logic of what you have been saying in relation to a post-revolutionary situation, but for people who are planning education policies for the immediate future - for people who are already at the broad end of the funnel - what sort of advice can you give? Is deschooling an appropriate...?

Dr Ivan Illich: Deschooling is not a policy. It

is something which is happening. I tell you that I am terribly worried about the havoc done by this word, of a title chosen by an editor.

Questioner: Alright. Would you say that the priority in a country like Australia, where there are relatively great distances between the rich and the poor in terms of the exercise of power, where the important decisions are made by the comparatively few people who have received the advantage of the education system...

Dr Ivan Illich: Yesterday, Mr Jackson pointed out very clearly to us that, instead of having 3% working class children, you have 5% of them among the decision makers. In most countries, being unionised, to be a worker means to belong into the exploiting upper quarter of society, because all people who are unionised have a certain chance to get their children through grammar school, and get access to a hospital, which three-quarters of society don't have. Being a unionist thereby means to be an exploiter.

Questioner: Alright. Two questions arise. One: should we have a greater public emphasis here within the present school system, on compensatory education, so that the base of the ladder is in a sense broadened?

The second major question that comes up is the fear that even in the long term the people who have the closest access to educational tools, as in the traditional education system, may still outdistance the poor who have access to the kind of educational resources which you have written about in your book, but who do not have the formal training.

Dr Ivan Illich: The real issue, if I were in your position, I would deal with it legally. There are three cases which the Supreme Court of the United States has decided this year which are fascinating from this point of view.

Exactly a year and two months ago, Chief Justice Burger, speaking for the unanimous Court, decided that the Duke Power Company committed an act of discrimination in denying a man advancement from coal shovelling to secretarial work for the simple reason that he did not have a high school degree and could not pass a high school equivalency test. The US Supreme Court said that the Duke Power Company had to show that, in this man's particular case, schooling was job-related.

You have here a first step to disestablish the measurement of people over consumption of education, or by the performance in analogy to people who do not know how to do a job but have an education.

Questioner: Can I comment on this first case. While we would all rejoice in this man's advancement because of what the court did, it still means that he is in a particular job situation which is likely to be inherited by his children, and their children.

Dr Ivan Illich: Of course. But the only way that I can recommend - this is very important - I would mostly be concerned with the rate of retention of any Australian to be submitted to a test of religion and logically therefore, to a test of education.

Questioner: I would agree with the logic of that, but isn't it going to mean that the disadvantaged and their children will suffer? While one would agree that they should be subjected to no legal penalty, and theoretically to no economic penalty, in fact they are not going to get the jobs because they are not going to be within striking position of them.

Dr Ivan Illich: Very few, increasingly few people from the rich will get the desirable jobs if we live in a world of constant progress, of constant amalgamation of corporations. There are increasingly fewer multi-national corporation presidents.

I cannot deal with this except through an entirely different retooling of society. Not deschooling, but retooling of society.

The second case was where the California court held that Mr Priest, the Superintendent of Schools, was discriminating against people where school tax was paid on assessed value but the education was worth only $1,000 a year, while in the neighbourhood next door in Hollywood somebody else paid only 1% tax and got $2,000 worth of education for his child. The court ordered that education expenditure be equalised and thereby threw the entire US education system into a crisis, which Mr Nixon now tries to solve by substituting for regressive education a major sales tax, which is a regressive form of taxation.

Third. In the Amish case, the court held that a man cannot be compelled to participate in any ritual, and that schooling constitutes a ritual.

I would therefore, if I were you, look in entirely different direction for allies.

Now, I want to mention one thing, since we now know each other. I have little papers here of things which come to my mind. There is still one question which I fully expected to get and which I was prepared to answer, but which I did not get. I was absolutely certain to get a question on women's lib., but none came up!

That surprised me very much, because I really left myself with a very important thing I wanted to say, and for which I would have used the case of women's lib.

Questioner from the crowd: What are your views on women's lib.?

Dr Ivan Illich: I expected, exactly, somebody to do me that favour.

In a society in which tools become increasingly more powerful, production becomes increasingly more capital intensive. Inevitably, there are fewer and fewer jobs to which we can impute high levels of productivity. These jobs are reserved for the elite, as is the one we have discussed - schooling. Another one is by introducing sex differences.

As long as we believe in unlimited growth of products and production, inevitably we produce also, structurally, more and more unemployment. This is because capital intensive productivity provides fewer jobs. It can create provisionally more jobs in the service sector, because we can create more need for schools.

And you can give me the argument that we need schools to create employment for the people whom we make unemployed by capital intensive production. But, what we are witnessing at this moment is really consumer resistance in the service sector. People cease to want to consume more of something which they find out is a sham commodity. The culturally privileged don't learn; they accumulate imputed values.

Now, I don't know anything about Australia, but in several other key countries one of the most interesting movements at the moment seems to be a new awareness of women and of their situation in the economy, which very frequently and in a combatant way, takes the form of saying: we have the same privileges to become destroyers, aggressors, as men have. We have a right to just as well-paid jobs, to which you can impute as much destructiveness or productivity or however you want to call it, as that to which men have access.

I do see in the women's liberation movement, very interesting instances of this already: an important base swell from the ground which says that neither men nor women can afford increasingly more capital intensive production: we must return to the type of life and everyday employment which at this moment in our society we call typically women's work. Caring, concerning, do it yourself, cleaning, shifting from one place to the other.

I simply wanted to point out that this 'deschooling' - the loss of legitimacy of schools - unless it goes hand in hand with a new revision of the sexual division of labour, cannot succeed.

I just want to leave you with this issue for discussion, about the relationship between the crisis in schools and the crisis which usually goes under the name of women's liberation.

When questioning the need for further schooling, I am really questioning the need for unlimited growth of the division of labour. One of the important forms of division of labour is rooted, not at all in schools, but in assumptions about sex roles.

Thank you. It was a real pleasure and honour.

15

W. SENTEZA KAJUBI

Is the school an obsolete institution?

Source: Educating the Young People of the World, edited by Alice Miel and Louise Berman, Association for Supervision and Curriculum Development, NEA, 1970.

* *

A voice from the Third World - Kajubi was Director of the National Institute of Education, Makerere University College, Uganda. This paper was given to the World Conference on Education at Asilomar, California, in March 1970. Kajubi reports: 'the school system is being criticised. It is regarded by many political and educational leaders as a means of disorienting the children from the realities of life as it is in developing countries, and as an institution which is failing to respond to the needs of society in the new nations.' But he concludes: 'there can be no question about the enormous value of the formal school, and the pivotal role it will continue to occupy in the educational systems of the world. ' See also Reading 20 - Julius Nyerere: Education for self-reliance, and Quotational Bibliography - BOWLES, Samuel; CASTLE, E. B. ; CALLAWAY, Archibald; FREIRE, Paulo; GRABOWSKI, Stanley; HUBERMAN, Michael; SCHOOL OF BARBIANA.

* *

Today, 'going to school' is one of the most important activities in which human beings engage. Of the $3\frac{1}{2}$ billion inhabitants of the earth, about 400 million, or the equivalent of the entire population of India, are engaged in full-time schooling. In 1970 there are probably 57 million youngsters in the public and private schools of the United States alone; and 90 per cent of all young people in that country remain at school until they are 17 years of age. In Africa the numbers are small; nevertheless, in 1963 over 26 million children, or about 10 per cent of the entire population of the Continent, were engaged in full-time schooling.

Large architectural firms around the world are becoming increasingly concerned with the designing and building of schools. The Five-Year Plans of Developing Countries devote disproportionately large sections to this aspect of national development. There is no doubt that the phenomenon of schooling has become a major preoccupation of all societies of the world and a first call on the resources of all nations. The human race has developed an unwavering faith in the power of education through formal schooling.

The enormous and growing commitment to school as the chief means of educating the young people naturally raises some questions: What is a school? For example, is the young girl in Africa who is learning to pound maize in a wooden mortar under the guiding hand of her grandmother, or the young boy who is learning to look after cattle with his father, going to school? Is the class under the tree in the bush a school, as well as Abington, Pennsylvania, High or Winchester Public School? What is a school? What can we learn at school that we cannot learn at home? If a definition of a school can be agreed on, what would be the implication of the continued reliance on the formal school institution as the chief vehicle of conveying education to the young people of the future in a rapidly changing and shrinking world? Do the amount of human effort and the commitment to, and involvement in, formal school education pay sufficient dividends for us to continue this exercise? In other words, should we continue in the future to place the same faith in and devote the same emphasis to the school as we have in the past?

This paper tries to examine the limitations of the school as a means of educating the young, and to make a few suggestions, in the light of these limitations, about alternative forms and processes of educating the young. While the role of the school in highly complex and industrialised countries of the world is kept in mind, the major emphasis is on the problems of developing countries, with particular reference to Africa, from which the writer draws his experience.

The school in the homestead

Education is often associated with schools and what teachers do. It is often thought that education starts at school and that the role of educating is confined to the formal activities of school. It is too often for-

gotten that education and the schools are not the same thing, and that what goes on inside the school is not necessarily always education.

All societies face the task of preparing their young for full membership in the adult community and all cultures include education as the principal means of perpetuating themselves. Education has, in fact, been defined as the process of enculturation. This process is accomplished in different ways and schools exist in varying degrees of 'schoolness'. These range from the unconscious and informal observations that children make of elders in the family to the more organised and formalised school situations. They include the 'bush schools' and the circumcision and initiation ceremonies as well as the modern classroom of Abington High with closed-circuit television and a dial-access system.

In pre-colonial Africa and indeed in all preliterate societies, there were no school buildings, but this did not mean that the children were not educated. They learned by living and doing. The homestead was the school. In the homes and on the farms, the children were taught the skills which would enable them to play their full part as adult members of their society. They learned by direct observation and imitation. By this method, the boys learned how to distinguish useful grasses and dangerous weeds, how to stalk wild game, and how to stock sheep and goats; and the girls were similarly taught the special skills related to their sex and age, such as the preparation of meals and looking after babies. All children were taught tribal history by oral tradition and were also helped to acquire the sacred cultural mores and attitudes as well as the modes of behaviour which were valued by their society.

While the mothers prepared the evening meal after a long working day, the grandmother kept the children awake by telling fireside stories and by asking them to find answers to riddles and puzzles. Through these stories, in which the hare outwitted the elephant, and the tortoise outran the hare, the youngsters learned that wisdom is better than physical strength, that good should be rewarded and evil punished, and that humility is more to be prized than ostentatiousness. There were many gods, but each had his own special responsibilities and his own locality, and there were seldom religious feuds between the worshippers of one god and those of another.

Let it not appear, however, that there is any attempt here to glamorise and romanticise tribal education. It was limited in scope, all children being given more or less the same kind of instruction according to their sex and age. It depended on custom and tradition and thus had a past orientation. Innovation and creativity were often ignored and, since there was no writing or reading, memorisation and recall of information played the key role in the teaching and learning situations.

Traditional education was, on the other hand, directly relevant to the needs and problems of the tribal society. It produced emotionally stable and economically productive members of the community and, above all, it was compulsory and free for all the children. There was no shortage of teachers, for every adult was a teacher to a lesser or greater degree. Every old man or woman was a reference library and resource centre. Nature itself was the playground.

The formal school

As societies become more complex, the processes of

socialisation and enculturation also become more intricate and specialised. Differentiated institutions become necessary to ensure the orderly transmission of culture from generation to generation. The most important among the institutions which have evolved is the formal school. As life has become more complex, the school has assumed more functions. The extended family, which was once the primary agent in shaping the child's interests, values, and personality, has given way to the school. The school has everywhere become the chief agent of educating the young.

In most African countries, the first schools were established by the various missionary societies. They had two main aims: first, to gain converts, and second, to train clerks, artisans, and other menial workers required by the newly established colonial administrations.

With the establishment of the mission schools, the task of formulating moral values and training youth in the proper ethical systems was relegated to the church and the schools. The churches, through the schools, aimed at extracting the children from the traditional 'heathen' communities and at giving them a new set of values - the Western values of individualism and social class and the Christian core of values based upon human brotherhood, monogamy, chastity, and all the beatitudinal teachings of humility and the life hereafter. Most aspects of the cultures of the indigenous people, such as traditional music and dances, all forms of artistic self-expression, and even their names were regarded as more or less evil influences which must be kept away from those who went to school. In Luganda - one of the vernacular languages of Uganda - the word for 'mission station', the centre where the church, the boarding school, and (usually non-African) priests and teachers were found, is 'Ekigo' or 'fort', with the inevitable implication that the school, built on top of a hill apart from the community, aimed at fortifying the students against the influence of the community. The values and skills taught in school were frequently at variance with current practice at home and in the community as a whole.

With the attainment of political independence, the time-honoured official sanction given to missionary enterprise in the field of education and the role played by the former colonial powers as the chief source of values have been questioned. Deliberate attempts are being made to bridge the gap between home and school, to draw inspiration from the past, and to plant the roots of African education in African soil. Indigenous music, art, folklore, and riddles are being incorporated into the curricula of schools. History, geography, and science syllabuses and teaching materials which take account of the local environment are also being developed.

Yet, despite these improvements, the school in its present form is giving only a partial and poor response to the needs and problems of developing countries. Some African countries are already spending a very high proportion - six to eight per cent of their Gross National Product and 25 to 30 per cent of their annual budgets - on education. Despite this zeal and commitment of public funds to education, only about 50 per cent of the children in the primary school age group are receiving more than a few years of schooling and only about two to four per cent of the children in the secondary school age group can be accommodated in the high schools. Education in its present form is proving to be a very expensive com-

modity relative to the ability of the economies of developing countries to pay. Philip Coombs has demonstrated that most developing countries, like Alice in Wonderland, will have to run as fast as possible just to keep in one place, in other words, to maintain the current participation ratio of about 50 per cent.

Therefore, a large percentage of the children in these countries will remain out of the formal school system and may thus be condemned to the world of permanent illiteracy, cultural deprivation, and unemployment from which there appears to be no escape.

In these circumstances, the conventional school of one teacher standing before one class of children behind their desks cannot meet the challenge of taking education to all the children who are demanding, and are entitled to, education throughout the world. In developing countries, for a long time to come, about half the children of primary school age, and 90 per cent of the children of secondary school age, must stay out of the school system, if the formal school alone is going to be relied upon in its present form. The question which is difficult to answer in these circumstances is this: When there is only one chair for every two children of primary school age in the country, and only three or four stools for every 100 children waiting outside the door of the secondary school, how do you select those who should get in and those who should stay out? Every parent naturally feels that his own child must get in and that it must be the other man's child who should stay out of the school.

In their last year of primary school, the children must sit tests in English (or another foreign language) and mathematics, the purpose of which is to sift the lucky few who are thought worthy of benefiting from secondary education from those who are considered unworthy of this privilege. Through these examinations, which in the case of an individual child may mean the difference between becoming a medical doctor, on the one hand, and an unemployed street loafer, on the other, the children acquire a highly competitive and sometimes selfish spirit, which is in contrast with the community of self-help, national cooperative movements that these countries are trying to foster.

Despite the fact that the majority of the children in these countries never see the inside of a secondary school, primary education is generally academic and literary in character, aiming at the preparation of children for secondary school, and the secondary school is only a narrow footbridge to the coveted university.

Teachers are in short supply and are inadequately trained or even untrained. Teaching methods in most schools are still formal, emphasising drill and the transmission of information, instead of stressing understanding and creativity. In other words, school children spend most of their school time accumulating and storing what Whitehead referred to as 'inert ideas that are merely received into the mind without being utilised, or tested, or thrown into fresh combinations'.

Consequently, the school system is being criticised. It is regarded by many political and educational leaders as a means of disorienting the children from the realities of life as it is in developing countries, and as an institution which is failing to respond to the needs of society in the new nations.

The overconcern of schools with book learning

and examinations tends to divorce the school from the world of reality. The school extracts the children from their social and cultural milieu and prepares them for a future which often does not exist in their country. It encourages in them a distaste, if not contempt, for manual labour. The result is that the children educated in school expect to become dependent upon a particular type of white-collar employment.

The most serious limitation of the school in developing countries, however, is that it can reach only a small proportion of the school-age population. The majority must, for a long time to come, be unreached by this institution and, consequently, will remain illiterate and culturally deprived.

Current data indicate that 49 per cent of the individuals who populate this shrinking globe are illiterate, which means that one out of every two human beings can neither read nor write. Statistics further show that even the United States, the richest and most educationally and technologically advanced of the nations in the world, still has three million illiterates. Is this a normal state of affairs, a condition which the world can accept and survive within the next decade?

One hundred years ago, the greatest American President - a man who even today maintains an image of admiration and respect throughout the world - declared that this troubled nation could never survive, let alone prosper, half slave and half free. Now, when the world is more sophisticated and more technologically oriented, is it logical to expect that the human race can survive, let alone prosper, half literate and half illiterate, half sighted and half blind? If our answer is in the affirmative, then perhaps our assignment at this Conference is just an academic exercise.

Dr Milton Obote, President of the Republic of Uganda, has stressed this point:

...We cannot afford to build two nations within the territorial boundaries of one country: one rich, educated, African in appearance, but mentally foreign; and the other, which constitutes the majority of the population, poor and illiterate.

The conventional school is ill-equipped to combat this problem. Even if the primary school system could be extended to cover all the children in the relevant age group, this would do little in the short run to combat the problems of mass illiteracy throughout the world, and in the long run this solution would be too expensive and would take too long to have an impact. Schools open at eight in the morning and they close at four in the afternoon. They are open for only nine months in the year, the rest being school holidays. The school plant is thus under-utilised, and the teachers are in a way under-employed.

Moreover, the children to whom the school directs its attention take a long time to grow into adult men and women. Society cannot wait until the school children being educated today are grown, in order to get the economic and social development it desires. Means and techniques must be found which reach far beyond the confines of the school and encompass the majority of the adult population and out-of-school youth.

The school must integrate itself with the community. It must become a social and cultural centre where not only the children but also their parents come to receive continuing education. The school must shift its emphasis from the production of 'educated' men to the creation of educable societies.

The primary school leaver crisis

One other current problem facing developing countries centres on the stream of primary school leavers. The number of children who complete the primary school, but for whom neither further education nor employment opportunities in the modern sector are available, is increasing very fast. To take two examples: in Kenya, the estimated number of children completing the seventh grade, that is the top of the primary school, will rise from 150,000 in 1970 to almost 250,000, of whom only 10 per cent will be absorbed in publicly supported secondary schools. In Zambia, of the 63,000 1969 grade seven leavers, 50,000 will be unable to find places in secondary schools. It is estimated that this number will have doubled by 1975. One could go on ad infinitum.

Most of these children have high job expectations. They drift to the towns where they believe these jobs to be. Denied further educational opportunities, rejected by the urban labour market, but too young, and perhaps considering themselves too 'educated' to go back to the traditional semi-subsistence farming, they go out into the world like displaced persons.

These circumstances are forcing a number of countries to reexamine the curriculum, the functions, and the organisation of the school in agriculturally-based societies. The school, if it is to play its proper role, must inculcate in the children appropriate social attitudes of living and working together in rural communities. It must produce good farmers. In Tanzania, for example, the schools, especially secondary schools, are now expected to become economic communities as well as social and educational communities and to contribute to their own upkeep. Each school should have, as part of it, a farm or workshop which provides food for the community and makes some contribution to the total national income.

No one, however, should be under the delusion that the manipulation of the school curriculum per se to include agriculture will change the attitude of school leavers towards farming, and thus arrest the massive rural-urban exodus which is endemic in most developing countries. Efforts to ruralise the curriculum in several low-income countries have not induced this change.

Paradoxically, 'the problems of agricultural education are not primarily agricultural'. They have their roots in economic factors, basically in the wide gap in economic opportunities between the rural and urban sectors of the economy. The solution to these problems involves physical planning, provision of capital, organisation of the marketing of produce, and other facets of development planning aimed at the transformation of the rural areas to make life there more attractive. These are not matters of the school curriculum. As the Kericho (Kenya) Conference on Education, Employment, and Rural Development concluded, the only thing which can check the rural-urban drift is the visible evidence that farming really pays.

This is not to detract from the importance of ruralising the curriculum, but rather to suggest that the school should not be looked at in isolation from other aspects of life in the community.

Several African countries have formally organised national youth services to try to alleviate the problem of school leavers. These organisations seek to orient their members toward the task of national development. The specific objectives, according to the Kenya National Youth Service, are 'to inculcate good citizenship and provide an opportunity for education and training which will make them productive, skilled workers or farmers'.

Youth movements could play an important role in reaching out-of-school children, and school children out of school hours. Israel has experimented successfully with youth movements, and it is said that the Kibbutzim which are a remarkable feature of Israeli social and economic life were a product of youth movements. In Kenya, another experiment - the village polytechnic - is under way. This is a very simple low-cost training centre for school leavers to provide them with opportunities for developing their character and changing their outlook on life, also to provide them with skills, the exercise of which will fill a need in their home. The courses are primarily residential and are structured in such a way as to fit localised manpower requirements.

It is too early to assess the impact of national service, of the youth movement, and of the village polytechnics. They should be viewed, however, as worthwhile experiments aimed not only at supplanting, but at supplementing the formal school. They also attempt to achieve what the school has so far failed to do, that is to imbue the youth with a national we-feeling of identity, and to prepare them for the realities of life in their respective countries.

Is school not too late?

An impressive array of psychologists who have made intensive studies of the intellectual growth and development of children have come to the conclusion that the period from birth to about age six is of vital importance to the individual's future cognitive development. Benjamin Bloom, for example, estimates that half of mature intelligence is developed between birth and four years, and another 30 per cent by eight years. One-third of future school achievement is determined before the child enters school. O. K. Moore, a Yale sociologist, contends that the early years of life are the most creative and intellectually productive years of our lives.

Yet the conventional school system starts after these vital years. The school begins to play its part, as it were, after the die is cast. In a world which is becoming more and more complex and demands more highly skilled and talented workers, this neglect of the first five years of an individual's life is amazing. In some developing countries, because primary education is terminal for most children, it has been suggested that the age of entering school should be raised to nine or ten years.

What are the implications of leaving children at home in what is often a sterile and impoverished traditional environment during this critical period? In most homes there is a dearth or total absence of books, pictures, magazines, radios, and toys which would create a stimulating environment for the children. Moreover, the lowest academically qualified and least professionally able teachers are usually assigned to the lowest classes, thus making remedial instruction impossible. Bloom has suggested that deprivation in early years of childhood can have far greater consequences than deprivation in later years. Is this not an extravagant waste of talent - a scarce resource - which the world cannot continue to afford?

In the face of this evidence, what is the logical reason for taking the children to school at six or seven years of age after 'the most creative and productive years of their lives' have been wasted academically, perhaps never to be retrieved?

The studies mentioned above are based on observations in North America and Europe. No such extensive studies have been carried out in Africa, or perhaps in any other parts of the developing world. Let me suggest that there is a crying need for programmes of research in child growth and development in African countries to provide a framework of knowledge on matters such as these on which to build school curricula that are meaningful in terms of the social and physical needs of children in the African social and cultural milieu.

If we assume for the time being that the findings of Bloom and others have universal validity, then the implications are straightforward. We must pay far more attention to the early years than we have done before. In developing countries, this may take the form of the school's playing an active part in the education, not only of the pupils, but also of the parents, to help them to realise the importance of the home to the future education of the child. Village play centres also can be established to provide a more stimulating and creative environment for the 'preschool' child.

I cannot speak with any practical experience, let alone confidence, about the school situation in the highly industrialised and overdeveloped countries of North America and Europe, where education as everything else is in a state of ferment. Great strides have been taken in these countries in the direction of curriculum reform and classroom organisation, to accommodate the school to rapidly changing and more complex situations. The last ten years have seen some fantastic feats and startling changes in curriculum development which are a revolt or near-revolt against the time-honoured ways of teaching and school organisation. I am thinking of the development of the new mathematics, PSSC and Nuffield science, new ways of teaching foreign languages, team teaching, a more widespread use of educational television, programmed textbooks, and a host of other individualised self-instructional devices which teach the students how 'to go it alone'.

An increasing number of schools are successfully facing a great many of the problems which baffle us in the developing countries. For example, the best of them are now equipped to treat each student as an individual, making the most of personal strengths and working to correct weaknesses, and many of them are thus offering a first-rate education to all students - not just the college-bound. The traditional concept of the school as a set of classrooms in which instruction is given by individual teachers to groups of pupils of the same age or ability is beginning to give way to the concept of the school as a learning resource centre. Rigid classroom walls are crumbling before the impact of more flexible scheduling. Chalkboards and single textbooks are yielding to overheads, microfilm readers, tapes, dial-access systems, and a complex of mechanical devices aimed at helping the learner to paddle his own canoe.

These and other innovations, however, are still confined to the top few of the best schools, which have money combined with foresighted leadership. The idea of the school and the teachers as a learning resource centre has not yet caught bush-fire. In the majority of the schools the traditional patterns of classroom instruction and organisation still persist.

There is need for education to take 'a questioning look' at itself. For example, is it essential that all students must spend the same number of years to go through an elementary or secondary school course? Must all pupils sit still for six or eight hours a day before a teacher? Can we not seek ways of increasing the quality and quantity of educational facilities within the limits of the resources available - ways which would help to lessen and even to close the gap between the educational haves and have-nots? Is this possible? Or must we learn to live with the present situation where half the population of the world cannot gain access to the secrets of education closed behind the doors of the school?

These are difficult questions. Yet they all point to one conclusion, and that is that we must be prepared to do what we have not done before. The school cannot respond to the challenge of children who demand and deserve more and better education today, merely by doing well or better what was done in the past.

Television and/or radio, used in conjunction with self-instructional correspondence materials, may in the long run prove to be the only practical means of bringing education to all the children and adults who want to learn. The experience of American Samoa has already revealed the tremendous potentialities of modern instructional media in developing countries. Through television, which is installed in almost all Samoan primary schools, Samoan children receive education from master teachers whose teaching is more concerned with ideas, understandings, and insights than with memorisation of relatively unrelated facts, while the planning, presentation, and reinforcement of follow-up procedures are developed cooperatively with the regular classroom teachers. Through this 'team teaching', the children as well as their teachers can be exposed to good teaching techniques, which would be out of the reach of most children in the traditional school system. It is teaching and in-service education in one package. The same system can be used for instruction in adult literacy and general continuing education connected with the specific needs and problems of the community. A similar project is under way in the Ivory Coast, where it is expected that by 1980 all primary classes will be equipped for television teaching and that 80 per cent of the primary school age children will be taught through this medium. It may be noted in passing that many developing countries have already invested heavily in television and radio systems which are currently under-used.

In conclusion, there can be no question about the enormous value of the formal school, and the pivotal role it will continue to occupy in the educational systems of the world. If it is to do this effectively, however, there is need for the school to adapt itself to rapidly changing conditions. The community and the school must come closer together. This is not to suggest that parents should take over the professional role of the educators, or that the school should invade the home life of the students. It does mean that the school should become a social and community centre where pupils and their parents meet for life-long learning. In other words, the wall of separation which has existed between school and society must be broken down. School curricula must be increasingly more concerned with community needs and problems, as well as with the continuing education of the parents. If this transformation of the school is to be successfully achieved, we must pay special attention to the education of the teachers.

Finally, the school must modernise itself through the more systematic use of the means which modern technology has placed at our disposal, in order to make more and better education available to all the children of the world. We must not be satisfied with the situation where half of the human race is kept in cold storage in a world of permanent illiteracy and cultural deprivation, for we have discovered the truth of the Ki-Swahili saying that <u>Utajiri wa nchi ni Wananchi</u>, 'The wealth of the country is its people'.

16

IAN LISTER

Should schools survive?

Source: Working paper for the Loccum International Conference 'Towards a Freer School', West Germany, February 1971.

* *

This is a working paper and a period piece. During the course of 1970, at a time when I had never heard of Ivan Illich, I began to work on the question: Should schools survive? I think I was led to this position by a variety of things. I had lived in Austria (the extreme model of the schooled society) and I had visited Austrian schools and viewed them with the critical distance which comes from another culture and another language. (Perhaps the most memorable visit was to the school in Linz of which Adolf Hitler and Adolf Eichmann are both Old Boys.) For ten years, in the field of general education, I worked for a kind of curriculum reform that never happened. Other work with resources-based learning made me conclude that schools were deficient in resources and that many resources lay outside the school. And my work in political education made me suspect that schools, through their operational methods, structures and rituals, offered a political education in acquiescence to the majorities they pretended to serve. A visit to West Africa, where I saw families sleeping on the street surrounded by intellectuals quoting Emerson and Longfellow and ruling élites using schools to buttress their own power, drove me on. The arguments and assertions of the paper were tried on, and challenged by teachers all over West Germany at various seminars - although Hessen, the home of the progressive schoolmen, suffered most at my hands, as they were 'verunsichert' - made to feel insecure, as they could not tell whether it was 'progressive' or 'conservative', the two categories they use to save themselves the trouble of further thought. Teachers and students in England have suffered it too - and again it was the left-wing teachers who suffered most. Although I would now have reservations about many of the arguments, I would still defend it as a discussion paper.

* *

The argument will be in three sections:
(1) the cultural crisis and the school
(2) reforms, and reformism
(3) the case for deschooling society

I. The cultural crisis and the school

The cultural crisis has many aspects, including:

1. The realities of mass society; the aspiration to mass education (for the first time in English history); the search for mass democracy and, by some, for mass participatory democracy.

2. At the same time there is continued concern for the individual.

3. The recognition of cultural diversity within our society (particularly class cultures and 'racial' cultures - part of the challenge of immigration): recognition both in the sense that we see that diversity exists and in the sense that many believe that it ought to be encouraged rather than fought.

4. The growth of a technological, urban, more mobile society. The relative decline of the extended family; the weakening of the family, the community, the environment as educators. Unprecedented challenges are made to schools and schoolteachers - challenges which they are inadequate to meet.

5. There is a fundamental lack of agreement about what schools are for, and widespread dissatisfaction with schools as they are. For example, some of the arguments about the relationship/gap between the school and the world; the school and the community; the school and the home (the family); the school and the working class (the majority of the population; 'Half our Future'); the school and work; the school and leisure; the school and education. In short, the school is at the centre of many of our social dilemmas; it epitomises our crisis in social education: the essence of the argument concerns the relationship of school to society.

II. Reforms and reformism

'A political programme which does not explicitly recognise the need for deschooling is not revolutionary; it is demagoguery calling for more of the same. Ivan Illich.

'The educational reformers are racing against time, and they are losing the race. ' Ian Lister.

Reforms are generally of three kinds:
1. reorganisation of school systems (comprehensive schools)
2. reorganisation of teaching and learning systems
3. reform of the curriculum and the content of education (curriculum development).

1. REORGANISATION OF SCHOOL SYSTEMS

Arguments that the school should educate for community, for democracy. Not for leadership. The school system should not be socially <u>divisive</u>.

Pupils of different ranges of ability, and of different social classes (sometimes even of different sexes!) should go to the same school.

The stress is on <u>social</u> rather than <u>intellectual</u> education.

The ultimate argument is for the comprehensive university.

It is worth stressing that these reformers want to conserve the old <u>institutions</u>.

2. REORGANISATION OF TEACHING AND LEARNING SYSTEMS

One of the illusions 'on which the school system rests is that most learning is the result of teaching'. Ivan Illich.

There has been a general movement towards
(a) non-streaming, and
(b) individualised learning.

Non-streaming is the logical development of the argument that the school should not be socially divisive/should be a social mixer.

Individualised learning is supported theoretically by modern learning theory; it is demanded <u>practically</u> by the difficulties presented by having pupils of a wide range of ability in the same group.

3. CURRICULUM DEVELOPMENT

In England the curriculum developers are trying to improve/save the system by reforming the content of education. In general, they are part of a conservative attempt to prop up the system by limited reform.

Most projects have been funded by philanthropists (Nuffield Organisation) and the Schools Council (founded 1965).

Early projects (Science, Maths, Languages) largely reflected the major failures in skill teaching in English schools...

Later projects (The Humanities Curriculum Project, the Integration of the Humanities Project, the General Studies Project) largely reflected the major crisis in social education in the country. They involved not only the content of education, but also teaching and learning systems: one project Director even claimed 'the system is the message'.

4. MAJOR REFORM OF TEACHER TRAINING

The ultimate of all these attempts at reform is the Community School movement - with the school as a resource centre; open to the whole community; and a central part of the community. It is also the ultimate pretension of the school educators: the school will create the community, not the community the school.

III. The case for deschooling society

'The serious alternative to socialising the school is to deschool society.

THE SCHOOL AS METAPHOR

(a) <u>The school as prison</u>; the headmaster is the prison governor; the teachers are warders (one of the two things for which they can be dismissed is failing to check the list of the prisoners); the prisoners are the pupils, in the obvious instance, but the teachers are prisoners too. Pupils have to attend by law (the 'raising of the school leaving age' is, for some pupils, the 'raising of the school staying age'). Attendance is compulsory by law, during most of daylight hours (for teachers as well as pupils in state schools). The deprivations of school include being deprived of the company of human beings other than members of the pupil's peer group; in many schools being deprived of the company of the opposite sex; in many selective and neighbourhood schools being deprived of the company of children of different levels of intelligence, and of different social classes. The main message of many schools is passive obedience. There are, of course, some schools where the prison element is greater than in others. In some public boarding schools, lost in the feudal parts of the country, pupils are extracted not only from their families, but also from the industrial, urban society that created the wealth which made their deprivations possible. In some schools in England you can find windows nailed to their frames, so that the prisoners can't escape during exercise periods. When headmasters of some schools say that absenteeism without adequate explanation will be followed by expulsion, the real message is that the pupil/prisoner will be sent to a much worse school/prison. Those pupils who vote with their feet - the so-called 'early leavers' - often regard the school as a prison. Some social reformers want to help them by giving them a longer sentence.

(b) The school as military academy; this was true of many of the public schools of the 19th century - which trained pupils for leadership in the Army, the Church of England, and the Empire - three enterprises which have faced bankruptcy in the 20th century. Such efficient training depended on a clarity of objectives and a certainty in prediction of future occupations which now no longer exist.

(c) The school as hospital - which tends to individual and social problems. The selective/rejective school 'is a hospital which tends to the healthy and rejects the sick' (The School of Barbiana, p. 24). The comprehensive school is more likely to suffer from our social illnesses than to cure them.

(d) The school as museum; the practical responses of today, when institutionalised, become the sacred cows of tomorrow: yesterday's tomorrow is today. The school as museum has set opening hours; it shows the exhibits (Tudor England, the literature of past ages - Shakespeare, Corneille, Goethe). It abhors the applied science on which our society is based. It invites admiration, not participation. It teaches the skills necessary for living in a passing age or in a bygone society - handwriting, French for the Entente Cordiale. The school as a transmitter of culture usually means the school attempting to transmit the high culture (and the dead culture). A vital culture does not need to be transmitted by an institution (which is the one sure way of killing it): it transmits itself.

(e) The school as church; in England, of course, the connections between schools and the actual church are very great. There are many church schools - and traditionally the premium was put on affective rather than cognitive education. Many schools have the same architecture as churches. But that is not really the point. When Ivan Illich likens a school to a church he does so because it is institutionalised; fossilised; and on the defensive. He predicts: 'The school system... may soon face a problem which the churches have faced before: what to do with surplus space emptied by the defection of the faithful. '

The parallels between our schools and the Elizabethan church in late-16th-century England are striking:

(a) teachers must have certificates/ministers had to have a licence;

(b) there are arguments being made for super-teachers, and ordinary teachers (or auxiliaries)/the preaching ministry, and the non-preaching ministry;

(c) teachers are badly paid/as were ministers;

(d) teachers are often ill-educated/as were ministers, and many of the laity are/were better educated than the teachers;

(e) both teachers today and ministers before were important instruments of political and social control;

(f) both influence by ritual, at least as much as by content;

(g) both were threatened by new developments in communications - the Elizabethan church by the book, the school today by television;

(h) attendance was/is enforced by law, with fines for non-attendance;

(i) in the church debates of Elizabethan England and the education debates of today the conservatives were the nationalists, and the reformers were the internationalists;

(j) in both cases a huge array of vested interests - kings and governments, bishops and inspectors and education officers, the clergy and teachers, tried to keep the system going;

(k) the Elizabethan church was challenged by a consumer revolt - the Puritans. 'The Puritan revolt - its formal and conscious inception took place among members of the academic intellectual class' (William Haller). Today middle-class movements such as C. A. S. E. (the Confederation for the Advancement of State Education); W. H. E. R. E. (a consumer magazine on education); and the Playgroups Movement are challenging the traditional church. In 16th-century England the Separatists separated from the church. 'The citizenry were religiously instructing their own children' (Louis B. Wright, Middle-class Culture in Elizabethan England). The Puritans solved the paradox of individualism and community by setting up communities of their own exclusive individuals. The comprehensive school of today, though, is in the position of the comprehensive Elizabethan Church. If it gives way to some of the demands made on it it will no longer be comprehensive: if it remains comprehensive it will lose dynamism and social meaning, power and influence. The sequence of the Puritan attack was firstly on the vestments - the trappings of the church, 'the habits of the stage'; then on its rituals; then on its political structure. The mortarboard and academic gowns are on the way out; the vain repetitions of textbooks are condemned; the importance of teachers as political educators is beginning to be realised.

(f) The school as theatre; it is often said that someone is a good teacher because he can act or tell a good joke. The truth though is that if schools are theatres they are full of third-rate actors who, without compulsory attendance, would be without an audience. They often feel helpless in competition with other professional 'theatres' - such as television, advertising, and children's comics - which they fear, hate, and condemn as immoral manipulators.

(g) The school as factory; the economist's view of school education - as capital tied up in labour - does give a means of assessing school success. So does the qualifications race (by which the educational system actually justifies itself - virtually by printing its own money!). Many middle-class parents see money which they devote to the education of their children not as expenditure, but as investment.

(h) The school as alibi; by this is meant not

only the school as a baby-minder (Parkplatz für Kinder) but, more important, the way in which the school is used as a social excuse, and actually to divert attention from social problems. If there are things wrong with our society attention must be directed to those very things, not to schools which reflect society far more than they can change it.

SOME DEFENCES OF THE SCHOOL

Lucio (an Italian peasant boy) who has thirty-six cows in the barn at home, said: "School will always be better than cow shit. "' (Letter to a Teacher)

Schools can be defended if they can offer things which the family or other groups, including the community, cannot offer. They can be defended as:
1. intellectual educators
2. social educators
3. extenders of experience
4. resource centres (people and materials)

1. Intellectual educators - how efficient is skill teaching (why does private skill teaching flourish?) - what mastery do pupils have of the structure, concepts, approaches of disciplines/forms of knowledge? What mastery do the teachers have of these things?

2. Social educators - the more explicit the demand for the school to be a social educator, the more obvious the crisis in the culture. In many schools 'social education' is for the less able. Schools which suffer from bad buildings, a high turnover of staff, very limited exposure to pupils (probably no clubs or societies) are those which are consciously asked to socially educate.

3. Extenders of experience - the school can be an escape from the limitations of the family and the community. Through history, literature, art, etc. the school can widen and enrich the life of its pupils. In the ultimate form the school can be a liberator.

4. Resource centre - what resources do most schools have, other than a collection of teachers? Many learning resources are in the environment from which schools cut pupils off.

SOME PARADOXES AND CONTRADICTIONS OF THE MOMENT

1. In spite of the hopes of people like Husén, the country's economic resources are always decades behind being enough to satisfy the demand for institutionalised education.

2. Reformers have to force people to be free - to use Rousseau's paradox - and pass laws to force pupils to stay at school.

3. In many comprehensive schools the aims of social mixing and of individualised learning contradict: pupils breathe the same air in the same room, but they work on their own. 'What they learn there is how to isolate themselves in a group. ' The community of the language laboratory is the extreme sick joke.

4. Teachers are more and more confused about their role - are they more social workers? - if so, they are not trained as such. Or intellectual educators? - if so, many of them lack qualifications for the task. Should they supervise lunch, and pupils at play? At the same time, some reformers are confusing teachers further by thrusting new roles upon them.

5. The ultimate arrogance of the school educators is probably the community school movement. It

also poses some of the major problems: how do we think beyond traditional institutions (schools, universities)? How do we think beyond the romanticised communities of the past? (R. H. Tawney; F. R. Leavis; Richard Hoggart, etc.)

SOME HINTS FROM THE THIRD WORLD

In Africa in the 19th century, England exported its school ideas of the time; transplanted from one culture to another; ideas fossilised - anti-technological, pure academic - with the results that West Africa lacks doctors, engineers, agricultural experts, but many of its urban unemployed can quote Shakespeare as they die on the pavement.

Dilemmas (which are ours) are seen clearly in the Third World:
(a) the enormous cost of institutionalised education
(b) the problem of élite versus popular education
(c) the relationship between the formal education system and the culture.

John Wilson (in Education and Changing West African Culture) wrote: 'Education was not integrated with the economic, social and political facts of life. ' (Is it in England today?)

René Dumont (in False Start in Africa) wrote about 'the inadequacy of the present school system, entrenched in an unimaginative imitation of the European model', and argued that education in Africa must be decolonised. Have we not a need to decolonise our education from unchallenged assumptions?

Michael Huberman (UNESCO) has argued that Third World countries cannot afford our kind of education. Can we afford our kind of education?

A POSITIVE PROGRAMME

The general trend which needs reversing - as society has become more industrialised, urbanised, mobile, the demands made upon formal education have become greater and greater. At the same time schools have moved away from skill teaching (at which many are very bad) and attempted more and more explicitly to become social educators. To do this they cut children off from society, and social groups. Ironically, formal teaching methods were ultimately seen by some reformers to be ineffective and they advocated role-playing and simulation techniques. (Imagine you are in a family, city, etc.) The Humanities Curriculum Project took living in cities, the Family, Relations between the Sexes as some of its major topics... BUT

1. Work, leisure, politics, city living etc. should themselves become the means of education, i. e. we should attempt to informalise a lot of formal education. In short, we should use society itself, and the environment, as educators.

2. We should not abolish schooling suddenly, but we should begin and encourage a dismantling programme. The less effective parts of the school should then wither away.

3. We should encourage voluntary groupings (such as the playgroup movement) with financial support. We should encourage a variety of voluntary enterprises and alternatives (voluntary workshop groups, discussion groups, etc.).

4. We should promote the establishment of skill centres - for modern languages, mathematics, etc.

5. We should encourage self-learning (auto-didactism) by producing appropriate teaching materials and by creating opportunities for those autodidacts who want it to come together in groups, to discuss and to work in common enterprise.

6. We should encourage the Open University programme, and take it further to an Open School programme.

7. Schools should concentrate on an intellectual education - on the generalised elements of intellectual knowledge (structures, concepts, approaches, i. e. specific data will be used for its illustrative qualities, not as part of enculturation or a hurdle in a mental obstacle race).

8. Social education will be achieved in society (the only place where it can be achieved) and not in school.

9. The concept of 'school age' must be more and more open to question. Opportunities and readiness for learning will coincide more when we develop 'lifelong education'. Resources for learning, the chance to join voluntary groups, to master a particular skill at a skill centre (or through the agencies of a skill centre) should be available throughout a person's whole life. This will weaken the obsession of peer group organisation which we have in most institutionalised education, and lessen the problems of youth culture and the generation gap. Vertical groupings will unite people in common enterprises.

10. At the moment we are creating difficulties for ourselves by lowering the legal age of majority (in England to 18) on the one hand, and on the other hand extending the period and uncertainties of adolescence (and studolescence) by our systems of formal education. Perhaps adolescence and maturity would become blurred in the more spontaneous, voluntary and choosing society of the future. (If we are to retain the notions of youth and maturity we should create some kind of initiation - youths in West African tribes went out into the forest, proved themselves, and returned as men. Our youths could prove themselves by working in our forests - the asphalt jungles of the cities - in urban renewal programmes.)

11. One of the major objections to the kind of de-institutionalising of education which I am advocating comes from advocates of equality of opportunity - i. e. will not the deschooling of society favour privileged groups? Here we are discussing possibilities and probabilities. The traditional school system favoured the middle class - always well in the lead in the competitive consumption of institutionalised welfare. It attempted to destroy class cultures (and in many ways impoverished working-class culture). Today the reformers are often doing the same thing in their attempts at 'social education'. The Humanities Curriculum Project, according to its Director, has chosen the 'curriculum of the News of the World'. In fact, it has chosen the curriculum of The Observer. The new comprehensive schools will only promote equality of opportunity by their capacity to prevent pupils from learning. The social power of the educational system lies in its power to print its own money (certification) just as the social power of the church lay in its power to excommunicate and promise eternal life. It is in this light that certification needs to be radically reviewed, and the hold of the middle class over the system broken.

12. If one asks the general question: What can schools achieve that could not be achieved in other (and better) ways? The only possible answer (apart

from the case of boarding/day schools in foreign countries for nationals of a different country) is in terms of the school as an instrument of social and political control. The studies now being made of the school as a political educator are raising the question of whether it is the kind of political and social control we want, and whether it does not in fact contradict some of the major values and aspirations of our society. In the more flexible and dynamic education of the future we must help groups (families, and voluntary groupings) to aid the education venture: this is part of the general attempt to revitalise non-school education. In the words of Chairman Mao 'we should unfold the mass training movement...'.

All this would indeed be the great cultural revolution of our times.

17

IAN LISTER

The concept of deschooling and the future of secondary education

Source: Paper presented at the International Seminar of the European Cultural Foundation, Florence, in October 1971.

* *

This too was a 'pièce d'occasion' - a mixture of survey, critique, and speculation. Again I would not now agree with all of it. In particular, it accepted alternative projects too much at their face value; it suffers from romantic populism; and I now think differently about the underground - which I fear is more likely to be a complementary part of the dominant reality than a real challenge to it. The paper was used in work on future alternatives in education by the international curriculum group of the European Cultural Foundation, of which I am now a member, and whose researches will be published later; at present the book has the provisional title Has Education a Future? It was also used by R. H. Dave in Lifelong Education and the School Curriculum, 1973. A shortened version was published in Education and Culture No. 19, Summer 1972. The paper has the virtue of raising a central question - what are the implications for schools of the introduction of lifelong learning opportunities? The question of the relationship of the underground to society is also important. Theodore Roszak theorised about it in The Making of a Counter-Culture in 1968 (see Quotational Bibliography); Daniel Berrigan made positive assertions about it in 1972 (see Quotational Bibliography); Frank Musgrove, of Manchester University and Maurice Punch of Essex University are currently researching the area; and theoretical writings are being produced by the sociologists of deviance (see, for example, contributions in Politics and Deviance, edited by Ian Taylor and Laurie Taylor, Penguin, 1973). For me the most profound treatment of the question so far has been provided by Herbert Marcuse in Counter-Revolution and Revolt (Allen Lane The Penguin Press, 1972).

* *

Holmes: Look at those big, isolated clumps of buildings rising up above the slates, like brick islands in a lead-coloured sea.
Watson: The Board Schools.
Holmes: Lighthouses, my boy! Beacons of the future! Capsules with hundreds of bright little seeds in each, out of which will spring the wiser, better England of the future.

Sir Arthur Conan Doyle

'The mere existence of school discourages and disables the poor from taking control of their own learning. All over the world the school has an anti-educational effect on society.'

Ivan Illich

The problem

In England, since the real beginnings of a state system of education, it has come to be assumed that the extension of compulsory education is synonymous with social progress. The Whig view of history, in which liberty broadens from precedent to precedent and by Parliamentary Act, has now been rejected in most history teaching but it has had two curious survivals - in Commonwealth countries and in the History of Education as it is generally taught. There have always been challengers of this Whig view of education. The 'culture debate' of the nineteenth century included men like Ruskin and Morris who saw beyond schools, and who wanted to make all life an educational experience. In the twentieth century a line of related thinkers - from D. H. Lawrence through F. R. Leavis and Denys Thompson - have questioned the dominant assumptions in popular education: these thinkers, however, tended to be literary men, using literary evidence of doubtful validity. They recognised the impact of industrial society but their suggested escapes from the worst aspects of that society were usually romantic and reactionary. Professor Bantock is one of the last in this line. Recently new kinds of radical voices have been heard in the Old World, the New World, and the Third World. Michael Huberman has questioned the whole basis of UNESCO educational policy in 'under-developed' countries; in the USA Paul Goodman, Ivan Illich and Everett Reimer have argued for an end to compulsory schooling; and in Uganda W. Senteza Kajubi has asked: 'Is the school an obsolete institution?' The difference between the challengers of yesteryear and the challengers of today is that now anthropologists, sociologists, political scientists and social planners are in the debate. The deschooling of society, which is the major alternative to a continuation, in some form or other, of the traditional educational orthodoxy, is not only being taken seriously by theorists and administrators: alternative programmes are being drawn up and, to some extent, alternatives are already being fed into present systems. It is this which makes an examination of the concept of deschooling, and of its implications for

secondary education, a worthwhile task at the present moment.

The concept of deschooling

The concept of deschooling presupposes a concept of schooling, both in theory and practice. Generally speaking, when writers refer to the 'schooled society' they are talking about the universal and compulsory systems of education which have developed in several states during the last two hundred years. They are talking about the kind of formal education offered by institutions such as schools, colleges, and universities, as opposed to the informal and incidental education received from life and experience. Most of the deschooling writers tend to analyse schools in functional terms and then create a generalised stereotype of 'the school' or 'schooling'. Much of the argument is in terms of generalisations. However, there is no school of deschoolers: even in the Mexican deschooling Mecca of Cuernavaca there are differences in the thinking of Ivan Illich and Everett Reimer. Thus, the concept of deschooling can be approached from two other directions - first to see what the concept is not, and second to see the different use that different people make of the concept. Extreme criticism of schools, such as that made in the USA in the nineteenth century or by Bernard Shaw in his preface to Misalliance in 1910, cannot by itself constitute an argument for deschooling. This is because deschooling is not merely a negative concept: as used by the advocates of deschooling it implies a positive programme of alternatives - alongside the reduction in the role of schools goes an expansion of educational opportunities in order to achieve lifelong education and the learning society. Paul Goodman introduced many of the themes of the deschooling argument. He exposed education as the largest industry of modern society; the 'school-monks' as 'an invested intellectual class worse than anything since the time of Henry VIII' and argued that if we want to get education into society we must first get it out of the schools. He challenged the schools in moral terms: 'The schools less and less represent any human values, but simply an adjustment to a mechanical system.' And he challenged the whole existence of compulsory schooling: 'The belief that a highly industrialised society requires twelve to twenty years of prior processing of the young is an illusion or a hoax.' He used metaphors in his arguments - the school as prison, the school as concentration camp. He argued for an education which would be 'human' and 'natural' - which he thought school was not. He argued for a general deinstitutionalisation and deformalisation of education, and a growth in incidental education - learning by experience. Decades ago he was writing about the crisis of community which is behind many of our educational dilemmas. Most of these things reappear in the writings of Illich and Reimer. Illich's peculiarity, perhaps, is that as a left-wing Catholic he argues on a religious level: he talks of 'education or celebration' and applies the Catholic and Marxist concept of alienation to schools - 'School makes alienation preparatory to life, thus depriving education of reality and work of creativity.' Everett Reimer, whose background is as colourful as, but different from, that of Illich, speaks of deschooling as being necessary for our 'secular salvation'. Thus, deschooling is used to describe a process, or rather a number of allegedly related processes which culminate in some kind of religious experience. In brief, deschooling is not a precise concept, with clear delimitations - and nor would its creators wish it to be. It is less of a concept than a general drift of thinking. Nor could it be located within a discipline - such as sociology, psychology, or philosophy: indeed it is one of the greatest strengths of Goodman, Illich and Reimer that - unlike many education thinkers in England - they are not the prisoners of any single discipline. However, as persons, they may also have some weaknesses, which are suggested here because the concept, the reality, and the perceiver stand in an organic relationship. Goodman, who least of all would object to an argument 'ad hominem', is a socialist anarchist who sees good in people and evil in institutions. For evidence he tends to rely on school visits and the statements of others - 'A great neurologist tells me...', 'I have heard James Coleman...' - who agree with his own arguments. Illich, who has written that 'each of us is personally responsible for his or her own deschooling', has been schooled more than most - Vienna and Salzburg are particularly inauspicious beginnings for a sane education in the mid-twentieth century - and he has probably failed to deschool himself. He can't help preaching and he gets carried away by the flow of his own rhetoric. He confuses rhetoric and argument as accuracy is ritualistically slaughtered on the altar of the balanced sentence. Like Spengler, his general theory stands or falls by his own general theory, for that is the foundation on which it is built. Everett Reimer builds a stereotype of schools and probably used this negative reference point too much as a basis on which to build his programme of alternatives. Evidence is sparse, and Paulo Freire bears a heavy burden as an example of what might be achieved on a wider scale. Goodman, Illich and Reimer share two major weaknesses which need to be taken into account in any consideration of deschooling and educational planning. They are lacking in convincing evidence - particularly empirical evidence, and their programmes of alternatives tend to be speculative paper proposals. This weakness needs to be remedied by a series of empirical investigations (to answer such questions as: What do schools actually do? What do schools actually achieve?) and by a number of case studies of alternatives in education which already exist, both within and beyond the traditional system. The other major weakness of Goodman, Illich and Reimer is that, although they all accept that their proposals are politically revolutionary and challenge political establishments, they do not face up to the political difficulties involved in achieving their programme. Like most visionaries they are more interested in ends than in means, but the greatest danger of which we ought to be aware is that deschooling could happen, but in ways quite other than those which they intend. Illich's interpretation of the Supreme Court judgment in the case of Griggs et al. v. Duke Power Company suggests that in him the wish is father of the thought.

Present policy developments in secondary education

In England in recent years the two outstanding moves in secondary education have been the attempt to establish a system of comprehensive schools and the decision to raise the school-leaving age to 16. At the same time, and often connected with these, there have been attempts to reform the curriculum and the content of education; teaching and learning systems; and the training of teachers. Indeed, the widespread nature of the attempted reforms suggests a crisis in secondary education. The early curriculum projects, in Science, Maths and Modern Languages, partly reflect the low standards of achievement in skill learning in schools. The later projects, such as the Humanities Project, and the General Studies Project, reflect an uncertainty about what kind of social learning schools should offer to the majority and dilemmas about general education in modern society. Although it is too early to speak of the failure of the reform movement in England it is not unreasonable to predict that the kind of lament made by Silberman for educational reform in the USA will be matched within the next five years. This is because of contradictions inherent in the society and the planning and the practice of education as we now have it. The two main contradictions of the moment are: that many people desire a society which is 'participatory', 'horizontal', and 'creative' whereas most schools are non-participatory, vertical and passive: and that cultural diversity is a value of more and more people and no institution as yet has comprehended a diversity of cultures and norms within it. The aspiration underlying the first contradiction suggests much more decentralisation and deinstitutionalisation of education, along the lines favoured by Goodman: the reality underlying the second contradiction suggests that, in this respect, as Illich argues, schools are not feasible. The comprehensive school, like the comprehensive church of Queen Elizabeth I, is not a precursor and creator of a more unified society: rather it is the epitome of the contradictions within society. Like the Elizabethan church it is likely to be overtaken by more dynamic organisations. Not everyone would agree with my central thesis that there is a profound social crisis, with many related aspects, underlying the present crisis in education. However, they might agree with some aspects which I have stressed. These would include a crisis within the high culture which has made intellectual leaders uncertain about what schools should teach; the decline of former educators, such as the extended family, the church, and the community, and perhaps the loss of a shared language by the members of society. All these things have presented schools, and teachers, with challenges which they proved inadequate to meet. In this situation the Schools Council, with its programme of conservative, limited reform aimed to prop up the system, ignores the underlying problems, and can only promote the continuation of contradictions. The school as an institution contradicts cultural diversity; independent learning contradicts the needs of a collaborative society; the bureaucratic structure of education contradicts talk of a participatory democracy. Not only do the schoolmen reformers argue that schools would be all right if only they were different: they end up in paradox and pretence when they argue that schools should create communities, instead of communities create schools. It is the supreme virtue of the deschoolers that they have exposed the fact that, with present institutionalised schemes, resources are always well short of requirements for education, and that they have thought in terms of educational provision in society and not just in terms of a school system. In doing this they have shown that the present programme in secondary education based as it is on a projection, with adjustments, of present practice is leading up a blind alley. Even supporters of the system now admit the failures of the attempt to achieve mass education through the schools: until recently over half the pupils left at the earliest possible time; truancy rates are high; illiteracy rates are alarming; and there is significant damage to the buildings of many schools. Although impressive new schools have been developed in country areas, such as in Leicestershire and Cumberland, there has been no significant and successful innovation in an urban area: the sad history of Risinghill showed the difficulty of radical innovation in a metropolis. The extension of primary school education into the secondary sector, through the introduction of 'middle schools', only shows the poverty of our thinking in this field.

For the future in education two main alternatives now present themselves: one is a system which offers élite education for leadership for the few and life-adjustment education for being led for the majority - which would be a continuation of the present system; the other is a system which would stress voluntarism, participation, and variety. In terms of curriculum, the first would offer differential curricula for the élite and the mass, who argue for diverse activities appropriate to individual and group needs. The first argues for schools; the second argues for an end to compulsory secondary schools. Because of its inherent contradictions the first programme is, in my opinion, no longer possible. The second programme might be.

Alternatives

In searching for an educational system to take us beyond our present dilemmas Goodman has looked to ancient Athens, with its 'mini-schools' and to medieval Europe and its apprenticeships; Reimer and Illich have looked to technotopia, with voluntary learning groups brought together by the computer. Torsten Husén, perhaps the high-priest of the schoolmen, has linked the past and the future in suggesting that the personal tutor, available to past rulers, is now available to all. In considering the alternative of a cooperative and participatory future others have looked to the Kibbutzim of Israel and to the communes of China. What is certain is that eventually we will need a cross-cultural, comparative and inter-disciplinary approach: something which goes far beyond the projections of present practice which is offered by such bodies as the Schools Council and the James Commission.

The general lines of any alternative programme would have to include:
1. An end to compulsion and the promoting of voluntarism. This would also involve the provision of real choice for learners/consumers, which in turn would mean putting the funds, or the credit, for education in their hands; and an expansion of advisory services, which would offer consultancy to people on how to obtain their needs from the provision available in the more flexible and varied system of the future.
2. Deformalising instruction, and putting more stress on informal and incidental learning. This would involve using the resources of the environment - both things and people - much more than at present.
3. Creating opportunities for life-long learning (permanent education). This would involve adequate funding of institutions, and collaborative enterprises, and would have the ultimate aim of making life and society themselves educational experiences.
All this would demand a radical rethinking of the major problems which confront us in education today.

In sketching the details of an alternative programme, I would like to identify alternatives which already exist within, outside and beyond the traditional system in England, and assess their possibilities for the future.

In many parts of the country, such as Oxfordshire, Leicestershire and the West Riding of Yorkshire, the 'alternative' primary school is already victorious. Non-streamed, cooperative, participatory, and creative, these 'progressive' primary schools accord with the aspirations of our society. If education is the new World Religion, as Illich suggests, he must admit that it takes different forms in different places: planeloads of American pilgrims come to worship at the shrine of the English primary school, but there is little traffic in the other direction.

In the secondary sector, and within the system, Countesthorpe Community College in Leicestershire provides an example of an institution which relates to the local community, is democratically run, and which organises teaching and learning in a nonauthoritarian way. Wyndham School, Egremont, is an example of a successful community school, affording access and educational provision for all the people of the locality. Although both of these schools are in rural or semi-rural areas, and although the community school has not yet proved itself in an urban setting, it must not be forgotten that large numbers of people, even in Western Europe, do not live in cities.

Outside the system, there is the example of the Scotland Road Free School, in Liverpool - 'an alternative school for Liverpool' which seeks not to 'alienate people from their backgrounds... but to enrich and intensify their lives'. Its ultimate aim is 'to bring about a fragmentation of the state system into smaller, all age, personalised, democratic, locally-controlled, community schools'.

Also outside the system there are examples of voluntary group projects. The Playgroup Movement has responded to educational research in a way that the traditional system was too cumbersome to do; in Bradford the participatory projects of the Art College involve people in creating their own educative drama; and there are examples of artists, such as sculptors and potters, opening up their workshops to those who wanted to work and learn with them.

Within certain projects there are elements significant for the future alternative programme. The York University Immigrant Projects have used students in language teaching on a one-to-one basis. The Educational Priority Area Projects in Denaby, West Riding and Liverpool have involved ordinary people in the educational enterprise: educators have gone into the homes of the people, and have provided facilities for children to learn in a domestic, nonschool setting. The various humanities projects have exposed the limitations of schools as centres of knowledge, and difficulties of the storage and retrieval of information. At least one school is now making itself a resource centre and a centre of enquiry.

Beyond the system there are the examples of the Open University; of Youth Action organisers; Adult Education tutors; and of W.E.A. tutors acting as 'worker-priests', taking groups in laundrettes, working men's clubs, and tower-block flats.

The prototypes of Illich's 'skill centres' already exist. At York the Language Centre is available to all schools - it should be available to everybody - and offers a range of foreign language teaching which schools, because of institutional reasons, are unable to match. At Solihull, the Euro-Lang Centre, whose founder members include British Leyland and ICI, offers courses in six languages. In Cambridge efficient language schools for a long time have offered courses to the daughters of the European bourgeoisie, who in return offered learning opportunities to others in the locality.

The Advisory Centre for Education, and the ventures of 'Education shops' giving advice about the system, are an example of counselling services. The demand for them shows the need for a great expansion in this area.

In general, the elements of the future alternative system which might already exist, in embryo at present, are secure in direct proportion to how they are supported by the present political/economic system. Thus, the Euro-Lang Centre, enjoying big-business support, is secure. Countesthorpe College and the alternative school for Liverpool, whose whole organisation challenges the present political structure, are vulnerable. In a third category, the Open University, Youth Action Organisers, Adult Education and W. E. A. tutors, are in danger of being used as safety-valves - as concessionary fringe alternatives, fed into the system to keep the essential system going.

That said, these prototypes must be viewed as having, potentially, enormous importance, for not only do they indicate the shortcomings of present provision; they also provide clues as to what might happen during the transitional period, when voluntarism is at last achieved. Illich has written: 'The school system... may soon face a problem which churches faced before: what to do with surplus space emptied by the defection of the faithful.' In York, where we have more churches than congregation, one declining church was made into a hostel; another

is now a tourist information office. A third, however, got a dynamic teacher - and is still a church.

Towards the future

The strategy required for implementing the kind of changes we support has two dimensions - one methodical, the other inspirational. In the research field we need more empirical investigations, both of traditional and innovative practice in education, and many more case-studies of experiments in our own countries, and in other countries - particularly Israel and China. In practice, we need to support alternatives where they already exist, and to introduce a programme of alternatives to present provision. However, the advantage that we have over the traditional education machine is that we have a purpose and a vision and it does not. Edward Boyle has recently said: 'the major political differences in our national life are not so much between government and opposition as between government and everybody else. Governments "do", the rest of us talk.' In the case of educational innovation, where governments have often shown that they are incapable of 'doing', he is hardly accurate. Like the Independents of seventeenth-century England people in the localities are claiming more control over the conditions of their own lives. A cultural revolution, involving people in their own education would not only end the distinction between the rulers and the ruled, the planners and the planned. It could lead to an upsurge of the human spirit like that of the Movement to the People in Russia in 1874 when, it was said, 'there came to mind scenes of the first centuries of Christianity and the times of the great Emancipation'. Today in the catacombs of educational thought the deschooling underground might be revealing to us the outlines of tomorrow's world.

18

IAN LISTER

The whole curriculum and the hidden curriculum

Source: A discussion document presented to the Schools Council Project on the Whole Curriculum in June 1972.

* *

A discussion document aims to provoke discussion. The assertions stem partly from such exotic intellectual areas as political socialisation, labelling theory, curriculum theory, and the sociology of knowledge. However, it is a good question what kinds of investigations would have to be carried out in order to find evidence to support the assertions.

* *

The Schools Council has come under criticism for approaching the curriculum from its parts, and thus promoting 'reforms' which merely prop up the general structure.

Until recently the 'curriculum' was considered mainly in terms of the structure of knowledge.

Now people like Ivan Illich have pointed out the distinction between the explicit curriculum and 'the hidden curriculum of schooling'. This paper lists some points which might be considered when thinking of the relationship of the hidden curriculum to the whole curriculum.

'I am using the term hidden curriculum to refer to the structure of schooling as opposed to what happens in school in the same way that linguists distinguish between the structure of a language and the use the speaker makes of it.' Ivan Illich in 'After Deschooling, What?' Social Policy (Sept./Oct. 1971).

Some messages of the hidden curriculum

1. Schooling and education are the same thing.

2. The world is non-educational: the school is unworldly.

3. Learning is the result of teaching.

4. Economically esteemed knowledge is the result of professional teaching.

5. Learning is mastery of the curriculum. The curriculum is a commodity. Schools and teachers package and sell the commodity.

6. Knowledge is divided into packages (subjects/topics). Learning is linear - knowledge comes in sequential curricula and graded exercises. (Curriculum reform is the filling of the curriculum with new packaged courses).

7. Specialist knowledge is the kind which is most highly esteemed.

8. Other people make all the decisions. (You must accept 'the environment'. You cannot influence - never mind change - it.)

9. Life is a zero-sum game in which individuals and countries compete for scarce resources (university places, petroleum). One man's/one country's gain is another man's/country's loss. Competition, not cooperation, is the essence of 'life', and is therefore 'natural'.

10. Individuals and countries can be graded/degraded on a sliding scale. (IQ/'academic' - 'Newsom' children/restricted-elaborated code: 'developed'-'underdeveloped' countries.) The 'poor' are incapable of helping themselves and need to be helped by those who are 'better off'. Philanthropy is thus a 'natural' part of the system.

11. There is a phase of a person's life when he/she is at 'school age'. Education ends when schooling ends. In order to get more education we must therefore raise the school-leaving age.

Some challenges to the Schools Council

1. Could the Schools Council be deschooled and become instead an Education Council? Instead of asking the question of how it can keep the schools going (or keep a shaky service-industry in business) couldn't it ask the question: What kind of educational provision ought to exist in our society? (Could it ask the questions of the Wright Commission on post-secondary education in Ontario rather than those of the James Report?)

2. Could it investigate the relationship between schooling and education; analyse the positive possibilities of schooling and identify those areas in which the school might be anti-educational, and in which it might provide a bad learning environment? Could it identify valuable and effective learning outside schools? Could we investigate ways in which we can identify educational possibilities in the environment? Could we find ways of making the environment and life itself more educative?

3. Could it investigate the relationship of teaching and learning? Could we have more studies of learning and of learners? Could we concentrate less on how to produce teachers and more on how to create conditions for learning?

4. Could we find ways of validating knowledge, skills, experience acquired outside formal institutions?

5. What is the relationship of 'the curriculum' to learning and to education?

6. What are the alternatives to curriculum packages, and sequential curricula? Can curriculum reformers avoid setting up a curriculum development industry, with the language of General Motors, the alibis of nuclear scientists (spin-off), and in-built obsolescence?

7. Could there be such a thing as a 'generally educated man/woman'? If so, what would be his/her characteristics?

8. What are the areas in education where learners could meaningfully make their own decisions?

9. What are the possibilities of collaborative learning; of conviviality between people (an area where resources might be infinite); of concentrating on how resources might be justly distributed (between individuals, groups, state and private concerns) rather than on how much each competitor can get of the limited supplies available?

10. What are the possibilities of diagnostic assessment (aimed to help the learner) and descriptive references rather than grade assessment?

11. What are the possibilities of 'lifelong learning' and 'the learning society'? And what are the dangers - might it usher in the age of 'the global schoolhouse', indistinguishable from the global madhouse?

A statement and a question

Statement: Curriculum reform which involves real change, rather than a reshuffle of the old parts, clearly must involve a change in the hidden curriculum.

Question: Can a change in the hidden curriculum be achieved without putting in its place a new hidden curriculum, as insidious and as riddled with contradictions between itself and our social aspirations as the one we have at present?

19

ERIC MIDWINTER

Stick with the system

Educational reformers in Britain tend to regard themselves as working 'within the system', outside the system, or walking the tightrope. Eric Midwinter, who at the time of writing was director of the Liverpool educational priority area project, enjoys both a practical and mythological presence in English education. He has argued against a curriculum of arcane knowledge for the majority. Some accuse him of offering a new kind of life-adjustment education. Is his argument practical and down-to-earth, or more a mixture of ambivalence and opportunism?

* *

In a recent leader The Times Educational Supplement spoke sadly of the Liverpool l. e. a. 'missing an opportunity to support the kind of unorthodox innovation which only an independent venture can launch.' In the specific case under review - a gallant and inventive attempt to establish a 'free school' in an unpropitious area of Liverpool - the l. e. a. have now generously consented to give limited support.

This in itself is interesting, as the free school movement aims at the 'fragmentation of the state system'. Beyond the rather bewildering logic of an avowedly private venture wishing for public support, there is a mild amusement in the l. e. a. cheerfully volunteering this first step towards walking the plank. None the less, there may well be occasional worthy objects of public assistance of this kind. What is less believable is the bald statement that private enterprise is the sole mode of innovatory action.

Historically, the record of innovation from within the state system is a sound one, particularly since the war. It has increasingly been pointed out that a process of osmosis has been a principal factor in overall reform, with teachers actually seeing reforms succeed and with courses, in-service and student training, advisers, inspectors and so on acting as agents of change. Let me say at once that I am unimpressed by the speed of these alterations and that - progressive primary method is one illustration - the quantitative assessment of such change has been exaggerated. It is, however, on the acceleration of this solid gradual process that the radical restructuring of the education system depends.

Progressive independent schools have had less influence than some commentators have indicated. Teachers often regard such experiments as hothouse plants which blossom exotically and wither prematurely; they rarely see them as transferable to the more mundane allotments of the normal set-up. Indeed, they have sometimes proved counterproductive as teachers argue, with some validity, that they would not 'work' in real life.

It is the right wing of independent education that has had much more impact in, for instance, its influence on the stamp and character of the state grammar school. Private education has tended towards a deadening and elitist conformity, even when its original intentions have been charitable and humanitarian; many 'public' schools testify to this.

Conversely, there can be few educational structures more flexible than the English state system. This has disadvantages (such as the difficulty of altering 'bad' schools) but lack of opportunity for innovation is not one of these. A colourful and variegated pattern of innovation is being attempted across the nation at all times and in everyday situations.

One sometimes wonders whether the progenitors of private experiments have fully canvassed the possibilities of the public sector. This is not a dewey-eyed, naïve view of public education. In practice, the main course of action for those of us who wish to see a fundamental change in the state system is to operate purposefully within it.

To opt out of the public sector is to run a grave risk, if the aim of pilot experiment is to produce a broader response. It is not only a question of throwing out the baby with the bathwater, it is the hazard of throwing out the bath as well. The capital investment in our massive educational fabric is overwhelmingly huge - to turn one's back on this, as opposed to trying to change it from within, can be eccentric and woolly-headed.

It is an arduous task, but because of the versatility of the system, not impossible. Witness Priority, a national centre for urban education to be established in Liverpool next January. It will sustain and extend the Liverpool educational priority area project and attempt to act as a window for urban community education throughout the country. It will operate at base with some 35 schools, 30 playgroups, 250 teacher-students and 20 or so adult groups. It will be in touch with l. e. a. s, colleges and other agencies up and down the country.

Such is the flexibility of the state system that the Liverpool l. e. a. is able to provide housing and support, office services and personnel and much other assistance to embrace a composite agency including supporting elements from the Advisory Centre for Education, Cambridge, the Workers' Educational Association, the Liverpool Council of Social Service, the John Moores Family Foundation, the Oxford University Evaluation Unit and so on.

Paradoxically, it is where the innovation is most fundamental that the imperative need to proceed within the state system is most urgent. In our own field of community education we are anxious to 'communalise' the schools; we know that there exists a 'we' and 'them' image of educational organisation, as of most other social institutions, so much so that commentators can speak pejoratively of an establishment-oriented, bureaucratic entity far removed from the citizenry.

Nevertheless, the state is a conglomeration of individuals, most of them rate or tax payers, many of them parents and children, all of them with a stake in the schools. If the system is wrong, it needs to be changed, not abandoned. In theory, the state system is the people's system, and it is the task of all those interested in community education to render this genuine in practice.

My own radicalism is old-fashioned enough for

me to be an unrepentant devotee of the public system and a fervent proponent of the view that all available endeavour should be pressed into changing it at its many weak points and bases. Equally, I am a suspicious opponent of private education in all its facets.

Although, of course, one recognises how tempting it is to enjoy the indulgence of going it alone, one mourns the loss of talented and energetic educators who attempt to establish independent 'models', for these are too often dead-ends rather than short-cuts. My contention is that, not only is the state system capable of comprehending innovation, it is, effectively, the best and the necessary focus for it.

20

JULIUS K. NYERERE

Education for self-reliance

Source: Policy booklet published in March 1967, and reproduced in Julius K. Nyerere, Ujamaa: Essays on Socialism (Oxford University Press, 1968).

* *

'Tanzania's education is such as to divorce its participants from the society it is supposed to be preparing them for.' This piece by the President of Tanzania, who is generally known to the people as 'Mwalimu' - 'Teacher', is a classic. It raises first-order questions about purposes, and identifies the fundamental problems about education and society. Important questions which now need to be asked include: How does what Tanzania does relate to what Nyerere says? How appropriate is this approach to other Third World countries - in Latin America for example? And what can developed, and over-developed countries learn from it? Do people in those countries need to decolonise their assumptions about their own educational system?

* *

Since long before independence the people of this country, under the leadership of TANU, have been demanding more education for their children. But we have never really stopped to consider why we want education - what its purpose is. Therefore, although over time there have been various criticisms about the details of curricula provided in schools, we have not until now questioned the basic system of education which we took over at the time of independence. We have never done that because we have never thought about education except in terms of obtaining teachers, engineers, administrators, etc. Individually and collectively we have in practice thought of education as a training for the skills required to earn high salaries in the modern sector of our economy.

It is now time that we looked again at the justification for a poor society like ours spending almost 20 per cent of its Government revenues on providing education for its children and young people, and began to consider what that education should be doing.

For in our circumstances it is impossible to devote Shs. 147,330,000/- every year to education for some of our children (while others go without) unless its result has a proportionate relevance to the society we are trying to create.

The educational systems in different kinds of societies in the world have been, and are, very different in organisation and in content. They are different because the societies providing the education are different, and because education, whether it be formal or informal, has a purpose. That purpose is to transmit from one generation to the next the accumulated wisdom and knowledge of the society, and to prepare the young people for their future membership of the society and their active participation in its maintenance or development.

This is true, explicitly or implicitly, for all societies - the capitalist societies of the West, the communist societies of the East, and the pre-colonial African societies too.

The fact that pre-colonial Africa did not have 'schools' - except for short periods of initiation in some tribes - did not mean that the children were not educated. They learned by living and doing. In the homes and on the farms they were taught the skills of the society, and the behaviour expected of its members. They learned the kind of grasses which were suitable for which purposes, the work which had to be done on the crops, or the care which had to be given to animals, by joining with their elders in this work. They learned the tribal history, and the tribe's relationship with other tribes and with the spirits, by listening to the stories of the elders. Through these means, and by the custom of sharing to which young people were taught to conform, the values of the society were transmitted. Education was thus 'informal'; every adult was a teacher to a greater or lesser degree. But this lack of formality did not mean that there was no education, nor did it affect its importance to the society. Indeed, it may have made the education more directly relevant to the society in which the child was growing up.

In Europe education has been formalised for a very long time. An examination of its development will show, however, that it has always had similar objectives to those implicit in the traditional African system of education. That is to say, formal education in Europe was intended to reinforce the social ethics existing in the particular country, and to prepare the children and young people for the place they will have in that society. The same thing is true of communist countries now. The content of education is somewhat different from that of Western countries, but the purpose is the same - to prepare young people to live in and to serve the society, and to transmit the knowledge, skills, and values and attitudes of the society. Wherever education fails in any of these fields, there the society falters in its progress, or there is social unrest as people find that their education has prepared them for a future which is not open to them.

Colonial education in Tanzania and the inheritance of the New State

The education provided by the colonial government in the two countries which now form Tanzania had a different purpose. It was not designed to prepare young people for the service of their own country; instead it was motivated by a desire to inculcate the values of the colonial society and to train individuals for the service of the colonial state. In these countries the state interest in education therefore stemmed from the need for local clerks and junior officials; on top of that, various religious groups were interested in spreading literacy and other education as part of their evangelical work.

This statement of fact is not given as a criticism of the many individuals who worked hard, often under difficult conditions, in teaching and in organising educational work. Nor does it imply that all the values these people transmitted in the schools were wrong or inappropriate. What it does mean, however, is that the educational system introduced into Tanzania by the colonialists was modelled on the British system, but with even heavier emphasis on subservient attitudes and on white-collar skills. Inevitably, too, it was based on the assumptions of a colonialist and capitalist society. It emphasised and encouraged the individualistic instincts of mankind, instead of his cooperative instincts. It led to the possession of individual material wealth being the major criterion of social merit and worth.

This meant that colonial education induced attitudes of human inequality, and in practice underpinned the domination of the weak by the strong, especially in the economic field. Colonial education in this country was therefore not transmitting the values and knowledge of Tanzanian society from one generation to the next; it was a deliberate attempt to change those values and to replace traditional knowledge by the knowledge from a different society. It was thus a part of a deliberate attempt to effect a revolution in the society; to make it into a colonial society which accepted its status and which was an efficient adjunct to the governing power. Its failure to achieve these ends does not mean that it was without an influence on the attitudes, ideas, and knowledge of the people who experienced it. Nor does that failure imply that the education provided in colonial days is automatically relevant for the purposes of a free people committed to the principle of equality.

The independent state of Tanzania in fact inherited a system of education which was in many respects both inadequate and inappropriate for the new state. It was, however, its inadequacy which was most immediately obvious. So little education had been provided that in December 1961, we had too few people with the necessary educational qualifications even to man the administration of Government as it was then, much less undertake the big economic and social development work which was essential. Neither was the school population in 1961 large enough to allow for any expectation that this situation would be speedily corrected. On top of that, education was based upon race, whereas the whole moral case of the independence movement had been based upon a rejection of racial distinctions.

Action since independence

The three most glaring faults of the educational inheritance have already been tackled. First, the racial distinctions within education were abolished. Complete integration of the separate racial systems was introduced very soon after independence, and discrimination on grounds of religion was also brought to an end. A child in Tanzania can now secure admittance to any Government or Government-aided school in this country without regard to his race or religion and without fear that he will be subject to religious indoctrination as the price of learning.

Secondly, there has been a very big expansion of educational facilities available, especially at the secondary school and post-secondary school levels. In 1961 there were 490,000 children attending primary schools in Tanganyika, the majority of them only going up to Standard IV. In 1967 there were 825,000 children attending such schools, and increasingly these will be full seven-year primary schools. In 1961, too, there were 11,832 children in secondary schools, only 176 of whom were in Form VI. This year there are 25,000 and 830. This is certainly something for our young state to be proud of. It is worth reminding ourselves that our present problems (especially the so-called problem of the primary school leavers) are revealing themselves largely because of these successes.

The third action we have taken is to make the education provided in all our schools much more Tanzanian in content. No longer do our children simply learn British and European history. Faster than would have been thought possible our University College and other institutions are providing materials on the history of Africa and making these available to our teachers. Our national songs and dances are once again being learned by our children; our national language has been given the importance in our curriculum which it needs and deserves. Also, civics classes taken by Tanzanians are beginning to give the secondary school pupils an understanding of the organisation and aims of our young state. In these and other ways changes have been introduced to make our educational system more relevant to our needs. At this time, when there is so much general and justified questioning of what is being done, it is appropriate that we should pay tribute to the work of our teachers and those who support their work in the Ministry, in the Institute of Education, the University College and the District Councils.

Yet all these things I have mentioned are modifications of the system we have inherited. Their results have not yet been seen; it takes years for a change in education to have its effect. The events of 1966 do suggest, however, that a more thorough examination of the education we are providing must be made. It is now clearly time for us to think seriously about this question: 'What is the educational system in Tanzania intended to do - what is its purpose?' Having decided that, we have to look at the relevance of the existing structure and content of Tanzanian education for the task it has to do. In the light of that examination we can consider whether, in our present circumstances, further modifications are required or whether we need a change in the whole approach.

What kind of society are we trying to build?

Only when we are clear about the kind of society we

are trying to build can we design our educational service to serve our goals. But this is not now a problem in Tanzania. Although we do not claim to have drawn up a blueprint of the future, the values and objectives of our society have been stated many times. We have said that we want to create a socialist society which is based on three principles: equality and respect for human dignity; sharing of the resources which are produced by our efforts; work by everyone and exploitation by none. We have set out these ideas clearly in the National Ethic; and in the Arusha Declaration and earlier documents we have outlined the principles and policies we intend to follow. We have also said on many occasions that our objective is greater African unity, and that we shall work for this objective while in the meantime defending the absolute integrity and sovereignty of the United Republic. Most often of all, our Government and people have stressed the equality of all citizens, and our determination that economic, political, and social policies shall be deliberately designed to make a reality of that equality in all spheres of life. We are, in other words, committed to a socialist future and one in which the people will themselves determine the policies pursued by a Government which is responsible to them.

It is obvious, however, that if we are to make progress towards these goals, we in Tanzania must accept the realities of our present position, internally and externally, and then work to change these realities into something more in accord with our desires. And the truth is that our United Republic has at present a poor, undeveloped, and agricultural economy. We have very little capital to invest in big factories or modern machines; we are short of people with skill and experience. What we do have is land in abundance and people who are willing to work hard for their own improvement. It is the use of these latter resources which will decide whether we reach our total goals or not. If we use these resources in a spirit of self-reliance as the basis for development, then we shall make progress slowly but surely. And it will then be real progress, affecting the lives of the masses, not just having spectacular show-pieces in the towns while the rest of the people of Tanzania live in their present poverty.

Pursuing this path means that Tanzania will continue to have a predominantly rural economy for a long time to come. And as it is in the rural areas that people live and work, so it is in the rural areas that life must be improved. This is not to say that we shall have no industries and factories in the near future. We have some now and they will continue to expand. But it would be grossly unrealistic to imagine that in the near future more than a small proportion of our people will live in towns and work in modern industrial enterprises. It is therefore the villages which must be made into places where people live a good life; it is in the rural areas that people must be able to find their material well-being and their satisfactions.

This improvement in village life will not, however, come automatically. It will come only if we pursue a deliberate policy of using the resources we have - our manpower and our land - to the best advantage. This means people working hard, intelligently, and together; in other words, working in co-operation. Our people in the rural areas, as well as their Government, must organise themselves co-operatively and work for themselves through working for the community of which they are members. Our village life, as well as our state organisation, must

be based on the principles of socialism and that equality in work and return which is part of it.

This is what our educational system has to encourage. It has to foster the social goals of living together, and working together, for the common good. It has to prepare our young people to play a dynamic and constructive part in the development of a society in which all members share fairly in the good or bad fortune of the group, and in which progress is measured in terms of human well-being, not prestige buildings, cars, or other such things, whether privately or publicly owned. Our education must therefore inculcate a sense of commitment to the total community, and help the pupils to accept the values appropriate to our kind of future, not those appropriate to our colonial past.

This means that the educational system of Tanzania must emphasise cooperative endeavour, not individual advancement; it must stress concepts of equality and the responsibility to give service which goes with any special ability, whether it be in carpentry, in animal husbandry, or in academic pursuits. And, in particular, our education must counteract the temptation to intellectual arrogance; for this leads to the well-educated despising those whose abilities are non-academic or who have no special abilities but are just human beings. Such arrogance has no place in a society of equal citizens.

It is, however, not only in relation to social values that our educational system has a task to do. It must also prepare young people for the work they will be called upon to do in the society which exists in Tanzania - a rural society where improvement will depend largely upon the efforts of the people in agriculture and in village development. This does not mean that education in Tanzania should be designed just to produce passive agricultural workers of different levels of skill who simply carry out plans or directions received from above. It must produce good farmers; it has also to prepare people for their responsibilities as free workers and citizens in a free and democratic society, albeit a largely rural society. They have to be able to think for themselves, to make judgements on all the issues affecting them; they have to be able to interpret the decisions made through the democratic institutions of our society, and to implement them in the light of the peculiar local circumstances where they happen to live.

It would thus be a gross misinterpretation of our needs to suggest that the educational system should be designed to produce robots, who work hard but never question what the leaders in Government or TANU are doing and saying. For the people are, and must be, Government and TANU. Our Government and our Party must always be responsible to the people, and must always consist of representatives - spokesmen and servants of the people. The education provided must therefore encourage the development in each citizen of three things: an enquiring mind; an ability to learn from what others do, and reject or adapt it to his own needs; and a basic confidence in his own position as a free and equal member of the society, who values others and is valued by them for what he does and not for what he obtains.

These things are important for both the vocational and the social aspects of education. However much agriculture a young person learns, he will not find a book which will give him all the answers to all the detailed problems he will come across on his own farm. He will have to learn the basic principles of modern knowledge in agriculture and then adapt them to solve his own problems. Similarly, the free citizens of Tanzania will have to judge social issues for themselves; there neither is, nor will be, a political 'holy book' which purports to give all the answers to all the social, political and economic problems which will face our country in the future. There will be philosophies and policies approved by our society which citizens should consider and apply in the light of their own thinking and experience. But the educational system of Tanzania would not be serving the interests of a democratic socialist society if it tried to stop people from thinking about the teachings, policies or the beliefs of leaders, either past or present. Only free people conscious of their worth and their equality can build a free society.

Some salient features of the existing educational system

These are very different purposes from those which are promoted by our existing educational arrangements. For there are four basic elements in the present system which prevent, or at least discourage, the integration of the pupils into the society they will enter, and which do encourage attitudes of inequality, intellectual arrogance and intense individualism among the young people who go through our schools.

First, the most central thing about the education we are at present providing is that it is basically an elitist education designed to meet the interests and needs of a very small proportion of those who enter the school system.

Although only about 13 per cent of our primary school children will get a place in a secondary school, the basis of our primary school education is the preparation of pupils for secondary schools. Thus 87 per cent of the children who finished primary school last year - and a similar proportion of those who will finish this year - do so with a sense of failure, of a legitimate aspiration having been denied them. Indeed we all speak in these terms, by referring to them as those who failed to enter secondary schools, instead of simply as those who have finished their primary education. On the other hand, the other 13 per cent have a feeling of having deserved a prize - and the prize they and their parents now expect is high wages, comfortable employment in towns, and personal status in the society. The same process operates again at the next highest level, when entrance to university is the question at issue.

In other words, the education now provided is designed for the few who are intellectually stronger than their fellows; it induces among those who succeed a feeling of superiority, and leaves the majority of the others hankering after something they will never obtain. It induces a feeling of inferiority among the majority, and can thus not produce either the egalitarian society we should build, nor the attitudes of mind which are conducive to an egalitarian society. On the contrary, it induces the growth of a class structure in our country.

Equally important is the second point; the fact that Tanzania's education is such as to divorce its participants from the society it is supposed to be preparing them for. This is particularly true of secondary schools, which are inevitably almost entirely boarding schools; but to some extent, and despite recent modifications in the curriculum, it is true of primary schools too. We take children from their parents at the age of 7 years, and for up to

$7\frac{1}{2}$ hours a day we teach them certain basic academic skills. In recent years we have tried to relate these skills, at least in theory, to the life which the children see around them. But the school is always separate; it is not part of the society. It is a place children go to and which they and their parents hope will make it unnecessary for them to become farmers and continue living in the villages.

The few who go to secondary schools are taken many miles away from their homes; they live in an enclave, having permission to go into the town for recreation, but not relating the work of either town or country to their real life - which is lived in the school compound. Later a few people go to university. If they are lucky enough to enter Dar es Salaam University College they live in comfortable quarters, feed well, and study hard for their degree. When they have been successful in obtaining it, they know immediately that they will receive a salary of something like £660 per annum. That is what they have been aiming for; it is what they have been encouraged to aim for. They may also have the desire to serve the community, but their idea of service is related to status and the salary which a university education is expected to confer upon its recipient. The salary and the status have become a right automatically conferred by the degree.

It is wrong of us to criticise the young people for these attitudes. The new university graduate has spent the larger part of his life separated and apart from the masses of Tanzania; his parents may be poor, but he has never fully shared that poverty. He does not really know what it is like to live as a poor peasant. He will be more at home in the world of the educated than he is among his own parents. Only during vacations has he spent time at home, and even then he will often find that his parents and relatives support his own conception of his difference, and regard it as wrong that he should live and work as the ordinary person he really is. For the truth is that many of the people in Tanzania have come to regard education as meaning that a man is too precious for the rough and hard life which the masses of our people still live.

The third point is that our present system encourages school pupils in the idea that all knowledge which is worthwhile is acquired from books or from 'educated people' - meaning those who have been through a formal education. The knowledge and wisdom of other old people is despised, and they themselves are regarded as being ignorant and of no account. Indeed it is not only the education system which at present has this effect. Government and Party themselves tend to judge people according to whether they have 'passed school certificate', 'have a degree', etc. If a man has these qualifications we assume he can fill a post; we do not wait to find out about his attitudes, his character, or any other ability except the ability to pass examinations. If a man does not have these qualifications we assume he cannot do a job; we ignore his knowledge and experience. For example, I recently visited a very good tobacco-producing peasant. But if I tried to take him into Government as a Tobacco Extension Officer, I would run up against the system because he has no formal education. Everything we do stresses book learning, and under-estimates the value to our society of traditional knowledge and the wisdom which is often acquired by intelligent men and women as they experience life, even without their being able to read at all.

This does not mean that any person can do any

job simply because they are old and wise, nor that educational qualifications are not necessary. This is a mistake our people sometimes fall into as a reaction against the arrogance of the book-learned. A man is not necessarily wise because he is old; a man cannot necessarily run a factory because he has been working in it as a labourer or storekeeper for 20 years. But equally he may not be able to do so if he has a Doctorate in Commerce. The former may have honesty and ability to weigh up men; the latter may have the ability to initiate a transaction and work out the economics of it. But both qualifications are necessary in one man if the factory is to be a successful and modern enterprise serving our nation. It is as much a mistake to over-value book learning as it is to under-value it.

The same thing applies in relation to agricultural knowledge. Our farmers have been on the land for a long time. The methods they use are the result of long experience in the struggle with nature; even the rules and taboos they honour have a basis in reason. It is not enough to abuse a traditional farmer as old-fashioned; we must try to understand why he is doing certain things, and not just assume he is stupid. But this does not mean that his methods are sufficient for the future. The traditional systems may have been appropriate for the economy which existed when they were worked out and for the technical knowledge then available. But different tools and different land tenure systems are being used now; land should no longer be used for a year or two and then abandoned for up to 20 years to give time for natural regeneration to take place. The introduction of an ox-plough instead of a hoe - and, even more, the introduction of a tractor - means more than just a different way of turning over the land. It requires a change in the organisation of work, both to see that the maximum advantage is taken of the new tool, and also to see that the new method does not simply lead to the rapid destruction of our land and the egalitarian basis of our society. Again, therefore, our young people have to learn both a practical respect for the knowledge of the old 'uneducated' farmer, and an understanding of new methods and the reason for them.

Yet at present our pupils learn to despise even their own parents because they are old-fashioned and ignorant; there is nothing in our existing educational system which suggests to the pupil that he can learn important things about farming from his elders. The result is that he absorbs beliefs about witchcraft before he goes to school, but does not learn the properties of local grasses; he absorbs the taboos from his family but does not learn the methods of making nutritious traditional foods. And from school he acquires knowledge unrelated to agricultural life. He gets the worst of both systems!

Finally, and in some ways most importantly, our young and poor nation is taking out of productive work some of its healthiest and strongest young men and women. Not only do they fail to contribute to that increase in output which is so urgent for our nation; they themselves consume the output of the older and often weaker people. There are almost 25,000 students in secondary schools now; they do not learn as they work, they simply learn. What is more, they take it for granted that this should be so. Whereas in a wealthy country like the United States of America it is common for young people to work their way through high school and college, in Tanzania the structure of our education makes it impossible for them to do so. Even during the holidays we assume that these young men and women should be protected from rough work; neither they nor the community expect them to spend their time on hard physical labour or on jobs which are uncomfortable and unpleasant. This is not simply a reflection of the fact that there are many people looking for unskilled paid employment - pay is not the question at issue. It is a reflection of the attitude we have all adopted.

How many of our students spend their vacations doing a job which could improve people's lives but for which there is no money - jobs like digging an irrigation channel or a drainage ditch for a village, or demonstrating the construction and explaining the benefits of deep-pit latrines, and so on? A small number have done such work in the National Youth Camps or through school-organised, nation-building schemes, but they are the exception rather than the rule. The vast majority do not think of their knowledge or their strength as being related to the needs of the village community.

Can these faults be corrected?

There are three major aspects which require attention if this situation is to change: the content of the curriculum itself, the organisation of the schools, and the entry age into primary schools. But although these aspects are in some ways separate, they are also inter-locked. We cannot integrate the pupils and students into the future society simply by theoretical teaching, however well designed it is. Neither can the society fully benefit from an education system which is thoroughly integrated into local life but does not teach people the basic skills - for example, of literacy and arithmetic, or which fails to excite in them a curiosity about ideas. Nor can we expect those finishing primary school to be useful young citizens if they are still only 12 or 13 years of age.

In considering changes in the present structure it is also essential that we face the facts of our present economic situation. Every penny spent on education is money taken away from some other needed activity - whether it is an investment in the future, better medical services, or just more food, clothing and comfort for our citizens at present. And the truth is that there is no possibility of Tanzania being able to increase the proportion of the national income which is spent on education; it ought to be decreased. Therefore we cannot solve our present problems by any solution which costs more than is at present spent; in particular we cannot solve the 'problem of primary school leavers' by increasing the number of secondary school places.

This 'problem of primary school leavers' is in fact a product of the present system. Increasingly children are starting school at 6 or even 5 years of age, so that they finish primary school when they are still too young to become responsible young workers and citizens. On top of that is the fact that both the society and the type of education they have received led them to expect wage employment - probably in an office. In other words, their education was not sufficiently related to the tasks which have to be done in our society. This problem therefore calls for a major change in the content of our primary education and for the raising of the primary school entry age so that the child is older when he leaves, and also able to learn more quickly while he is at school.

There is no other way in which this problem of primary school leavers can be solved. Unpleasant though it may be, the fact is that it is going to be a long time before we can provide universal primary education in Tanzania; for the vast majority of those who do get this opportunity, it will be only the equivalent of the present seven years' education. It is only a few who will have the chance of going on to secondary schools, and quite soon only a proportion of these who will have an opportunity of going on to university, even if they can benefit from doing so. These are the economic facts of life for our country. They are the practical meaning of our poverty. The only choice before us is how we allocate the educational opportunities, and whether we emphasise the individual interests of the few or whether we design our educational system to serve the community as a whole. And for a socialist state only the latter is really possible.

The implication of this is that the education given in our primary schools must be a complete education in itself. It must not continue to be simply a preparation for secondary school. Instead of the primary school activities being geared to the competitive examination which will select the few who go on to secondary school, they must be a preparation for the life which the majority of the children will lead. Similarly, secondary schools must not be simply a selection process for the university, teachers' colleges, and so on. They must prepare people for life and service in the villages and rural areas of this country. For in Tanzania the only true justification for secondary education is that it is needed by the few for service to the many. The teacher in a seven-year primary school system needs an education which goes beyond seven years; the extension officer who will help a population with a seven-years' education needs a lot more himself. Other essential services need higher education - for example, doctors and engineers need long and careful training. But publicly provided 'education for education's sake' must be general education for the masses. Further education for a selected few must be education for service to the many. There can be no other justification for taxing the many to give education to only a few.

Yet it is easy to say that our primary and secondary schools must prepare young people for the realities and needs of Tanzania; to do it requires a radical change, not only in the education system but also in many existing community attitudes. In particular, it requires that examinations should be downgraded in Government and public esteem. We have to recognise that although they have certain advantages - for example, in reducing the dangers of nepotism and tribalism in a selection process - they also have severe disadvantages too. As a general rule they assess a person's ability to learn facts and present them on demand within a time period. They do not always succeed in assessing a power to reason, and they certainly do not assess character or willingness to serve.

Further, at the present time our curriculum and syllabus are geared to the examinations set - only to a very limited extent does the reverse situation apply. A teacher who is trying to help his pupils often studies the examination papers for past years and judges what questions are most likely to be asked next time; he then concentrates his teaching on those matters, knowing that by doing so he is giving his children the best chance of getting through to secondary school or university. And the examinations our children at present sit are themselves geared to an international standard and practice which has developed regardless of our particular problems and need. What we need to do now is think first about the education we want to provide, and when that thinking is completed think about whether some form of examination is an appropriate way of closing an education phase. Then such an examination should be designed to fit the education which has been provided.

Most important of all is that we should change the things we demand of our schools. We should not determine the type of things children are taught in primary schools by the things a doctor, engineer, teacher, economist, or administrator need to know. Most of our pupils will never be any of these things. We should determine the type of things taught in the primary schools by the things which the boy or girl ought to know - that is, the skills he ought to acquire and the values he ought to cherish if he, or she, is to live happily and well in a socialist and predominantly rural society, and contribute to the improvement of life there. Our sights must be on the majority; it is they we must be aiming at in determining the curriculum and syllabus. Those most suitable for further education will still become obvious, and they will not suffer. For the purpose is not to provide an inferior education to that given at present. The purpose is to provide a different education - one realistically designed to fulfil the common purposes of education in the particular society of Tanzania. The same thing must be true at post-primary schools. The object of the teaching must be the provision of knowledge, skills and attitudes which will serve the student when he or she lives and works in a developing and changing socialist state; it must not be aimed at university entrance.

Alongside this change in the approach to the curriculum there must be a parallel and integrated change in the way our schools are run, so as to make them and their inhabitants a real part of our society and our economy. Schools must, in fact, become communities - and communities which practise the precept of self-reliance. The teachers, workers, and pupils together must be the members of a social unit in the same way as parents, relatives, and children are the family social unit. There must be the same kind of relationship between pupils and teachers within the school community as there is between children and parents in the village. And the former community must realise, just as the latter do, that their life and well-being depend upon the production of wealth - by farming or other activities. This means that all schools, but especially secondary schools and other forms of higher education, must contribute to their own upkeep; they must be economic communities as well as social and educational communities. Each school should have, as an integral part of it, a farm or workshop which provides the food eaten by the community, and makes some contribution to the total national income.

This is not a suggestion that a school farm or workshop should be attached to every school for training purposes. It is a suggestion that every school should also be a farm; that the school community should consist of people who are both teachers and farmers, and pupils and farmers. Obviously if there is a school farm, the pupils working on it should be learning the techniques and tasks of farming. But the farm would be an integral part of the school - and the welfare of the pupils would depend on its output, just as the welfare of a farmer depends on the output of his land. Thus, when this scheme is in operation, the revenue side of school accounts would not just read as at present - 'Grant from Government...; Grant from voluntary agency or other charity...'. They would read - 'Income from sale of cotton (or whatever other cash crop was appropriate for the area)...; Value of the food grown and consumed...; Value of labour done by pupils on new building, repairs, equipment, etc...; Government subvention...; Grant from...'.

This is a break with our educational tradition, and unless its purpose and its possibilities are fully understood by teachers and parents, it may be resented at the beginning. But the truth is that it is not a regressive measure, not a punishment either for teachers or pupils. It is a recognition that we in Tanzania have to work our way out of poverty, and that we are all members of the one society, depending upon each other. There will be difficulties of implementation, especially at first. For example, we do not now have a host of experienced farm managers who could be used as planners and teachers on the new school farms. But this is not an insuperable difficulty; and certainly life will not halt in Tanzania until we get experienced farm managers. Life and farming will go on as we train. Indeed, by using good local farmers as supervisors and teachers of particular aspects of the work, and using the services of the agricultural officers and assistants, we shall be helping to break down the notion that only book learning is worthy of respect. This is an important element in our socialist development.

Neither does this concept of schools contributing to their own upkeep simply mean using our children as labourers who follow traditional methods. On the contrary, on a school farm pupils can learn by doing. The important place of the hoe and of other simple tools can be demonstrated; the advantages of improved seeds, of simple ox-ploughs, and of proper methods of animal husbandry can become obvious; and the pupils can learn by practice how to use these things to the best advantage. The farm work and products should be integrated into the school life; thus the properties of fertilisers can be explained in the science classes, and their use and limitations experienced by the pupils as they see them in use. The possibilities of proper grazing practices, and of terracing and soil conservation methods can all be taught theoretically, at the same time as they are put into practice; the students will then understand what they are doing and why, and will be able to analyse any failures and consider possibilities for greater improvement.

But the school farms must not be, and indeed could not be, highly mechanised demonstration farms. We do not have the capital which would be necessary for this to happen, and neither would it teach the pupils anything about the life they will be leading. The school farms must be created by the school community clearing their own bush, and so on - but doing it together. They must be used with no more capital assistance than is available to an ordinary, established, cooperative farm where the work can be supervised. By such means the students can learn the advantages of cooperative endeavour, even when outside capital is not available in any significant quantities. Again, the advantages of cooperation could be studied in the classroom, as well as being demonstrated on the farm.

The most important thing is that the school members should learn that it is their farm, and that their living standards depend on it. Pupils should be given an opportunity to make many of the decisions necessary - for example, whether to spend money they have earned on hiring a tractor to get land ready for planting, or whether to use that money for other purposes on the farm or in the school, and doing the hard work themselves by sheer physical labour. By this sort of practice and by this combination of classroom work and farm work, our educated young people will learn to realise that if they farm well they can eat well and have better facilities in the dormitories, recreation rooms, and so on. If they work badly, then they themselves will suffer. In this process Government should avoid laying down detailed and rigid rules; each school must have considerable flexibility. Only then can the potential of that particular area be utilised, and only then can the participants practise - and learn to value - direct democracy.

By such means our students will relate work to comfort. They will learn the meaning of living together and working together for the good of all, and also the value of working together with the local non-school community. For they will learn that many things require more than school effort - that irrigation may be possible if they work with neighbouring farmers, that development requires a choice between present and future satisfaction, both for themselves and their village.

At the beginning it is probable that a good number of mistakes will be made, and it would certainly be wrong to give complete untrammelled choice to young pupils right from the start. But although guidance must be given by the school authorities and a certain amount of discipline exerted, the pupils must be able to participate in decisions and learn by mistakes. For example, they can learn to keep a school farm log in which proper records are kept of the work done, the fertilisers applied, or food given to the animals, etc., and the results from different parts of the farm. Then they can be helped to see where changes are required, and why. For it is also important that the idea of planning be taught in the classroom and related to the farm; the whole school should join in the programming of a year's work, and the breakdown of responsibility and timing within that overall programme. Extra benefits to particular groups within the school might then well be related to the proper fulfilment of the tasks set, once all the members of the school have received the necessary minimum for healthy development. Again, this sort of planning can be part of the teaching of socialism.

Where schools are situated in the rural areas, and in relation to new schools built in the future, it should be possible for the school farm to be part of the school site. But in towns, and in some of the old-established schools in heavily populated areas, this will not be possible. In such cases a school might put more emphasis on other productive activities, or it may be that in boarding schools the pupils can spend part of the school year in the classroom and another part in camp on the school farm some distance away. The plan for each school will have to be worked out; it would certainly be wrong to exclude urban schools, even when they are day schools, from this new approach.

Many other activities now undertaken for pupils, especially in secondary schools, should be undertaken by the pupils themselves. After all, a child who starts school at 7 years of age is already 14 before he enters secondary school, and may be 20 or 21 when he leaves. Yet in many of our schools now we employ cleaners and gardeners, not just to supervise and teach but to do all that work. The pupils get used to the idea of having their food prepared by servants, their plates washed up for them,

101

their rooms cleaned, and the school garden kept attractive. If they are asked to participate in these tasks, they even feel aggrieved and do as little as possible, depending on the strictness of the teacher's supervision. This is because they have not learned to take a pride in having clean rooms and nice gardens, in the way that they have learned to take a pride in a good essay or a good mathematics paper. But is it impossible for these tasks to be incorporated into the total teaching task of the school? Is it necessary for head teachers and their secretaries to spend hours working out travel warrants for school holidays, and so on? Can none of these things be incorporated into classroom teaching so that pupils learn how to do these things for themselves by doing them? Is it impossible, in other words, for secondary schools at least to become reasonably self-sufficient communities, where the teaching and supervisory skills are imported from outside, but where other tasks are either done by the community or paid for by its productive efforts? It is true that, to the pupils, the school is only a temporary community, but for up to seven years this is the group to which they really belong.

Obviously such a position could not be reached overnight. It requires a basic change in both organisation and teaching, and will therefore have to be introduced gradually, with the schools taking an increasing responsibility for their own well-being as the months pass. Neither would primary schools be able to do as much for themselves - although it should be remembered that the older pupils will be 13 and 14 years of age, at which time children in many European countries are already at work.

But, although primary schools cannot accept the same responsibility for their own well-being as secondary schools, it is absolutely vital that they, and their pupils, should be thoroughly integrated into the village life. The pupils must remain an integral part of the family (or community) economic unit. The children must be made part of the community by having responsibilities to the community, and having the community involved in school activities. The school work - terms, times, and so on - must be so arranged that the children can participate, as members of the family, in the family farms, or as junior members of the community on community farms. At present children who do not go to school work on the family or community farm, or look after cattle, as a matter of course. It must be equally a matter of course that the children who do attend school should participate in the family work - not as a favour when they feel like it, but as a normal part of their upbringing. The present attitudes whereby the school is regarded as something separate, and the pupils as people who do not have to contribute to the work, must be abandoned. In this, of course, parents have a special duty; but the schools can contribute a great deal to the development of this attitude.

There are many different ways in which this integration can be achieved. But it will have to be done deliberately, and with the conscious intention of making the children realise that they are being educated by the community in order that they shall become intelligent and active members of the community. One possible way of achieving this would give to primary school pupils the same advantages of learning by doing as the secondary school pupils will have. If the primary school children work on a village communal farm - perhaps having special responsibility for a given number of acres - they can

learn new techniques and take a pride in a school community achievement. If there is no communal farm, then the school can start a small one of their own by appealing to the older members to help in the bush-clearing in return for a school contribution in labour to some existing community project.

Again, if development work - new buildings or other things - are needed in the school, then the children and the local villagers should work on it together, allocating responsibility according to comparative health and strength. The children should certainly do their own cleaning (boys as well as girls should be involved in this), and should learn the value of working together and of planning for the future. Thus for example, if they have their own shamba the children should be involved not only in the work, but also in the allocation of any food or cash crop produced. They should participate in the choice between benefit to the school directly, or to the village as a whole, and between present or future benefit. By these and other appropriate means the children must learn from the beginning to the end of their school life that education does not set them apart, but is designed to help them be effective members of the community - for their own benefit as well as that of their country and their neighbours.

One difficulty in the way of this kind of reorganisation is the present examination system; if pupils spend more of their time on learning to do practical work, and on contributing to their own upkeep and the development of the community, they will not be able to take the present kind of examinations - at least within the same time period. It is, however, difficult to see why the present examination system should be regarded as sacrosanct. Other countries are moving away from this method of selection, and either abandoning examinations altogether at the lowest levels, or combining them with other assessments. There is no reason why Tanzania should not combine an examination, which is based on the things we teach, with a teacher and pupil assessment of work done for the school and community. This would be a more appropriate method of selecting entrants for secondary schools and for university, teacher training colleges, and so on, than the present purely academic procedure. Once a more detailed outline of this new approach to education is worked out, the question of selection procedure should be looked at again.

This new form of working in our schools will require some considerable organisational change. It may be also that the present division of the school year into rigid terms with long holidays would have to be re-examined; animals cannot be left alone for part of the year, nor can a school farm support the students if everyone is on holiday when the crops need planting, weeding or harvesting. But it should not be impossible for school holidays to be staggered so that different forms go at different periods or, in double-stream secondary schools, for part of a form to go at one time and the rest at another. It would take a considerable amount of organisation and administration, but there is no reason why it could not be done if we once make up our minds to it.

It will probably be suggested that if the children are working as well as learning they will therefore be able to learn less academically, and that this will affect standards of administration, in the professions and so on, throughout our nation in time to come. In fact it is doubtful whether this is necessarily so; the recent tendency to admit children to primary schools at ages of 5 and 6 years has almost certainly meant that less can be taught at the early stages. The reversion to 7 or 8 years entrance will allow the pace to be increased somewhat; the older children inevitably learn a little faster. A child is unlikely to learn less academically if his studies are related to the life he sees around him.

But even if this suggestion were based on provable fact, it could not be allowed to over-ride the need for change in the direction of educational integration with our national life. For the majority of our people the thing which matters is that they should be able to read and write fluently in Swahili, that they should have an ability to do arithmetic, and that they should know something of the history, values and workings of their country and their Government, and that they should acquire the skills necessary to earn their living. (It is important to stress that in Tanzania most people will earn their living by working on their own or on a communal shamba, and only a few will do so by working for wages which they have to spend on buying things the farmer produces for himself.) Things like health science, geography, and the beginning of English, are also important, especially so that the people who wish may be able to learn more by themselves in later life. But most important of all is that our primary school graduates should be able to fit into, and to serve, the communities from which they come.

The same principles of integration into the community and applicability to its needs, must also be followed at post-secondary levels, but young people who have been through such an integrated system of education as that outlined are unlikely to forget their debt to the community by an intense period of study at the end of their formal educational life. Yet even at university, medical school, or other post-secondary levels, there is no reason why students should continue to have all their washing up and cleaning done for them. Nor is there any reason why students at such institutions should not be required as part of their degree or professional training, to spend at least part of their vacations contributing to the society in a manner related to their studies. At present some undergraduates spend their vacations working in Government offices - getting paid at normal employee rates for doing so. It would be more appropriate (once the organisation had been set up efficiently) for them to undertake projects needed by the community, even if there is insufficient money for them to constitute paid employment. For example, the collection of local history, work on the census, participation in adult education activities, work in dispensaries, etc., would give the students practical experience in their own fields. For this they could receive the equivalent of the minimum wage, and any balance of money due for work which would otherwise have been done for higher wages could be paid to the college or institution and go towards welfare or sports equipment. Such work should earn credits for the student which count towards his examination result; a student who shirks such work - or fails to do it properly - would then find that two things follow. First, his fellow students might be blaming him for shortfalls in proposed welfare or other improvements; and second, his degree would be down-graded accordingly.

Conclusion

The education provided by Tanzania for the students of Tanzania must serve the purposes of Tanzania. It must encourage the growth of the socialist values we aspire to. It must encourage the development of a proud, independent and free citizenry which relies upon itself for its own development, and which knows the advantages and the problems of cooperation. It must ensure that the educated know themselves to be an integral part of the nation and recognise the responsibility to give greater service the greater the opportunities they have had.

This is not only a matter of school organisation and curriculum. Social values are formed by family, school, and society - by the total environment in which a child develops. But it is no use our educational system stressing values and knowledge appropriate to the past or to the citizens in other countries; it is wrong if it even contributes to the continuation of those inequalities and privileges which still exist in our society because of our inheritance. Let our students be educated to be members and servants of the kind of just and egalitarian future to which this country aspires.

21

JOHN OHLIGER

Adult education: 1984

Source: Article in <u>Adult Leadership</u> (January 1971).

* *

John Ohliger, who is a Professor at the College of Education, Columbus, Ohio, is one of the few who have warned about the growth of compulsory adult education in the USA and the kind of permanent education in which individuals would be dehumanised by being 'resocialised' and recycled to adapt to the changing needs of the economy. Here he gives his answer to the question raised by another American critic - Is there school after death?

* *

A child is born in the United States in the year 1984. He can never look forward to getting out of school. From the 'infant school' he starts attending at the age of six months to the 'geriatric learning centre' he dies in, he finds himself going to school all his life 'for the good of society'. From 'infant school' he goes on to elementary school, then to junior high school. At the point he might 'graduate' from junior high school, he takes a series of tests. These tests of his mental abilities, social adjustment potential, and motivation determine whether he will go on to a high school which will prepare him for 'higher schooling' and a career as a professional or whether he will go on to a vocational school which will prepare him for life as a worker. Let's say he is sent to a vocational school. After graduation perhaps he is placed in a job, or perhaps he is sent to a technical school to prepare him as a paraprofessional, or perhaps he is sent to a 'job bank school'. Many 'job bank schools' exist in the late 1900's because there are so few jobs available, since the great strides of automation.

The 'permanent school district' in which the young man resides has experts to make the important decisions for him. It is called a 'permanent school district', because by 1984 it was recognised that all people must go to school all their lives - permanently. The 'permanent school district' is run by a 'board of lifelong education' which has some of the characteristics of the old local board of education, the old draft board (because it is now accepted that we will be continually at war fighting 'Communism' all over the world), and the old board of regents or board of trustees for what were formerly called universities or colleges. By 1984 there are no more universities or colleges as we know them. Their buildings and remaining funds have all been turned over to the local 'permanent school districts', and the institutions have been renamed 'higher schools'. The private colleges ran out of resources years ago, because few rich people or corporations would contribute money to such 'disruptive' and 'permissive' institutions. The public universities found they could no longer get appropriations from the state legislatures, for the same reasons. Most of the faculty members of the old universities or colleges have long since been fired, sent to 'retraining camps', or to mental institutions for 'the good of society'.

So let's say our young man, who was born in 1984, is sent to a 'job bank school'. There he learns, along with some 'worthwhile hobbies', some skills that experts think he might just possibly use a few years later, in new jobs that just might exist then. Let's say our young man is lucky, the job he is preparing for does develop. He gets that job, and what is the first thing he does? He goes back to school. This time the school is in the factory where he works. Though he has learned the skills of the job, he still needs orientation to that particular factory, still needs to learn the unique demands of his particular task in relation to other functions in that factory, and needs to learn how to 'adjust' to the men and women and computerised robots working around him.

Suppose he does well at that job after attending the 'factory school'. He saves up some money and decides he wants to get married. His local 'board of lifelong education' gives him permission to marry, provided he and his fiancee attend a 'School for Marital Adjustment'. After attending the school the couple are married, settle down in a house which they are allowed to purchase after going to a 'School for Home Ownership Responsibilities', and decide they want to have children. They apply for permission to have babies and are put on a long waiting list, because there are the necessary controls on births to keep the population within manageable limits.

One of the controls is that every male child, at an early age, has a reversible vasectomy performed on him. Finally after waiting a few years the couple is told they may have one baby. But first, before the operation is performed on the husband to reverse the sterilisation, the couple must attend a 'School for Child Care'. After attending the school the couple is permitted to have the baby. Six months after he is born the baby is placed in an 'infant school', and the cycle begins all over again.

Meanwhile, the father finds that the job he has

been performing is now obsolete. Back to the 'job bank school' he must go to prepare for another position the experts predict will exist in a few years. Incidentally, all this time the young man, along with the rest of the adult population, is required to attend a 'citizenship institute' as part of his employment, which keeps him up-to-date on current political issues so he can vote intelligently, which is now compulsory.

At the age of 40, our young man, no longer young, is required to attend a 'geriatric preparation academy'. There he learns how to get ready to 'retire', which he must do at the age of 55. At 55 he leaves his job (the seventh he has held and gone to 'job bank schools' to prepare for), and enters a 'geriatric learning centre' where he is taught the arts and crafts which he is told will keep him 'happy' and 'out of mischief' until he dies.

When he does die, a minister eulogises him over his grave. By the way, the minister has gone through a 'higher school' and has been required to go back to the 'higher school' every two years for refresher courses in order to keep his license to preach. The minister delivers a beautiful eulogy. He points out that this man was very lucky, for he was born in 1984, the first year that the national 'Permanent School Law' was in effect. The minister extols the wisdom of the late President Spiro Agnew, who in the last year of his second term of office was able to get such a great law passed. 'And so we bid goodbye to this lucky man', the minister chants, 'firm in the conviction that he will go to heaven where he will attend a 'school for angels' into eternity. '

22

DAVID A. REIBEL

Language learning analysis

Source: Article in the International Review of Applied Linguistics in Language Teaching, Vol. VII, No. 4, 1969.

* *

Teachers of foreign languages in schools often live with failure on a saddening scale. Deschooling theory has criticised the structures in which they operate (and argued for more special skill centres to be set up) and the methods which they use. In this article David A. Reibel, who has been Visiting Professor at the University of Hawaii and who is currently Senior Lecturer in Language at the University of York, raises a central question for language teachers. Is language learning 'more exponential than linear' and, if so, what are the implications of that? The question also applies to those in other fields who construct a linear, sequential, and graded curriculum in contexts where it is not appropriate, something which more often provides a rationale for teachers than an aid to learners. (For this Reader the academic references and notes of the original text have been omitted.)

* *

This paper is an attempt to show that a widely held view about the requirements for a successful language teaching and learning programme is incorrect. The principle in question is that the course designer must write his teaching material on the basis of a detailed analysis of various parameters of texts of the target language, such as frequency, usefulness, basicness, or productiveness, of lexical or structural items. I will try to show that this principle is neither necessary nor sufficient to guarantee successful language learning and that it is furthermore mistaken on linguistic grounds alone. At the beginning of the paper I will try to present a fair and accurate outline of how this principle might be applied to the selection and sequencing of lexical items. I will then discuss some considerations that, I think, argue against the need for constructing special language teaching texts that reflect in a deliberate way various parameters of natural language use.

Let us first consider the language teacher's goals, and how to achieve them. A fair characterisation of the language teacher's commitment is that he wants the learner to achieve the ability to perform in the language that we observe in the native speaker. In providing the learner with the materials and activities that he needs to accomplish his purpose, the teacher normally wants to use the most efficient means available. This leads the teacher into a detailed and exhaustive analysis of all the components of the language learning situation. Methodological and linguistic elements of the language teaching programme are all subjected to the most searching kind of inquiry.

Let us look at what categories of things the teacher does need for a successful programme. First, taking the one well-attested constatum of psychology, that learners by and large learn to do what they do, we give the learner language learning materials that represent real language being used in real situations. That is, the language he learns from should be as much like the language he himself is going to produce as possible. Second, the teacher has some appropriate means for presenting this material to the learner, and getting him to use it. That is, the teacher has some method for modelling the language in life-like presentations which the learner imitates until his performance matches that of the model as closely as possible. Such techniques form the teacher's language teaching methodology.

Now the question I would like to raise is this one: In creating life-like language taught in life-like situations, is it also necessary, or even possible, for the teacher to exercise some control over the selection and sequencing of phonological, lexical, or grammatical elements? The assumption, often stated as fact, that the learner can or should learn only one thing at a time, has, apparently, led many language teaching analysts to the conclusion that the course designer himself has to decide what these items are, and the order in which they are to be learned. Since the behaviour of the fluent native speaker is very complex and presents structural and lexical features in an apparently random way, the language teacher feels encouraged to ease the path of the learner by limiting the complexity that he en-

counters at any one moment by some process of selection and ordered presentation.

This selection procedure can be generalised in the following way: The language teaching analyst selects typical examples of the language the learner is expected to learn to use; the relevant elements are analysed out; then a programme is constructed that presents the parts or pieces n at a time so that they can be effortlessly learned. The first step, then, is the selection of the texts themselves - the limitation process - on the basis of the appropriateness of the texts, either to the kind of language - e. g. scientific, commercial, literary - the learner is expected to be able to use, or to the use - reading, speaking, writing - to which it is expected the learner will be putting his knowledge of the language. It is not, of course, always easy to maintain this distinction. The criteria that are used for the analytical procedure involve considerations of frequency, complexity, over-all usefulness, congruence - or lack of it - with the learner's native language, and other notions such as productivity or basicness of patterns. The third part of the procedure is to arrange the elements into a progressive sequence according to the selection criteria (and of course also according to others, such as length of learning unit, number of new items per learning unit, ordering of items with respect to each other, number of repetitions, types of learning aids, etc.). Reduced to its essentials, the assumption is that there is some kind of weighted value that can be assigned to textual elements and that this weighting then provides the course designer with a well-motivated, non-arbitrary method of determining automatically the order in which the elements are to be presented. This weighting is the language course designer's basis for including any item in his teaching material, and provides the rationale for the sequencing of the items. For purposes of illustration and simplification the rest of the discussion is limited to the selection and sequencing of lexical items.

Of course, if one tries to operate simultaneously with all possible weighting criteria, then certain difficulties arise. For example, the Russian word for 'teacher' is a frequent item in some class-room context, let us say, and would be weighted so as to appear early and frequently on that account. It might be weighted just the other way, however, on grounds of phonological or morphological complexity, and hence would be destined to appear very late. In other words, it is no solution to say that 'in practice' one must balance the various criteria off against each other, since there is, as far as can be determined, no criterion for weighting the various criteria themselves with respect to each other that does not imply abandoning the criteria entirely.

Now let us take a detailed look at this selection process, as represented in the diagram. The diagram is merely a schematisation of the interpretation being given of the lexical selection procedure.

First, a corpus of texts known to have some desired characteristic, such as naturalness or representativeness, is assembled. This is the Primary Corpus of Texts, Box 1 in the diagram. These texts can be thought of as the out-put of the Grammar, Box 1B in the diagram. The discourse Content, or set of meanings, represented in the diagram by Box 1A, operates in such a way that, together with the rules of the grammar, the sentences of the corpus are produced in some way.

Then, the Analytical Selection Procedure, Box 2 in the diagram applies the weighting criterion to the

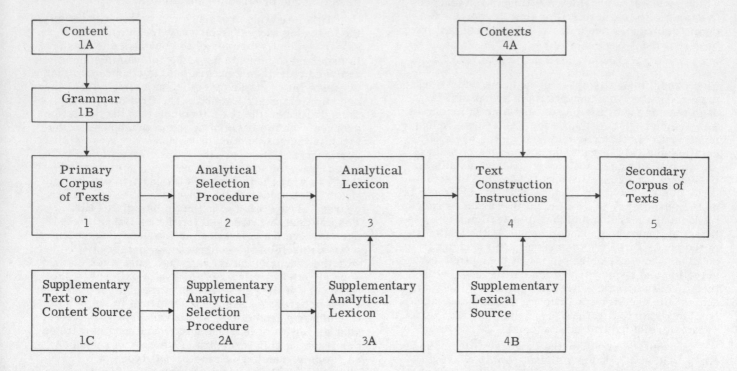

lexical items of the corpus, yielding the Analytical Lexicon, Box 3. The Analytical Lexicon stores the lexical items, along with a code indicating the weighting assigned to each entry. We can think of this process, 1 to 2 to 3, as the primary item-selection procedure.

In practice, however, the Analytical Lexicon must be supplemented from other sources, using other weighting criteria. For example, it is often recognised that 'useful' words may show up rather low down on the frequency scale. Thus a Supplementary Text or Content Source, Box 1C, is added to the primary corpus of texts, and a Supplementary Analytical Selection Procedure, Box 2A, weights the lexical items there, to form the Supplementary Analytical Lexicon, Box 3A, whose contents are then added to the main Analytical Lexicon, Box 3.

The analytical lexicon now serves as the source of lexical items that are the input to the set of Text Construction Instructions, Box 4. These instructions control the sequencing of the lexical items according to the weighting provided in the analytical lexicon. The selected items then trigger the selection of appropriate contexts that provide the situational basis for the texts that are constructed according to the Text Construction Instructions. Of course, the analytical lexicon may not even now contain all the lexical items that are needed for the procedure to operate. Suppose that the weighting associated with some lexical item indicates that it should now be introduced into language teaching texts. The context triggered by the selection of that lexical item might dictate that for the sake of naturalness, or for some other reason, another lexical item not presently in the analytical lexicon must be introduced. Hence the need for a Supplementary Lexical Source, Box 4B in the diagram. Finally a Secondary Corpus of (teaching) Texts, 5, will be produced which can serve as the basis of the teaching programme that has been the language teaching analyst's and programme designer's goal all along.

But now notice an interesting consequence of the

selection and sequencing process. According to the principle that motivates this procedure, the elements of the output texts should now be characterised by a certain set of parameters, such as frequency, usefulness, basicness, etc. But these parameters, which are regarded as so indispensible for successful language learning, are already present as properties of the primary corpus of texts. This claim, that both the input texts, Box 1 in the diagram, and the output texts, Box 5 in the diagram, have the same set of characterising parameters, is important. If it is true, then the whole selection and sequencing process can be dispensed with! The principle that the language which the learner learns from should reflect the natural parameters of language use makes it unnecessary for the language course designer to provide a special mechanism to ensure that the texts he uses have these characterisations.

What is being claimed is that, if what is required is a set of texts from which to teach the language, texts which reflect some particular aspect of language use, such as frequency, collocability, usefulness, or whatever, then the primary corpus of texts already has these properties, and on that account alone, the procedure implied by steps, 2, 3, 4, as well as their output, 5, can be dispensed with entirely.

Now notice that all along we have been saying nothing about the learning strategy that the learner might be following when he uses, that is, performs and learns from, the language teaching texts which are the final output of the text-construction procedure we have just discussed. In other words, what we have been discussing is language teaching analysis, what the teacher does. What does the learner do? I would like to assume that he has a language learning strategy that governs the process whereby he constructs the internalised grammar of the target language that will, under ideal or near-ideal conditions, approach or be isomorphic with the internalised grammar of the native speaker. Like the native speaker, he can do this on the basis of experience with sentences of the target language used in meaningful situations.

I am not suggesting that we know very much about the nature of this strategy. All I would like is a name for whatever it is that enables the adult learner to learn whatever part of the target language he does learn. I do not think it unreasonable to impute such a learning strategy to the learner, and furthermore, to assume that, to whatever extent it differs quantitatively from the language learning capability of the child, it is nevertheless qualitatively the same, that is, it operates in the same way.

In any case, despite our relative ignorance of the operation of the mechanism by which the learner accomplishes his progress, we can nevertheless discern some surface aspects of his learning strategy. For example, the more of the language the learner knows, that is, the more complete and complex his internalised grammar of the target language, and the greater his skill in using what he knows, the longer are the learning units that he can handle. It is probable that the difficulties that the learner faces when unedited, or raw language texts are presented to him at the initial stages are at least as much a function of their length (and manner of presentation) as of their complexity.

The principle of selection is often justified on the grounds that it is more economical to have the learner learn just the useful, frequent, basic elements of the language. It seems to assume that the learner's proficiency can be measured in terms of number of language parts known. For this reason, these should always be the most frequent, useful, basic elements of the language. But the learner's proficiency in the target language, like that of the native speaker, is not just the linear, additive sum of all the language parts he knows. It is a function of his skill in using those parts to express himself appropriately, to say what he wants to say without effort. But skill in use, as I conceive of it here, is not a grammatical parameter. It is the speaker's ability to make appropriate use of his knowledge of the grammatical form of his language. That is, the parameters of frequency, basicness, etc., which are said to characterise natural texts of the target language are not linguistic parameters at all. They are simply reflections of the native speaker's ability to make appropriate use of his internalised grammatical knowledge of his language. If 'skill in use' is not a linguistic feature of some language part, say a lexical item, it cannot be learned automatically along with that part - except through practice in using it. That is, the learner can acquire the native speaker's skill only when he, too, like the native speaker, has had appropriate practice in using the language parts that are being taught to him. The learner, then, uses his language learning strategy to internalise a grammar of the target language, and his proficiency in the language increases as he acquires more and more knowledge of the language and increases his skill in using that knowledge. Thus his learning is more exponential than linear, and we can account for the observed fact that some adults can and do acquire remarkable proficiency in a foreign language in a very short time, say, nine months. His proficiency in the language then consists of his internalised knowledge of its structure, plus his skill, acquired through practice, in using it in speaking, understanding, reading, writing, typing, translating, interpreting, etc.

To summarise, then, the analytical lexicon such as I have described it constitutes no part of the linguistic description of a language. Skill in using

language parts is not an independent parameter. In constructing sentences that have semantic interpretations that correspond with what he wants to say, it is very doubtful that the speaker makes use in any way of notions of frequency, usability, disponibilité. Rather, such properties of texts are effects, not causes. The frequency of lexical items is controlled, for one thing, by the semantic features of the context of use of sentences, and is not a part of the grammar. Context operates, and very indirectly, on the grammar to produce the sentences of the language. A corpus of sentences may reflect certain statistical properties, but these properties are contextual rather than grammatical or linguistic in nature.

It has been noted that unedited texts of the target language contain in natural form the important, frequent and useful phonological, lexical and grammatical elements of the target language. The course designer's energies should be spent in making such texts usable as learning instruments, not in studying such texts for clues on how to build others just like them. If we can assume a language teaching methodology that increases the usefulness of short texts, and given a characteristic of the learner's language learning strategy that enables him to segment, analyse and store for re-use the lexical and grammatical features of already learned sentences, it may then be claimed that it is possible to dispense entirely with the elaborate analytical apparatus implied by the principles of selection, and its corollary notion, sequencing, without thereby losing the other insights of the language teaching reformers of the early 20th century.

23

EVERETT REIMER
Networks of people

Source: Extract from School is Dead (Penguin, 1971).

* *

Everett Reimer has carried on a dialogue on de-schooling with Ivan Illich over a period of more than fifteen years, and he ran the seminar at Cuernavaca on 'Alternatives in Education'. Here he presents an argument for alternative educational provision, based on network theory. An important question raised by the blueprint is whether deschooling demands the emergence of super-educators.

* *

Although people could learn a lot in a world where things were freely accessible to them, it would still be helpful to have the assistance of other people. Each person might eventually learn to type, given a typewriter, but each might learn to type in a different way. Having a typist who could demonstrate the skill would help to avoid this, especially if more than one learner took advantage of the same model. If that happened, those two could compare notes and, thus, learn something from each other. If, finally, there were in addition to the skill model and the two learners, someone who had taught typing before, had compared the progress of various learners, and drawn some valid conclusions, this person might also be useful in reducing the time required to learn to type.

The indispensable resource for learning to type is, of course, the typewriter itself. The skill model, while not indispensable, might, nevertheless, reduce the learning time by quite a bit and improve the final product as well. The fellow learner, the peer, is also important, especially in providing motivation to learn and the opportunity for practice. Less important than the others is the typing teacher.

Schools reverse this kind of logic. They do not, it is true, try to teach typing without a typewriter, but they frequently try to teach foreign languages without the help of anyone who can speak them, without anyone to speak to in them, and without anything to say in them that could not just as well be said in the native language of the learner. Geography is similarly taught without benefit of people who come from the places in question. Music is taught without instruments or musicians, science and mathematics by people who do not know them. Schools assume that the indispensable resource for learning is the teacher. Ideally this teacher should have the essential equipment for the practice of the skill and should also be able to demonstrate the skill, but these are secondary considerations. The need for learning peers is given lip service but little use is made of peers in the learning process.

Schools are not just wilfully perverse. Learning a skill, learning to practise it with someone else who is learning it, and learning how others have learned it are three different things, sometimes related but also frequently not. Schools try to find teachers who combine all three kinds of learning but, understandably, they often fail. The combination is much scarcer than its elements. When they do succeed in finding the scarce combination, schools use it as if it were not scarce at all. The experienced teacher is required to act as skill model and as practice partner for individual students, to say nothing of the many duties which are unrelated to learning or teaching. The scarcest skill of the teacher is usually the ability to diagnose learning difficulties, a skill acquired by observation of learning under various circumstances. In school, the use of this scarce skill must share time with all of the other functions built into the teacher's role. This is how schools succeed in taking plentiful learning resources and making them scarce. They package them all together, then stand the package on its head.

What schools do, nevertheless, provides an excellent model for the organisation of educational resources. The model has merely to be used in reverse. Educational resources must be administered independently of each other, and given priority in reverse order to that of the school. First, attention must be given to the availability of information in the form of records, the instruments which produce and interpret these records and other objects in which information is stored. Second priority must be given to the availability of skill models, people who can demonstrate the skill to be acquired. Third priority

must go to the availability of real peers, fellow learners with whom learning can actually be shared. Fourth and last priority must go to the provision of educators who by virtue of experience can facilitate the use of the more essential learning resources. It might appear that educators are of first importance, if only to see that the other resources are properly valued and used. It is evident, however, that this is what educators when incorporated into schools do worst, not because they are educators, but because schools give them powers which corrupt their judgement.

Skill models are different from educational objects in two important respects. First, they must personally consent to their use as educational resources. Second, they frequently have enough additional flexibility and other secondary advantages to make it worth the trouble of gaining this consent. In this technological age they are not strictly necessary, since their skills can all be demonstrated on records of one kind or another, but they are convenient. The superior flexibility of human models was recently demonstrated in Patrick Suppe's experiment in computerised instruction at Stanford University. The computers were programmed to teach reading and numbers to beginning first graders. The computers worked well - so long as one teacher stood behind each child to deal with his unexpected responses. Typical of these was the insertion of a pencil under the keys which operated the computer. The computer could, of course, be programmed to deal with each one of these unanticipated reactions but at the end of the third year of the experiment the programmers were lagging further behind the children than at the beginning. Computers may be able to teach other computers but it appears that human learners may, for a time at least, continue to be better served by human models.

Skill models are in plentiful supply. There are almost always more people in any vicinity who possess a particular skill than there are people who want to learn it. The major exceptions are when a new skill is invented or imported into a new territory. When this happens, skill models proliferate rapidly and are soon in balance with the demand for their services. Only schools and similar monopolistic institutions make skill models scarce. Schools try to forbid the use of models who have not joined the teachers' union. Some of the most famous musicians in the world, who fled from Germany at the time of the Nazi terror, were not allowed to teach music in the schools of the United States. Unions and professional associations also restrict the unauthorised use of skills, frequently creating serious shortages of vital services. Nurses, for example, are scarce in the United States, primarily because the training curriculum has been extended again and again by schools of nursing, placing the cost of training beyond the means of the girls for whom the profession offers opportunities for social mobility. Restrictions on the practice of a skill are usually justified in terms of professional standards and protection of the public. Sometimes these claims are true, but more often they are patently false. The best skill models are frequently those who have just learned a skill. Children learn to read from older siblings, sometimes with ridiculous ease. English schools were really economical for a time, when Joseph Lancaster introduced the systematic use of older students to teach younger ones. This system was better than schools usually are and was very much cheaper. It shares with other forms of schooling the fatal flaw of not allowing the learner to choose his model, his subject matter and his place and time of instruction.

Skill models should be organised as an educational resource so as to give each learner the widest choice of models and each model the greatest latitude in accepting or rejecting learners. This requires first an absence of restrictions and second a directory of skill models of all kinds. Ideally, there would be no special restrictions of any kind. Model-pupil relationships are subject to risk and abuse as are any kind of human relationships but the general laws and customs which cover all such relationships provide the best available protection. Learning in and of itself creates no additional hazards. The advantage of permitting the learner to seek and find a model from whom he will learn is, in general, worth all the additional risk that such latitude entails. Not learning what needs to be learned is likely to involve the greatest risks of all.

Developing directories of skill models is not intrinsically difficult. Truly convenient and comprehensive directories might be so valuable, however, as to warrant considerable investment. Responsibility for developing and administering such directories should probably be vested in a public utility. Skill models willing to offer evidence of their skills would be offered free registration. Those who chose not to do this would, nevertheless, retain the freedom to make such arrangements as they could, using their own means of publicity.

The financing of skill training contracts can best be dealt with after the organisation of other educational resources has been discussed. It may be that skills which seem to be required for intelligent participation in the modern world should be taught at public expense. In this case the public utility which maintained the directory of skill models could also be charged with paying them. Public payments should not be made, however, except upon evidence that an essential skill had been learned to an acceptable standard. Private contracts could be left to the wishes of the contracting parties.

Having learned a skill, people need someone with whom to practice. But peers are important even before practice. Who would bother to learn a skill unless there were others with whom to share it, fellow explorers of the new ground opened by the skill? Many skills are learned primarily with peers, taking advantage of the skill models in the general environment. Often peers and skill models are hard to distinguish. In ordinary interpersonal relations there is no need, nor advantage, in distinguishing skill models from peers. On the contrary, learning occurs best when such distinctions are not made. There is, however, an important distinction which can be ignored only if the individuals involved are willing to ignore it. Peers are, by definition, equals deriving mutual benefits from their relationship. They can play tennis together, go exploring together, study mathematics together, or build a camp together. If they are peers, they contribute more or less equally to each other's objectives. Helping a smaller brother or sister learn what he wants to learn is different. It may be equally enjoyable for a while, but the enjoyment palls more quickly. Peer relationships are freely chosen, freely kept. Skill modelling frequently requires some sort of compensation for the model, if the relationship is maintained as long as the learner would like. A method for compensating skill models is needed, therefore, which is not needed in relationships of peers.

Finding peers is merely a matter of knowing where they are and being able to get there, write or call on the telephone. Neighbourhoods free of automobile hazards are all that most children need for the purpose. As skills develop, however, the better ball players go farther afield to find worthy competitors, the botany bug outgrows his neighbourhood pals, the serious ballet addicts find their ranks thinning out.

Schools supplement neighbourhoods, as things are now organised, but schools create as many barriers to peer groups as opportunities for them. In schools, peer groups form around the goals of teachers or around the interests of dope-pushers. Student-initiated groups have a hard time competing with either. But for teenagers the neighbourhood no longer serves as an adequate base for contacts. If it did, the telephone and the automobile would be more dispensable. These instruments are often charged with breaking up the face-to-face community, but actually, along with Main Street and Peyton Place, they mainly expose its limitations.

For adults, with their frequently highly specialised interests, even the largest cities cannot always provide true peers. The best illustration of this is the scientific community, which must be world-wide for the most fruitful peer encounters to occur. The scientific community also illustrates how peer matches can be fostered or frustrated.

The logical structure of science provides a framework for identifying persons of similar interests. Its journals provide means of communication. Its rules of logic and criteria of evidence provide the parameters for fruitful encounters. Its achievements unfailingly generate new problems which beckon explorers with common interests. All these advantages of science, as a network of related interests which provide an ideal basis for peer-group formation, have now been offset by institutional barriers. National and corporate interests now dictate who may speak or write to whom, in what terms, when, how and where. Only the model of a scientific community is left, available for other interest groups which have been less successful in forming fruitful peer groups than scientists used to be.

The advantages of science in fostering communication among peers are no more natural than the forces which have now disrupted them. The modern 'logical' structure of science did not exist a century ago. Neither did its current journals, nor its present rules of logic or standards of evidence. The beginnings were already there but, two centuries ago, even those were only dim foreshadowings.

Fortunately, other communities of interest do not have to retrace the steps of science. Her example, as well as her products, make it possible to shortcut these steps. Today any area of interest can be so described that a computer can match the persons who share it. Learners in search of peers need only identify themselves and their interests in order to find matches in the neighbourhood, city, nation or world. The computer is not indispensable. In the neighbourhood a bulletin board will do, in the city a newspaper, in the nation a national magazine, in the world an international journal. All of these media and others are and should be used to find peer matches, but computers can make the matching easier and more flexible.

The operation of a peer-matching network would be simple. The user would identify himself by name

109

and address and describe the activity he wanted to share. A computer would send him back the names and addresses of all who had inserted similar descriptions. People using the system would become known only to their potential peers.

As in the case of skill models, a public utility might provide free service for the finding of peers. This would be justified not only in educational terms but also as buttressing the right of free assembly. The same right should also be extended to include prohibition of involuntary assembly, in the form of compulsory attendance at school. If freedom of the press and free assembly were taken seriously and public means provided to make them available to everyone, compulsory school attendance, military service and other common current compulsions would become unnecessary.

As schools are replaced by networks of educational objects, skill models and peers, the demand for educators, rather than declining, will increase. These educators will perform different functions from those now performed in school and not all of them will be the same people. The need for people with real ability in administration, teaching and scholarship will increase, and their rewards in terms of educational achievement, professional freedom and income will also increase. Schoolmen whose skills are primarily in the hiring, supervision and firing of teachers, public relations with parents, curriculum making, textbook purchasing, maintenance of grounds and facilities and the supervision of inter-scholastic athletic competition may not find a market for their skills. Neither will all of the baby-sitting, lesson-planning and record-keeping teachers, unless they have skills which can be turned to other uses, or unless they leave education for more honestly designated employment..

At least three kinds of professional educators will be in strong demand: first, architects and administrators of the educational resource networks which have been briefly described; second, pedagogues who can design effective individual educational programmes, diagnose educational difficulties and prescribe effective remedies; and third, leaders in every branch of learning.

24

CHARLES E. SILBERMAN
The failures of educational reform in the United States

Source: Extract from Charles E. Silberman, Crisis in the Classroom (Random House, 1970; Wildwood House, 1973).

* *

Silberman's book was an instant classic when it appeared in the USA. It was both critical of present practice, and it kept the American dream alive. The style was evangelical, moralising, didactic and discursive, reminiscent of the Talmud and the Old Testament. Generalisation is heaped on generalisation, adorned by parables and fables. The problems come over as real enough, but the ways beyond the problems are simplistic - importing progressive primary schools from England; finding better teachers. Silberman seems to believe that the faith, and the synagogue, will be all right if only we can get a good rabbi. The work cost over $300,000 and stretches to over 500 pages. It is the classic schoolman's lament.

* *

What happened? Why did a movement that aroused such great hopes, and that enlisted so many distinguished educators, exert so little impact on the schools?

A large part of the answer is that what was initially regarded as the curriculum reform movement's greatest strength - the fact that its prime movers were distinguished university scholars and teachers - has proven to be its greatest weakness. In part because the movement was based in the scholarly disciplines, in part because it grew out of the scholars' revulsion against the vulgarisation of progressive education and against the anti-intellectualism that that vulgarisation in turn had spawned, the reformers by and large ignored the experiences of the past, and particularly of the reform movement of the 1920s and '30s. They were, therefore, unaware of the fact that almost everything they said had been said before, by Dewey, Whitehead, Bode, Rugg, etc.; and they were unaware that almost everything they tried to do had been tried before, by educators like Frederick Burk, Carleton Washburne, and Helen Parkhurst, not to mention Abraham Flexner and Dewey himself.

One result of this failure to study educational history, particularly the history of progressivism's successes and failures, was that the contemporary reformers repeated one of the fundamental errors of the progressive movement: they perpetuated the false dichotomy that the schools must be either child-centred or subject-centred. Ignoring the warnings of men like Dewey, Boyd Bode, Harold Rugg, and

Carleton Washburne, the progressive reformers had opted for the former; their preoccupation with child-centredness made them content, in Dewey's phrase, 'with casual improvisation and living intellectually hand to mouth'. It was this 'absence of intellectual control through significant subject-matter,' Dewey wrote, 'which stimulates the deplorable egotism, cockiness, impertinence and disregard for the rights of others apparently considered by some persons to be the inevitable accompaniment, if not the essence, of freedom.'

The reformers of the 1950s and '60s made the same mistake, except that they opted for the other side of the dichotomy. They placed almost all their emphasis on subject matter, i.e., on creating 'great compositions', and for the most part ignored the needs of individual children. As Dewey wrote of the progressive educators whose one-sidedness he deplored, the new reformers 'conceive of no alternative to adult dictation save child dictation'. Reacting against the banality that child-dictated education had become, they opted for adult dictation. They knew what they wanted children to learn; they did not think to ask what children wanted to learn. Some of the reformers, however, now realise their error. Thus it was Zacharias, at the 1965 White House Conference on Education, who made a passionate plea that educators think about children and their needs.

Because the reformers were university scholars with little contact with public schools or schools of education, moreover, and because they also neglected to study the earlier attempts at curriculum reform, they also tended to ignore the harsh realities of classroom and school organisation. The courses they created were, and are, vastly superior to the tepid and banal fare most students now receive. But without changing the ways in which schools operate and teachers teach, changing the curriculum alone does not have much effect.

To some degree, this error reflected the reformers' innocence and naïveté. Because they had so little firsthand experience with the elementary or secondary school classroom (in contrast to most of the great figures of the progressive movement), they somehow assumed that students would learn what the teachers taught; that is, if teachers presented the material in the proper structure, students would learn it that way. Thus, they assumed implicitly that teaching and learning are merely opposite sides of the same coin. But they are not.

The error reflected academic hubris as well: not content with ignoring the classroom teacher, the reformers, in effect, tried to bypass the teacher altogether. Their goal, sometimes stated, sometimes implicit, was to construct 'teacher-proof' materials that would 'work' whether teachers liked the materials or not or taught them well or badly. 'With the kind of casual arrogance only professors can manage, when they conceived of lower schools,' Dean Robert J. Schaefer writes, the curriculum reformers' goal was 'to produce materials which permit scholars to speak directly to the child.' They viewed teachers, if they thought of them at all, as technicians, and they conceived of the schools, Schaefer suggests, as 'educational dispensaries - apothecary shops charged with the distribution of information and skills deemed beneficial to the social, vocational, and intellectual health of the immature. The primary business of a dispensary,' Schaefer continues, 'is to dispense - not to raise

questions or to inquire into issues as to how drugs might be more efficiently administered, and certainly not to assume any authority over what ingredients should be mixed.

The effort was doomed to failure. For one thing, the classroom teacher usually is in an almost perfect position to sabotage a curriculum he finds offensive - and teachers are not likely to have a high regard for courses designed to bypass them. For another, many of the 'teacher-proof' curricula have turned out to be more difficult to teach than the courses they replaced; certainly the 'discovery method' makes far more demands on the teacher than does rote drill or lecturing. But insofar as they thought about in-service education of teachers, the reformers tended to assume that the problem was to get teachers to know - to really know - the subject they were teaching. This was crucial, of course, but experience with National Defense Education Act Institutes and the like have made it painfully clear that mastering the subject matter does not begin to solve the problem of how to teach it.

The failure to involve ordinary classroom teachers in the creation and modification of the new curricula, moreover, tended to destroy, or at least inhibit, the very spirit of inquiry the new courses were designed to create. Curriculum designers are not likely to attract students to the life of the mind if they fail to entice the students' teachers as well. 'How can youngsters be convinced of the vitality of inquiry and discovery,' Dean Schaefer asks, 'if the adults with whom they directly work are mere automatons who shuffle papers, workbooks, and filmstrips according to externally arranged schedules?' Since the spirit of inquiry 'necessitates a live sense of shared purpose and commitment', the teachers must participate in the scholar's search if the effort is to succeed.

The most fatal error of all, however, was the failure to ask the questions that the giants of the progressive movement always kept at the centre of their concern, however inadequate some of their answers may have been: What is education for? What kind of human beings and what kind of society do we want to produce? What methods of instruction and classroom organisation, as well as what subject matter, do we need to produce these results? What knowledge is of most worth?

There is considerable irony in the fact that the contemporary reformers did not put these questions in the foreground, for certainly they did think about them. Bruner's The Process of Education is full of reflections on these questions; so is his essay 'Character Education and Curriculum' in Learning About Learning, and several of the essays in On Learning. Other reformers, such as Jerrold Zacharias and David Hawkins, have also thought seriously and hard about these fundamental questions. But because the reform movement was university-based and grew out of dissatisfaction with the teaching of specific subjects, e.g., physics, chemistry, biology, math, social studies, the reformers never really attacked the curriculum as a whole. Indeed, academic provincialism made the reform movement a good deal narrower than some of the reformers had wanted. For example, Jerrold Zacharias and Francis Friedman originally intended to create a course in the physical sciences, hence their organisation was named the Physical Sciences Study Committee. But the university chemists refused to go along; they were only interested in reforming the teaching of chemistry. And so it went; as a result, the reformers never worked on more than a course at a time. But a curriculum, as Lawrence Cremin writes, 'is more than a succession of units, courses and programmes, however excellent; and to refuse to look at curricula in their entirety is to relegate to intraschool politics a series of decisions that ought to call into play the most fundamental philosophical principles. '

25

MICHAEL STORM
The community and the curriculum

Source: Specially commissioned for this volume. The article is based on a talk given to the Conference of the General Studies Association in September 1972.

* *

Michael Storm is Head of Geography at Berkshire College of Education. This paper links some Third World problems with those of developed countries, and it raises some fundamental challenges to the community school movement. In England that movement began in rural areas, such as Cambridgeshire, Leicestershire and Cumberland, although now major projects are being operated at Coventry, Manchester, and Sutton-in-Ashfield, Nottinghamshire. The movement has consistently evaded such political questions as: Who are the community? What different perceptions of 'the community' exist? And whose perceptions win, in practice? Michael Storm points out that to most people the school is peripheral, and that 'community' is sometimes something that middle-class people think that working-class people ought to have. Storm asserts that in some societies geographical communities are now less important than network communities. What are the implications of this for educational provision?

* *

Writing in a recent issue of 'Dialogue', John Rennie of the Schools Council Social Education Project affirmed that 'it seems clear that a radical approach to the problem of the community and the school. . . is increasingly needed'. Two recent experiences suggest that this need is widely recognised. In the summer of 1971 I was at the official opening of a new junior secondary school at the western end of Jamaica. The school had in fact been open for two or three years, and the formal opening was a blend of openday exhibitions, school concert, prizegiving, and political occasion, for the opening speech came from the Prime Minister, who took the opportunity to announce plans for future public investment in the western region, the least developed part of an underdeveloped island. But it was the principal's report that was most memorable. In it, he explained that, without the permission of the Ministry of Education in Kingston, the school was allowing its school leavers to return to school, staying on after the statutory leaving age. This was because he, his staff, and the school governors could not bear to see bright, determined youngsters become disillusioned drifters in a matter of months, as they joined the rural underemployed or the urban shanty-dwellers. Back at school, these older, unofficial, pupils developed practical skills which the school itself could employ, even if the wider society could not. Thus, the boys were responsible for carpentry, painting, and minor constructional work on the campus; the school paid them in tokens, with which they could buy clothes made by the girl 'returners', meals made with vegetables grown in the school grounds, and so on. The picture that emerged was at once heartening and depressing; heartening, because of the school's bold and anti-bureaucratic reaction to the glaring inadequacies of its own socio-economic setting - yet depressing, for the school-based 'commune' that seemed to be emerging could hardly shelter these young people permanently. Nevertheless, this Jamaican episode illustrates one approach to 'the problem of the community and the school', involving an attempt to build an alternative community within the institution, to replace, albeit temporarily, the inadequate larger society outside.

An entirely different approach was being tried at the teacher training college at Port Vila, in the New Hebrides, an island group in the western Pacific where I spent a month working in 1972. Here, room had been found in a crowded curriculum to develop a community service project, which involved small groups of first-year students being taken by the college bus to a shanty area on the edge of the little town. With them they took balls, building bricks, and other toys. As the bus approached over the rutted track, mothers could be seen sluicing their children down with buckets of water (one water tap for eighty families). The students were deposited in a dusty little hut and eventually a few small girls emerged shyly from the nearby shacks. The students organised some games in a desultory sort of way for an hour or so, but were probably relieved when the bus reappeared to take them back to their well-ordered campus on the other side of the town. The organising tutor agreed that the dice were rather heavily loaded against the success of the scheme. Most of the students came from other islands and had no way of communicating with the shanty dwellers. Clinging precariously to their own hard-won niches on the ladder leading out of the subsistence economy, the students were perhaps unlikely to take readily to a Lady Bountiful role. The college supplied more students than the settlement supplied clients, and as far as I could tell no contact was made with adult members of the community. This New Hebridean experiment will however serve to illustrate another, very different approach to school-community relations - in this case, an attempt was being made to use the institution, not to replace, but to repair the deficiencies in the social situation. The college students were envisaged as functioning as a supplementary welfare resource, whilst simultaneously enriching their own personal higher education in a meaningful way. (Community studies unfortunately admits no rival when it comes to the output of cloying gobbledegook.)

I hope that these two vignettes will have established the two main meanings traditionally attached to the phrase, 'the community and the curriculum'. Educators have always been concerned with the school or college community (in the Jamaican sense); its size, its esprit de corps, its tone, its democratic or arbitrary rule-making. But, increasingly, they have tended to turn their attentions away from the building of the utopian community within the school - either because that task has been satisfactorily completed, or abandoned as hopeless, I'm not sure which - and have become more preoccupied with the community outside the school, as in the New Hebridean example.

'The community and the curriculum' is the sort of phrase that arrives trailing clouds of conventional wisdom. So it seems appropriate to isolate, initially, those sentiments which every right-minded educator would expect to discover under such a heading. J. K. Galbraith explained the notion of 'conventional wisdom' thus: 'Just as truth ultimately serves to create a consensus, so in the short run does acceptability. Ideas come to be organised around what the community as a whole or particular audiences find acceptable.' What are these acceptable, regularly-reiterated ideas concerning community and curriculum? I suppose we should place first the academic aspect; it is widely believed that there should be an emphasis upon the local population and its environment as affording ideally-appropriate study material in every sector of the curriculum. Local investigations are inevitably more interesting, more enjoyable, more relevant than narrowly academic, bookish studies. It is often implied that local work is somehow even more enjoyable and stimulating for the less academic students, but in any case, close links with the locality are recognised as an unequivocally Good Thing, in the Sellars and Yeatman sense, and schools display their locally-oriented activities as a sort of emblem, denoting an authentically enlightened approach to education.

A second element in the conventional wisdom concerning community and curriculum might be termed the amenity aspect. I refer to the increasing rejection of the school as a specialised institution, and the advocation of its transformation into a multi-purpose centre, a focus for a wide range of local activities, a boost to the neighbourhood's sense of identity, and its community-consciousness. This idea is rooted deep in the history of town-planning, in Ebenezer Howard's wards and Clarence Perry's neighbourhood units; more recent manifestations would include the Leicestershire community colleges. Thirdly, educators thoroughly attuned to school-community discussions would expect to find some stress on the ability of a truly community-oriented institution to identify and repair deficiencies in local community life. This ameliorative objective is expressed in two ways. Sometimes students are engaged in specific, direct repair functions - weeding gardens for old people, helping with pre-school playgroups, and so on. Then there are wider repair functions, in which the school and its curriculum is regarded as an effective mechanism for solving - or at any rate, holding at bay - the problems of the locality, especially if it is a deprived locality. This expectation

links together the EPA concept, bussing in America (and Ealing), programmes of compensatory education, and the attempts to design specially relevant curricula to suit particular areas.

Finally, we might expect to find, under the heading 'community and curriculum', a bundle of sentiments more concerned with diagnosis than with actual educational strategies. We might confidently expect to find the words 'alienation' and 'organic' bandied about, with Mumfordesque anatomical analogies about cancerous overgrowths, and so on. There would normally be some evidence of a veneration of small communities, especially villages, and a central notion, lurking about even if not announced, would be that of optimum size. I think that most people would employ this concept if asked what they meant by 'community' - an ideal community generally tends to be a somewhat smaller group than the one in which one is currently operating. The question of optimum size is surely one of the commonest areas of debate within educational institutions themselves, and indeed is one of the very oldest notions around, with a respectable lineage from Aristotle, whose ideal community 'must have a population which is self-sufficient for the purpose of living the good life after the manner of a political community, but not so unwieldy that the members cannot maintain personal contact with one another' to the Ecologist's 'Blueprint for Survival' which argues that 'the small community should be the basic unit of society and that each community should be as self-sufficient and self-regulating as possible'. It is sometimes implied that schools could, or should, do something about this - either by creating an ideal community within the school, where every member is consulted and listened to, or by arranging the curriculum so that the children, in John Rennie's words, 'feel a sense of identification with their community', or, at the least, by ensuring that pupils are equipped with appropriately wholesome ideals concerning community size and participation.

A critique of the conventional wisdom of community education would have to begin by assessing claims to academic relevance. Here the greatest danger lies in the yawning gap between curriculum development language - never less than grandiloquent, and increasingly overarching - and what actually happens. Thus, 'rediscovering the heritage of their own locality, strengthening their sense of identification and pride in the community' might turn out to describe the sketching of thirty-seven almost identical pieces of flint in a dusty glass case in the local museum, or copying out from the Victoria County History a list of villeins and ploughs operating roughly where the scrap metal yard now abuts onto the sewage works. 'Focusing on the contemporary characteristics of their own immediate environment, gaining a deep understanding of the ways in which people live and work in the local community' might mean the colouring of chemists shops blue, grocers green, off-licences purple, supermarkets blue, green and purple, on a big map taking twelve sheets of cartridge paper and one and a half terms. Or it could mean rediscovering the pleasures of counting cars and lorries, a pastime last enjoyed at the age of three (when it was pursued with rather more dedication). Unfortunately, even 'using techniques of direct observation and active discovery to replace the dreary bookishness of traditional academic education' can mean that students spend hours pestering local inhabitants, whose mounting annoyance is only matched by the extreme unreliability of the information - on population, ages of buildings, and so on - which they provide. There is a vein of anti-intellectualism in the community/curriculum movement; the sort that enables a school to claim that it is running extensive local study programmes whilst not possessing any local planning reports, census volumes, or even large-scale maps.

I've argued elsewhere that most local study programmes fail on two counts. They often encourage the amassing of fortuitous, unrelated and unimportant facts in a parochial ragbag - Saxon coins were found near the 'Dog and Partridge' in 1873, an ornamental bench in the park was donated by the Townswomen's Guild in 1953, and so on. Furthermore such studies don't necessarily do anything to reinforce those school-neighbourhood links so strenuously advocated, and can easily damage them. There is well-documented resistance to local surveys from those surveyed and, increasingly, from the young surveyors.

What about that part of the community-curriculum movement which stresses the need to replace the school as a specialised institution, by a multi-purpose social centre, with library, committee rooms, sports facilities, and so on? This is a well-established notion, and on economic grounds - the 'use of plant' argument - virtually irrefutable, although there are gritty and sometimes intractable wranglings concerning caretakers, financial responsibilities, and siting (a fully-used community school in a residential area can have an effect on noise and traffic levels comparable to that of a light industrial estate). The range of facilities envisaged generally tends to allot more community functions to the secondary schools; but their catchment areas are usually rather larger than those of the local 'community', however defined. Significantly, in Perry's classic working-out of the neighbourhood unit idea, the focal school (which defined the size of the planned neighbourhood) was a primary school. Quite often schools are not sited at the real focal points of the community, such as local shopping centres. Schools require too much land to be able to compete for locations endowed with genuine centrality, which are necessarily expensive. Libraries, clinics, evening classes, are all rather peripheral activities, involving only a minority of the local population. If we ever become really serious about planning communities around the school, we'll have to permit commercial contamination, placing the pub and the shops in the campus, next to the basket-weaving and flower-arrangement workshops. As the American sociologist Herbert Gans points out (repeatedly) in discussing the school-centred community, 'the school, which is the centre of the planner's neighbourhood, actually impinges on only a minority of the residents. Its activities affect only the compulsory clientele (the students), the parents of those students who take an interest in the school, and other adults who participate in the organisational activities that are centred in the school. Residents without school-age children, and those without interest in their children's schooling or in organisational participation, are little touched by the school.' It seems that this 'amenity' argument affords another illustration of the gap between the teacher's perception of his job, and how the rest of the community sees him. The endemic pedagogical disease is surely role-inflation. Rather as a recent survey showed the space between teacher objectives (developing awareness, citizenship, rounded personalities, and so on) and pupil/parent expectations (specific skills, examination successes), so there is a parallel gap between the teacher's vision of the

school as the nub of the locality, regularly thronged with elderly chrysanthemum-growers and youthful disco-addicts, and the public view, that the teachers should get on with their specific job, i. e. teaching (thereby facilitating upward social mobility) and not worry too much about jacking-up the local community spirit, whatever that is.

To be critical of the third community/curriculum strand - the ameliorative function, using school projects to assist the dependent populations in the area, whether infant, elderly, or hospitalised - seems unacceptably churlish. But there has been a rapid escalation of activity in this field, from the traditional harvest collection of tinned pineapple and the fund-raising carol-singing, to situations where massive courses in moral education or social studies devote considerable time to placing adolescents in various voluntary work situations, rather like a miniature Cultural Revolution dispersing the intelligentsia into the countryside. The speed and scale of these developments is producing murmurs of dissent from a variety of sources. Teaching colleagues may object to the time spent on charitable projects, especially if they can produce evidence of time frittered away, or actual malingering. Parents may see incipient conflict between worthy local causes and their children's career prospects, or may feel disquiet at the institutionalising of voluntary work within the curriculum. Radicals may object to the apolitical manner in which gaps in the social services are filled by children in school, who may derive from their experiences an unhelpfully simplistic view of the causes and solutions of social problems. The more ambitious 'factory work study projects' may attract unenthusiastic trade union attention, whilst the pupils themselves may wonder why it would be wrong for them to leave at fifteen and go into the decorating, window-cleaning, or gardening business full-time, thus learning accountancy as well as social studies.

But this repair function is merely one expression of a wider concept of community education. By devising an appropriate type of curriculum, involving members of the local community in the work and life of the school, involving school pupils in the problems of the local community, it is argued, schools themselves can help to solve the problems of deteriorating inner urban areas, declining rural areas, or suburban wastelands. Only the essentially romantic and apolitical value system found in teacher education, which is characterised, according to William Taylor, by 'a lack of interest in political and structural change', can explain the placing of such faith, against all the evidence, in a schools system as a serious agent of change. A recent American study alleges that society is regularly 'asking too much of its schools, expecting schools to solve problems - such as segregation - that the larger society is unwilling to tackle directly', and that 'if educational egalitarians continue to assume that public policy cannot contribute to economic equality directly, but must proceed by ingenious manipulations of marginal institutions like the schools, then progress will remain glacial'. The aspirations of curriculum development theorists in inner urban areas, which almost invariably look for salvation in ever closer links between community and curriculum, seem to me to have a curious Canute-like quality, defying some relentless socio-economic tides such as the long-established and accelerating exodus of population from such areas. This process dates back to the early nineteenth century in most cities and virtually every town of over fifty thousand can show steep declines in its inner wards. There is surprisingly little consideration of the implications of this trend in most discussions of curriculum development. A picture emerges of idealistic teachers attempting to assist young people to put down roots, to identify with an environment, whilst the young people themselves are primarily concerned to exchange their environment for a more satisfying one, with better housing, amenities, wider job opportunities, higher income levels. Those educators who are preoccupied with the need to design forms of teaching especially relevant to working class culture are after all making fairly sweeping assumptions about future trends in society and the likely life-patterns of their pupils. As J. H. Westergaard observed recently, 'it has become almost fashionable to deplore the dilution of traditional working-class culture per se - a reaction which reflects an odd, conservative nostalgia for a way of life moulded by insecurity, local seclusion, and crude deprivation, both material and mental'. Too great an emphasis on a localised, community-based curriculum is likely to erode the school's traditional function - rejected by many teachers, but not by society at large - as a relatively impersonal escape-route or channel of social mobility. Advocates of intensifying the input of place-flavoured work, whether orthodox local study or social service, should at least consider that many young people cordially dislike their home environment. This must tend to impair their enjoyment of local work.

But if we reject the idea that the schools, by re-orienting curricula onto community concerns, can effect changes which in reality could only be achieved by political, legislative, fiscal measures, we are still left with the argument that school programmes can help to foster 'local community spirit'. People rarely acknowledge any obligation to explain what they mean by this. Ray Pahl offers a useful discussion of the concept in his book, 'Patterns of Urban Life', in which he points out that the only certain characteristic of the community, and community spirit, is that it is universally agreed to be a Good Thing -

'Priests, ministers, social workers, and teachers frequently use the word "community". As a notion it is generally held to be a "good thing", particularly when it has a "spirit" attached to it. Social leaders and public persons are usually very ready to pass judgments on the quantities of this spirit that they can detect. Local groups are congratulated when they have lots of it and preached at when they are said to lack it. In other words, the notion of community, or community-spirit, is value-loaded.' An important strand in Pahl's argument is that the better-off have never lived in spatially-fixed communities, but in network systems. Thus, the main social contacts of landowners, vicars, doctors, solicitors, were not the people in their vicinity, but their opposite numbers - other landowners, vicars, doctors, solicitors, over the hill. Only below this level did people, perforce, live in communities where their contacts were restricted by propinquity; Pahl characterises these as 'communities of deprivation' whose key characteristics are the absence of occupational, social or geographical mobility. These are the sort of communities which Oscar Lewis has studied in rural Mexico, and found to be characterised by mutual distrust, meanness, and paralysing conformism. Pahl argues that the place-based community is a rapidly obsolescing phenomenon - 'with greater affluence and more "choice", there has been a slow and steady move from community to social network as the meaningful arena for social relationships. '

No sociologist would endorse the view that any given settlement, or part of a settlement, will necessarily contain anything definable as a 'community'. Yet the feeling remains that if it doesn't, it ought to; put very crudely, that there is something fundamentally wrong if we don't know the people on the other side of the avenue.

Clearly, increased mobility is one of the most powerful factors contributing to the demise of the place-based community; almost 10% of secondary school pupils move house every year. Additionally, increased mobility leads to the use of a widely-dispersed set of destinations, for work, shopping, leisure pursuits. Physically, my own home area would appear to be unequivocally suburban to Reading; yet only 37% actually travel into central Reading to work, and the rest are linked to over ten other workplace destinations within a 35-mile radius. For many people, the significant social group is based upon work, and thus regular social contacts are quite reasonably more likely with a colleague and his family ten miles away than with the people in the same street. Another factor destroying the place-based community is scale; the target levels for new planned settlements have risen from 25,000 (Welwyn) to 250,000 (Milton Keynes). And this is not just a pragmatic response to population growth. The services and amenities that people expect, from transport networks to shopping facilities, become increasingly uneconomic below an ever-rising population threshold. Only the larger settlements can offer that expanded range of choice which for most people is part of a higher standard of living. An increasingly large proportion of the people living in small settlements are there because they are rich enough to be able to have the best of both worlds - the pleasures, real or imagined, of life in a small community, together with swift access to more centralised facilities.

A third factor eroding the place-based community is the steady fall in the average densities at which people live. Contrary to popular mythology, people are not steadily becoming more crowded together; outward dispersal, both planned and 'spontaneous' has resulted in a continual lowering of overall residential densities in this country, from 61·5 acres per thousand population in 1901 to 86·8 acres in 1961. Arguably this is the most dramatic single indicator of rising living standards, since most popular aspirations - car, garden, space, privacy - really add up to a demand for lower densities. Although there's no clear-cut link between residential densities and the degree of community spirit detected, most of the classic community studies, whether Willmott's Bethnal Green (150 to 200 persons to the acre) or Williams's Gosforth village, were of people living rather more cheek by jowl than will be likely in, say, Milton Keynes (20 to 40 persons to the acre).

Pahl is only one of many social scientists who have pointed to the decline of the community. This is what Melvin Webber wrote in 1963 in a seminal essay called 'Community without Propinquity'; 'the communities with which modern man associates and to which he "belongs" are no longer only the communities of place to which his ancestors were restricted. People are becoming more closely tied to various interest communities than to place communities, whether the interest is based on occupational activities, leisure pastimes, social relationships or intellectual pursuits. ' Or on age groups, one might add.

Now all this might seem to be stating the obvious, but teachers and planners continue to operate in the belief that they can restore, or create, place-communities, if they try hard enough. In the case of planners, this belief is expressed in the school of architectural determinism, the theory that given a certain arrangement of buildings, spaces, routes, amenities, and a certain population, then a community, or neighbourhood, can be expected to emerge. But as Gans points out, 'the portions of the physical environment with which city planners have traditionally dealt do not have a significant impact on people's behaviour... economic and social structures are much more important than spatial ones.' The failure of planners to create communities is also documented by Willmott, whose study of Stevenage showed that 69% of his respondents could not even name the carefully-designed neighbourhood unit that they lived in.

But if architectural determinism is largely outmoded, a variety of educational determinism, in the form of the community-curriculum movement, is alive and well. Adherents would not accept that Willmott's assessment of the neighbourhood unit in Stevenage as a 'functional unit which does not necessarily have any social significance in promoting

'community' or 'neighbourliness' could apply to that other functional unit, the school. In a fervent plea for a community-based curriculum throughout the secondary school, John Rennie warns that such work should not involve 'attempts by teachers to inculcate their values into the children'. And yet the decision to centre the work on the local community is surely, inescapably, the teacher's, and according to Pahl, 'so-called community consciousness remains predominantly a middle-class ideology'. Undoubtedly the most obvious evidence of 'community consciousness' in action today owes little to the schools, and is overwhelmingly middle-class. I refer to the ever-expanding numbers of civic societies, ratepayers associations, and the like, normally triggered by some defensive reaction against a new development; but the type of community feeling which produces sporadic rashes of coffee evenings seems to have relatively little momentum in it for fifteen-year-olds and their curriculum. Elsewhere, unexamined assumptions about the actual and/or desirable relationships between people and places may yet turn out to be the Emperor's New Clothes of the community school.

26

GASTONE TASSINARI

The 'Scuola and Quartiere' movement: a case study

Source: Paper presented at the International Seminar of the European Cultural Foundation, Florence, in October 1971. This version is a text specially edited for this Reader.

* *

Gastone Tassinari is an Assistant Professor of Education at the University of Florence, and besides working in the city he was also involved with the Barbiana School project. The 'Scuola and Quartiere' work is one of the Italian projects that have moved in a deschooling direction - the others include the Barbiana project, and the work of Mario Borrelli in Naples. In taking the life-situations of the learner as the starting point for educational planning Tassinari is similar to the West German Jürgen Zimmer and the Brazilian Paulo Freire. His general analysis proceeds from the assumption, shared by Antonio Gramsci, that there is a dominant culture, which oppresses the majority and which must be overcome. The dilemmas of all people who think like this, and who go in for action work, come out clearly in this account. On the one hand they try to help working-class children to operate more efficiently within the traditional structures: on the other they believe that those very structures oppress the children. The

school acts as a focus for those who seek to create alternatives to the present system, but the context for building the alternatives is found outside, and not within, the school itself. The path towards a better future to Tassinari involves participation and dialogue within a dialectic of change. See also Readings 3 and 30, FREIRE, Paulo and ZIMMER, Jürgen; and Quotational Bibliography - FREIRE, Paulo; GRAMSCI, Antonio; SCHOOL OF BARBIANA; ZIMMER, Jürgen; and ZINNEKER, Jürgen.

* *

Introduction: The Italian context

The 'Scuola and Quartiere' (School and Quarter) movement began in Florence in 1968. Many of its aspects resulted from the social, political and cultural conditions in the town, but it would be wrong to lay too much stress on its local nature. Since its beginning the movement has aroused remarkable interest beyond the town and the region; it has given rise to similar experiments in other towns and has established contacts with groups of people who share some of the basic political, social, and educational interests of the movement. Although the directions in which the movement has developed - 'doposcuola' -

(i. e. after-school activities), evening schools, quarter committees, parents' associations, contacts with the working class through its basic associations - appear to be focused on the local problems of the town, in practice they set these problems in a wider perspective. These directions are suggested by an analysis of the actual local conditions which identifies in them the effects of structures that are characteristic of society in general. In education these directly involve some of the basic problems of progress in Italy and in other countries where similar conditions exist. These problems concern:

- the persistence of inequalities in the educational opportunities of different social classes;

- the involvement of education in the contradictions and conflicts that are peculiar to the present stage of social change;

- the development (or the rediscovery) of a pedagogy capable of appraising the cultural resources peculiar to the environment the pupils come from, together with the pupils' creative and intellectual powers other than their capacities to live and work together and to promote social action;

- the necessity for new management systems for schools which would facilitate continuous education where children, adolescents and adults would be present and participate together.

The 'Scuola and Quartiere' movement does not propose curricular and structural changes in the whole of general secondary education. The correlation between the movement's action area and the existing Italian educational system is at the 'scuola media' level - the three-year school following the elementary course, which is the completion of compulsory education and the lower level of secondary education. The choice of this area by the movement was by no means fortuitous. The common 'scuola media' has been established in Italy for over ten years with the specific purpose of providing an education common to all children, regardless of their social-cultural environment or their future aspirations. In practice it is highly selective. Although hidden by efforts to modify the school curriculum and structure there is evidence that education is still viewed as a matter of privilege that benefits only a part of the population. The last Italian census (1961) revealed that only 18% of the entire Italian working population had received an education beyond the five grades of the elementary school.

However, this situation is rapidly changing: the sixties saw a remarkable increase of students at almost every level of the education system, from the 'scuola media' up to the university - 'an education boom'. This emphasised the contradictory situation in which the 'scuola media' operates. Although it was set up as a means of improving the cultural, educational, and social level of the country, it did not fulfil these goals. Instead it was engaged in maintaining 'education privilege' through selection processes that in practice resulted in the segregation and drop-out of students from the lower social classes.

That contradiction, and its inevitable consequences, are the main points on which the movement criticises the official school, and form the basis for the action which it carries out in the community.

Although reorganisation of the 'scuola media' would undoubtedly be one of the main ways to renew the Italian school structures, we cannot disregard the fact that reform at this level of the education system also necessitates a radical modification of the successive courses of study. This need for modification is further supported by the probability that education will in the future become compulsory to the age of sixteen. The proposals for the reform of higher secondary education, which have been suggested by the Government and political parties or by educational experts, have firstly called for a new structure for this level of the school system: either a unitary or multi-trend school; the organisation of optional courses to be added to the basic curriculum; the possibility of switching from one type of school to another, and the establishing of links between general and vocational education.

The activities of the 'S. and Q.' movement do not indicate many remedies for these main problems. However, the potential contribution of these activities to the reform of higher secondary education cannot be disregarded if we consider, for example, the demand for social management of school administration - one of the fundamental aspects of the experiment in which the movement is engaged. There is also another contribution which we think should be pointed out when taking the scope of this study into consideration. This is evident when one considers what the 'S. and Q.' movement means to the young people who have been the promoters of the movement itself as well as for those who have joined the movement later. These young men, most of whom had just graduated from higher secondary schools or were university freshmen, wanted through this work to reveal the defectiveness of the school they had just left and to supplement - or even amend - the education they had received. While teaching the 'scuola media' pupils attending the after-school activities, these young men have actually taught themselves by making the role that teachers and students play in education a matter for discussion by trying to weaken the myth of a school that - because it is considered a 'temple of wisdom' - stands apart and ignores the social and cultural reality of today, and by trying to replace that myth with a school open to influence from the outside world. In such a school the essential components of the educational process should be the use of critical thinking on the basis of deep consideration of the problems arising from community life, the awareness of the conflict situations existing in present society, and participation in social action to remove the causes of such conflicts.

Some of the recent experiences of the 'S. and Q.' movement confirm the interpretation we have given to their significance even beyond the 'scuola media' level. In some 'doposcuole' which have experimented with techniques of enquiry and communication that the present official school neglects, young people of different ages and levels of education have actively cooperated and enjoyed a kind of collaborative life and integration of experience which the traditional fragmentation of the school system discourages.

In these perspectives the 'S. and Q.' movement points towards some ways for renewing the entire structure of general secondary education, based on a school which is open to the surrounding community as well as in its own management and internal organisation.

1. Economic, social, and cultural context

The 'Scuola and Quartiere' acquires a particular meaning not only educationally but also socially and politically because the Italian political parties and the workers' unions have shown in practice that they are only interested in innovations within the ruling

117

institutions. The 1963 reform of the lower secondary school failed to renew substantially the general education system, or to provide the necessary new cultural outlets for the problems and the needs of the working class. The 'doposcuole' which were established in Florence are the result of an initiative independent of the political powers and the unions, even the school unions. The initiators of the 'doposcuola' start from the fact that the Italian school is a class-school that selects and discriminates against peasants' and workers' children: from the beginning, the book Letters to a Teacher, written by the students of the Barbiana school, has been regarded as the 'red book' by the young promoters of the 'doposcuola'.

They are also aware that exploitation occurs not only in the factory, but also outside the factory all over the country, through high rents and the lack of public parks, adequate social and educational services, and leisure-time facilities. All this means that the struggle and the perspectives spread from the factory to the country and particularly to the district, the 'quartiere'. The quarter committees formed during the floods in November 1966 did not last long, although they succeeded in showing what the people could achieve by working together and how this could be done. In the quarter the workers meet other workers belonging to different trades (craftsmen, small shopkeepers, clerks), who do not experience the daily struggle in the factory even though they suffer from the same kind of exploitation.

The 'S. and Q.' movement is set in the general context of the struggle that shook Italian society in the late sixties which began in the universities and went on with the strikes that took place in the factories during the 'Hot Autumn', although it did not attain the intensity of the workers' struggle in Northern Italy. The need for direct participation that rejects delegation policies and rediscovers the great importance of holding meetings at places of work and study, has found in Florence the strong support of the groups that operate in the quarters. As political tools, these groups have chosen either the 'doposcuola' or the evening school, because the education problem lends itself to the organisation of new forms of co-operation and consciousness which point towards new schools and new forms of community relationship as alternatives to the official school. Why do these new forms of social and political action develop in the quarters more readily than in the factories or in universities? It is connected with the social-economic structure of Florence, the main characteristics of which are:

- an almost total lack of important industries (except for two factories with 2,000-2,500 people);
- a high concentration of small industries;
- a large number of handicraft businesses, mostly family managed, which flourish with the tourist trade and rely on hundreds of apprentices. This situation is peculiar to the historical quarters;
- the presence of large building concentrations (Isolotto, Vingone, Sorgane) which were founded mainly as 'dormitory suburbs' on the outskirts of the town;
- the presence of old quarters in the middle of the city where one can no longer find the old habits and traditions that used to distinguish one quarter from the other. Only a major transformation which took into consideration the people's interests and suggestions could give new life to these quarters.

It is evident that such a structure reveals many problems:

(1) from a union standpoint, the extreme vulnerability of the workers at their places of work due to the fragmentation of the production process;

(2) the phenomenon of commuting workers and an almost complete lack of working-class suburbs near the places of work. The workers, who are separated from one another during work, find themselves far more separated when they are away from work. This explains why the workers' struggle in Florence is rather backward in comparison with that in Milan and Turin, and why the need to meet together is so urgently felt;

(3) the very high percentage of children between 12 and 13 years old who stay away from compulsory school and the low attendance at the general education level of children between 13 and 15 years old. This is mainly due to the presence of a large number of handicraft businesses where children of 13 to 15 years old start working as underpaid apprentices after leaving school. This is another important feature which encouraged the choice of the 'doposcuola' and the evening school as the field of action in the quarter;

(4) the absence of a true community life in the 'dormitory suburbs' and the lack of essential services to develop community life. Exceptions are found in a few quarters where the church and the 'Casa del Popolo' (People's House) have started to revitalise community life;

(5) a continuing attempt by the town administration to renovate old-fashioned quarters by transforming the old houses into offices and shops or into luxury apartments.

To understand properly the 'doposcuola' one also needs to know something about the social and cultural context in which it arose.

For a long time Florence has been the scene of new catholic trends. Giorgio La Pira, Mayor from 1951 to 1966, provided a point of reference for many young Catholic men who found inspiration in his 'Christian Socialism', his deep concern for the poor, the homeless, the unemployed, the workers struggling for their jobs and his proposals for increasing participation in social and political life. Early in the sixties, La Pira's and his followers' experiments in administration were interrupted by the Christian Democratic Party. They then looked for other outlets for converting their evangelical principles into social activity. The quarter committees, and later on the 'doposcuola' and the evening schools, offered them the best opportunities.

To understand how things developed one should bear in mind the open atmosphere established by some groups of the Florentine church. Among them were people like Don Borghi, a worker priest, who fought against exploitation in factories; Don Milani who, with the Barbiana school, promoted a new and, in some ways, revolutionary experiment in education; and Don Mazzi, who put the organisational and administrative structures of the parish of Isolotto into the hands of the people. The initial impetus came from the Catholic forces who made an important contribution to the 'S. and Q.' movement. The movement grew and spread because the original forces joined with other elements, finding a common meeting-place in the 'Casa del Popolo'. (Very few parishes have allowed the development of 'S. and Q.' activities after they discovered the political ideologies behind them.) These belong mainly to the Marxist camp. Encouraged by the new ideas shaking society as well as by suggestions from the most advanced groups, the Communists and Socialists looked for new ways of dealing with policy through more direct contact with the needs of the people. At first the new view met with some resistance within the parties inclined as they often are to favour institutional means rather than social action; but its supporters eventually succeeded in introducing new features into the action to be undertaken by the parties themselves.

The 'Case del Popolo' fulfil a very important function because they are the only organisations which in most cases allow the 'doposcuola' and the evening school to be held on their premises or even allow them to develop their activities further. The groups at the grass-roots dealing with school matters, which were accepted and tolerated from the beginning, contributed later on by encouraging a new interest in the 'Case del Popolo' which often operate only as recreation centres.

The 'doposcuole' are also attended by many students who have been discouraged by the lack of outlets in the struggle carried out inside the university (in Florence this is characterised by a very low level of practical action in spite of much more revolutionary talk than elsewhere). Thus they apply to the quarters in the hope of obtaining specific opportunities for political and social action.

To understand the trends, the limitations and the possibilities for development, one needs to examine the activities and the aims of these experiments.

2. The main weaknesses of the school system according to the 'Scuola and Quartiere' movement

The structures on which the whole Italian school system is based, from primary to higher secondary schools and universities, are the same as those introduced by Gentile's reform in 1923. The successive attempts to reform the programmes (in 1945 and 1955 for primary school; in 1963 for the lower level of secondary education) did not modify the fundamentals of Gentile's school reform. Even though the school has to a certain extent become aware of problems related to the psychological and environmental backgrounds of the children, it has remained fixed on a kind of cultural and pedagogical pattern based on authority, selection and class discrimination, with the intention of producing an élite able to provide the future managers of the economy and policy makers.

One of the greatest causes of the failure to renew the school is the teachers' training system which offers teachers no real opportunities of keeping up to date after the completion of higher secondary education or university courses. The task of carrying innovation from theory to practice was entrusted to teachers who were moulded by the cultural and pedagogic standards of the old secondary education system. On the other hand, the school organisation itself would have hindered any attempts at improvement even had they been undertaken with the best will in the world. In many cases, in the country and mountain villages, the peasants' and shepherds' children attend one-teacher schools, with one, all-grade class. In the immigration areas the special classes for maladjusted children are open mainly to children coming from Southern Italy and from the country after they have been uprooted from their customary way of life. In the town quarters where there is a high concentration of workers and lower middle-class people, the classrooms hold 30 to 35 pupils and are used by different class grades in rotation during the morning and the afternoon. All this, plus the teachers' incapacity to escape from strict rituals

and dessicated rules that make no sense when compared to the real problems the children face in everyday life, has erected a wall against which the innovations of the Italian school have banged ineffectively.

In the middle of this mess the first stage of the selection process encouraged by capitalism takes place. By providing the children with a culture that is useless for the analysis of the problems they experience, the first class selection is carried out. Such a selection, even though a cultural one, operates inside a social stratification system already determined in the organisation of work. The school fails to give the proletarian children answers to their requirements and interests; these children are immediately neglected and discouraged in their desire to be socially integrated. At most they are compelled to look for integration by denying their own class values; in practice they either put up with being neglected by the social organisation of the school or achieve integration by twisting the values of their own social class by overwhelming their fellows through competition and individual success. The type of culture forced on them does not give them any possibility of teaching social maturity; it serves just to ensure that the one who receives it is worthier than the one without it. That kind of culture does not solve any real problem, nor does it serve any real need; it is only a function of the social rank aspired to. Therefore, it can only be provided by a series of oppressive and authoritarian tools; it requires a mnemonic bent rather than critical participation; it allows no personal re-arrangement of the subjects, only passive retention and conventional repetition; it does not help the development of logical and creative thinking, but is embodied in formal schemes determined once and for all. The only form of self-determination and degree of flexibility within the school is given by the subdivision of the study into subjects. However, each subject is separated from the others and tends to be established as a container in which to keep the elements that have been poured into it from day to day. The subject is imposed as something extremely abstract, conventional and always the same throughout the years. Moreover, it is needed only for school and is useless for understanding and acting on the social reality outside the school. The result is that the child never identifies himself with what he studies; he is never able to recognise himself and his people and to find connections between community problems and the subjects he is taught. In other words, the school system is based on bourgeois standards and its main value is still the intellectual and cultural superiority of one individual over another. This is realised through obedience to the principle of authority in all its cultural and disciplinary aspects.

3. Aims and objectives of the 'doposcuola'

The general features of the 'doposcuola' activities have taken two main directions: one towards the parents and the other towards the children. The parents are involved not as 'owners of the children', but as members of the working class, who, away from their places of work, are even more disunited and vulnerable to the modern means of capitalist exploitation. The involvement of the parents in the 'doposcuola' activities may become an important way of developing their social lives through working together and of increasing their awareness of the social processes realised through education. Here the 'doposcuola' clearly shows its political aspect. The

119

'doposcuola' must be run by the workers who live in the quarter; the educational programmes as well as the pedagogic practices must reflect the social problems which the parents and their children experience in their environment. Only in this way can the culture that emerges from the 'doposcuola' activities be a working class culture and thus an alternative to the bourgeois culture on which the official school is based. The other perspective is towards the children and the recovery of all those whom the school, through its selective procedures, predestines to a poor education and a premature working life. The starting point is the official school curriculum but with the scope enlarged. The 'doposcuola', with the help of both the educators and the pupils, aims to experiment and to work out new cultural and pedagogic models as alternatives to those of the school, and as a means of achieving far-reaching social change. On the whole, the 'doposcuola' represents a kind of community education which involves the children as well as the adults, according to objectives which result from the integration of education and politics. These objectives place the 'doposcuola' in direct opposition to the present education system and clearly prove that a change in the present social and economic structures is a precondition of any transformation of that system.

4. The initiators of the 'doposcuola'

At the time that the 'doposcuola' started its activities, there were some indications of a crisis within the student movement in Florence which prevented it from changing from a movement with a few politically involved students into a mass movement. The most active members then looked for new outlets for political action. These they found in the small groups belonging to the extra-parliamentary leftists or in the dying quarter committees that were set up soon after the floods of 1966 and which lost their capacity to improve the people's circumstances and meet their needs. The first 'doposcuola' was founded in the parish premises of the Ponte Rosso Quarter by Catholic students, who have always shown ability and determination in organising recreative activities for the children of the parish.

Other quarters followed this example and founded their own 'doposcuola'. The initiators were once again students, always in conflict with themselves, looking for new space permitting social development which the school had never succeeded in giving them and which, through the student movement, the university had stimulated but failed to satisfy. These students acted both as an impetus and a brake to the 'doposcuola' experience. They, too, suffer - just as the teachers of the official school do - from the consequences of the traditional education they have received. However, through the university disputes, during their preparatory meetings, their debates and discussions, these students have experimented with forms of active and personal participation which have aided their own human and social development. They take into the 'doposcuola' the results of an authoritarian education together with an anarchic potential springing from repressed rage against their previous education. They arrive en masse at the beginning of the school year, decrease in February/March and disappear in May/June to prepare for their university examinations. They have been culturally and intellectually educated according to bourgeois patterns; in spite of that, they have chosen to be socialists although most of them have not understood or grown up in a socialist culture. They teach in the 'doposcuola' by replacing the traditional heroes with socialist ones; they try to treat the children as friends and ask them 'what would you like to do?' or 'what would you like to talk about?' and always end up talking about fascism, resistance, Vietnam and the Middle East no matter what the children's requests are. They talk on these topics just as the school teachers used to, and although the 'doposcuola' pupils are somewhat noisier than ordinary pupils their participation remains passive. For these reasons most of the 'doposcuole' are short-lived, opening and closing within a few months. This new experience, which has probably left the children emotionless, comes as a shock to the student organisers. Many of them disappear from the 'doposcuola' movement and meet other university comrades in the small extra-parliamentary groups where it is easier to theorise on revolution, political practice and the methods to be used in the struggle against capitalism.

Those who continue with the 'doposcuola' experiment see the urgent need to open up the educational institutions - particularly the secondary school and the university - towards community problems, and above all, to overcome the split between those institutions and the working world. Without this the 'Scuola and Quartiere' movement may merely be a way of satisfying a sentimental need for social engagement. The working class need to be inside the school organisation, so that the relationships between the students and the working and quarter worlds can become an essential element in the educational process.

5. The main forms of educational practice of the 'doposcuola'

Although the ideas on which the students founded the quarter 'doposcuole' are based on the book Letter to a Teacher, the actual environment where the groups operate is quite different from that of Barbiana, where Don Milani created a full-time school, completely independent from the official school, and its range for cultural action was practically boundless. In Florence the quarter 'doposcuola' cannot disregard the official school which the children must attend. Therefore the 'doposcuola' operates in a contradictory situation: it must help the children to make up for ground lost and at the same time experiment with new forms of education as alternatives opposed to the bourgeois culture for which the school stands. This is a contradiction that often leads to the downfall of some 'doposcuole'. However, in those cases where the 'doposcuole' carry on and are not overwhelmed by the initial failures, the contradiction is gradually overcome. Then a framework for action may be developed.

In June 1970 a national meeting of all the groups operating in different parts of Italy was held in Florence. There the futility of discussing the false dilemma - teaching activities versus alternative cultural activities - was pointed out. At the beginning of their coming year's activities (October 1970), the Florentine group held a seminar to discuss the problem as presented during the June meeting and tackled the root of the problem: it was useless to regard tutoring as an alternative to the bourgeois cultural patterns; the tutoring and the alternative activities should be separated and the tutoring should remain for as long as the school continued to reject the workers' children through its selection procedures.

This activity should in any case remain marginal in comparison to the basic discussion on education which requires the development of a new socialist education. An educational framework capable of meeting the new requirements can only arise from a radically new conception of the culture-environment relationship. We cannot confine ourselves to a child's logical relationship to the environment. Class-conflict is part of the environment and through education a child must find his answers to the social problems which exist in the environment in which he lives. In other words, it is a question of giving a political perspective to the entire discussion about the culture-environment relationship. Within his own environment a child suffers, even though in a different way from the adults, all the contradictions suffered by the subordinate class: the family, the social structures, the school are fields where he undergoes a process of depersonalisation as well as human and social alienation. Education must enable the child to analyse and think critically about such contradictions in order to discover appropriate ways of changing the situation without deserting his own social class.

Techniques such as photography, newspapers, theatre performances and drama have been included in the 'doposcuola' activities in order to develop the ability to analyse the social reality and encourage communication. The children are stimulated to think about their conditions in the context of their social environment. Photographic displays are organised, children's newspapers are published and theatre plays are prepared so that the children may express the social problems to the people of the quarter. The children's theatre in particular proved to be a powerful instrument both for cultural expression and reforming teaching methods. A series of activities leads up to the dramatisation. The subjects concern the family, the school, the places of work, building speculation and the lack of public parks, justice, world-wide starvation. They are very different problems and sometimes (for instance, starvation) they are remote from the child's experience. The approach used ensures that the child actively participates. The problem of world-wide starvation was analysed by drawing up a questionnaire which the children took round the quarter to get the people's opinions on this matter. The answers were then set out and extensively analysed. The subject was dealt with by a problem-solving approach and took various perspectives: historical, geographical, economic, scientific. Finally the children had to choose a kind of language appropriate for the audience. The project is based on group cooperation and not competition among the cleverest children. Its results are 'open': they expand and take on different features when they are communicated to others. The existence of many 'Case del Popolo' in the town and in the surrounding province allows the performances (as well as the photographic displays and the children's newspapers) to be presented in several town quarters and in the province too. The children then have an opportunity to meet new people, have a chance to test their proposals in the light of different situations, gather new experience from each performance. Maybe one of the main aspects of the whole experience of the 'doposcuola' lies in the fact that it satisfied the children's need to communicate,

to present their problems and requirements in a wider social context.

In a society where the opportunities for communication are precluded and discouraged with more and more subtle tools, the chance of making oneself known and understood through many and various forms of expression allows a whole range of problems to be brought out into the open. The success of the 'doposcuola' in helping the participants to discover their personal value as well as the value of their social class establishes the real contribution of the 'doposcuola' to the cultural and social recovery of the children and the grown-ups. The 'doposcuola' not only improves the critical and creative capacities of the children, but also provides an opportunity for the continuing and collective education of the other members of the community.

The general lines and the activities of the 'doposcuola' are discussed and worked out by the children and educators together with the parents and all the workers and students living in the quarter who are interested. The research work, the analysis of the social problems and the expressive activities of the children are fed back to the quarter and community and lead to discussion about the subjects and the ideas developed by the children. For instance, the lack of a playing field has encouraged the children to work together to locate a spot where the playing field could be laid out and to develop a proposal on how that area could be organised according to their and other children's needs. Adults also get involved, and when this occurs we may speak of an actual experience of continuing and collective education.

6. The contribution of the 'Scuola and Quartiere' movement to a new image of society

The requirements of a new socialist orientation in education can be deduced from the foregoing experiments. In Florence we discovered the basic community dimension which may be seen as the social management of the school. If the construction of a new society means mainly the education of new men, participation and individual and collective responsibility at the grass-roots are very important. Decision-making should be decentralised in as wide and detailed a manner as possible to allow workers to participate in making political choices and to create both in the school and in the other branches of public administration, new forms of decentralisation and self-management, even within the bourgeois system.

The new arrangements are neither invented nor haphazard: they are constructed gradually through research and experimentation as well as trial and error. It is essential to establish a connection between the research and experimentation and the gaining of a full control of the means of production by the working class. By doing so it may be possible to avoid a repetition of some other socialist examples where power is centralised and bureaucratic and does not permit a full realisation of each man's capacity and everybody's actual participation. The true socialist society will be achieved only if its structures are wide and articulated, and if it results from direct democracy, self-management and a continuing education in the factory, in the school and in the quarter.

27

JOHN VAIZEY
Anti-anti school

Source: Review in <u>New Society</u>, 21 October 1971.

* *

'The diagnosis of the American educational problem is almost wholly inapplicable to the British situation. ' 'Much of what (these writers) say seems to me to be wildly reactionary. ' - the reaction of one English socialist and university professor to the arguments of some of the American educational radicals. A letter from W. L. Wood, in a subsequent issue of <u>New Society</u>, said: 'I teach in an Educational Priority Area, and it would seem to me that children who, through the arbiter of social stratification, face the complexities of socialisation with little or no grounding and consequently no confidence, can find little in the way of aids to survival in a set of values which begins and ends with the Holy Trinity of home, family, and possessions. ' Maybe the view from the Educational Priority Area is different from the view from the professorial chair but the problem goes deeper than that - and probably isn't that at all. Deschooling theory presented progressive socialists with a dilemma. On the one hand it made them admit that their traditional policies had achieved relatively little in the way of democratisation. On the other, they felt that deschooling alternatives might well be worse (and create greater inequalities) than present practice. Those who now argue for a policy of 'positive discrimination' have to ask themselves if a large-scale redistribution of wealth, which is the precondition for that policy to be successful, is a political possibility.

* *

I find education an immensely interesting subject to think about and to take part in, but it is often boring and tedious to read about - an odd admission, perhaps, from someone who has written several books on education.

There is no doubt that the six authors of five books recently published by Penguin are also people of tremendous and passionate concern about the society that they live in and the part that education plays in that society. But I not only disagree with them: I disapprove of them.

On the whole, it is also my view that a reviewer should fundamentally be in sympathy, either with the author of the book he is reviewing, or with the subject that the book is about. So I have only agreed to review these books reluctantly. In a sense what I have to say is not in the form of a review proper at all: but I hope that New Society will publish this cry.

There is a further emotional problem for me. I am deeply involved with America, both by the fact that I frequently go there and am, so to speak, a personality on the American scene in the sense in which I am not in England; and I have an American wife and my children have American passports. So I feel very proud of America in some senses, and deeply involved in it. At the same time, I am reluctant to draw the analogy, which the publication of these books in Britain implies, between the crisis in American society and the situation in the United Kingdom, grave though it is, because I believe there are profound and important differences.

And in particular I would say that the diagnosis of the American educational problem is almost wholly inapplicable to the British situation. In addition to this, and to add further to my tale of disqualification as a reviewer, there is the fact that as someone in his early forties, who bore a pale pink flag in his twenties and thirties, I could easily put myself into a sort of Malcolm Muggeridge stance in which I regard these revolutionary writers as beneath contempt because I am out of sympathy with the revolution which follows the one that I was engaged in. Fortunately, however, most of the writers of these books are considerably older than I am (and I also believe that we have not yet begun to win the revolutionary fight in which my pale pink flag was occasionally seen to be waving).

Broadly speaking, the view that I have taken in the past about education in this country is that whatever the forms or structures that were developed, or whatever kind of teaching went on, we were engaged essentially in bringing the best of middle class standards to the whole community. I do not mean by this that we were necessarily seeking to inculcate into the working class 'grammar school values' in the sense in which Brian Jackson and Dennis Marsden attacked them. What I mean is that the abundant resources of money and time, of care and consideration and compassion, that are available to the most fortunately placed middle class professional families, should be the birthright of every English child.

I think, for example, that every child should have its own, separate, well-heated bedroom; that it should have enough to eat; that it should have a certain degree of emotional security derived either from the presence of its parents, or from parent substitutes such as aunties, grandmas and so on, who tend to be around in well-organised, moderately prosperous houses. I think that each child should be able to take part in intelligent and frank discourse, that the radio should occasionally be tuned to the music programme, that visits to the theatre and to the ballet and opera should be part of the normal activity of the household; that an annual holiday should be an event, but an expected event; that there should be books and newspapers lying around and a reasonable supply of well-cared-for pets; that the children should have access to gardens; that the parents should expect to be consulted about their child's progress at school, and that their own views, idiosyncratic though they may be, should be paid attention to by the schoolteachers and in particular by the headmistress and headmaster.

Now I am fully aware, if only from reading the autobiographies of unhappy middle class children, that this is an idealised picture of much middle class life; but I still think that it represents, broadly speaking in the given context of the (to my mind broadly acceptable) social democracy in which we live, the ideal that I would wish for most children. I would hope, for example, that for most children it would be unthinkable that they should leave school before 16, and normal that they should be expected to go on till 18 and to take some form of further training, whether that training takes the form of going up to a university or taking part in some kind of well-conducted apprenticeship.

Now what is quite clear is that in America this form of ideal is consciously rejected by those who are concerned with the education of ghetto children. They interpret the whole situation in much more radical and apocalyptic terms. I can well understand that a well-trained marxist, which I am not, could regard my view of the ideal social and educational set-up as hopelessly alienated from what the reality would be in the classless society after the end of alienation. I have never had any desire, to put it mildly, to live in a kibbutz, and therefore I am quite prepared to believe that my vision of the future is not compatible with that of a real radical.

What I find deeply distressing is that whereas most of my political activity in education has been consciously designed to try to raise the financial and physical standards of working class children in the broadest context - new housing, more open space, much better wages for their parents, better social security and schools with small classes, good buildings and well-trained teachers, and access to what I still regard as the essentially valid English middle class culture - that these new radicals in the United States would regard that sort of concern as a side issue, while they talk about the overthrow of the educational system as part of the general overthrow of the ghetto structure in the United States.

Much of what they say seems to me to be wildly reactionary. For example, the proposal for educational vouchers in this country must be seen as part of the process of dismantling the public education system and the reversal to 19th century manufacture and utilitarianism, whereas it is presented in one of these books as a radical breakthrough to a new social order. Similarly, with the whole attitude to Freudian psychoanalysis, which I must confess in the American context strikes me as a profoundly reactionary doctrine. It is an attempt to attribute to social problems a personal dimension and offer a personal cure for a situation where a social solution is desirable.

28

LUDO WATSON

Deschool off

Source: This article first appeared in issue no. 4 of a student-teachers' magazine entitled Blackbored, which ran for four issues in 1970 and 1971 and which has now merged with the socialist teachers' magazine Rank and File, which appears five times a year, and is distributed from c/o 221 Westcombe Hill, Greenwich, London, SE 10.

* *

'The idea of deschooling is a dazzling distraction'... 'The schools are in a state of crisis... merely to abandon the school system at the point of crisis would be a huge historical anticlimax... Our job is to democratise the schools...' 'It is only because the outside world is exploitative and hierarchical that school is too.' The case for 'the long march through the institutions' and 'working from within'.

* *

One of the most apparently radical ideas to arise in recent years is deschooling. It is American writers such as John Holt, Paul Goodman and Ivan Illich who have developed this idea. What exactly deschooling means is difficult to find out. Often if seems to mean not the abolition of schools but smaller, neighbourhood schools. This wish is natural in the American context, where you sometimes get schools of 7,000, but is less relevant to England, where not many schools exceed 1,000. It is interesting that the debate on deschooling occurs just at the moment when the mass media have developed to the extent where they are capable of taking over the conventional role of schools (Sesame Street to teach basic concepts, for example). As a socialist, I accept that schools have an indoctrinating and controlling function on behalf of capitalism. But if schools were abolished, television, commercial radio, etc. would perform that same indoctrinating function, and firms would no doubt run their own training schemes. The deschoolers evade the issue of who wields power in society, and at times seem to see deschooling as a more efficient way of running the present system. Illich argues that schools are an inefficient way of organising the transmission of knowledge, and that 'organisations which nobody now classifies as educational would probably do the job much better. I think of restaurant owners, publishers, telephone answering services, department store managers and even commuter train executives, who could promote their services (my emphasis - LW) by rendering them attractive for educational meetings.' This sees deschooled education as part of the repertoire of capitalist gimmicks.

The real meaning of deschooling is that society has developed to such an extent technologically that it no longer needs to make separate, formal provision for children to be socialised in its values and trained in its skills. This is assumed by John Holt when he says 'With children living in an environment full of print, newspapers, magazines, writing on television, signs, advertising, I cannot imagine how any child who has not been made to feel he was too stupid to learn to read, would not do so.'

Even if this is true - and I doubt if many infant teachers would agree - it only means that children would read enough to be docile consumers. Holt also says 'My own bias is that education is going on spontaneously anyhow, is itself part of the kaleidoscope of the society'. The word kaleidoscope betrays a confusion about society, not seeming to recognise its exploitative nature. The deschoolers make a distinction between school, which is said to be destructive of human freedom and creativity, and the world outside, which is said to offer valuable educative experience. This is a false dichotomy. It is only because the outside world is exploitative and hierarchical that school is too. Although the deschoolers might accept the necessity for revolutionary social change, they put things in a false perspective by presenting problems such as alienation, lack of creative fulfilment, etc. as educational problems, caused by schools. This distracts attention from the social and economic system, which is the source of both the problems and the schools.

The idea of deschooling, then, is a dazzling distraction. The schools are going to go on and we are going to go on having to work within them. However, we are working to change them. Admittedly the teacher with genuine good intentions towards the kids is the front line shock troop used by the school to soften the impact in both directions: he makes school just about tolerable for the kids, and, by allowing them free expression in his lessons, acts as a safety valve protecting the heavily repressive teachers from the consequences of their own tyranny. (Though they, of course, hold him in contempt for 'not being able to control his classes'.)

The schools are in a state of crisis. Truancy and petty sabotage (indiscriminately called 'violence' by the heavies) are rife. Merely to abandon the school system at the point of crisis would be a huge historical anticlimax. For, in spite of all the iniquities of school, this is the period when, for the first time, progressive education is actually beginning to bite. The isolated points of real teaching are beginning to crystallise into a network.

To abandon the school system in its present form is an idea which, some day soon, may have a great appeal for the moneylords and joblords as a way of avoiding an explosive situation. However, they won't be able to carry it through. The entire Labour movement, for whom the right to education has always been a first principle, would fight it. The entire teaching profession would fight it purely on grounds of job protection. And the mentality of conservatism itself, which is often too inert even to see its own interests, would fight it simply because it's a radical idea.

This should not cause us to agitate for it. Our job is to democratise the schools; to pursue new teaching methods to the point where they really work; to win over the kids not to school life but to our interpretation of it; to give them skills not just for fitting in with society but for criticising it; to help develop their skills of discovery and self-expression beyond what mere job-survival demands of them; and to help them see that a better society can be won through collective conscious action, not indiscriminate sabotage. Deschooling would simply mean a dispersal of the energies which are at present crystallising.

29

DOUGLAS T. WRIGHT and D. O. DAVIS

Post-secondary education in Ontario

Source: Extract from Post-Secondary Education in Ontario: A Statement of Issues, originally published by the Ontario Commission on Post-Secondary Education in 1970; reprinted as an appendix in the final report of the Commission The Learning Society, Ontario, Ministry of Government Services (Toronto, 1973).

* *

This Commission has produced the most radical general plan for education yet to come out of a post-industrial society. The extract is from a paper circulated in Ontario in 1970 when the Commission was commencing its public hearings. The extract shows that the Commission was not afraid to ask very fundamental questions, and to invite ordinary people to participate in dialogue and help to create the future. In its man-centred approach, its stress on pluralism and diversity, and its proposals for life-long learning opportunities, the Commission's proposed plan, embodied in its final report, reflects some of the best elements of deschooling theory. With the U-68 Plan in Sweden, it merits serious study by anyone concerned with possible alternative futures in education. Douglas T. Wright was Chairman of the Commission from 1969 until 1972; D. O. Davis was then Chairman until the Commission concluded its work early in 1973. See also Quotational Bibliography - WRIGHT, Douglas T.

* *

One of the impressions that the Commission has formed about post-secondary education is that there is abroad an air of genuine doubt about current efforts in post-secondary education. It is not only that the government is unhappy about the costs, that the students rebel, and that the public is bewildered by it all. For the first time in a long while - perhaps for the first time ever, and definitely for the first time in the memory of all living - the very foundations of our education, and especially of our educational structure, are being questioned. Perhaps it is not even the questions themselves that are new; what is new, rather, is the earnest sense in which they are being asked. The Commission shares many of these doubts and, in particular, is struck by the relevance of the following questions:

1. Why do we keep piling one year of schooling after another upon our students? Why is it necessary to have up to twenty years of continuous schooling? Why not break it up and, if necessary, space the years over a lifetime? What, indeed, are the emotional and social costs we are imposing upon our youth and ourselves when we, in fact, 'conscript' them into

our educational institutions (or, as some observers have it, 'minimum security prisons') for so many years? By tolerating and encouraging forms of master-apprentice and officer-cadet types of relationships for young men and women in our educational institutions, are we not doing something to our social fibre as well?

2. Why is it necessary to assume that 'learning' must take place only when institutionalised? Why would it not be possible to have, in place of segregated and fragmented institutions, a plethora of educational services available to all, at any age? Is going to x number of theatre performances less 'academic', less for 'credit', than attending one course in English offered by a university or a college teacher? Is 'research' possible only at the graduate level?

3. Why should professional associations be allowed to stipulate formal educational requirements instead of administering tests regardless of educational backgrounds? Why should there be any formal links between educational requirements and occupations? Why, indeed, do we use degrees and diplomas for certification purposes? And if we must, why not issue such degrees and diplomas for only a limited period - say for five or ten years? After all, why should one certification last for a whole lifetime?

4. Is there any justification for the 'academic year'? Do we still believe that students must go back to the farms to help with the harvest - hence the need for free summers? Why is the trimester the only alternative? Why not two six-month periods of schooling?

5. What are the true implications of universality for post-secondary education? Even if it is assumed that universality does not mean attendance by all but merely an equal opportunity of access for all, how 'far up' - for how many years - should this be? All the way to the Ph.D.? Why should society invest this kind of money in one person and not in another? Merely because one is being 'educated'?

6. Do our post-secondary institutions really contribute to a better, fuller, life? Or should we, perhaps, be asking the same questions about 'more' education as are beginning to be asked about 'greater' economic growth?

It is dubious whether the Commission will ever arrive at answers to these questions; it is equally questionable whether any reasonable and realistic answers can be found by considering merely the financial and organisational issues, important though they may be. But if we are to have a debate over post-secondary education, it should be on issues that are fundamental to the quality of life in Ontario. Only after a basic appreciation of the present reality and beliefs can we be prepared not only to anticipate the inevitable but also to facilitate the desirable.

Finally, it is clear that if the Commission is to be at all successful in its task, it must have the help of the people of Ontario. It is our hope that via briefs, public hearings and other fact finding, Ontario citizens will engage in a fruitful public debate with the Commission. Our Interim Statement is meant as an invitation to such a debate.

30

JÜRGEN ZIMMER

A curriculum for working-class children

Source: Extract from an essay in <u>Schule ohne Klassenschranken</u> (Rowohlt, 1972).

* *

Jürgen Zimmer was a schoolteacher; he later worked with Saul B. Robinson in the Max Planck Institute for Educational Research in Berlin; he is now director of the pre-school education section of the Federal Jugendinstitut in Munich, where he plans deschooled curricula, and puts them into practice with pre-school children. Although the curriculum was part of a general plan for a model school for Solingen, and was never put into effect in that town, many similar projects - particularly those related to institutions, and the newspaper, and theatre projects -

have now been put into practice. Zimmer has similarities with Freire and Tassinari: the life-situation of the learner is the starting point of educational planning; learning hard-knowledge is part of the projects; and social change is the ultimate aim of the curriculum. Apart from the question of <u>how</u> the projects actually work in practice, two other major questions need to be raised: Is Zimmer working with <u>politically</u> marginal groups? And, is this the Marxist social-psychologist's version of the old romantic dream - of a society reformed by children?

* *

The general rules about aims, content and methods

1. There would be no more class teaching. Everything would be done through projects.

2. The projects should fulfil the needs of a working class which aims to achieve self-determination.

3. The principle of self-determination should also apply within the school, and in the choice of projects.

4. The school should not live in a world of its own, but should move back into society in those areas where change is needed.

5. The children should be given every chance of self-fulfilment. They should be happy, and their needs should be satisfied, as far as this is possible within a school context.

6. The children should not be cut off from society - otherwise they might apply their demand for self-realisation to only their own, limited environ-

ment. They should argue for their interests in the light of the interests of society as a whole, and they should negotiate and achieve their interests in a democratic way.

The general strategy

1. Pupils, teacher, parents, and educationists must change the present curriculum. Even taking into account the social control over aspects of the curriculum - for instance the children would need to be able to acquire recognised certificates, so as not to be condemned to the fate of drop-outs - quite a lot could be achieved. We could take advantage of the vague manner in which official documents talk of 'freeing the child'. We could relate this general aim much more specifically to what is actually done.

2. The acquiring of basic, and socially important, skills could probably be achieved in 20% of the time taken up hitherto. Unimportant parts of the curriculum could be omitted altogether. Those parts of the old curriculum considered to be still valuable could be carried over into project work, or combined with projects about to be developed. In this way a considerable amount of time could be gained and scope found for innovation and change.

3. Projects would have two important aspects - (a) as an operational method and (b) as a means of relating parts of the curriculum, and learning, to the life-situations of the learner.

4. Project development would be based not on the revision of traditional subjects but on these life-situations for which every school should prepare its pupils. An examination and analysis of those life-situations would be the precondition for determining the kind of qualifications and behavioural qualities that the learner would need to acquire.

5. As the projects aim to equip pupils to act freely in real-life situations, their development would have to be based on situations of social conflict, and we would have to be on the side of those whose interests are suppressed, and who produce social wealth but lack the power to decide on its just distribution.

6. A curriculum which is concerned with the needs of working-class children (i. e. ultimately, the abolition of domination of one class over another, and of social injustice) and which is not satisfied with educating working-class children according to bourgeois concepts of education, would be based on fundamental contradictions in our present society, such as the contradiction between the social nature of production and the private appropriation of the products. It would have to equip the children with the kind of qualifications they would need to fight against the disadvantages that society has inflicted on them, and for them to insist on the abolition of those contradictions which are a root cause of the conditions they suffer.

7. In order not to fall victim to utopian hopes we must ask ourselves what might be realistically achieved through the school curriculum and what aims can be achieved only through society as a whole.

8. An educational approach which concentrates on social conflict, and which takes sides, would have to prepare people for various kinds of strategic action. It would not be enough merely to be able to observe critically social reality. A curriculum in which the pupils only see, interpret and understand, does not go far enough. The important thing is to be able to convert knowledge into the capacity to act, with purpose and with objectives. However, projects

could not end in blind orders for action: nor should they create direct rules for action. Action would be considered before being taken, and evaluated while it was being taken, and social and material constraints, and questions of relative political power, would be important factors in these calculations.

9. Education through projects would mean education towards joint action. It should promote the solidarity of the pupils with the oppressed, and against their oppressors.

10. Project development would be part of school life. The projects themselves should both enable pupils to acquire necessary qualifications and make a contribution to curriculum development.

Examples of some possible projects

(a) CONFLICT AT THE FACTORY

Let us take a life-situation in industry, where employers and the management keep to themselves important information about financing, investment, and accounting. For the project the basic problem would be that workers and the works' council would want to gain access to the data, and start an 'open the books' campaign as a means of achieving this aim and as part of a democratisation programme within the works related to requirements laid down by the Basic Law of the Federal Republic. The questions to be answered would include:

Which data will be made public?
What do they express, and what do they distort?
What important things do they say nothing about?
What data are important for the employers?

How can the interests hidden in this abstract information be exposed?

How are the interests of the employers being realised, both through the organisation of and the technology used in the enterprise - for example, in the way these data are processed?

What kinds of knowledge and skills would workers and the works' council need in order to decide which data are essential for them to have?

What would they need to know about the origins of the data in order to be able to estimate their relative significance?

Part of the project could be a simulation. The information that a partly-fictitious business makes generally available could be compared with the kind of information that the employer keeps to himself. Works newspapers, and other sources of information connected with the business, could be studied, and knowledge of political economy or sociology could be applied. Those parts of the project aimed to develop powers of action could involve the simulated planning and carrying out of an 'open the books' campaign.

We would need to explain to the workers the aims of the campaign, and what it might achieve; the legal nature of the campaign; the political obstacles; the defining of levels of action both in and outside the business; the kind of organisation needed; and the resistance to be expected. Parts of the project should actually be carried out in a factory. This could be done by working with workers' representatives, and listening to and evaluating statements made by the management.

School will frequently take place outside the school building, not in a naïve application of 'learning by doing', but in the sense of deschooling which, in this case, means challenging theory by practice, and practice by theory, by the direct use of the world outside the school.

(b) THE SOCIAL WELFARE OFFICE

This project could be based on the argument that, in our society, non-profit-making social institutions, such as schools and hospitals, are permanently at a disadvantage compared with profit-making enterprises.

The work of a social welfare office in the community could be studied to find out the kind of contradictions which exist between clients' desires for the immediate satisfaction of basic needs (and, in the long run, for the removal of the social causes of their condition) and the inclinations of local politicians to keep expenditure down.

The following would be a suitable project for middle-school pupils. We can presuppose that in the locality where the school is situated the child-care institutions will display the same kind of faults as those of such institutions in the country as a whole, such as the social and emotional neglect, through hospitalisation, of babies and small children, and, at a certain age, moving them from one institution to another, causing social and emotional desolation. We might then find that in spite of assertions made by social workers, in the light of their experience, about the effects of neglect and hospitalisation, that changes in organisation and personnel have not been brought about, even though, by the standards of private business, they would have meant long-term savings.

The project should analyse such facts, and consider theoretical statements about the Lumpenproletariat. It should discuss the social control functions of social work, particularly the way in which it treats the symptoms rather than the causes of social problems. It should give the pupils some practical experience of such institutions. Finally, and most important, it should try to find out how far the bureaucratic structure itself contributes to the sad situation.

Afterwards pupils, teachers, parents and social workers could petition the local authorities with proposals to turn the child-care institutions into communes for young people, in which lasting emotional relationships would be possible. Studying the course of such a proposal as it went through the hierarchical, decision-making machine, would show whether and how such an application was blocked, altered, or had the teeth taken out of it.

The way that the decision-making process had worked in real life should be contrasted in the school by a simulation of how people might arrive at decisions in democratic institutions. Questions of strategy for effecting change in the future, and of the practical possibilities, should be discussed: could an alliance of the social workers themselves speed up the process of democratisation?

(c) FOLLOW-UP PROJECTS

Both the factory and the welfare office projects offer possibilities for parallel and follow-up projects. In the first one could study mathematics and its contribution in the production process, not regarding it as a matter of transmitting mathematical skills in isolation from their possible application in everyday life.

People should learn how to analyse how values which lie outside mathematics can be transformed into mathematical symbols, rules, and processes. Conversely, people should be able to recognise the nature and the values of the things that lie behind the formal mathematical symbols. People need to be able to do this particularly in situations where the technological processes and the mathematical activities associated with them give an impression of objective rationality, while the interests which lie behind them remain hidden. The second project could be made into a joint effort between social workers, the school and the pupils. The ways in which groups from outside the school participated would have to be critically assessed, especially in the light of the failure of some recent schemes.

(d) PROJECTS TO HELP THE PUPIL'S SELF-DEVELOPMENT AND SELF-RELIANCE

We should also try to free both teachers and pupils from the inhibitions formed by their previous way of life. This would strengthen that sense of self-respect that is the basis of all political action aimed at abolishing contradictions caused by the conflict of interests between different groups in society. Experiments would be carried out involving bargaining, trial living, and attempts to overcome barriers, which have been internalised and are recognised as repressive, and to overcome them here and now, by action, and not - as in group therapy - only with words. These would anticipate a concrete utopia in which people live together and help each other. The experience of such living might later make people oppose social repression and fight for the realisation of such a utopia in everyday life. All this attempts to help pupils to be no longer mere objects of others set in educational authority over them, but to become more self-reliant and to gain more and more control over their own social development.

Through role-playing, and other methods of gaining experience of ourselves or of working off our feeling (such as action-oriented forms of art, psychoanalysis and behavioural therapy) we could promote this process. In order to do this teachers would have to give up their traditional role-distance, and any inclination to lecture to their pupils.

Other projects could include newspaper production and television production. Pupils could produce a newspaper whose contents are determined, not by the editors, but by the readers. Pupils of all ages could take part in such a project, and they could work in editing, printing, and distributing the paper, according to their various qualifications. Children could also produce television programmes for children, as well as teaching materials, picture books, and reports about their own work.

The general principles of this project-curriculum can also be applied with pre-school children. The kind of pre-school curriculum where a world of the rich man in his castle, the poor man at his gate is presented as part of the natural order of things is a political curriculum, albeit a conservative one. To ask questions about the world is not to subject children to indoctrination before they are able to think for themselves. The approach must be one of making them aware of a variety of positions, so that later they might take up a position themselves. In all cases they must have the right to choose projects, and to refuse to take part in projects they do not like.

Further reading: a quotational bibliography compiled by IAN LISTER

ADAMS, Paul et al.: Children's Rights, Panther, 1972. Argues that 'the denial of certain very basic rights to our children... results in a society of adults sick with neurosis...'. Includes contributions by A. S. Neill and Michael Duane. Libertarian and therapeutic. Paul Goodman wrote about it: 'It is touching that the English can still talk about such profound issues.'

ARCHER, Margaret Scotford (editor): Students, University, and Society, Heinemann, 1972. Contributors analyse the crisis in education in various countries, including West and East Europe, Japan and the USA. They show how, viewed as phenomena, events in the various countries grow more and more alike. Systems fail to democratise, attempting both to expand and to retain the traditional, elite structures. Paradigm incident: in 1968 the magnificent rector of Turin University lectured surrounded by policemen while six officers tried to persuade one student to take his hat off.

ARIES, Philippe: The Centuries of Childhood (trans. by R. Baldick of L'Enfant et la Vie familiale sous l'Ancien Régime, Paris 1960), Cape, 1962. 'In medieval society the idea of childhood did not exist... as soon as the child could live without the constant solicitude of his mother... he belonged to adult society.' 'Medieval society... had no idea of education.' Later it was thought that 'the child was not ready for life and that he had to be subjected to special treatment, a sort of quarantine, before he was allowed to join the adults'. 'Family and school together removed the child from adult society. The school shut up a childhood which had hitherto been free within an increasingly severe disciplinary system which culminated in the 18th and 19th centuries in the total claustration of the boarding school.' The origin of much of the argument that childhood is a modern invention.

BANTOCK, G. H.: Culture, Industrialization and Education, Routledge and Kegan Paul, 1968. Analysis of the education crisis as reflecting a crisis in the culture. 'If we are honest, we have to admit that a great deal of our popular education is an almost total failure.' 'The school has come to take its major role in the distribution of life chances...' 'The school can stand as a conservative force (literally conserving) in a disintegrating world.' A conservative's view of the crisis. Bantock has written elsewhere: 'Two major issues in education for our times are (a) the need to civilise the intellectual proletariat, and (b) the need to civilise the meritocracy.' (Position paper for the European Cultural Foundation Conference, Education 2000, York University, 1972.)

BECKER, Howard S.: 'A School is a lousy place for learning anything in', in Learning to Work, edited by Blanche Geer, Aldine, 1972. 'I think it likely that the similarities between schools are much greater than conventionally supposed...' 'Students apparently do not learn what the school proposes to teach them.' 'Students often attend school for some purpose other than learning: to avoid being charged as a truant, to secure a draft exemption, or to meet a legal require-ment for some other desired activity.' 'On-the-job training... seems on balance more likely to produce educational successes.' The essay is about the comparative chances of learning via school or via apprenticeships, but is gloomy about the prospects of both as at present organised. 'My pessimistic conclusion is that on-the-job training does not do a very effective job either...'

BEREITER, Carl: 'Schools without education', Harvard Educational Review, Vol. 42, No. 3 (August 1972). Distinguishes between education - 'which in its largest sense is the deliberate development of the human personality, the making of citizens' - skill training and custodial child care, and maintains that only skill training and custodial care are legitimate functions of the elementary schools. 'I have said nothing about schooling beyond the elementary years. It is not at all certain that the high school will survive as an institution. The pressures toward its disintegration are much stronger and the reasons for its survival much weaker.' 'An alternative school plan... should carry with it a diminished rather than an inflated notion of the importance of schooling... If we want schools to be brought down to human scale, we need to conceive a role for them that is also of human scale - a modest role that ordinary people can handle by themselves. To conceive of such a modest role is to conceive of schools without education.'

BERG, Ivar: Education and Jobs: The Great Training Robbery, Praeger, 1970. Against himself, Berg came to the conclusion that there is a negative correlation between levels of certification and subsequent job performance. 'The conclusions do not give much comfort to those who argue that educational requirements serve managers well as a screening device with respect to either potential or actual performance.' Argument shares an ambivalence with Illich - it uses a conservative, functional analysis in order to reach a radical position - i. e. it could be argued that dysfunctional job performance, and 'disruptive qualifications', ought to be welcomed in certain economic and social systems.

BERRIGAN, Daniel: America is Hard to Find, SPCK, 1973. Testimony of a de-churched priest - a view from the priest-hole, the underground, and the prison. 'Our prisons do not rehabilitate, because our society is destitute of a vision of man.' In the United States 'reformism is dead' but so is revolution. 'We should aim at the slow reduction of the encroaching state.'

BETTELHEIM, Bruno: The Children of the Dream, Paladin, 1971. A study of the educational experiments of Israel's kibbutzim by a man whose own education included Dachau and Buchenwald. A humanist and a schoolman-reformer, with a concern for the deprived. 'Throughout their schooling... we must provide the kind of experience that will keep them from looking at school as something alien to their existence.' Of the kibbutzim alternative he comes to the conclusion: 'Even the most cursory inspection convinces me that kibbutz society could not survive economically without drawing on the high technology of surrounding Israel.' And 'all efforts to create kibbutzim among urban groups who work in large-scale production have failed. '

BOWLES, Samuel: 'Cuban education and the revolutionary ideology', Harvard Educational Review, Vol. 41, No. 4 (Autumn 1971), or CIDOC Document No. A/E 71/343. A critical but sympathetic study of the Cuban alternative, where 'the school plays a central role'; where there are some elements of job-rotation - teachers go cane-cutting; impressive literacy programmes; and an attempt to 'universalise the university'. 'The Revolutionary content of Cuban education is conveyed primarily outside the classroom. It is in the fields and the factories, at least as much as in the schools, that one finds the development of a new concept of education...' Castro is quoted: 'Revolution and education are the same thing. '

BOWLES, Samuel: 'Contradictions in US higher education', CIDOC Document No. A/E 71/346. Argues that 'the student movement and radicalism among young professionals is the manifestation of structural weaknesses endemic to the advanced capitalist system'... 'The two main functions of schooling in a capitalist society are the expansion of the forces of production and the reproduction of the social relations of production. '

BREMER, John and **von MOSCHZISKER, Michael**: The School Without Walls, Holt, Rinehart and Winston, 1971. The story of Philadelphia's Parkway Program. The school goes on to the street and into the city. One student writes: 'Parkway is an experience of growing, caring, frustration, sadness and joy. It is these very things because we are in the world of reality where learning has no special geographic setting or time. '

BUCKMAN, Peter (editor): Education without Schools, Souvenir Press, 1973. 'Education is not schooling... By education I mean a process of understanding the world, or acquiring the confidence to explore its workings... The emphasis of this book is on education as a lifelong experience. ' Includes contributions by Ivan Illich (The Deschooled Society); Ken Coates (Education as a Lifelong Experience); and Brian Winston (Self-help: the Media).

CALLAWAY, Archibald: Educational Planning and Unemployed Youth, UNESCO, 1971. 'There may now be required greater emphasis on out-of-school education more closely attuned to the economic scene: farm-extension, on-the-job training, functional literacy programmes. ' 'The less charted area, to which educational planners must now give greater concentration, lies beyond schools and universities. ' A humanist-economist's critique of societies, both in the 'developed' and the 'under-developed' world, where many students are destined to become 'graduates without jobs' or 'surplus youth'.

CASTLE, E. B.: Education for Self-Help: New Strategies for Developing Countries, Oxford University Press, 1972. Leans heavily on Philip Coombs, Julius Nyerere, and the author's own experience in East Africa. 'To continue enlarging existing systems of education which have evolved from the earlier concept of general educational growth in all sectors of education... is a recipe for educational and economic confusion. ' Includes a case for an intermediate technology. Economy-centred, rather than man-centred; revisionist not radical.

DAVE, R. H.: Lifelong Education and the School Curriculum, Unesco Institute for Education, Hamburg, 1973. An attempt to analyse the implications that lifelong educational opportunity would have for schools. Like much UNESCO material it attempts to co-opt contradictory ideas, and carefully evades conflict issues.

DENNISON, George: The Lives of Children: The Story of the First Street School, Random House, 1969; Penguin, 1972. One man's answer in a world that is not fit for children - a free school for deprived children in New York. Influenced by Rousseau, Tolstoy, and A. S. Neill. Funny, sad, posing most of the dilemmas. The hope - 'our schools could be used in a powerfully regenerative way. ' The reality - 'the children had acquired allies and havens, and this is no small thing in the hostile streets of New York'.

DROUARD, Alain: 'Education', in Europe Tomorrow, edited by Richard Mayne, Fontana, 1972. 'There is every reason to think that the fundamental crisis in all educational systems will last for many years to come...'

ENTWISTLE, Harold: Education, Work and Leisure, Routledge and Kegan Paul, 1970. 'Our more chronic educational ills are not ultimately to be healed by a direct attack upon the symptoms within the schools... The transformation of our culture in vocational terms may still be necessary. ' Argument for 'an education which equips all men to find in work a creative personal experience'.

ENTWISTLE, Harold: Political Education in a Democracy, Routledge and Kegan Paul, 1971. A review of the problems of the school as a political educator. Like his other book, it only scratches the surface of the problems.

FAURE, Edgar et al.: Learning to be, UNESCO/ Harrap, 1972. 'We propose lifelong education as the master concept for educational policies in the years to come for both developed and developing countries. ' Written in UNESCO prose, it co-opts many of the ideas of deschooling, and tries to accommodate the challenges raised by Michael Huberman in his paper on Democratisation.

FOUCAULT, Michel: Madness and Civilization, Random House, 1965 (a translation by Richard Howard of Histoire de la Folie, Plon, 1961). The great lock-up theory. 'The seventeenth century created enormous houses of confinement... The phenomenon has European dimensions... In several years, an entire network had spread across Europe. ' 'Confinement... is a "police" matter. Police, in the precise sense that the classical epoch gave to it - that is, the totality of measures which made work possible and necessary for all those who could not live without it...' 'Throughout Europe, confinement had the same meaning, at least if we consider its origin. It constituted one of the answers the seventeenth century gave to an economic crisis that affected the entire Western world... But outside of the periods of crisis, confinement acquired another meaning. Its repressive function was combined with a new use. It was no longer merely a question of confining those out of work, but of giving work to those who had been confined...'

FREIRE, Paulo: Pedagogy of the Oppressed, Herder and Herder, 1970; Sheed and Ward, 1972; Penguin, 1972. A rediscovery of the humanising vocation of the intellectual and a framework for action in which the twin poles of 'oppression' and 'liberation' form a dialectic of change. An approach which focusses on contradictions in society, and on the life-situations of the learner, in which 'Liberation is a praxis: the action and reflection of men upon their world in order to transform it'. Searches for emancipatory strategies, and develops a theory and practice of dialogue between teachers and learners as a way towards the future.

FREIRE, Paulo: 'Letter to Will Kennedy', in Seeing Education Whole, World Council of Churches, 1970. 'The "liberating" educator... cannot be a libertarian, (and) he cannot be an authoritarian either.'

FREIRE, Paulo: Cultural Action for Freedom, Penguin, 1972. Language learning as 'an act of knowing and not of memorisation'. Against 'the "digestive" concept of knowledge, so common in current educational practice...' Freire's method for adult literacy - 'the literacy process, as cultural action for freedom, is an act of knowing in which the learner assumes the role of knowing subject in dialogue with the educator'. Critical of literacy campaigns which are 'humanitarian - but not humanist'.

FREIRE, Paulo: 'A few notions about the word "Conscientisation"', in Hard Cheese, No. 1, 1973. 'Cultural action, cultural revolution, is the way in which we attack culturally in our own culture. It is to take culture as always problematic...' 'Conscientizaçao... is disturbing in its beginning as if we were born again.'

FROMM, Erich: Fear of Freedom, Routledge and Kegan Paul, 1942 and 1960. 'Only if man masters society and subordinates the economic machine to the purposes of human happiness, and only if he actively participates in the social process, can he overcome what now drives him to despair - his aloneness and his feeling of powerlessness.' A classic work which raises some dilemmas for deschooling theory.

GAMM, Hans-Jochen: Kritische Schule, List Verlag, 1970. Analysis of present school problems, and a plea to make a radically restructured school a centre for the emancipation of teachers and pupils and of enlightenment in society.

GARNETT, Emmeline: Area Resource Centre, Arnold, 1972. Account of an experiment in Leicestershire County. L. C. Taylor says the book shows, about Teachers' Centres, 'how profitable a trade, when given a chance, they might ply'. His metaphor, not mine.

GOFFMAN, Erving: Asylums, Anchor, 1961; Penguin, 1968. Classic analysis of inmates and staff in total institutions, much of which is applicable to schools. 'Rationales for mortifying the self are very often merely rationalisations, generated by efforts to manage the daily activity of a large number of persons in a restricted space with small expenditure of resources.' 'An important kind of leverage possessed by the staff is their power to give the kind of discharge that reduces stigmatisation.'

GOODMAN, Paul: Growing Up Absurd, Gollancz, 1961; Sphere, 1970. A classic. See Introduction.

GOODMAN, Paul: Compulsory Miseducation, Horizon, 1962; Penguin, 1961. The first major confrontation with 'a mass superstition'. Also see Introduction.

GRABOWSKI, Stanley M. (editor): Paulo Freire: A Revolutionary Dilemma for the Adult Educator, Syracuse University Publications in Continuing Education and ERIC Clearinghouse on Adult Education, 1972. Essays by various adult educators on the challenges raised by Freire - especially that they themselves are domesticated within institutional frameworks which prevent them from doing what they

seek to do. By far the most valuable item is the Quotational Bibliography, by Anne Hartung and John Ohliger, which contains selections from 184 pieces by, or about, Freire.

GRAMSCI, Antonio: 'On Education', in Prison Notebooks, Lawrence and Wishart, 1971. Written by an Italian Marxist when in Mussolini's prisons before the Second World War. Plea for a common school: 'Studies should be carried on collectively.' 'The active school is still in its romantic phase, in which the elements of the struggle against the mechanical and Jesuitical school have become unhealthily exaggerated...' 'It was right to struggle against the old school, but reforming it was not so simple as it seemed. The problem was not one of model curricula but of men, and not just of the men who are actually teachers themselves but of the entire social complex which they express.' 'In education one is dealing with children in whom one has to inculcate certain habits of diligence, precision, poise (even physical poise), ability to concentrate on specific subjects, which cannot be acquired without the mechanical repetition of disciplined and methodical acts.' '...It will always be an effort to learn physical self-discipline and self-control; the pupil has, in effect, to undergo a psycho-physical training. Many people have to be persuaded that studying too is a job, and a very tiring one, with its own particular apprenticeship - involving muscles and nerves as well as intellect.' By implication, a serious challenge to the bourgeois-individualist, and hedonistic elements of Deschooling theory.

GRAUBARD, Allen: Free the Children: Radical Reform and the Freeschool Movement, Pantheon, 1972. Critical, sympathetic, committed. A clear exposition of free school dilemmas. 'There is no simple solution; hiding behind a freedom ideology or the notion that anything one does is learning is a cop-out.' Points out the conservative possibilities of some alternative education schemes, which might privatise education and depoliticise educational questions - 'the issues would be eliminated because criticisms of schools would not longer be a publically arguable concern'. This critique applies equally to the privatising elements of deschooling.

GREENE, Maxine: 'Existentialism, Literature and Schooling', CIDOC Document No. A/E 71/337. An existentialist's view of deschooling, sympathetic but seeing practical problems. 'The individual, here at Cuernavaca, as well as in his school or college, must struggle against the temptation to acquiesce, to be a believer, to sit at the feet of a guru. He must rebel against the charisma of someone like Ivan Illich, who - I am convinced - has not chosen himself as a cult-figure, who has pointed out explicitly the dangers in claiming to be a prophet of any sort.' '...If we ponder what Illich and others mean by our being "schooled", we cannot blandly assume that consciousness can be easily changed (or "raised") through exposure to social deficiencies for the first time rationally displayed'.

GROSS, Ronald and Beatrice (editors): Radical School Reform, Simon and Schuster, 1969; Gollancz, 1971; Penguin, 1973. Contributors include James Herndon, Jonathan Kozol, Jules Henry, Marshall McLuhan, Edgar Z. Friedenberg, Neil Postman and Charles Weingartner. Mainly libertarian schoolmen-reformers. No Illich; no Reimer.

HAJNAL, John: The Student Trap, Penguin, 1972. Sees the problems of 'the conveyor belt' and argues for 'à la carte curricula' as a way beyond present troubles.

HENRY, Jules: Essays on Education, Penguin, 1972. Social-anthropological analysis of education and schools by the author of Culture Against Man. 'In education the group most strategic for social change is the teachers, and we know that the teachers are a vulnerable group. '

HENTIG, Hartmut von: Cuernavaca oder: Alternativen zur Schule? Klett/Kösel, 1971. An exposition and critique of deschooling by one of West Germany's leading schoolmen-reformers. Argues for deschooling the school: 'society needs a school which is quite different from the one it now has. '

HILL, Christopher: The World Turned Upside Down, Temple Smith, 1972. About seventeenth-century England, but provocative of many insights if schooling is viewed as the state church of today. 'The function of a state church was not merely to guide men to heaven: it was also to keep them in subordination here on earth. ' 'Priests and scholars would have liked to keep interpretation of the Bible the monopoly of an educated élite. ' 'Necessarily only a select group have the economic status, the education, the leisure to master this (new) theology; only a minority can be free... ' (Danger of deschooling?) 'If the elect (today, those born intelligent) are chosen from all eternity what do priests take our money for?' So 'the oligarchy of grace was democratised... ' Freeschoolers (groups meeting in inns and boats); demands for community control; the setting up of communes; the claim that more religion (education) might be found in the ale-house and even the whorehouse than in the church (school); and the popular demand of salvation for all - these were all there. There was 'a breakdown of confidence on the one hand, and prevalent millenarian enthusiasm on the other. ' Illich talks of 'counter-foil research' and the need for 'inversion'. Hill records: 'radicalism passed into rationalism'; the early Quakers - perhaps the deschoolers of the time - became respectable; Naylor lost, Fox won; they were a group 'which had failed to turn the world upside down'. The historical parallel raises the question what might happen if schools lost their powers of compulsion and expulsion. Hill: 'The right to exclude from the sacraments was the last priestly control left in England. '

HOFSTADTER, Richard: Anti-intellectualism in American Life, Jonathan Cape, 1964. William Franklin Phelps (1870): The schools 'afford the sad spectacle of ignorance engaged in the stupendous fraud of self-perpetuation at public expense... ' Joseph M. Rice (1892) '... elementary education has become in many places a vaudeville show. The child must be kept amused and learn what he pleases. ' Hofstadter: 'The figure of the schoolteacher may well be taken as a central symbol in any modern society... ' By one of America's greatest humanist-scholars. Traces influence of anti-intellectualism, and how it led to 'de-intellectualised curricula' and the early disappointments of the schoolmen. A book for quarrying.

HUBERMAN, Michael: Reflections on Democratization of Secondary and Higher Education, UNESCO, Paris, 1970; version of text, under same title, also available in The Times Educational Supplement, 21 August 1970. 'A small, élitist educational system that must expand and democratise cannot cling to patterns and norms of an earlier age and created for a different purpose. ' '... The secondary and higher education systems seem to discourage those who do not conform to the place and content of the school programme. ' 'We must begin to look at the educational structure not as a chronological sequence, but as a sort of configuration. ' 'How much longer can countries, especially developing countries, afford to support school and university systems whose curriculum is abstracted from the activities of life and divided into texts, lessons, scheduled learning periods and graded promotions?' 'The idea that the only way people get educated is by being enrolled in institutions is part of the unfortunate mythology that has complicated our educational crisis. ' 'In the majority of countries, the university has created and - through its control over certification for high-level jobs - strengthened the myth that no one can learn unless he goes to school. '... 'The main reason schooling is confused with education is certification. '... 'We judge our success by whether a pupil stays, not by whether he learns. ' 'The student movement has been politically radical while remaining educationally conservative. '... 'The time is ripe for an ambitious programme in reverse technical assistance, whereby specialists from developing countries in community development, second-language teaching, polyvalent out-of-school education, family education and rural "animation" can help solve the most acute over-development problems in highly industrialised countries. ' A piece full of radical questioning and by implication a criticism of much UNESCO policy to date. Permission to reproduce the paper in this Reader was refused by UNESCO - 'For reasons of general policy Unesco does not wish this study to be published again... ' Huberman has written a new paper specially for this Reader, taking the argument further.

HUSÉN, Torsten: 'Useful functions for the Schools of the Future', in Educating the Young People of the World, edited by Alice Miel and Louise Berman, NEA, 1970. 'What are the institutions that will be rendering contributions to tomorrow's educational systems? It stands to reason that the school in its traditional sense will continue to play the dominant role. ' A schoolman's vision - technotopia version.

HUSÉN, Torsten: Skolans kris, Almqvist and Wiksell, 1972. The school crisis mediated.

HUTCHINS, Robert M.: The Learning Society, Penguin 1970. 'A world community learning to be civilised, learning to be human, is at last a possibility. ' Man-centred - 'Man makes himself'. A classic.

ILLICH, Ivan: Deschooling Society, Harper and Row, 1971; Calder and Boyars, 1971; Penguin, 1973. 'For most men the right to learn is curtailed by the obligation to attend school. '... 'The disestablishment of schools will inevitably happen - and it will happen surprisingly fast. ' The classic work on deschooling. A book to be read, not mediated. See also the Introduction.

ILLICH, Ivan: Celebration of Awareness, Calder and Boyars, 1971; Penguin, 1973. Illich writes: 'Each essay was written in a different language, addressed to a different group of believers, meant to hit home as a particular crisis of confidence. ' Includes calls to declericalise the church; to recognise the futility of schooling; to see the ineffectiveness of 'Aid' programmes, as currently organised, both to the 'socially deprived' and to 'under-developed countries'. It ends with a call for cultural revolution. It includes his address, as Vice-Rector, to graduands of the University of Puerto Rico: 'The "age of schooling" began about two hundred years ago. Gradually the

131

idea grew that schooling was a necessary means of becoming a useful member of society. It is the task of this generation to bury that myth. Your own situation is paradoxical. At the end and as a result of your studies, you are enabled to see that the education your children deserve, and will demand, requires a revolution in the school system of which you are a product. '

ILLICH, Ivan: 'After Deschooling, What?', Social Policy (September/October 1971). 'If the school continues to lose its educational and political legitimacy, while knowledge is still conceived as a commodity, we will certainly face the emergence of a therapeutic Big Brother. '... 'Unless we guarantee that job relevance is the only acceptable criterion for employment, promotion, or access to tools, thus ruling out not only schools but all other ritual screening, then deschooling means driving out the devil with Beelzebub. '

ILLICH, Ivan: 'Anglo-American Law and a convivial society', CIDOC Document No. I/V 72/7. 'From the juristic point of view what remains is the task of recognising and incorporating into our law the principles that the present problem of society is limiting not increasing productive efficiency. The legal tools to set these limits are already at hand. '... 'If mankind cannot accept limits, disaster will set them within the next generation on gruesome levels which the Club of Rome tries to predict. Such studies lay the groundwork for an even worse nightmare: survival within limits set and enforced by a bureaucratic dictatorship. '

ILLICH, Ivan: 'Re-tooling Society', CIDOC Document No. A/E 72/369. 'Politics in a post-industrial society must be mainly concerned with the development of design criteria for tools rather than, as now, with the choice of production goals. '... 'Three years ago it took courage to question the value of schools, and by now it has become a fad to do so. But unfortunately, the loss of legitimacy of the tool has only increased concern with the achievement of the goal for which the tool has proven to be ineffective. The decreasing reliance on school as the choice instrument to condition men for life among modern tools has led to a search for less hypocritical, more ruthless and more effective ways to tool men for their tools all during their lives. The public has now become aware of a need for protection against schoolteachers. Protection against other "educators" is even more important. '... 'Industrial society as such - and not just its separate institutions - has outgrown the range of its effectiveness. ' A working document. Book now published as Tools for Conviviality, Harper and Row, Calder and Boyars, 1973.

JAMES, Eric: Teacher Education and Training, H. M. S. O. , 1972. The Report's 'argument for fundamental change is not based upon any false assumption that the present system has, in some total sense, failed or is in imminent danger of doing so... Nevertheless, there is abundant evidence that the system is no longer adequate to its purposes... Changes must be made if the needs of the schools and of society over the next 20 years are to be met, and the system cannot be expected to reform itself as rapidly and as fundamentally as the situation requires. ' Harry Judge, a member of the Committee which produced the Report, wrote elsewhere (The Higher Education Supplement, 28 January 1972): 'Whatever happens to these proposals, it must by now be painfully obvious that positive action of some kind must soon

be taken: if it is not, the present system will collapse. '

KOHL, Herbert: 36 Children, Gollancz, 1968; Penguin, 1972. A view from the classroom of a ghetto school by a dedicated teacher who sees both the humanity of his pupils and the system as a whole. The pupils' behaviour is 'a direct response to the institutionalised hypocrisy that is characteristic of schools in the United States today'. 'The thirty-six children are suffering from the diseases of our society. '

LABOV, W. : 'The logic of nonstandard English', text available in Language and Education, Routledge and Kegan Paul and The Open University, 1972. 'It may seem that the fallacies of the verbal deprivation theory are so obvious that they are hardly worth exposing... That educational psychology should be strongly influenced by a theory so false to the facts of language is unfortunate; but that children should be the victims of this ignorance is intolerable. ' An antidote for those who draw simplistic conclusions from the work of Bernstein et al.

LIPSET, Seymour Martin: Rebellion in the University, Routledge and Kegan Paul, 1972. A man who wrote in 1958: 'The fundamental political problems of the industrial revolution have now been solved' now writes: 'The brief look presented here into the history of campus-related unrest and protest should force us to be humble both about our ability to understand and to predict waves of discontent. '

LISTER, Ian: 'The Deschoolers'. Two articles in The Times Educational Supplement, 9 July 1971 and 23 July 1971.

LISTER, Ian: 'Radical Alternatives in Education', in Rights of Children, N. C. C. L. , 1972.

LISTER, Ian: 'Towards an Educative Society: Getting there from here' in Education without Schools, edited by Peter Buckman, Souvenir Press, 1973.

LISTER, Ian: 'Pluralism and Diversity for a Learning Society: an analysis of the Ontario Report, with comments by adult educators on the analysis', Adult Education, Vol. 45, No. 4 (November 1972).

LISTER, Ian: 'A Conversation with Paulo Freire', The Times Higher Education Supplement, 13 June 1973.

MARTIN, Bernice: 'Progressive education versus the Working classes', Critical Quarterly, Vol. 13, No. 4 (Winter 1971). 'Increasingly I have come to suspect that current reforms in school structure, curricula and teaching methods are not merely not assisting their main intended beneficiaries, the working classes, but may well be hampering them further. '

MUSGROVE, Frank: Patterns of Power and Authority in English Education, Methuen, 1971. A witty book - a cherished rarity in the dreary steppes of educational literature. 'The theme of this book is that schools are underpowered in relation to the goals they try to attain. '... 'Most teachers live in a state of constant crisis and chronic apprehension... Although the teacher lives constantly with crisis, it is his crisis'... 'Informal education is a neglected factor in the equation of power. ' 'One reason why schools are impotent is that they are a bore. ' 'Teachers are relatively powerless because they have little to offer that their pupils urgently want. ' 'Any goals for schools may soon be pointless. '

National Council for Civil Liberties, 'Children Have Rights', 1971. A series of working papers. Items include: Children in Schools, Children at Home, and Compulsory School Attendance. Reveals the legal confusions about children, and that 'it is still tacitly assumed that children are the "property" of someone - if not the parents, then the state. ' On compulsory school, when the compulsion is felt and resented: 'There is immense strain on all concerned; teachers feel threatened and pupils de-humanised. Incipient paranoia thrives on both sides. ' A useful starting point but there is still a long way to go in this field of juristic counter-research.

NISBET, Robert: The Degradation of the Academic Dogma, H. E. B. , 1971, laments the invasion of the community of scholars by 'the higher capitalism of the campus' and asks: 'Is the university today undergoing some possibly irreversible decline, comparable perhaps to what happened to the guild, the landed aristocracy, and village community in earlier ages?'

OECD, Towards New Structures of Post-Secondary Education, Paris, 1971. 'Most countries are at an intermediary and critical stage between élitist and mass higher education, the former having been abandoned under the pressure of numbers and a series of socio-economic factors, the latter requiring structures, content and organisational arrangements which have not yet been developed and only partly identified. The major challenge to policy-planning is to ensure that this transition takes place smoothly. '

OECD, Alternative Educational Futures in the United States and in Europe, Paris, 1972. 'Those who wish not only to fit in with the future, but also to participate in the choosing of it, need to understand what is at stake in the choices - the "issues beneath the issues"... '

OHLIGER, John and McCARTHY, Colleen: Lifelong Learning or Lifelong Schooling? Syracuse University Publications in Continuing Education and ERIC Clearinghouse on Adult Education, 1971. An introductory essay on Illich and deschooling, and a quotational bibliography of 157 items. Invaluable.

PLUMB, J. H.: 'Children, the Victims of Time', in In the Light of History, Allen Lane The Penguin Press, 1972. Childhood as a modern invention. 'Rarely do we look far enough into the past for the roots of our present problems. This revolution of youth has been building up for decades, because we forced the growing child into a repressive and artificial world, a prison, indeed, that was the end product of four centuries of Western history, of that gradual exclusion of the maturing child from the world of adults. '

POSTMAN, Neil and WEINGARTNER, Charles: Teaching as a Subversive Activity, Delacorte, 1969; Penguin, 1971. Plea for the school as a centre of social criticism and renewal. 'The new education is new, not because it offers more of anything, but because it enters into an entirely new "business": fundamentally, the crap-detecting and relevance business. ' 'School, after all, is the one institution in our society that is inflicted on everybody and what happens in school makes a difference - for good or ill. ' 'Unless our schools can switch to the right business, their clientele will either go elsewhere (as many are doing) or go into a severe case of "future shock"... Future shock occurs when you are confronted by the fact that the world you were educated to believe in doesn't exist. '

PUNCH, Maurice: Dartington Hall School 1926-1957, Ph. D. thesis, University of Essex, 1971. A small island of empirical evidence in the sea of assertions about the effects of schooling. Dartington regarded itself as the nearest thing to a deschooled school. Punch interviewed graduands who had left either between 1935 to 1940 or 1950 to 1954, and who had stayed in the senior section of the school for a minimum of three years. 'The general impression... was of almost semi-retreatist, home-centred, "privatised" individuals avoiding formal institutions and political-social activism. ' Currently the trustees of Dartington are refusing Punch permission to publish the work, but it is available through the Inter-Library loan service. In case of difficulty contact the Department of Sociology, University of Essex.

REIMER, Everett: School is Dead: An Essay on Alternatives in Education, Penguin, 1971. 'Alternatives to school, as opposed to mere reform, require going beyond the experience of individuals to an analysis of the essential characteristics of schools. ' With Illich's Deschooling Society the classic statement of deschooling. See also Introduction.

RICHMOND, W. Kenneth: The Free School, Methuen, 1973. 'In practice, deschooling has already begun in many places, not necessarily under that name, of course, and not necessarily in extreme forms. ' Includes a section on 'Deschooling in Action'. Suffers from a failure to distinguish between deschooling, free schools, and community colleges. Takes a schoolocentric view of the present crisis.

ROSZAK, Theodore: The Making of a Counter Culture, Faber, 1970. Includes a chapter on Paul Goodman. 'Well before either the beats of hippies had begun to sabotage the middle-class American "reality" principle, Goodman... was laying the theoretical foundation of the great dropout. '

RUSK, Bruce (editor): Alternatives in Education, University of London Press, 1973. Papers given at the Ontario Institute for Studies in Education and published in Canada in 1971. Includes contributions by Neil Postman (The Language of Education); Jean Vanier (Educators and the Mentally Deficient); and Ivan Illich (The Deschooling of Society). Now has a somewhat faded look.

SCHAEFER, Robert J.: The School as a Centre of Inquiry, Harper and Row, 1967. One of the most impressive works of the schoolmen-reformers. Practical suggestions on how to make the school a place which is educative for teachers as well as pupils, 'an institution characterised by a pervasive search for meaning and rationality in its work'.

School of Barbiana: Letter to a Teacher, Penguin, 1970. Written by the peasant children of Barbiana who, with the help of a left-wing priest, organised their own school. Their project was a protest against the Italian educational system. School 'is a hospital which tends to the healthy and rejects the sick'. 'School, with today's timetable, is a war against the poor. ' 'It remains a school cut to measure for the rich. For people who can get their culture at home and are going to school just in order to collect diplomas. ' 'Nothing is more unjust than to share equally among unequals. ' 'Teachers can always find excuses for forgetting. The missing child (who has been failed and expelled from the class) has the defect of not being there. At his old desk there ought to be a cross or a coffin, as a reminder.' A plea for better schools, beautifully written and showing the power of Christian-humanism. Already a classic among teachers in many countries. See also Reading 26 by Gastone Tassinari.

SCHWARTZ, Barry N. (editor): Affirmative Education, Prentice-Hall, 1972. Includes 'A Conversation with Ivan Illich'. Illich: '...it is a ghastly thing, this coining of new words. I almost wish I had not spoken of deschooling. Do you know where I learned it? There was a meeting in the Urban Training Centre in Chicago...I started to tease some of the people from the Black Economic Development Corporation because of the consumer orientation in their development plans. And when we spoke of school I wanted to try to get from them what people feel schools do...some guy said, "Yeah, you are right. Schools are made to screw you." But I understood that he had said schools are made to school you. When I repeated this everybody laughed...In the afternoon we all showed up with buttons: "School You". We then began to speak of the deschooling of society.'

SEARLE, John: The Campus War, Penguin, 1972. Tries to analyse a crisis which has seen cops on the campus from Kraków to Kent State, and the killing of students in many countries. 'The members of each new generation inherit an institutional framework for conducting their lives that was created by earlier generations. Sometimes the problems which the institutions were designed to cope with have been solved or have become irrelevant to contemporary worries, and yet the institutions continue, though lacking much of their original purpose.'...'We are living in one of those periods, like...at the end of the 18th century, when traditional forms of authority are being challenged everywhere.' Searle excludes England from some of the general analysis: 'most things in England...are about a century out of date.'

SHAW, Bernard: various works well worth revisiting. The Preface to Misalliance (1910) - the school as prison; the Preface to Androcles and the Lion (1913) for an analysis of de-synagogued religion - 'John went into the wilderness, not into the synagogue' and Christianity as the first comprehensive school - 'bringing the Gentiles (that is the uncircumcised) within the pale of religion'; and in the Yearbook of the Workers' Educational Association (1914): 'The government of the world by people who have been longest at school has been so far an organisation of ignorance, unsociability and terrorism, exploding from time to time in such monstrous smashes as the present war...'

SILBERMAN, Charles E.: Crisis in the Classroom, Random House, 1970; Wildwood House, 1973. 'It is not possible to spend any prolonged period visiting public school classrooms without being appalled by the mutilation visible everywhere - mutilation of spontaneity, of joy in learning, of pleasure in creating, in sense of self. The public schools - those "killers of the dream"... - are the kind of institution one cannot really dislike until one gets to know them well. Because adults take the schools so much for granted, they fail to appreciate what grim, joyless places most American schools are, how oppressive and petty are the rules by which they are governed, how intellectually sterile and aesthetically barren the atmosphere...' The classic statement of the American Reform Movement. Like many other reformers Silberman went on pilgrimage to the English progressive primary school and, although

one reformer comments 'It is easier to put man on the moon than to reform the public schools', Silberman ends up as a schoolman-reformer and subtitles his book 'The Remaking of American Education'.

SIMON, Brian: 'The raising of the school-leaving-age and deschooling', Forum for the Discussion of New Trends in Education, Vol. 14, No. 3 (Summer 1972). 'It is ironic that, just at the moment when a reform fought for many decades by the labour and progressive movement generally is about to be implemented, the deschooling movement in the United States, arising from the sharp social contradictions there, has been accorded massive publicity in the press and TV. Clearly the schools need changing... but the alternative presented, that of destroying the publicly provided system of education, is a counsel of despair.'

SOBEL, Harold W. and **SALZ, Arthur E.:** The Radical Papers: Readings in Education, Harper and Row paperback, 1972. A number of contributors, including Neil Postman on 'The Politics of Reading' ('Teachers of reading comprise a most sinister political group...'); Ira Glaser on 'Are children people?'; Christopher Jenks on Education Vouchers. Also reports from some American alternative schools. Many of the items do not get beyond progressive rhetoric. Two important exceptions are Peter Marin - 'Whatever happens is shrouded in folds of propaganda and rhetoric. It goes on and on...the grasping for paradise lost, paradise now. If this is not the kingdom of the apocalypse, it is at least an apocalyptic condition of the soul.' And Jonathan Kozol: 'We should not fool ourselves about the nature of the task before us...We turn in desperation to complex technologies (called systems), new phantasies of "open schools" within closed buildings, new phrases ("Discovery", "The Integrated Day") for old deceptions. What is the realistic meaning of alternatives "within the system", if the system is the primary vehicle of state control?...The public schools may be inept, archaic, old and unattractive, but they are not suicidal.'

STORM, Michael: 'Schools and the community: an issue-based approach', Bulletin of Environmental Education (May 1971). A practical attempt to define learning resources in a locality, and to face up to conflict-issues.

STORM, Michael: 'Where the Left is Right', in the Guardian, 28 July 1972. 'The deschooling movement probably presents the most exciting potential for Left-Right alliances.' Argues that deschooling would lead to increased bureaucratisation. 'Children need protecting from the hazy millenarianism of the educational Left.' A vigorous polemic which scores some hits, but which also suffers from its own confusions.

TAYLOR, L. C.: Resources for Learning, Penguin 1971. A plea for more independent, resources-based learning. 'One wonders whether...we have exhausted the possibilities of "the Gutenberg technology" or have yet to explore them seriously.' 'The argument of this book is that we should test independent learning thoroughly as an alternative method to teacher-based learning in our secondary schools.'

TOLSTOY, Leo: On Education (translated by Leo Winer), Chicago University Press, 1967. Includes classic pieces 'On Popular Education' and 'The School at Yasnaya Polyana'. 'Schools which are established from above and by force are not a shepherd for the flock, but a flock for the shepherd.'

'All agree that schools are imperfect (I, on my side, am convinced they are injurious)...' 'everywhere the greater part of one's education is acquired, not at school, but in life.' 'If we by all means must educate the people, let us ask them how they educate themselves, and what their favourite instruments for attaining this end are.' 'The popular school must respond to the exigencies of the masses... What these exigencies are, only a careful study of them and free experiment can teach.' 'The school has no right and ought not to reward and punish.' 'We personally are not yet able to renounce the tradition that grammar, in the sense of the laws of language, is necessary for the regular exposition of ideas; it even seems to us that the pupils have a need of grammar, and that in them unconsciously lie the laws of grammar.' Practical parallels with the free schools of today; theoretical parallels with Freire in general strategy, and perhaps Chomsky in language. Christian, humanist, populist; by a genius, and a great educator.

WRIGHT, Douglas T. : Draft Report of the Commission on Post-Secondary Education in Ontario, The Queen's Printer, Ontario, 1971. 'We must ask ourselves whether we wish to allow the trend towards universal and sequential education to continue, or whether we should provide viable alternatives.' 'Education must be man-centred.' 'We must never forget that the basic purpose of education is learning; that learning cannot but be, ultimately, a highly individual matter.' 'If the individual is at the centre, he must have the opportunity and the responsibility to decide what educational experience is best for him.' 'Educational services should be available to all citizens throughout their lives.' 'Where student intake quotas are for the present unavoidable admission should be determined on the basis of a lottery conducted among... qualified applicants...' 'Legislation should be enacted to prevent discrimination in employment because of attendance or non-attendance at educational institutions.' The basis for educational planning in the province of Ontario. University critics wrote of the Report: 'This philosophy seems to have reached them through Ivan Illich.' The most radical analysis of problems of Education and Society yet produced by any post-industrial country.

YOUNG, Michael F. D. (editor): Knowledge and Control, Collier-Macmillan, 1971. Raises key questions about knowledge in modern society - its organisation, transmission, and control. Berstein: 'How a society selects, classifies, distributes, transmits and evaluates the educational knowledge it considers to be public, reflects both the distribution of power and the principles of social control.' So far the sociologists of knowledge share with phenomenologists the major limitation that they offer critiques without also offering operational strategies and alternative programmes.

ZIMMER, Jürgen: Aspects of a curriculum for working-class children from the example of a planned model school in the German Federal Republic, European Cultural Foundation, 1971. 'The Summerhill experiment aimed at establishing the happiness of pupils but did not offer through a curriculum the chance of communicating the personal claim to self-liberation in a united front...' At the School of Barbiana - in spite of its analytical insight into the class character of the Italian school system - the pupils still had largely to submit to the educational canon that was opposed to their interests.' With 'project development... the starting point is no longer the correction of syllabuses used hitherto, but those life situations for which the school has to prepare its pupils.'

ZINNECKER, Jürgen: 'Chancen für Gegenschulen?' in Schule ohne Klassenschranken, Rowolt, 1972. Argues that the school is a structural part of capitalist society, and reflects weaknesses in the capitalist system, and the inabilities of the system to overcome those weaknesses. The concept of learning in such a society itself contains a contradiction, for at the same time it aims to liberate and captivate the learner. Anti-schools and free schools have a utopian character, but can reveal the inhuman limitations of learning in capitalist society. One of the preconditions of achieving this is that they must 'present a contribution to the deschooling of learning'.

Notes

Introduction

1. Philip H. Coombs: The World Educational Crisis, Oxford University Press, 1968.

2. Edward Britton, leader of the National Union of Teachers in Britain, Easter 1972.

3. Michael Pollard: Anti-educationists find a hearing among some parents and teachers. The Times, 19 April 1972.

4. Julius Nyerere: Education for Self-Reliance, 1967. See Reading 20.

5. Archibald Callaway: Educational Planning and Unemployed Youth, UNESCO, 1971. See Quotational Bibliography.

6. W. Senteza Kajubi: Is the School an Obsolete Institution? 1970. See Reading 15.

7. Alain Drouard: 'Education', in Richard Mayne (editor): Europe Tomorrow, Fontana, 1972.

8. School of Barbiana: Letter to a Teacher, Penguin, 1970.

9. Gastone Tassinari: The Doposcuola and Quartiere Movement, 1971. See Reading 26.

10. Hartmut von Hentig: Cuernavaca oder: Alternativen zur Schule? Klett/Kösel, 1971. See Reading 7 and Quotational Bibliography.

11. Torsten Husén: Skolans Kris, Almqvist and Wiksell, 1972.

12. Paul Goodman: Growing Up Absurd, Gollancz, 1961; Sphere, 1970.

13. Paul Goodman: Compulsory Miseducation, Penguin, 1971; p. 19.

14. John Holt: Reformulations, 1971. See Reading 9.

15. John Holt: How Children Fail, Pitman, 1964; Penguin, 1969.

16. John Holt: How Children Learn, Pitman, 1967; Penguin, 1970; p. 8 Penguin edition.

17. John Holt: The Underachieving School, Pitman, 1970; Penguin, 1971; p. 26 Penguin edition. See Reading 8.

18. John Holt: What Do I Do Monday? Pitman, 1970.

19. Ivan Illich: Deschooling Society, Harper and Row, 1971; Calder and Boyars, 1971; Penguin, 1973. Most of the quotations are taken from here.

20. Everett Reimer: School is Dead, Penguin, 1971.

21. Michael Huberman: Reflections on the Democratization of Secondary and Higher Education, UNESCO, 1970. See Quotational Bibliography.

22. Ivan Illich: 'After deschooling what?' in Social Policy (September/October 1971).

23. Philippe Ariès: The Centuries of Childhood, Cape, 1962. See Quotational Bibliography.

24. Paulo Freire: 'Education: domestication or liberation?' in Prospects, 1972. See Reading 3.

25. Rupert Wilkinson: The Prefects: British Leadership and the Public School Tradition, Oxford University Press, 1964.

26. Horst Ueberhorst: Elite für die Diktatur, Droste, 1969.

27. Eric James: Education and Leadership, Harrap, 1951, is the classic statement.

28. James S. Coleman (editor): Education and Political Development, Princeton University Press, 1965.

29. Leo Tolstoy: On Education, Chicago University Press, 1967, p. 12.

30. L. B. Namier: Facing East, Hamish Hamilton, 1947, p. 46.

31. Matthew Arnold: Reports on Elementary Schools 1852-82, H. M. S. O., 1908, p. 41.

32. Lutz Lehmann: Klagen über Lehrer F. und andere Schulbeispiele, S. Fischer, 1971, p. 10.

33. J. Gus Liebenow: Liberia, The Evolution of Privilege, Cornell University Press, 1969, p. 104.

34. Richard E. Dawson and Kenneth Prewitt: Political Socialization, Little, Brown and Co., 1969, pp. 158-60.

35. Philippe Ariès: The Centuries of Childhood, Cape, 1962.

36. J. H. Plumb: 'Children, the Victims of Time', in In the Light of History, Allen Lane The Penguin Press, 1972.

37. Michel Foucault: Madness and Civilization, Random House, 1965, pp. 38ff. See Quotational Bibliography.

38. York Playspace Project leaflet, 1972.

39. A. S. Neill: Summerhill: A Radical Approach to Child Rearing, Hart, 1960, p. 4.

40. Douglas T. Wright (Chairman): Draft Report of the Commission on Post-Secondary Education in Ontario, The Queen's Printer, 1971.

41. Howard S. Becker: 'A school is a lousy place to learn anything in', in Learning to Work, Aldine, 1972. See Reading 1 and Quotational Bibliography.

42. Erving Goffman: Asylums, Anchor, 1961; Penguin, 1968; p. 73 Penguin edition.

43. James Herndon: The Way It Spozed to Be, Simon and Schuster, 1965.

44. School of Barbiana: Letter to a Teacher, Penguin, 1971, p. 32.

45. Robert Silman: 'Teaching the medical student to become a doctor', in Counter Course, Penguin, 1972, p. 271.

46. Ivar Berg: Education and Jobs: The Great Training Robbery, Praeger, 1970. See Quotational Bibliography.

47. Booker T. Washington: Up From Slavery, Grant Richards, 1904, pp. 6-7.

48. School of Barbiana: Letter to a Teacher, Penguin, 1971, p. 68.

49. Paulo Freire: Pedagogy of the Oppressed, Herder and Herder, 1970; Sheed and Ward, 1972; Penguin, 1972; p. 23 Penguin edition.

50. Edward Boyle: Foreword to Half Our Future, H. M. S. O., 1963.

51. Michael Huberman: Reflections on the Democratization of Secondary and Higher Education, UNESCO, 1970. See Quotational Bibliography.

52. Peter Newell: A Last Resort? Penguin, 1972. The teacher's other obsessive concern is 'motivation' of pupils. Stick and carrot.

53. Christopher Hill: The World Turned Upside Down, Temple Smith, 1972, p. 136.

54. Ian Lister: 'The deschoolers', The Times Educational Supplement, 23 July 1971.

55. Ian Lister: The Concept of Deschooling and the Future of Secondary Education, European Cultural Foundation, 1971. See Reading 17.

56. Daniel Berrigan: America is Hard to Find, SPCK, 1973, p. 97.

57. Robert M. Hutchins: Toward a Learning Society. See Reading 11 and Quotational Bibliography.

58. Piffl Percevic: Continued Education, Ministry of Education, Vienna, 1965, p. 1.

59. E. W. Sudale: Continued Education, Council of Europe, 1971, p. 114.

60. Bertrand Schwatz: L'Éducation Permanente en l'an 2000, current working papers for the European Cultural Foundation.

61. William M. Rivera: Recurrent Socialization: A New View of 'Adult' and 'Education' in the Life-long Education Concept, ERIC document, 1971.

62. Rocco Gambacorta and John Rosser: Discussion papers for the meeting of the National Council of State Directors of Adult Education, New Orleans, March 1972.

63. Dragomir Filipovic: Permanent Education and the Reform of the Educational System in Yugoslavia, Convergence Vol. 1, No. 4, 1968.

64. John Ohliger: Adult Education: 1984. See Reading 21.

65. Hermann H. Frese: Permanent Education: Dream or Nightmare? See Reading 4.

66. David G. Gueulette: 'Is there school after death?' Adult Leadership (September 1972).

67. Peter Laslett: The World We Have Lost, Methuen, 1971, p. 3.

68. Dennis Kavanagh: Political Culture, Macmillan, 1972, p. 68.

69. Robert E. Dowse and John A. Hughes: Political Sociology, Wiley, 1972, p. 215.

70. Max Weber: 'Major features of world religions', in Sociology of Religion, edited by Roland Robertson, Penguin, 1969, pp. 25 and 22.

71. Ivan Illich: Anglo-American Law and a convivial society, CIDOC document, 1972.

72. Ivan Illich: Re-tooling Society, CIDOC document, 1972. Book forthcoming, Harper and Row, 1973.

73. René Maheu, commenting on the programme: 'Student unrest in traditional universities has been evident throughout the world. The need to experiment with new forms of higher education is urgent.' UNESCO document, June 1971.

74. Jarl Bengtsson: The U-68 Committee and the Future of Secondary Education, European Cultural Foundation, 1971.

75. Douglas T. Wright and D. O. Davis (chairmen): The Learning Society: Report of the Commission on Post-Secondary Education in Ontario, Ministry of Government Services, 1972.

Reading 5

1. Illich himself does not use the term 'commodity fetishism.' I shall do so, however, as it is more felicitous than 'institutionalised values' in many contexts.

2. Throughout this paper, I restrict my analysis to capitalist as opposed to other economic systems of advanced industrial societies (e. g. , state-socialism of the Soviet Union type). As Illich suggests, the outcomes are much the same, but the mechanisms are in fact quite different. The private-administrative economic power of a capitalist elite is mirrored by the public-administrative political power of a bureaucratic elite in state-socialist countries, and both are used to reproduce a similar complex of social relations of production and a structurally equivalent system of class relations. The capitalist variety is emphasised here because of its special relevance in the American context.

3. The main elements in Illich's left-convivial 'learning web' alternative to manipulative education are all fundamentally dispersive and fragmenting of a learning community:
    (1) Reference Services to Educational Objects - which facilitate access to things or processes used for formal learning. Some of these things can be reserved for this purpose, stored in libraries, rental agencies, laboratories, and showrooms like museums and theatres; others can be in daily use in factories, airports, or on farms, but made available to students as apprentices or on off-hours.
    (2) Skill Exchanges - which permit persons to list their skills, the conditions under which they are willing to serve as models for others who want to learn these skills, and the addresses at which they can be reached.
    (3) Peer-Matching - a communications network which permits persons to describe the learning activity in which they wish to engage, in the hope of finding a partner for the inquiry.
    (4) Reference Services to Educators-at-Large - who can be listed in a directory giving the addresses and self-descriptions of professionals, paraprofessionals, and free-lancers, along with conditions of access to their services.

Reading 10

1. C. A. Anderson, 'Patterns and variability in distribution and diffusion of schooling', in Anderson and Bowman (eds.), Education and Economic Development (Chicago: Aldine, 1965), p. 341. You may recall Plato's version in the Republic: 'Citizens... you are brothers, yet God has framed you differently. Some of you have the power to command, and in the composition of those he has mingled gold, wherefore also they have the greatest honour; others he has made of silver, to be auxiliaries; others again, who are to be husbandmen and craftsmen he has composed of brass and iron, and the species will generally be preserved in the children. '

2. J. Coleman, 'The concept of equality of educational opportunity', in Harvard Educational Review, Vol. 38, No. 1 (1968), p. 9.

3. Ibid. p. 10.

4. This trend is analysed very well in M. B. Katz, Class, Bureaucracy and Schools: The Illusion of Educational Change in America (NY: Praeger, 1971).

5. R. Turner, 'Modes of social ascent through

education', in Halsey, Floud and Anderson (eds.), Education, Economy and Society (NY: Free Press of Glencoe, 1961), pp. 121-39.

6. E. Mishan, The Costs of Economic Growth (Harmondsworth: Penguin Books, c. 1967).

7. B. Bloom, 'Learning for Mastery', in Evaluation Comment (Los Angeles: UCCA Center for the Study of Evaluation of Instructional Programs), Vol. 1, No. 2, 1968.

8. These traits, in fact, probably determine high academic performance. To be sure, they are culture-bound, i.e., many of the children who do well at primary school on tests of non-cognitive behaviour tend also to do well on aptitude and intelligence tests.

9. Bereiter has a brilliant paragraph on the nature of schooling as an initiation rite, in which he points out indirectly how children from lower-class backgrounds can be confused and alienated by the experience: 'The situation in a traditional school has much similarity to the situation in a peacetime army. Both child and the peacetime soldier are being readied for future activity, but in both cases the future activity is too remote and unforeseen to serve as adequate motivation of purpose on a day-to-day basis. There being no real accomplishments to strive for, an artificial world is generated in which work of no actual consequence becomes invested with importance by being used as a running test of merit. All aspects of life become highly ritualised and so much emotion becomes attached to the rituals that even minor deviations from them are seen as threatening to the whole structure of life. The guiding purpose in life becomes not that of achieving any external objective but that of being a good pupil or a good soldier as the case may be.' (C. Bereiter, 'Schools without education', in Harvard Educational Review, Vol. 42, No. 3 (August 1972), pp. 398-9.)

10. See the discussion of R. Dreeben in On What is Learned at School (Boston: Wesley-Addison, 1969), pp. 22-38.

11. We are reminded of the recent history of testing adolescents' motivations. Adolescents who lacked the desire to earn a great deal of money or to compete with others for executive posts were categorised as listless or unmotivated. In fact, their real motivations were not being tested by the items used in the battery, which had been chosen uniquely in accordance with norms of material achievement and consumption.

12. This point has been made consistently and well by E. Gordon in his writings on socially handicapped children. See, for example, his chapter on 'Programmes of compensatory education' in Deutsch, Katz and Jensen (eds.), Social Class, Race and Psychological Development (NY: Holt, Reinhardt and Winstow, c. 1967), pp. 381-410.

13. B. Bloom, Stability and Change in Human Characteristics (NY: Wiley, 1966), p. 105.

14. See the discussion of Bloom in Stability and Change, pp. 215-16.

15. See C. Stendler-Lavatelli, 'Environmental intervention in infancy and early children', in Deutsch, Katz and Jensen, op. cit. p. 360.

16. However, children of senior cadres and professionals end up enrolled disproportionately in the prestigious university faculties (medicine, law, natural sciences, engineering), in the urban universities (Moscow, Warsaw, Prague) and in the full-time rather than in the more arduous part-time degree programmes.

17. E. Reimer, An Essay on Alternatives in Education (Cuernavaca: CIDOC, Cuaderno no. 1005), 916.

18. I have often observed that in countries where schools were run in a severely authoritarian and directive manner, a group of persons spent much of their free time meeting to talk about classroom self-management and non-directive teaching. Few were or had been teachers; all were intolerant of any reform which fell short of their orthodox version.

19. M. Huberman, Understanding Change in Education (Paris: UNESCO, 1973).

Published by the Syndics of the Cambridge University Press
Bentley House, 200 Euston Road, London NW1 2DB
American Branch: 32 East 57th Street, New York, N. Y. 10022

Introduction, selection, Readings 10, 16, 17, 18, 25,
the English translations of Readings 7 and 30 and Quotational
Bibliography © Cambridge University Press 1974

Library of Congress Catalogue Card Number: 73-92784

ISBNs: 0 521 20409 7 hard covers

       0 521 09845 9 paperback

First published 1974

Printed in Great Britain
at the University Printing House, Cambridge
(Brooke Crutchley, University Printer)